BEYOND EUPHRATES

'That she so triumphantly holds our attention and makes us long for more is due to her sensibility, her courage, her honesty and, above all, to her gift for writing good English, a gift that must leave all other travellers and writers desperate with envy.' *The Listener*

Dame Freya Stark has recently become a nonogenerian and has fascinated the world for years with her intrepid travels to the Middle East, and the lively accounts of her trips.

In *Traveller's Prelude* she described the beginnings of her travels: being carried over the Alps in a basket aged 2½, her cosmopolitan upbringing against a background of parental conflict and her youthful struggles.

Beyond Euphrates takes up the tale at the start of her Eastern travels, on which she embarked in 1928, undeterred by the illness which had threatened to semi-invalid her for life. Through the medium of her delightful letters and snatches of diary, she describes her life in Baghdad and her experiences of living in a harem in Damascus, her journeys in Persia and her treasure hunt in Luristan, besides her visits to England and Canada and her life in Italy.

'*Beyond Euphrates* is a book that leaves behind it feelings of gratitude and wonder.' *The Observer*

'Miss Stark . . . is a perpetual source of interest, entertainment and lasting pleasure.' *Daily Telegraph*

'The peoples and landscapes of Iraq and Persia are evoked vividly and with spontaneous understanding.' *Sunday Times*

Beyond Euphrates

AUTOBIOGRAPHY 1928–1933

FREYA STARK

CENTURY PUBLISHING

LONDON

First published in Great Britain in 1951 by
John Murray (Publishers) Ltd
This edition published in 1983 by
Century Publishing Co. Ltd
76 Old Compton Street, London W1V 5PA

ISBN 0 7126 0275 5

Cover shows a painting from the collection at the Mathaf Gallery, 24 Motcombe Street, London S.W.1.

Printed in Great Britain by
Richard Clay (The Chaucer Press) Ltd
Bungay, Suffolk

To Jock Murray
The gentlest companion

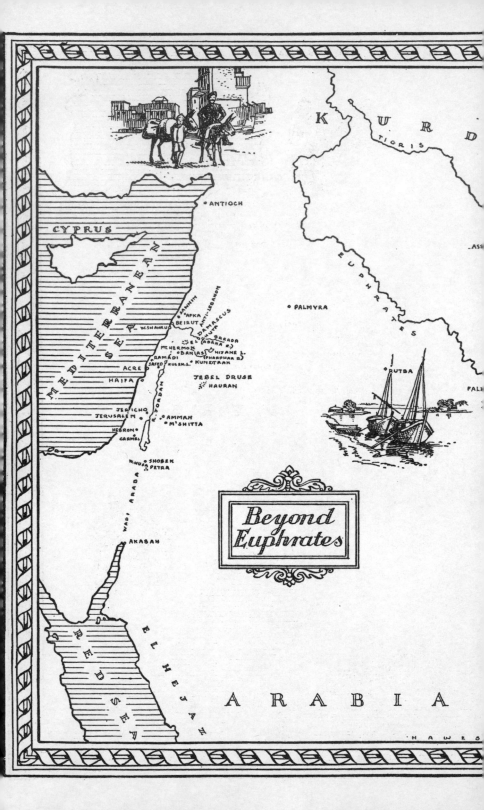

K U R D

TIGRIS

ASS.

EUPHRATES

• ANTIOCH

CYPRUS

• PALMYRA

M
E
D
I
T
E
R
R
A
N
E
A
N
S
E
A

YAMMIN
• AFKA
• ANTI-LEBANON
BEIRUT • DAMASCUS
W.SHAHRUR • ABANA •
• EL BARADA
(ABANA ?)
ME HERMON • BANIAS
RAMADI
SAFED HULEN.L.
ACRE •
• KUMETRAH
HAIFA •

ABANA

• RUTBA

FAL.

JEBEL DRUSE
• HAURAN

JERICHO
JERUSALEM •
HEBRON •
CARMEL
• AMMAN
• M'SHITTA

JORDAN

W.MUSA • SHOBEK
• PETRA

WADI ARABA

AKABAH

Beyond
Euphrates

R
E
D
S
E
A

E
L
H
E
J
A
Z

A R A B I A

HAWES

CASPIAN SEA

MARAND

RESHT
MAZANDERAN
RUDBAR
ROCK OF ALAMUT
SHAHSAVAR
KHURRAMABAD
LAMIASAR CASTLE
SHAHRUD
NEVISAR SHAH CASTLE
SALAMBAR
AB GARM
CHALA
GARMUD
BADASHT
ELBURZ MTS
TALAGHAN
KALAR DASHT
CHALUS R.
JOISTAN
DOHTAR QAL'A
THRONE OF SOLOMON
QAZVIN
MT DEMAVEND

NINEVEH
OSUL

KIRKUK

TEHERAN

SAVEH
SENNA
QUM
HAMADAN

KANGAVAR
KERMANSHAH
HARSIN

NIHAVEND

MANDALI
KADHIMAIN
HASANABAD
BAGHDAD
DUSHT-I-MUH
KHANIKIN
LURISTAN
CTESIPHON
ALISHTAR
BEDRAH
PERSIA
TIGRIS
BELAD
NEJF
BABYLON
HILLAH
KUFA
EUPHRATES
URFA
NASIRIYAH
EL BASRA

KUWEIT

PERSIAN GULF

Scale of Statute Miles

5 0   10 0   15 0   20 0   35 0

Je suis profondément convaincu que le seul antidote qui
puisse faire oublier au lecteur les éternels Je que l'auteur
va écrire, c'est une parfaite sincérité. (Mero, 20 juin, 1832.)
STENDHAL: *Souvenirs d'Egotisme*

Contents

Foreword

THE insertion of letters into biography is a difficult thing to manage: there is a continual holding up of the narrative while people say good morning and good-bye. I have tried to solve this problem by taking away from my correspondence all that impedes the story, and by doing so I hope to give a contemporary picture of myself as true as an autobiographer—a biased person inevitably—can make it. Our letters portray us, for better or worse, as we were at the time they were written: and I have put before them, at the beginning of every chapter, an introduction, written as it were by myself today, from this present vantage-point of time. With all fairness of selection, the letters of the past often seem crude and sometimes regrettable: yet they have their own life: the reader can compare the two ages—a thing which I myself am not sufficiently disinterested to do.

1

The First Journey, 1928

" LET us now praise famous men, and our fathers that begat us": this could be the beginning of all biography, for there are no single events in our world. They have been made by famous men and moulded to our size by our fathers; and the smallest thing we do is both a result and a cause. Deviations and accidents that might have made life different are forgotten, or half obliterated like prints in the desert where the wind has passed; and our self alone can recognize those dim beginnings curving outward, faint wheel-tracks under the surface of oblivion, which might have led—had we followed them—to what oasis or what mirage, impossible to tell. Our life is in the visible track we made; but autobiography holds a memory of those ghost tracks, can tell something of the moments of choice endlessly repeated. The recurrent decisions move back into the origins of ourselves; they belong to forebears and climates of the past, and lead into a complication of private history in which there is no beginning later than the first cause of all. The autobiographer can sometimes detect the decisive instant— probably in some silent, sudden blossoming of thought, itself the result of unassessed years or ages; there, and not in its outer and and later aspect, the event is born, and made inevitable by un- awareness; and thence it unrolls until it clothes itself in facts, strangely unexpected. The recorder's business is to remember this phantom world which gives perspective to the living show. In the *Traveller's Prelude* I described the background to my first eastern journey, which emerged out of conflicts, histories and dramas, and embodied itself on board a Lloyd Triestino steamer to the Levant in November 1927.

It was like the prince's story in the Arabian tale, who shot his arrow farther than he knew and then went out to find it. I had prepared for this journey during many years. I had walked for hundreds of miles along the Ventimiglia highroad and sat in many dusty trains to learn Arabic, eking it out with snatches of time at the London School of Oriental Studies. It had taken me a very long effort to organize my mother with some sort of financial stability and to build up a barely sufficient income of my own—three hundred pounds a year had been my aim: and this had been accomplished with so much strain and anxiety, so many accidents, deaths and family stresses, that illness had come, a burden never again to leave me for very long. All this was the price of freedom. I did not think it too heavy as we steamed down the Adriatic in the night.

I could look back with a fairly quiet mind on the landscape of the past as I left it. There in the foreground was beloved Asolo, its castle and small hills like the stitching on a sampler, and the Dolomites behind it—all within sight of the campanile of St. Mark's in Venice on a clear autumn day. The eye of imagination could see our home, with poplar leaves falling about it in yellow showers, and Herbert Young clipping his hedges in the last days of the sun. The house and garden were mine, for he had given them to me, and I left my mother in comfort and with his company, a happy thought for many years to come. She was busy with a small weaving industry, started by Mrs. John Beach, and quieter times were slowly smoothing away the sharpness of the memories of Dronero.

That stern little medieval city of the Alpine foothills was still fairly clear-cut in our landscape, for Mario my brother-in-law was there with most of our property in his hands and all his debts unpaid, with my dead sister's four children tightly clasped in a jealous grip well out of our reach, and his strange baleful influence over my mother liable to appear in unexpected ways: this was a dark corner, but mercifully and increasingly remote.

[2]

Closer and happier, was the blue and ochre, olive and pine-clad Riviera, with the corniche road winding towards the French border, and Mortola tower on its hill like a candle in daylight, white in the depths of sky: and below it, in a small bay, our vineyard and the cottage of L'Arma, which we had built up as Naboth must have built, in poverty and love, so that my heart is tied up in that landscape even now. At the time, however, the place was a problem, difficult to provide with peasants, equally difficult to let, and much more expensive than we could afford to keep in absence.

The English part of my life had receded since the death of my godfather, W. P. Ker. His loss made an emptiness there, partly and gradually filled by his brother Charles and his two sisters. I thought of these in Scotland and not in Gower Street, and London was chiefly connected with Viva Jeyes, who grew less happy as she grew older, suffering in the way of women whose life had been made easy by their beauty, and adding to this a puritan preference for unhappiness and failure in her friends. I dislike being an anvil for the hammering out of other people's virtues, and was too delighted in my emancipation to please her. I had to remind myself of her great kindness in the past: but that provides a poor climate for intimacy, and London was shadowed for me for some years to come.

Far nearer than England and ever in my thoughts with a constant pain, was the Canadian landscape, with my father's fruit farm and the timber cottage on the hillside where he wrote cheerful, laboriously pencilled little notes to reassure me as he rallied from his illness. Financial difficulties, and his own advice, and the accumulated impetus of all the years of preparation and desire for the East, had kept me from going out to him at once: but there was to be a recurring ache at the back of my thoughts, and the remorseful knowledge that it was his generosity alone which kept me away in the free and open world.

At the back of all this, pervading it and making a general atmosphere with which I was only too familiar, was the perpetual absence, rather than shortage, of cash. But enough had been collected for the voyage to Beirut, and most moderate terms were arranged with Mlle Rose Audi for my stay with her in the Lebanon village of Brummana; the financial situation could be forgotten for the moment; and indeed, as the Levant opened out day by day before me, everything else was also forgotten.

The word ecstasy is always related to some sort of discovery, a *novelty* to sense or spirit, and it is in search of this word that, in love, in religion, in art or in travel, the adventurous are ready to face the unknown. As we zigzagged down the Adriatic, with that double current which already the ancients recognized as unpleasant, I roused myself at every shore interval to feel interest and pleasure, in Fiume, Split, Bari and Brindisi: but it was Ithaca in the twilight that first revealed the magic word. We had been soothed by quieter waters in the lee of Cephalonia and were slipping in among islands across the Ionian sea: and I asked a name casually, and—steep and unexpected, with all her legends about her—Ithaca was there on the starboard bow.

Every day after that was enchanted. The gulfs of Patras and Corinth, the light of Athens washed in milk and honey, islands in sapphire seas, Rhodes where history lies sleeping— her streets and walls still surrounded by Turkish cemeteries, turbaned headstones askew among the iris—the first of the East, friendly, dingy, dignified and unknown, in Alexandretta and Antioch; and the drive through the stridency of Beirut into stony valleys, to the ridges of Lebanon. The account of my winter there has been published in *Letters from Syria*, so that I shall say little about it here.

The life I left behind me had given, without my knowing it, some of the necessary ingredients for travel. In the first place, I had learnt to rely on myself; not in matters of ordinary efficiency such as the reading of time-tables (which I have never been able to master) and catching of trains, but in a more subtle way: my mother had lived many years out of England, in a voluntary exile, doubtfully received in Italy, and this existence, separated from all the usual props external to ourselves by which we are supported, gave, I think, a certain directness of judgement both

[4]

to my sister and to me. Without anything particular in the nature of a 'setting', we had nothing but our own intrinsic selves to rely on, and came to look naturally at the intrinsic qualities of other people. Perhaps this is the most important of all assets a traveller can possess, for it minimizes barriers, whether of nationality, race or caste; and in fact I have never been able to feel that human beings differ except in things far more deeply rooted than their manners, habits or outward appearances or colours.

Another quality, produced at first by my father's rigorous teaching of endurance, and secondly by the financial ups and downs of our youth, was a certain indifference to circumstances. I had realized, by wanting them, how desirable many things are, but had also come to see how much of life can be enjoyed without them; and had learnt and have continued to learn that comfortable things like incomes are the servants and not the masters of our days (especially in a good climate).

Brummana, sung by Flecker, lay like a brown lizard on its ridge, and its climate through the winter was bitter. The Turkish wind swept it like a scimitar, and most people who could afford to do so moved to the town of Beirut, in sight but far below. Mlle Rose Audi in her little square house was surrounded by mats, curtains, cushions, and table centres—but they were all frustrating by being too thin, or too hard, or too small: the curtains never reached the sides of the windows where the draughts were, the marble floors were as persistent as Banquo's ghost through the ornamental little bits of things that floated about upon them, the table mats were all devoted to pictorial art rather than to the covering up of surfaces, and the cushions, deceptively frilled round their edges, seemed to be granite at heart. I sat at my table and studied verbs and nouns, wrapped in more clothes than I wore to climb the Matterhorn, and looked with a wary eye at the sunshine outside, dazzling and hard, and able to freeze one to the bone. In spite of this inclemency I flourished, attended to by Mlle Rose with the same care as that which she devoted to her begonias; they flowered in the middle of the winter on her marble floor. I was still very delicate from my last illness; I must lead a very quiet life, the doctor said in Italy, and would never be able to walk for more than half a mile. This gloom I made up my mind to disregard.

For the first few months of that winter I was still racked with pain through half the week or more; I walked about notwithstanding, with tiny steps to keep to Mlle Rose's pace, muffled to the ears in the midday sun, beside me; or alone up and down the steep stony slopes where sudden rains wear away the limestone into holes and all the wild flowers open in sheltered corners in the spring. I had nobody's business except my own to attend to, no anxiety, no decisions, no work except the learning of Arabic: and this and the active simple life cured me. A last attack of sickness caught me in Damascus, where I went down with dysentery in a squalid house near the gate of St. Thomas. When that was over I began to enjoy the Syrian spring: the El Azm family, to whom I had an introduction, were charming and friendly; they took me to their villages in the Ghuta, the oasis of Damascus, where acres of apricot blossom fluttered in the sun. My friend Venetia Buddicom reached me on her way home from India, and we travelled together through the borderland of the Druses, the first difficult journey I made. I had learnt already, in Alps and Pyrenees, that the foundation of such travel is careful planning; I read all I could, plotted out days and distances, and found a guide who had friends in the country, before Venetia came: and we slipped by the French guards one early morning, off the Damascus–Palestine highroad, into a country where feelings still ran high, where fighting had recently ended and martial law ruled, and where the French authorities showed no noticeable pleasure when, a few days later, they found us in the remotest bit of their territory, petted and feasted in an irritating way by all the people they thought most dangerous.

We reached Jerusalem, tired and loaded with as much novelty as could be taken in at one venture, and ready to relax at home. Egypt and Rhodes and Athens revisited, left only tourist

[6]

traces. In Cairo we lunched with Dr. Shahbender, who was a brother-in-law of my Damascus friends, an honest and I think a wise man, since murdered. His views on the international politics of Syria stirred in me an interest in the Levant which has never left me—an interest akin to that awakened by Greek drama where the unappeasable powers are too strong for the puny efforts of the stage. At that time the meeting passed without much attention though it made British authorities notice me as possibly 'subversive', and Venetia and I were shadowed through the streets of Cairo by a detective; we embarrassed him by lingering at every purely feminine shop while he had to dangle at a corner. We left Alexandria, and early in June landed in Venice, before the Doge's palace in a white summer mist, and departed each to her respective home. I had been away nearly seven months, and had spent £200: and came back with a feeling, dim but insistent, that the whole of my future must be rearranged.

The slowness with which I came to this conclusion, and adopted a life of my own now seems to me very remarkable. For years my old life faded, like Eurydice but very gradually, from my arms. This was not due to timidity, for I was morally brave by nature, and physically by will—nor did it happen through a lack of interest in the unknown. It came I think from a feeling which still influences me greatly, whose beginning I cannot remember and whose origin I cannot trace—a feeling for the value of affection in itself, and a reluctance to waste any of it that happened to come my way. This has little to do with one's own capacity for affection; my mother, the most exuberantly expansive of human beings, never hesitated to toss by the wayside what seemed to me the most precious and delicate possessions. Perhaps it was the sight of her recklessness, and the knowledge that I had no such command of riches; perhaps, and I think more probably, it was merely pity, the sight of something beautiful wasted, which made me feel towards love in general as one might towards a piece of porcelain forgotten in the middle of a road: one would go out of one's way to find it a safer place. It is a niggardly feeling, for the wealth and variety of love can be counted upon to overflow all loss: the general richness will compensate those who cross hither and thither on our path, while we make straight for the targets of our heart. But I cannot do so even now. The friendliness of a tramp will make me pause on my way, and I am happy to rub a donkey's ears in the sun. To be asked, and not to have it in me to give affection, is a pain; and only the brevity and tread of Time force me to renounce anything of the varieties of human friendship. My mother and Asolo, my father in Canada, the four children, the opening East—for as long as I could I tried to keep them all.

During this summer of 1928, and indeed before, in the leisure of Syria and Brummana, I realized that I was at one of those corners where the compass bearing must point to new landmarks. For a year or more before my Syrian travel I had been unhappy and perplexed, loving and loved by a man who had other claims: for some time we stood on an edge, between our own happiness and that of others. When it comes to the point, it is difficult to choose one's own; we did not, and the result was eventual tranquillity—but for those few years I was bewildered, with a pool of sadness in my heart, below the level of its ordinary life; and I came back from the Levant without knowing that my new road was found, and my feet already moving in its dust.

In 1926 and 1927, I had considered being a missionary. This unsuitable career was avoided by the discovery that I hate philanthropy and am averse to teaching, in a world where the pleasant occupation is to learn. The only level at which I could teach would be that of one schoolgirl to another at the same desk.

Yet my thoughts, such as were not taken up with the novelties of things around me, continued through the Syrian winter and spring to take an abstract turn. Mr. D was in Brummana —an intelligent young schoolmaster to whom teaching came easy; and he introduced me to Rudolph Steiner's books. I worked through them conscientiously for the rest of the year, till they led to such esoteric worlds that I turned back—not because of improbability, but out of a preference for this world as it is, and an inclination to deal with things one after another, even if they happen to be time and eternity. There is little leisure to discover what lies around us, and so much—presumably—for what is beyond; and it has long seemed to me to be the behaviour of a rather ill-mannered guest on this planet, to wolf his earlier courses and ask for port and coffee straightaway.

Mr. D gave me stuff to think about for which I was grateful. Rudolph Steiner's description of how an object—a tree for instance—is quite a different object if other eyes regard it, the eyes of an ant or a man—is one of the most useful things in everyday life to remember; and no doubt the practice of concentration did me good. When I returned to Brummana in 1929 and saw him again, he was absorbed in a new and promising pupil; she was younger than I was, and much prettier, and a visible proof, I felt, of how difficult it is to keep to the abstract in this world.

All the summer I wrestled in these depths, hoping for a direction; I kept most of my trouble to myself, for there was no one except Bismarck's niece, old and beloved Mrs. Robertson, to whom I could talk, and she was away in Bordighera. The months in Asolo passed with their usual gentleness—a Jane Austen sort of world with summer hats and dresses, neighbours and friends strolling between the roses, and the deep spring grass of the garden cool and varied with flowers, scythed away to smooth burnt summer lawn. From the open windows of my mother's little factory, the click of the shuttles and the thread of her five silk-looms came like the voices of pigeons in the East, harsh but blurred, monotonous as water, and now and then, like a break of wave above it, a snatch of song. We played badminton when the shadows lengthened after tea under the trees; we talked of politics and art, and mixed Italian, American and English friends: I wrote the first thing of mine that ever came to be published, an article on the Druses in Syria, and sat with my embroidery. Everyone was settled, and no one very young; their lives seemed to stretch away like those well-laid railway lines, varied with sun and shadow between banks built by human forethought—their corners expected and rounded and their stations known. Herbert with his human kindness, free from all arrogance of bestowing, gathered together a part of his small income and took us round the Dolomites for a few days, driving over high green passes where the summer pastures are slung like hammocks and the sunlight seems nearer to earth.

In August I went to Dronero, heavy with shadows for me, and the darkness of my sister's burial place. She lies there, suspended in a leaden coffin, untouched by the kind earth, in a family vault with her alien relations around her. The place, too, was full of perplexities at the time, for the children were growing up wild, though gay, with no one in particular to educate them. A note of exasperation, with my mother especially, creeps into my letters from that tainted house. "What one does badly is no good to anyone," I write acidly, though perhaps with truth. My mother had suggested that she might leave her little factory—which was doing extremely well—and help the domestic finance by taking in paying guests, a prospect which anyone who knew her must contemplate with dismay. I felt it would be better if she could bring herself to induce my brother-in-law to pay the sums he owed her, and begged her, unkindly and in vain, to "canalize her emotions".

"You have the luck to be doing the work you like. It is not basking in the sun, still it is *great luck* and worth sticking to. I have not yet got it, for I have to do all the jobs I don't like in between, and shall not reach my own work till I am about forty: I do however hope to reach it eventually, if there is anything of me left."

As I leave Dronero, the tension and the bitterness disappear. The children came to bathe at L'Arma, and the late summer drew to autumn there with long and easy days, neighbours and vineyards, the troubles of peasants, the last warmth of the mornings on the shore, the ripeness of grapes and figs and their sweet sticky scent, and the gossip of all the hillside that lies open to the sun, from Castel d'Appio in the west to Bordighera.

In the autumn I left for Canada, to go to my father, and on my way passed through Evian where David Horner was nursing Bernard d'Hendecourt; it was like a gateway opening into a sad but very dear northern world.

*   *   *

HOUSE OF HALIK 'AĪD, DAMASCUS,
16 March, 1928.

Dearest Pips,[1]

It is not all joy living with a native family. I had my first lunch with them: I was given a plate and fork—the rest just dipped their bread in the dish: it is very rich food, pepper, onion, grease, all the most deadly things. I have confessed to being an invalid, eat just the milky things, and even so am wondering how the experiment will get on. The family is mother, aunt, and three nice children, full of life and spirits: the father only appears in the evening when we gather in one of the bedrooms and sit—callers coming round and the men handing each other the hubble-bubble. I wish I understood more: all the really interesting conversation escapes me.

You would enjoy these bazaars. I was disappointed at first, as the big ones have a horrid mixture of cheap European stuff, but this morning I found my way into the real East and it was remarkably like the Arabian Nights. I went along where the town is still in ruins after the bombardment—such a desolation, a whole district practically razed.[2]

You do see lovely horses here now and then; and the coloured trappings and the blue beads make them look magnificent. I think we are getting the last of the proper East; the silks you now buy are artificial, the pretty headdresses come from Manchester, and the cheap stuff combined with the incredible dirt and untidiness has nothing to redeem it.

[1] My father: Robert Stark.

[2] From the Druse rebellion of 1925.

19 March, 1928.

This afternoon we went into the narrowest blackest streets, with overhanging rooms and a slit of daylight: I say we, because I had a charming, and so handsome, Moslem cavalier to whom I had an introduction. He belongs to a good family here, and came along in a flowing brown and gold cloak given by Ibn Sa'ūd to his brother, and we discussed religion. We wandered by Saladin's tomb, close to one of the marble water basins in a little garden of orange and blossoming almond: then wandered through the ruined town, sad and horrible. They say the French are going to rebuild it, and I think it would be as well, for it must rouse a lot of vindictive feeling.

To-morrow is the last of Ramadhān. Everyone is saying their prayers at a great rate in the big mosque cloister—big as a piazza—full of people coming and going. How I wish I could sketch, to give you some idea of it all. At every corner I wish you were there too, and wish I could at least describe it all to you. There is so much; such a jostle, and variety of types: fair blue-eyed hill people, every degree of black, and the beduin in their rags and big strides swinging their rough cloaks, their dingy little tattooed women behind them, donkeys with panniers jostling among the people (sometimes with skins of oil, not at all pleasant to be near), camels in long strings: occasionally a horse with handsome red and yellow tassels and blue beads: and all in the half light, for the bazaars are roofed over, and the little shops open on to them about two feet off the ground, like the rooms of dolls' houses or a row of boxes at a theatre which the merchants can enjoy all day long.

21 March, 1928.

Here we might not be having spring, except for the lovely skies and blossom, for the wind is like ice and I am perpetually cold and have not yet been able to shed my fur. I went out this afternoon with all the family to see the arrival of the new Vizir—the head of the government, though under the French Commissioner. Such a crowd—not as interesting as might be, for it was mostly Christians, and their costumes are getting sadly European. We went at two and sat on somebody's wall just in front of the triumphal arch which was made out of long poles and carpets slung over—very effective, especially as there was sword dancing going on underneath, to the beating of two tom-toms. The way the swords are twirled about,

[12]

so fast that you can't see the movement of the wrist at all, is very fascinating; in the other hand they hold a tiny brass target: they move their arms about, first very slowly, then gradually faster with the music, moving and suddenly springing and getting nearer and nearer —always keeping in harmony with each other—till they close up, twirling the swords about so that it seems impossible to avoid being hit; at the close one of them brings his weapon neatly horizontal between them and they kiss above the blade very prettily. There was another dance with three of them at it, one in the middle with two swords, defending himself against both the others; he was an elderly fat man, and very clever at the whirling, and went back to his friends awfully pleased and puffed, patted on the back by all who were near enough. It was amusing watching for the first hour: then I was told the Vizir wouldn't arrive till four, so I left the family and walked along the road, and then branched off. I found myself in actual Paradise—flat country all grass of brilliant green corn, all filled with running streams and speckled with shadows of old olives and blossoming fruit trees. It was so delicious. The Moslem peasants were saying their prayers, their spades stuck into the ground, their coats spread out, and their shoes beside them while they knelt with their face to Mecca: it seemed a good and pleasant way of praying, by oneself in the lovely country: here in the town you have to select, see the good things, and constantly turn away from some European horror: but there, there was nothing to disturb the picture: the villages all flat, baked clay—a lovely ochre: long walls all one colour with the dust of the street—with nail-studded doors here and there and few windows—all useful for defence: and the women in their bright clothes, like Tanagra come to life, the beautiful line of the draped head and shoulders, and their little blue or red frilled trousers showing underneath. One group was so lovely that I peered round their courtyard door and they all came and showed me the baby—not a month old and its eyelashes already blackened for beauty, wrapped up tight like a little Italian baby, and a blue bead for luck on its forehead: I remembered just in time to say, 'In God's name' before praising it, so as not to cast any evil eye on its poor little puckered face. The women with their lovely brilliant eyes and white-swathed faces, and every conceivable colour of dress, and bright orange-tinted finger-nails, made such a picture.

I stopped at a little shop and had some leban, and answered

questions; I then left amid blessings—for I gave two sweets to each of five children. And this is the country I was told a woman could not possibly be alone in. My Muhammadan friend here says one can go practically *anywhere*. I do believe however that a little of the language is rather necessary.

When I got back at four-thirty the Vizir was just arriving: a huge green banner in front, frantic singings and brass bands, soldiers, drawn swords in the air, and he himself a young man, quite round and amiable, with a turban and about two hundred motors behind him. All the old Fords of Asia it looked like. Good-bye dearest Pips—I am going to bed to try and get warm.

30 March, 1928.

I got the most ramshackle Ford you ever saw and a toothless dilapidated chauffeur in a dilapidated waterproof and ancient tarbush and in this outfit called on my aristocrat friends. The pretty sister came in her black veiled headdress and the two brothers with guns and topees and a charming retriever dog—or was it pointer—that had somehow got woolly, but was good at the quails all the same. We then went through the length of the Arab town—Maidan—where all the grain comes in from Hauran on long camel strings and you see it heaped in vaults on either side the street, the merchant sitting like a spider at the door. Then we got to the last suburb—where the prophet left his footprint when he turned back from Damascus—and out through the bombarded débris and barbed wire into the country. It is like a huge soup-plate, shallow, with a rim of shallow hills, the bottom of the plate all fertile, the hills all bare, Damascus leaning against one red barren slope down into the green plain, and Hermon, shining with snow, rising on the South. The country was wheat, here and there fallow, old shells still lying about (some unexploded); and here and there slow water flowing below the level of the plain, between high banks, all choked with green plants, and tortoises lying about on the edge. We got out and wandered in the wheat watching the hunting of the quail: the two men very neat at getting it on the wing. It makes a *whirr* almost like grouse and gets its name from it. All was so lovely: soft colour: the villages lost in each its plantation of olives and apricots, walnuts, figs, and poplars—all against the background of Hermon.

My friends brought the lunch, and we went to one of their villages,

[14]

and were greeted by three women in blue breeches and red head-sheets (each village has its own colour and pattern). And then we left the road, and the old Ford took a wobbly bridge—no room for more than three wheels—and then took us across the wheat and into a ditch and out the other side—all like a two-year-old, the chauffeur simply refusing to let us funk the ditch and walk. We did refuse the bridge, for fear our extra weight would sink it beneath us. You can't imagine the lovely prosperous peacefulness of all this country. The apricots had all been planted in perfect even rows by these people's grandfather. We looked down avenues of blossom, with an avenue of cypress in between. We went to one of the slow streams and picked cress out of its depth while the men shot more quails—and then returned to their little *pied-à-terre* (which was looted but luckily not razed down during the war) and there we found that the headman had spread a carpet in the shade, and lit a fire, and brought me leban in a wooden case—ordered from him the day before by my kind friends. And we roasted meat over the fire, and said a Moslem grace, and were very happy. In the country Miss Azm needn't bother to keep her face covered: she looked very pretty with the black veil thrown back. We had the delicious coffee to finish with, and sat about, and then wandered across fields to where the water creeps under ground, and climbed down what looked like a quarry pit to see it come out of its cavern, all hung with maidenhair and inhabited by innumerable small fish.

I tried to pick you flowers, but they don't last to carry home and there was nothing very special except a tiny mauve or crimson thing like a dwarf anemone—its petals fall as you pick it—and lots of camomile, do you remember Falstaff says "the more you tread on it the faster it grows"? It was there thick as can be on the path.

7 April, 1928.

I have been to Lake Hijane south of Damascus; one has to go nearly an hour across the desert with no road, and the white water is nearly invisible on the white soil. We had difficulty to get the guide; everyone was afraid of us; and when we got him—a fierce-looking fellow with his old German military coat looted from Damascus, and ragged white swathing his face, and rakish black camel-hair chaplet which never seems to slip off at whatever angle they clap it on to their heads—when we finally got him, my sheikh didn't seem too confident for he told me in his crisp English "This man will not play tricks, for if he does I will beat him: and now when we get out I will see if he has a revolver." As the poor man was one to five, I did not feel much alarm: but when we started walking towards the water I heard the sheikh's sister murmur to him: "Would it not be better to make the guide walk in front?" She then told me that her cousin had been killed by his guide from behind—a Druse too, and his ally during the war.

There were a lot of white birds like small gulls. They got two of them: Shahir, the sheikh's young brother, plunged into the lake to the waist, and they shot them as they were flying high up, looking beautiful with white wings in the sky. When one was shot the others hovered about, making a very sweet shrill song, and it seemed a great shame. We also got thirteen small partridge, and one other desert bird. Both men are very good shots and fearfully excited over it: one does feel in this country that a gun is an extremely useful weapon.

What I wanted to see was a ruin however, marked on my map, and apparently near. We had to go back near the village, where our guide instantly deserted. I don't quite know what happened, for I wasn't attending and only vaguely heard the sheikh telling him that he was an animal and a creeping creature, and then saw him stalking back with a dignified air: what it was all about I never discovered, but noticed that we took the back road by the village on our way home. What with the map and the desert road, however, we thought we could find the citadel for ourselves. The road is just a bit of desert cleared of scrub, and marked with two lines of stones like a Dartmoor avenue, only small. In fact the *feeling* of the landscape was very like Dartmoor before the heather begins to show anything but brown. The place of the Tors is taken by sudden little volcanic mounds—Tells they call them—which are thick as mushrooms.

We saw our citadel in the distance, a black square thing on top of a little hill; and it went on being in the distance: the wind began to blow, a horrid barren sort of wind, lashing furiously: we left the road and made across country, rather anxious because there were rushes and we feared soft ground and stickiness; we looked very incongruous—like a motor suddenly appearing by the Wallabrook say. At last we got to my ruin, climbed up over the stones, and had lunch in its shelter. The others were all disappointed in it, for there was not an inscription, or anything of special interest: but I was happy enough.

BRUMMANA, 25 April, 1928.

Damascus finished up in the best possible way with a day in the desert. How you would have liked it. It wasn't like the moor this time, but immensely vast—like the desert in fact: and beduin in it. I saw one of them waving and his horse running to him across the scrub and sand, a beautiful sight. If you wave your sleeves (they wear very long trailing ones) it is a sign of friendship, and this man, standing like a wonderful draped statue in the lovely land, made this signal as our car jolted along the rough ground.

We went all round the lake where the Abana finishes exhausted —a rushy big lake full of wild boar they say (though where the creatures hide I couldn't imagine), and full of wild duck, heron, and wonderful other birds some with crested heads, some with copper wings; and buffaloes we saw going by—quantities of them. A few people come from Damascus here to shoot: and merchants come to buy beduin sheep or camels; you see their motor tracks criss-cross here and there in the sand. Some leave their sheep on a sort of *mezzadria*[1] system, dividing the lambs and the wool with the beduin.

JERUSALEM, 22 *May,* 1928.

(After the ride through the Jebel Druse.)

We think we know now something of desert hardships, riding in dazzling light over the waste lands, without refuge from the sun: when the wind came off those stony slopes it was like the opening of an oven door. There were lots of birds, eagles and larks, swallows in the houses flitting in and out; and strange lovely little birds—yellow with brown heads, or black and white (called warwe) and many other kinds. No other animals we saw except one wild cat (we think) and hares, and lots of fat lizards with yellow marks down their backs, jumping from stone to stone in the most active way with all four fat feet at once. Also gigantic green and yellow frogs in the great tanks near villages.

[1] The sharing of harvests between peasant and landowner.

There were flowers, too; I tried to pick for you, but it is hopeless: this climate wilts them as they are picked. In the stony parts of the land there was nothing but a little sickly white flower on a low bush and the prickly sort of thistle that grows a yellow ball. Lots of scrubby wormwood everywhere. But in the corn land we came on pink dianthus, and near Shahba on a lovely sweet-smelling white dianthus I have never seen before. Chickory, and a tiny pink mallow, a tiny poppy with crinkly leaves: I could not decide whether it is poppy or anemone and the Arab name is the same for both. There was nothing else till we came to Trans-Jordania and found a valley full of tall pink mallows, and then looked down from the high mountain road into the narrow cuts of streams where they wandered like snakes among the yellowy brown hills, their courses nearly hidden in pink masses of oleanders.

The sight of a living stream came to us as sweetly as music after our wandering. There is a stony wilderness south-east of Damascus: the Black Mountains, the Hills of Brass, their very names tell you how grim they are. The river Pharpar flows there, but after that you come on practically no water except the village tanks which the Romans built and which still feed the inhabitants with yellow water out of their depths of black hard stone: you go down to them by the half broken Roman steps, and see the great blocks still neatly placed in mortarless rows, well fitted and joined: and I suppose this ancient craftsmanship has kept what little life the country has, for the trees have vanished, long since burnt as firewood by Arab raiders, and half the old cities have crumbled into indistinguishable heaps of black lava stone, and all their riches have gone: where the people still live, their poor houses are surrounded by old ruined houses, mostly now dwindled to low walls: you go through streets of these half-crumbled stones, enclosing emptiness: here and there some little bit of ancient ease and opulence, some carved lintel or Corinthian acanthus built into the rough masonry. The life is grim too. The people come down from the rocky plateau of lava where the villages stand—solid rock about thirty feet above the plain, on whose dismal edge nothing grows at all—and they sow the stony plain, and hope for rain: this ye r no rain has come, or little, and the harvest is practically withered: we went through a dead land and saw the people pulling up the yellow wheat, which had turned to straw long before it could ripen. They were crouching in the fields, pulling it up with their hands, while one

man or woman stood among them chanting a monotonous repetition
of a song whose cadence helped them on. They have no doctors:
when they fall ill they die, but they do not often fall ill, and look very
handsome and strong: fine fighters. Now there is a lull—the whole
country is policed under French martial law; but normally the Arabs
raid from the desert and every village has its posts where guards are
set to give warning of approaching beduin. Even as we rode along
the eastern fringe we had a curious feeling that it was the very edge
of settled law: and our guide was careful to be very ready with a
greeting for all we met on the road. "Peace be upon you." "And
upon you be peace." "And where do you come from?" And they
do not give a town or village, but say from north, or south, or east, as
the case may be. The men have fine straight looks, and ride finely,
their headcloths wrapped round like helmets covering mouth and
nose from the heat, their old tattered cloaks falling magnificently
round them. When life is so precarious, and held by one's own
virtue always, there is great dignity with it. Their manners as hosts
were perfect, rich and poor alike.

We had no real danger till we left our donkeys and drove through
Trans-Jordan down here with the most incompetent chauffeur
imaginable: just stopped him in time on the edge of a ravine near
Jordan; he was tilting us over into it in the dark, having mislaid the
road.

JERUSALEM, 25 May, 1928.

Dearest B,[1]

We shall both be rather glad to leave Jerusalem to-morrow. It
is not entirely the fault of the Holy City, although there is a great
deal of suburbia about it, but we have both been feeling rather ill
—whether accumulated indigestions or the return to western food
we cannot decide. What with packing, mending, finding our
luggage, getting money, etc., we are being reduced to the harassed
state of mind of the ordinary tourist.

We had a pleasant time for tea this afternoon, going to call on the
Bentwichs. He is legal adviser here, and they were both agreeable,
and told us that we might have been murdered any time on our
trip—which is always pleasant to hear—afterwards.

[1] My mother: Flora Stark.

Dearest Pips,

It hardly seems believable that I shall be in Venice to-morrow, and my Grand Tour over and done—and, except for a certain thinness and insatiable appetite due to starvation in Damascus and Jebel Druse, no bad effects are visible. I rather enjoyed Cairo : things like public gardens with well-kept grass and tidy flowers were very restful, and trees along the boulevards, and tarred roads and beautiful shops, people talking in refined low voices and not eating with their fingers or spitting at table. Venetia had only had three weeks of the unadulterated East, but after five months the charms of civilization are extraordinarily charming. We climbed a Pyramid; I think too that it was more dangerous to me than many another climb, for my muscle has not come back after the dysentery, and my knees began collapsing under me whenever I bent them—for it is a good climb to the top, 410 feet and over, and the steps high : the wind blowing too, strong from the desert, and the desert itself a loveliness of colour, as if a rosy fire were burning inside it. I wished we had brought our sacks to sleep out on the sands. We climbed down in the twilight, then waited till the moon came up and wandered out among the huge straight slopes, and sat and looked at the Sphinx with her great lion paws that seem too big and give an extraordinary animal feeling to her. There is a thrilling sense of vigilance, of repressed motion, about her : she really is more astonishing than any statue I have ever seen : in the moonlight now and then the shadow on her neck seemed to move, and if it had really done so I should hardly have been surprised. And as she is exactly the same colour, built of the actual desert, she seemed its very embodiment : also the embodiment of all life, rising from its huge animal foundations to the questioning human face, the chin just tilted up, as if it were looking out with immense courage and steadfastness into the spaces of stars. All the miserable traffic of tourists, and donkeys, and guides cannot spoil all this; and somehow it seemed merely suitable that eight or nine of them should fall off the pyramid and get killed every year : an offering in the old style.

We didn't think much of native Cairo, after our life in the real East, but we did have a good afternoon the first day of the feast going to the Cemeteries with the whole population, male and female, women in black on carts, crowds of children, with palm leaves, camping apparatus, tea baskets or the equivalent, all going to sit in the family tombs. The Cemetery is a town of narrow streets with small square domed houses each containing its tomb or more of them, and it was a curious mixture of cheerfulness with the natural loveliness of its uninhabited streets. We went to see the Sultans' tombs, all shut up together with the 360 (if that is the number) Mamelukes whom Muhammed Ali first murdered and then politely buried in his own mausoleum. They are a little crowded, five or six marble turbans stuck in groups on one tomb, but still there they are in a little room beside the gorgeous gold and blue sarcophagi of the Sultans; it is an impressive place. The sarcophagi all the same shape only varying in the decoration; on the ladies' tombs, two long plaits are painted down the back of the upright stone slabs; they are better treated than the poor queen of Cheops who is given a very inferior room in the big pyramid, not nearly so expensive as her husband's up above.

We had to wait a whole day in Alexandria for loading maize, and the perversities continued, for at Athens we found they were holding their Greek Pentecost and the Acropolis was closed. The young man at the Embassy to whom I had a letter had left months ago—we got on board again feeling that Providence was no longer to be trusted.

BELLEGARDE, 27 September, 1928.

Dearest B,

I am here waiting for the train for Evian [to see Bernard d'Hendecourt who was ill], after a very comfortable night. I shall reach Evian at two and leave in the evening at nine, and get to Paris to-morrow morning. I had meant to get here a day earlier, but could not rescue my luggage in Turin so had to wait there, and spent the time with Clot [De Bottini de Sainte Agnes]. She is going to be as bad as H about her clothes. A dreadful fate to be shortsighted when one gets older and unable to see if one's collar is right or not.

I was sorry to leave the children and particularly troubled about Bébé. She *must* go to school, or she will be quite quite spoilt and nothing later will ever be able to make up for it. I have spoken out to Mario [my brother-in-law] as strongly as I could and shall write again. He has promised to look for a school, but his promise isn't worth much. Eva backed me up, but she will not see it through. Perhaps you can do something when you go. I suggested Switzerland if he wants languages and does not like nuns, and you might find out from Mrs. Rose and have a concrete suggestion ready with prices and all so that you *might* be able actually to carry the matter through and take her yourself after Xmas for the winter term? I will gladly find the money for the journey for a matter so important. She is getting to live so entirely to herself, and also her personal habits and manners are getting bad. The others are all right for a year or two. I shall write to Mario and you will find the ground all ready prepared. Poor man. He was very glad to have me, and everyone was nice. But I do just suffocate. It is only the children who keep one happy there.

It is lovely being here in the grey northern light again. A nice damp morning, smelling quite different from the other side of the Alps.

I went to Gallia and resisted a new hat, but she is doing up my old black and blue one again, so I shall do.

2

Canada, 1928–1929

IN this chapter I include, together with my letters, a diary
of notes written in 1929. More accurately than I can do
at this distance, they picture the things and thoughts in
which I was interested, and what there was of growth during
those interludes of time which seemed so hard to bear. And
they show that delight in the visible world which still increases,
to be, I hope, one of the deepening pleasures of age.

I am grateful for the leisure of my years, whether voluntary or enforced—for long stretches of sickness or of holiday,
and also for small snippets like those produced by the habit
of dressing for the evening. It meant a casting away as it were
of the day's business. After dinner, in Asolo, Herbert Young
would read aloud while we embroidered; later on he and
my mother took to bridge; in any case all solitary activities
were laid aside and a sort of emptiness built about the folding of
the day. My father, too, on his farm, was an incarnation of
leisure, for his business depended on the seasons, whose movements encouraged no feelings of hurry except at harvest-time
when I was never there. Perhaps the unreckoned atmosphere
was less that of my elders than of the age to which they belonged.
I chafed under it for years, and longed to be at the things for
which my time seemed short; yet, now that I have seen how
people drug themselves with occupation, that daily uncrowded
ending, with its small discipline of courtesy, appears in a gentle
light. It freed me from the fallacy of believing that busyness
must be good. And I am sure that it is partly because of this
feeling that I like the Arab nomad, who receives his world as it

comes from Allah and is not concerned to alter it more than he need, even though the working side of life gets less attention from him than it deserves, and arts as well as comforts go by the board. Here in North Africa, where I am writing, our Lybians, who still have the desert within them, squat over their small glasses of mint tea through nearly all the hours for which we pay them. Although it is our work they are supposed to be doing, they feel my sympathy and offer a share of the tea when I find them out; and I find myself hoping that a certain amount of eastern leisure may loiter in my heart through all its western activity.

In January 1928 I wrote to my father, suggesting that he might take "an occasional winter off, possibly somewhere in the East with me, where (if ever I can live as I like in this world) I shall probably end by finding some little cranny."

Now the summer was over. Syria and Arabia were far away, and Canada approaching. After that, an operation threatened which I did not mention, and of which I was reminded by frequent pain.

In a diary of this year I find written, in January in Brummana: "No one believes I come here and work so hard merely for pleasure. What do I come for? If I had my health I should know, though I would not tell; but as it is, I fear I shall not have the strength. No one can know without experience how hard it is to have to live as it were separate from your body, trying always to abstract your own pleasures and interests from its incessant pains and clamours. If I felt sure of immortality, how gladly would I die, only to be free from this constant fight against pain."

Pain, and the journey away from all my desires, and my father waiting at the far end with nothing but weakness and death before him, gave a sadness to this autumn very different from the last. I bought a tourist ticket for British Columbia in August, and started in October, leaving myself with a balance of £3 10s. in the bank. The Atlantic seemed, as it still seems to me, a mere obstacle to human intercourse, so opposite to the

Mediterranean's ballroom floor meant for perambulation. The tourist class in the *Athenia* was a distraction of wailing children and howling winds. I dislike the sea anyway when it is anything more than something blue that wraps itself round islands. Yet as I lay in my bunk between distasteful meals I read the *Odyssey* for the first time in Butcher and Lang's translation; and the roar and hiss of the waves was a part of its music. I was so transported with delight that I leapt up at intervals to walk about the narrow cabin floor, in an ecstasy that had to be expressed somehow, or choke me. Except Shakespeare, who grew from childhood as a part of myself, nearly every classic has come with this same shock of almost intolerable enthusiasm: Virgil, Sophocles, Aeschylus and Dante, Chaucer and Milton and Goethe, Leopardi and Racine, Plato and Pascal and St. Augustine, they have appeared, widely scattered through the years, every one like a 'rock in a thirsty land', that makes the world look different in its shadow.

The *Odyssey* continued to sing itself inside me up the St. Lawrence's smooth cold stretches—where the wind tastes of ice from Labrador; where the sunsets look immense and remote in their green sky, and the sparse New Brunswick fields, in tiny clusters round the pointed wooden spires, seemed smaller and more touching than anything made by man that I had ever seen. The aloofness of Canada, not less inhabited perhaps, but so far less humanized than Asia, struck me with awe, and an immense admiration for the courage that had tackled it. In the people I noted "a keen look of having to take responsibility, different from the Arab keenness—the one in motion, the other stationary—the one for attack, the other for resistance: the latter makes the finer old men". And indeed, after more than twenty years, I continue to admire the fineness of the old men in the East.

At small, forest-swallowed stations, women came in and out "with rough hands, tinsel hats, chiffon dresses, fur coats—the girls with pink cheeks from the keen air, the older women plain with hard work". Lakes and forests, poor on the shallow soil,

[25]

fled by like pages turning over—dark firs, and birches fluid and bright as water. The prairie opened out with heaps of chaff from the harvested straw "like little tells tawny as the desert and with the same volcanic look". After four days we came to the Rockies; cold green rivers carried slabs of ice in the sun; russet larches appeared among the firs: and my father stood on Creston platform to meet me, looking old as I had never seen him, his face more wrinkled than the bark of an elm, his clothes creased, folded and fallen into a sort of permanence of age, his movements difficult—and only his blue eyes shining in this ruin with a tranquil clear transparency, gay if it had not been so quiet. He lifted the end of his stick slightly, from far away. A group of his friends were discreetly in the background. Tom helped us into the farm-cart which was waiting, threw the luggage in behind, and settled Betty, a small, white, insinuating, feminine and temperamental poodle, at our feet.

We drove along a straight street where three shops and two banks, with gaps of timber yards and garden patches between, made the beginnings of a centre for the valley; up-hill along a road with wooden sidewalk and small bungalows, the main street perhaps of a future Winnipeg, for these western towns take scarcely a generation to grow. For a mile or so we were in country, between fruit farms on the hillside and the Kootenay valley below, whose twin streams met and separated and interlaced. My father himself drove, though Tom had had to put the reins in his hand. Tom and Alice had been with us when my sister and I had been children in Devonshire and they were glad to see me. The soft Devonshire speech was pleasant to hear in the kitchen, and cream in a big bowl clotted slowly at the back of the fire. Alice was in despair over my father's clothes. "It's no good darning, Miss—just wastes the thread—and he won't wear no new ones." Tom's gun hung on the kitchen wall and my father's in the sitting-room corner where, whenever he was not out of doors, he sat in a deep window-seat. It gave him one of the few essentials of his life—a view; and I made a small place for myself opposite, and spent most of the next four winter months there, in a quiet companionship that shone like a miniature, very small and bright, in a great melancholy frame.

One can say of the more reticent British that, as you come to know them, some are discovered and some are found out. My father was of those who are discovered. *The Times* came to him regularly, and he had a small shelf of books which he read over and over, admitting a newcomer now and then, after much deliberation. The whole of George Borrow and of Charles Darwin, Hodson of Hodson's Horse, Buckle's *History of Civilization*, White's *Selborne*, Benvenuto Cellini, and Sismondi's Italian Republics are what I remember. Out of this slight and very individual store, and out of a life of observation interested, selfless and detached, he distilled a quiet sort of conversation which blossomed among his intimates, full of colour, prejudice and humour, free of affectation, and slow: it was like a cycle of nature that cannot be hurried, the seed fell, took root, grew, and appeared in its season, and if the surrounding talk was too quick for it, my father found it just as easy to say nothing and keep his thoughts for another time.

To me, in the long winter evenings, Time itself seemed to burn like a still candle without a wind, consuming the waxen minutes imperceptibly; and only now and then, a gust from the outer world, the thought of the best years wasted, the operation still to be faced, the precious East attained only to be lost, and the impossibility of writing or studying in the little window-seat when interrupted—even by the best of talk, came like a crisis of frustration and made the huge country round me, the immense separation of prairie, forest, lake and Atlantic beyond, seem like those fabled landscapes by the Styx, an unbridgeable waste of desolation, fit only to be peopled by the dead. These thoughts came in the night, or when I was alone; the sight of my father's old face, where—among all the wrinkles—the years had never been able to trace a line that was not noble, filled me with tenderness—and thankfulness too that I had reached him: one's good angel has such hard work to make one do the right things, that I have a feeling of gratitude independent of myself when he succeeds.

At this time, if it had not been for sickness hanging over me, I think I would have stayed, or tried to do so, though my father himself spoke of my future travels, and took perhaps more pleasure in the thought of them than in most things: and who shall assess the part of our joy that is taken up with dreams? Those who can distribute this happiness are not to be despised, though their own share of merit may be small enough. At this time, however, I had not to decide, but only to let the months pass, and wait for London and my operation in the spring. I took part in the life of the Canadian winter, and liked the kind, courageous people, more heroic than they knew. I learned to skate, went sleighing with my father, or watched the wood-cutters sawing up our trees on the 'mountain'. I walked home with Alice from late service in our small wooden church (there were more churches and chapels than shops in Creston I believe), through fir plantations stiff as Napoleon's grenadiers in Russia, under the frozen stars; and before sleeping joined with my father in giving Betty the poodle her evening game—a hunt in every cranny of the room for an old glove which we hid. When this was over, my father went to his cubicle, where a mattress was laid on boards, "easier to get up from than a bed"; in the dark before daylight, he would shuffle around to light the iron stove and in a very cold night would peer in to see that my blankets covered me securely: the feeling of peace, the warmth of love, would wrap itself about me, snatched out of the icy winter, and strange.

Apart from their timelessness, at which I chafed and fretted, these winter months live with a sort of icy brightness in my mind, a purely external glitter caused by climate. The Canadian snow is not that of the European lowlands: it is packed and frozen so hard that it squeaks like an unoiled cartwheel underfoot. But the Canadian winter held more than snow. It gave me my first sight of a river so darkly and solidly frozen that carts and horses carried their loads across; and, sleighing over the Kootenay,

near the ferry which was kept open, I watched the ice re-shaping
'like new skin over a wound', even as the commotion of the
paddle died away, leaving formless chunks, glaucous and black,
piled up on either side. A cart on the lake had once by ill-luck
hit the yesterday's track of a paddle steamer, and had sunk
like a stone, horses and all, where the ice was still too thin: I
thought I had never seen the grip of winter so cruelly shown,
draining the light out of water and forcing it to flow below,
voiceless and dangerous, blind under a slippery security, and
separated from the living air.

The heavy trains too, with their snow-ploughs like breast-
plates to the engine and sad bells tolling from the roof to warn
not human beings but herds of animals, came sounding through
the valley, bearded with icicles down all their length. And
when I left Creston, on February 1st, and made for New York
on my way home, I stopped for a day at Niagara, and saw
winter triumphant, and mountains of round ice below the
falls. The woods there were coated, even to the smallest
twig, with clear chandeliers of jangling drops whose still liquid
sisters hung in coloured rainbows of spray over the thunder
below: and the immense mass of water came tearing down
rough and victorious, tossing loosened ice-floes half-submerged,
until it turned over its ledge in one smooth, irresistible curve.

"There is no creature that Allah does not hold by the fore-
lock": I think of the verse of the Quran when I remember that
impetus of water. As I bent over to see the curve, so immensely
powerful, so strangely silent, between its two tumults—the
guide caught hold of me: many people, he said, are fascinated,
and throw themselves in if they can, and are drowned.

And when I had spent three very happy days with Lucy
Beach in New York, and had crossed the misery of the Atlantic
and welcomed the Mull of Kintyre pale in the morning sun,
and reached Scotland, I found there a winter almost as cold,
though less heartlessly brilliant than in Canada. The Lake of
Menteith was frozen over, and we skated across to the island:
and even south of the border taxis were plying on the surface of

the Dee. It was one of the coldest winters over Europe, and it killed our oleanders in Asolo, though they were gnarled old trees.

I stopped with Car and Penelope Ker in the Campsie Fells, in a house whose warmth and kindness shines unfadingly, to me as to many hundreds of passers-by and friends. I spent a night or two with Venetia in Wales, on my way; and reached London to be X-rayed and told that the operation, which had overshadowed my whole winter, was not necessary after all.

With this relief, and the prospect of the East again before me, I spent a very happy English spring.

My article on the Druses had appeared, and *The Cornhill* took my second effort also—*Canada and the Odyssey*. The first had procured me the friendship of Miss Doughty, a cousin of the explorer. I visited her in Lowestoft, and saw the Doughty home, empty and rather neglected, at Theberton in Suffolk. This was the first friendship brought me by my writing, and its memory still preserves—like many of the things I did during that English spring, and indeed most things afterwards—a faint Arabian enchantment built by association. A new venture mixed with the known ingredients of one's life makes a sort of patina like that of bronze or marble, or the lustre of ancient glass, an iridescence created by one layer of time on another, where both shine through. So, after riding with friends on Dartmoor by old ways known and loved since childhood, I would sit on their tennis court through the afternoons and read Philby's Arabian journeys, and lift my eyes from the brown desert-horizon of the pages, to see the Teign valley below me, the gentle steepness of slopes where every patch of warm gorse, every singing of heather or bending of grass in the south-west wind was known to me, with the voice of the hidden river slipping through forest pools. Philby the stranger and his deserts soon grew familiar inmates—to me—of that landscape which he may never see; and it is one of the pleasures of authorship to imagine into how many places one's words may wander, unknown to oneself, to become friends.

In London too the usual life with Viva Jeyes in Grove End

Road was mixed with mornings in the British Museum, reading *Brunow and Dussaud* on Roman roads in Moab and Edom; I spent time with Joan Ker buying a prismatic compass; and became aware of archaeology from the air, the discovery of sand-buried sites in Iraq and Transjordan.

* * *

S. S. ATHENIA, 26 *October*, 1928.

Dearest B,

To-morrow we should be crossing the Straits of Bellisle and getting to Father Point in Newfoundland, and a blessed thing it will be to see anything in the way of land at all. The Atlantic really is an objectionable ocean: 'How shall I meet thee? With Silence and Tears' in February. Everyone practically has been ill; we had two blizzards, one decent morning with a rainbow, and the rest damp rain. Now it looks like fog for the St. Lawrence.

The 3rd accommodation is perfectly comfortable and the stewards most kind and obliging. The only real advantage in 1st class is the people; the hectic effort at pretending to love your fellow creatures for nine days when the boat rolls about and they are all so dull and with so many babies. They are all good city folk, with lots of virtues, only not trimmed up. I tried to be interested in a young man who had Lawrence's book in his hands and has a lady friend who writes poetry, but his socks looked so like what the sea was making me feel that I had to give him up.

To-night we are going to have a whist drive. We are all reviving a little as we get into the shelter of the Continent. I am fairly happy, chiefly thanks to Car's oilskin and sou'wester and my gumboots which allow me to tramp up and down the slippery decks along which the other people have to skip in silk stockings. There is a cold air coming off Labrador, but not so bad as Syria. The sea is grey, exactly the colour of the seagulls with the white under their wings. They are still following us—lovely creatures. I have the joy of the *Odyssey*: it made me forget even the roll of the waves, such is the triumph of beautiful words. It is a revelation; to think that I reached 35 without reading it.

[31]

The orchestra is on its first sea voyage, with the result that when not overpowered by its sensations, it plays the same three tunes over and over: we always clap.

28 October, 1928.

We are in Quebec. The ship standing most harmoniously still. The sunset up the St. Lawrence last night was very grand—the blue sheet of water rushing down in a cold clear light. For a long way only one coast was visible: the right bank, sloping down in smooth lines, powdered with snow, or wooded, or cut into squares of fields, all very bare and simple lines, and here and there sparse villages and pointed spires. On the other side, there was a cold rippling sea, and a green and pink sky, very cold, and the air cold and thin from Labrador, with the taste of ice·in it and crisp and exciting: it was so clear even the little waves seemed chipped off and frozen in sharp ridges. Then we had a round moon in the middle of the smoke-trail of our funnel, and an evening star over New Brunswick.

Quebec has not shown herself till just now in the dusk—strings and clusters of lights, and spires here and there piled up in the grey of the water and the evening. We came up to her through thin rain and sleet, and it was too miserable to want to see anything at all.

Towards the end of the voyage our drooping spirits revived. We had a concert, almost all provided by various stewards who did their best very creditably. There is something lovable and innocent in most British gatherings for amusement—the only set-off to their appalling mediocrity. We were all quite happy, and every single item except one was incredibly bad. The best, however, was the bagpipes which started off hissing themselves (and you know what a terrible discord that is) and wouldn't stop: the poor boy with the red hair stood manfully trying to reduce them to order, or at any rate silence, screwing round the stops frenziedly while they groaned and squeaked and wailed, and the audience rocked with laughter all except the only 'foreigner' on board, who listened with a set and tortured face and evidently thought it part of the music.

CRESTON, 4 *November*, 1928.

Dearest Herbert,[1]

I think it is your turn for a letter. I thought I should write many

[1] Herbert Young.

[32]

in the train, but it was too jolty and I was busy looking out at Canada.
I was glad to arrive, with a vile cold produced by the meeting of
hot radiator air and the icy current off the window-panes; but now
I have had two nights rest and am spending a lazy day indoors with
the big stove going and two puppy dogs lying about like woolly
mats. Pips' gun is in the corner by the door and all the genuine
atmosphere of the Wild West—except that I haven't got to cook the
dinner. It is a cosy little log hut, four rooms and a veranda, and we
look down hill to the roofs of the barns and stable and a little three-
roomed hut where Tom and Alice now sleep—all cedar-wood slats,
very neat in the landscape; and then across a low undulation of cleared
land, brown and yellow stubbles with patches of forest here and there,
to the wide valley: they call it the 'Flats' and the mist lies there in the
evening, and the Selkirk range comes out of it steeply, with the
sunset straight behind it, we face due west. There is a little powder-
ing of snow fallen last night on the tops, and a filmy grey sky drifting
over the blue, and smoke from various fires going up in long streamers.
The forest is all small, Douglas fir, pines, birches, larches and the
cedar which is really a cypress: it is very thick for going through, but
not grand as timber. Pips himself came to meet me at the station:
he is stiff and cannot raise his arms much, but he can walk quite well,
and it was lovely to see him, looking as if all these years he had been
busily growing more and more a bit of the landscape; at a few yards
distance his dear old clothes would just melt into it invisibly. He
has a few books (nearly all I sent at various times) and a gramophone,
a bath, a stove and some Chippendale chairs he picked up from a man
who was leaving, and a geranium in a tin in the window, and these
are all the luxuries except the telephone, which seems very out of the
picture, but is indispensable.

The village is hidden behind the hill, and has two shops. Neither
of them provide clothes-hangers, which is all I have badly wanted so
far, but they provide groceries and whisky, if you can get a government
permit for which you pay four dollars a year. A Calabrese shoemaker has just been to call, with a bottle of cherry wine—very good
indeed: "Fatta la legge, trovato l'inganno."[1]

There are seven or eight neighbouring ranches visible from our
window, and nearly every one belongs to a different nationality—

---

[1] "Make a law and find the way round it."

Swede, French, German, English—they are all mixed, and Nature is such a big enemy that all the rest become insignificant.

There is really no means of describing the immensity of this great lovely country. This is comparatively inhabited, and Montreal is a very fine city, with beautiful buildings, banks and such-like, far more ornamental than any of their kind I have seen in England. The big shops are also impressive: you walk through marble colonnades in a restful silence (only too hot) with lots of space to move about in, and it is all beautifully organized and made so as to rest the jaded city-mind and avoid unnecessary trouble. Then your train starts and soon you are out in the endless flat stretches of woods and lakes, solitary as anything you can imagine. The train slips along for two days, and it is always the same: the long stretches of water where the ice is now forming at the edge: the thick pines and white birches, and here and there a sandy road with perhaps two lonely little square boxes of three or four rooms, or some little shanty by the water's edge with a canoe drawn up for the winter. People get lost in these woods and can never find the way out again. They go to shoot moose, or fish in the lakes. The monotony of it adds extraordinarily to the sense of remoteness and of the valiancy of men's effort who live here and make the land habitable.

At Winnipeg I suddenly heard myself greeted by my name, and there were two Scotch boys off the *Athenia*: two twins just leaving school and sent out to make their way with an introduction to some fruit growers here on the Kootenay lake. They came along with me all the way, and grew more and more pathetic over the beauties of Scotland as we got nearer the end of the journey: poor boys—I left them almost weeping with homesickness as I, the last link with the Old Country, got off and waved good-bye. The people they are going to are making them give £5 a week besides their work while they learn, which seems unfair, but I think they will look after themselves. "They'll soon find we're no so green," they assured me.

30 *November*, 1928.

Dearest B,

Your letter came just as I was leaving for Nelson, which is our only comparatively near city (six hours by train and boat). I spent a night in the hotel there, and last night on the boat and am now, just after breakfast, steaming back along the lake, the hill-tops hidden in

[34]

cold snowy mists, and one lonely wooded snowy promontory after the other unwinding slowly. The landing-stages are little wooden platforms floating in a framework of great poles, like huge bunches of asparagus half out of the water: as the snows melt and the lake rises, the platform rises too till it reaches the tops almost of the poles. The steamer is one of those shallow draughty paddle boats that they adopted for the Tigris during the war: it can lie right in with its snout on the beach like a crocodile and back out again into deep water.

Nelson is a pleasant little town with a high street and two trams, and a few stone houses among the wood. It clambers steeply uphill, with the lake—there as narrow as a river—below it and steep hills on all sides shutting it in. It is the only town of any size (and I suppose is smaller than Ventimiglia), between us and Vancouver, six hundred miles away. The whole of Canada has only nine million people and three thousand miles of continent for the railway to cross before it can touch coast again: if one thinks of this, the expense of the voyage across does not seem so great after all.

I was glad to hear prospects of L'Arma sale, for I shall need money badly if I have to come out to Pips at frequent intervals: and this will be inevitable. Thank goodness I foresaw at the time and managed to get at least partially ready for the emergency, for he of course can do nothing in the matter or in the way of finance: in fact, I very much doubt if he will be able to suffice for himself later on: however, sufficient for the day. He is I think a good deal better since I came. I have started little bridge parties for him, sending the people off at 11 (they used to go on till 3 or 4 a.m.).

I am trying to write another Druse article, but not getting on very fast. Pips has no particular occupation indoors, which is fatal for any concentration in our little sitting-room. Also there is always some ancient rancher or other dropping in. A poor Irishman, ex-officer on a P. & O. now sold out at Creston and going to try his luck with five hundred dollars in New Zealand, at sixty-three: it is rather pathetic. Indeed there is none of the buoyancy of prosperity in Creston: everyone is hard up and a little wistful. The energy and *joie de vivre* of the young country seems only to flourish in the towns. The country seems to rise on stepping stones, not of its dead selves, but of its dead pioneers, and the first lot who do the cleaning and the real hard work seem usually to succumb: then their successors get on.

[35]

CRESTON, 3 *December*, 1928.

Dearest Herbert,

This is exactly timed by your letter and Mama's, so that it *should* arrive on Christmas day and bring you my Christmas wishes, a whole bundle of them. We shall be thinking of you and wishing for that magic carpet—at least I shall—for though I like the interest and excitement of a new and empty country, I do feel myself *European* to the very bottom of my heart: or at any rate I feel that I belong to the Old World; partly because of the climate of the New, which is twenty-two below freezing this morning, and twenty-six below zero just a little east of us. If I happen to forget a hand, or bit of shoulder outside my eiderdown, I wake up with a violent ache all over it, and that is sleeping with closed windows: and though we keep the room up to seventy or more, the little cold airs manage to get in somehow. Yesterday I came home just about supper-time, the road hard with wide frozen ruts of solid ice: and it was so cold that I had no sensations at all below the knees.

I am depressed, having tried to write a second article which has been born as flat as a pancake—which just shows that I am not really meant by Destiny for an author.

14 *December*, 1928.

I must describe a dance in the Wild West to you. It is really rather fun. Imagine a cold clear night, Orion swinging up over the pines, and the planet of the season blazing away like a bonfire: the mud frozen hard, and me with overshoes and a flashlight, all warm in furs except where an icy zone encircles my silk stockings, making my lonely way through the wood to the parish hall. It is not more than half a mile away, all built of pine planks and cedar, and already very cosy with a roaring stove and red paper streamers down the windows: two gasoline lamps buzzing from the ceiling and the orchestra tuning up. Mrs. Lister, the wife of our provincial M.P. runs the orchestra; she has thin ankles, and a short white skirt, a striped blazer coat, and carries on with immense verve till any hour of the morning. Mrs. O, whose husband acquired from his wife a copper mine just above us on the hill, plays the piano; and a fair young man with a blue shirt

[36]

and intellectual forehead plays the banjo and also owns the garage here. The man at the drum looks as if he ought to be a producer of revues, but, of course, he isn't. I got there long after we were supposed to begin, but no dancers were there except a few of the young men in tartan shirts and the ladies whose business was to look after the supper. We slowly began to collect however, sitting ourselves in one long row. We all wear home-made dresses and pink stockings and really look very pretty especially when the colour we bring in from outside has stopped interfering with what we so carefully applied before starting. The young men don't come up unless they happen to know you, so that your social status can be gauged by the darkness of the coat or the amount of polish which has been given to the shoes that come up to dance with you. As soon as the music stops, you start walking round the room in procession till the orchestra takes pity and sets to again: when it remains obdurate, your young man takes you back to the row of chairs, deposits you among the other pink legs and retires. No sitting and flirting in corners: it would be difficult anyway in a bare square room. The men smoke at one end: Mr. Hester alone, who is a schoolmaster's son ranching out here and has the social nerve which lets him do bold things, comes up to talk to us occasionally. A little special knot of intimates sit round the stove in the kitchen, where the pretty cooks are. Now and then however there is a wave of democracy: someone in the hall shouts out "All change partners": and one is suddenly abandoned, and seized by the nearest young man, and whirled round till the next order is shouted out. Sometimes one's partner is tapped on the back by someone who wants a dance, to whom one is immediately handed over. It is amusing to be switched suddenly from a drawing-room step into say the latest from a Liverpool suburb, or the backwoods here. When the supper waltz starts, everyone remains firmly seated on their chair till it comes to an end and the young men and women in charge begin handing down tables across the platform. I was taken up to sup with the orchestra and acted umpire while the drum and Mrs. O played dice with the sugar lumps, and we handed our mugs to be filled with café au lait out of big kettles. It was very like the Wild West of the movies to look down through the smoke and the gasoline lamps to the young women with their shingled curls (a little more rebellious than on our side) and the young men in the tartan shirts. At two we broke up, and packed ourselves back into

[37]

furs and galoshes and snowshoes. Some kind person offered to see me home, but they all have to get up early to milk cows and things, so I resisted and came by myself through the snowy stillness of the pinewood—very lovely.

[Note-book] 17.12.28.

Nothing is more useful to a woman traveller than a genuine interest in clothes: it is a key to unlock the hearts of women of all ages and races. The same feeling of intimacy is awakened, whether with Druse or Moslem or Canadian. I wonder if men have any such universal interest to fall back upon?

19.12.28.

Forty years ago in the prairie, Winnipeg was little more than a village. The eating houses there used to have a bell tolling over their doors so that they might be recognized in the snow. The temperature goes to fifty below zero.

Notice how talkative the lonely life makes people. Have observed how people can go on, talking a long time to say nothing in particular —and perhaps it is a trait descended from the pioneering days. Mr. Garland told me that "talking to oneself" is the recognized sign among trappers and all these lonely people; when they catch themselves at it, they pack up their things and come down for a while to civilization to get their balance again.

20.12.28.

Delightful dream—floating by ancient cities along a broad river— only outlines visible: white water, pale sky, dim azure visions of temples, pillars, great buildings. In my dream I knew I ought to know it all and that I had been there before, but could not remember. But I had the feeling of real happiness, pure and light as the scene. Usually all emotion and colour is a little sombre in sleep, as if felt and seen in shadow.

21.12.28.

The self-reliance we hear of in the New World is a fraud: it is just the opposite, a want of experience and fear of letting it be seen: they are not sufficiently sure of themselves to be able to be humble. Note,

[38]

one of the benefits of religion—to inspire humility in people not advanced enough to attain it for themselves. Does not exist here, religion, except in first generation from Europe.

22.12.28.

Mrs. S: met her in the post office. Told me she wanted to return to Europe to be treated with deference: just what is so nice to get away from, says I. Told me all her family history and love affairs, and how she was a governess and now works the ranch with her husband. And the price of apples is too low this year for a holiday at Penticton. Dr. Henderson came in and went on talking through her interruptions like an ocean liner with a head sea.

26.12.28.

Usefulness of chess in general philosophy. No good to attack till all the forces are out and ready to concentrate if necessary. Very risky to attack while you yourself are threatened or in danger of being threatened. (Napoleon however was an expert at this unorthodox tactic.) The actual struggle is often for quite a minor piece, on which all energies of both sides have to concentrate. To have all your tools handy: to have your own safety guarded; to concentrate fully on the object even if it is not the final one—not a bad plan for the campaign of life. To keep the end in view, but not to be pedantically determined on the precise patch of attainment.

27.12.28.

Out with Tom and the two dogs in the cutter sleigh, pulled by the team. Pleasant sound of bells, and hoofs on the soft snow. Pleasant smooth motion. Danger of corners: easy to overturn, and impossible to back. Look out for ice clods flung from the galloping hoofs backwards. Betty and Peggy ran all the way. Betty's paws and legs like a bunch of snowballs at the end.

Various sounds of snow: the patter of ice when you cut steps on a glacier is exactly like the patter of the foam with a sea breaking against the ship's side.

28.12.28.

C's to tea. Talking of Hudson Bay, and the Swan River, and all the North to be opened up possibly with the railway next year.

Muskeg is bog-land. The railway must cross miles of this, but they build on the frozen land in winter, and it never melts under the hard road.

29.12.28.

Thawing—the new snow dripping off the roof in the night. Resilience of the sound: because each drop drops in its own little puddle. They are skating with torchlight on the Flats, however.

1.1.29.

So far as my personal object in life goes, I should wish to attain two things: first the confidence of more time, not to be confined within the narrow limits of one life: secondly the sense of death as a new and wonderful adventure. If these two can attain to a real sense of certainty, my own inner life will have succeeded—and I hope to succeed. It will mean the absolute liberation from fear, which is a form of slavery.

It is for this reason I am willing to risk my life, not from any natural fearlessness or recklessness. I am careful of the things that I need to enjoy life: careful of money, health as far as may be, and time as far as I can: these are necessary. But to be careful of life itself is to assume that it is more important than what is beyond life. To risk one's life seems to me the only way in which one can attain to a real (as distinct from a merely theoretic) sense of immortality unless one happens to be among the lucky people in whom faith is born perfect.

2.1.29.

The sun is out to-day with the peculiar beauty of this green-blue sky of the north. We walked up the road to see Tooke and Harris cutting up trees for logs—got them sliding down from our mountain. One of the big trunks hit a tree and split. Luckily the split went the whole length and the trunk came down in two enormous splinters: it would be very difficult to get it off otherwise. These trees hardly ever live to much more than 150 years.

5.1.29.

Abstract thought, not thought pure and simple, distinguishes man from other animals, i.e. a hen will count up to five, will notice if one of five chicks is missing: but only a human being will realize that there is a quality of 'fiveness' which is the same whether it be

[40]

chicks or pebbles. The distinction from animal to human, therefore, (as usual in nature), seems to be gradual and not absolute, and the only line open to further development seems to be along the lines of *abstract* thought.

According to this reasoning the artistic sense would be inferior to the philosophical in so far as it appeals to the senses—thought in its animal stage so to say, or little beyond it. All the arts in fact appeal in various degrees to the primitive mind. The art becomes higher the more abstract it becomes: poetry most of all: music also can become almost all intellectual.

Steiner's idea that a new philosophy of life should find a new art of form and colour to express it is pure nonsense: art has to express tangible objects, not ideas, and the very fact of its being lower in degree than philosophy also means that it can be perfect without superior aid: just as we prefer an 'artistic' and not a 'philosophical' cook.

Helen Blair to lunch to-day—fifteen years—not shy but so self-conscious, feeling the eyes of the Universe upon her. So small a Universe, at fifteen, and so much of it outside oneself. In spite of all that is said, it is happier later where the joy and the value of learning about it all is discovered, and our self comes to count for so little that its unhappiness scarcely troubles one. The ageing body need not impede the spirit very much. But never for a moment, if one desires this true contentment, can one think in terms of this life only: the proportion with eternity must be kept.

6.1.29.

I am just re-reading Gertrude Bell's *Syria,* and comparing her route with ours. She however travelled with three baggage mules, two tents, and three servants: so I consider we were the more adventurous. She also says that the water in the Jebel Druse 'is undrinkable by European standards', so I suppose our standard cannot be European: or perhaps an Italian education has hardened us.

6.1.29.

The king said: "I desire a maid than whom is none in her time more beautiful. Perfect in loveliness, excellent in judgement, and of a sweet disposition." The great men of the kingdom said: "This is not to be found for less than ten thousand dinars."—From *The Arabian Nights.*

[41]

Finished Gertrude Bell's *Syria*. Papa's criticism true: she did not have enough adventures: perhaps because she went with her own tents, and also—to get to the heart of things—one must stay longer in one place. If I live and I am free, I should like to have a little shop for a time somewhere in an eastern town. Say Hama or Aleppo? Great possibilities for observation—in fact the ideal for a meditative life.

7.1.29.

Watching the tits at the bacon hanging from the veranda post. Their swift, impulsive movements—quick as thought indeed, for nothing else in this world can compare with this kind of rapidity made of quick changes. The mind makes these sudden movements, darting from one side to the other, a short flight, a hop to one side: so it will do, when we should like it to take the large and soaring flight.

8.1.29.

Extraordinary veracity of *The Arabian Nights*. I think the secret is that they are all stories which have long been *told* before they were written. The same reason for the force of the Psalms: all the non-essentials are dropped during long repetition. Same for ballads. I believe W. P. [Ker] says so à propos of *Count Arnaldos*. The second charm of *The Arabian Nights* is their total want of any ethical aim. Only when reading them do we realize how all-pervasive this microbe is in European literature, i.e. in Boccaccio, who can be compared with the Arabian authors, there is always the undercurrent of satire; in Chaucer, satire or sentiment comes in. And where there is no ethical preoccupation, as for instance in some of R. L. Stevenson, there is a personal tinge given by the author, which interferes with the pure force of the story. "Keep your eye on the object," was W. P.'s literary advice: this is what the Arabian author does, eliminating all that might come between the reader and the tale. It is the same charm as one finds in some books of travel.

9.1.29.

Bridge at the W's. Wonder why he is so obviously devoted, and she is evidently a difficult and not a good-tempered woman. Decide it is because she is unexpected—one of the chief virtues in a wife, if one considers the monotony of most existences. Virtue in a husband too, and explains why so many quite valueless men are adored by

[42]

their women. Having a talent for the unexpected myself I would rather have a steady husband, but if one had not 'resources in oneself' like Miss Elton—why, anyone who gives the little shock of variety is invaluable. And hence Mr. W does not mind being hen-pecked.

10.1.29.

Alice always has her meals alone, after Tom has finished. Very reminiscent of the Druses. To treat women on a real equality only belongs to a *very* small class even in Europe: and I rather think this particular form of good breeding comes originally from good French society. Chivalry on the other hand, which is after all a respect for weakness, is found I imagine all over the world.

One of the advantages of visiting a Dominion, is that one comes to meet on equal terms people into whose life one never could enter in England. In the towns one is absolutely relegated to one's own class: in the country this is widened if you are a sportsman or woman. But people like our neighbour the watchmaker, or Sutcliffe the old huntsman and his family—we could never know them as they are in England simply because they would feel a distance between classes which here is disregarded. And what a fine reliable lot of people.

13.1.29.

Small squirrel to-day has carried off eight eggs. Tom saw him in the shed, carrying the egg in its front paws and holding it in place under its chin, toddling along on its hind paws and tail: so agitated when it saw Tom that the egg bumped against a corner of the shed and broke, and the little beast sat a little way off and chittered furiously at Tom.

14.1.29.

Looking out on this perpetual grey drizzle of snow I am haunted by Victor Hugo's verses in the Châtiments—the retreat from Moscow. Magnificent rhetoric:

> *Au seuil des bivouacs désolés*
> *On voyait les clairons à leur poste gelés,*
> *Restés debout, en selle et muets, blancs de givre,*
> *Collant leur bouche en pierre aux trompettes de cuivre.*

What a picture. Perhaps not absolute inspiration, but very wonderful.

[43]

15.1.29.

I often think how heavy a responsibility we should feel it, how careful we should be, if we realized how great an influence casual words may have. When one is young, one's whole life is waiting to be swayed, without as a rule any very definite bias on one's own part: and the most important things are often settled by the chance remark of someone we love or admire. I often think of this when I am with young people, who always seem to take to me and trust me very quickly: I suppose because they know that I do love youth not grudgingly as elders are apt to do. Their trust is so magnificently generous: one would like to deserve it by saying now and then something which in moments of doubt or difficulty may be of use to them: at least one would wish to avoid anything which might hinder instead of helping their sense of the proportion of things. If one's words have been ever a help and never a hindrance, that surely is a useful life and no other justification needed for it, even if it has accomplished nothing more tangible.

16.1.29.

Sleighing down the goat hill, absurdly unable to get rid of the fear of a fall. I can make myself run the risk of it, but cannot avoid the instinctive stiffening against it, which shows that one should never let oneself get out of the practice of these moral tests, any more than of the physical. To regain fearlessness is no small matter. The tumble was on a hard bit of road too, which does not make the future attempts really easier.

18.1.29.

Watched Alice coming up from the cottage through the blizzard. The snow whirled in the Flats like sandstorms. "Awful," says Alice getting out of shawls like a cocoon. She never speaks with emphasis, like many deaf people. We had the fire going and water nearby boiling. And the blizzard died down in the morning. All footprints nearly flattened out in the snow and the snow squeaking like new boots when you walk in it—so cold and hard packed, and it is enough to make anyone squeak too.

19.1.29.

"Not a climate to live in," said Alice this morning. I found her warming one foot after the other in the oven. Two below zero out-

side and my breath as I walked froze on my fur and tipped every hair
with ice. Ice in the kitchen wherever a drop of water touched glass
or metal on the outer wall, and the kitchen temperature is 70°. I like
the bright glittering air, and a tree top full of birds was twittering
shrill as can be for spring. *"Per l'aer freddo sui nudati rami"*—only
after plucking a goose do I realize how warm a bird is in its down and
the feathers over: like living in the centre of an eiderdown, with no
draughts.

Charming dog at the Blairs—has learnt that things come to you
if you sit on your hind legs for them: drove a mouse into a hay stack
and, when all else failed, sat down and put his paws up in front of the
hole, hoping to see it come out.

20.1.29.

A lot of observation lies under common figures of speech. One's
heart stands still, or sinks, or leaps; one sees red, or is frozen with horror:
no more accurate words could be found to describe what actually
these feelings are. And it is ever our figurative thinking that is
accurate, gives, that is to say, the unmistakeable picture of what we
intend. When they carry a picture, the simplest words can hold an
extraordinary weight of meaning. Who for instance but one accustomed to the desert horizon could say like the Psalmist that the Lord
has removed our sins from us "as far as the East from the West".
When we think of the words, we see what the Psalmist saw, and it is
the fact of his having seen it that makes it live—not a deliberate skill
with words which can never take the place of real vision.

21.1.29.

Perseverance is often praised, but it is not so often realized that
another quality must accompany it to make it of any value—and
this is *elasticity*; perseverance in only one direction very often fails:
but if one is ready to take whatever road offers, and to change the
chosen way if circumstances change, and *yet* to keep the end in view—
then success is infinitely more probable. The elemental forces, water,
fire, air, have this quality—ever ready to be deflected, ever taking the
line of less resistance, they make irresistibly for their natural level.
Meredith has a good passage about the Countess de Saldar which
illustrates the theory.

[45]

CANADA, 1928-29

Mrs. Brown at tea talked of early days on the prairie when the mounted police used to give dances in barracks and the prisoners were used to hand round the refreshments. She says their thumbs always seemed to fill the plate.

24.1.29.

Mrs. A's tea. Four ladies we were, for Mr. A fled after trying several anecdotes which I rather think were not considered refined. We sat over a white crochet table mat and discussed the Church Guild, which is wearing out its members with entertainments. The Presbyterians are cross, for every Friday is taken up by Church of England gaiety, and nothing is left for deserving Presbyterian objects: but soon will be Lent, and then the Presbyterians will have every week to themselves without a rival. Meanwhile the parish hall has to be decorated for a masquerade and only five dollars to do it with: Miss W thinks one could run to red cardboard hearts with paper streamers: and Mr. G has hung up sacred pictures on the walls. The hearts must not be put right over the sacred pictures, but it wouldn't matter if they were in between—say one heart over each window and a big one over Mrs. O at the piano, and the sacred pictures on the brown bare walls. Mrs. W suggested that they might come down and away altogether, but Mrs. A thought the vicar would not like a dance at which the sacred pictures could not assist as it were. And the hearts will be there for the Sunday school next morning, so that the sacred and profane will have an equal innings.

27.1.29.

Everyone is extraordinarily tired out by this weather, far more so than if it were in Europe, and I feel certain that this is because all have to do their own work. When these blizzards and cold days come, there is more work and it is all harder to do. Our kettle was frozen this morning, though the stove was roaring last night: my jug and hair lotion frozen in my room, and ice in *lumps* on the inner side of my bedroom window. But it is only five below zero or little more.

28.1.29.

Yugo-Slav dictatorship. This makes six or seven since the war. I think my generation should live long enough to see the end of this

[46]

experiment—possibly its success, but at any rate the definite result. England will probably benefit, for while she avoids the danger and disadvantages of having an actual dictator herself, the fact of there being so many of them in Europe will generalize the good they do accomplish and discredit the abuses whose existence has brought them into power. Parliament for instance will not be abolished in Britain, but the fact that other countries are doing without them will cause people to examine more closely into their merits and defects. In fact the success of a new principle of government is a challenge which can only be met by increased efficiency of the old—and therefore all to the good as far as we are concerned. It is perhaps one of the great reasons of our success in government that we are so slow in acting so that we can profit by other people's mistakes: the loss of time at the start is usually more than made up for by the comparative security in our direction, since the question for a government to ask is far less "*how soon* can we get there?" than "*where* are we going?"

29.1.29.

The Arabian Nights are really far more like real life than many stories. There is the wonder and strangeness; the unexpectedness which is so much more frequent in life than in the 'realistic' novel. The wonder of meetings and partings above all; you go out one morning, and the chances of life seize you, and half a generation goes by before you see your own people again: how many of the men you see strolling up and down the Creston street would bear out the truth of this? Quite a number.

31.1.29.

Palfreyman told us his ear was frozen on Saturday as he walked home (quite a short walk). It became soft and flapped over: very unpleasant, but worse if it happened to one's nose. They have it 60° below zero in Calgary—an uncivilized climate. I notice people do not seem to get more hardened to the cold. The only way to be hardened to uncomfortable conditions is not to know of a comfortable one.

"*Sà piu il matto in casa sua che il savio in casa degli altri.*" (Alick Mirabelli's proverb: "The fool knows more in his own house than the wise man in someone else's").

[47]

2.2.29.

In the *Odyssey* the phantom of Iphthime (Bk IV) is made to pass in by the thong of the bolt. The Nosairis north of Antioch still have holes for the spirits to go in and out of their houses. I think the ornament set over doors in Bosra may have had that idea.

WINNIPEG, 3 February, 1929.

Darling B,

Here I am on the way home again, in the middle of the snowy prairie, nearly 30° below zero, but it is so dry one does not feel it more than at Creston—only has to look out for one's ears and nose, etc. I feel I am quite lucky to have kept my nose. I felt it going rather queer and rubbed it hard in time. I do think it is a horrid climate where bits of you die off like this without your noticing.

It was rather miserable leaving. I hope all may be well till I return next year and possibly find Pips well enough to come back with me, though I rather doubt it. He came down to the station, and Mrs. and Miss Hamilton came, and the bank manager, and the Italian shoemaker with a bottle of rum wrapped in newspaper as a parting gift. I never expected to be given a bottle of rum on the platform. Then he rushed home and came back with sugar plums as an afterthought.

I had the train more or less to myself, as they had an accident and the service was a bit disorganized, and also people do not travel unless they have to now. One is nearly suffocated by heat *in* the trains, and frozen outside—and they are a wonderful sight, huge heavy engines and carriages, the lower part where the steam comes out all congealed in blocks of ice, and a long sort of beard of icicles all the way down dripping from the roofs so that they look like inventions for Christmas cards. They go along clanking a bell, to frighten away cattle I suppose, but it has a most lugubrious tolling sound.

[Note-book] 4.2.29.

"All this the Gods have fashioned, and have woven the skein of death for men, that there might be a song in the ears even of the folk of aftertime" (*Odyssey* VIII).

5.2.29.

Day at Niagara Falls; the sun and the ice made the enchantment. A Turner picture,—the spray, and the smooth sheet of water rushing down into it, the rainbow rising from it, and the iron suspension bridge like a phantom through the mist behind. The woods and gardens were frozen, every twig a white bar of ice bending under the weight: looking over the spectacle of tossing water and ice, to the icy trees behind, not a soul nor a building was in sight, nor anything but the elements, except black flocks of wild duck among the floes. The middle fall, churning on to an invisible ledge and boiling over, looks like an avalanche at close quarters: the same frothy milkiness. The noise down below, half smothered under the mounting range of ice mounds, goes on like those huge wooden hammers that beat the cloth out in old mills in the Alps: the same regular thudding. I saw the white water at night too, lit up by two (or whatever it was) billion candle power: vulgarity to make the forces of nature play parlour tricks.

[New York] 7.2.29.

As we passed Wall Street, saw two nuns coming out of the Stock Exchange building. Found in the City Hall, sitting at George Washington's desk, an old wizened lady who might have come over in the *Mayflower*. Her mother came from England in 1850 in a sailing vessel taking six weeks, and never dared face the ocean again.

In the evening we went to see 'Wings over Europe', with what is supposed to be a picture of the British Cabinet. Realize how entirely insular our standards of conduct are. The English express almost every feeling by *not* giving words to it, so that all the essential information is given by their pauses and silences: this point was completely missed by the American playwright.

9.2.29.

"He regarded love as a sort of cruel malady through which the elect are required to pass in their late youth and from which they emerge, pale and wrung, but ready for the business of living. There was (he believed) a great repertory of errors mercifully impossible to human beings who had recovered from this illness. Unfortunately there remained to them a host of failings, but at least (from among

[49]

many illustrations) they never mistook a protracted amiability for the whole conduct of life, they never again regarded any human being, from a prince to a servant, as a mechanical object." (*The Bridge of S. Luis Rey*.)

One of the secrets of the style of this book is its objective treatment of abstract things: the thoughts and feelings are described in absolutely the same way, with the same objective visualizing, as the landscape. Also a wonderful selective discrimination: the description is cut down to one or two points always concrete, usually dramatic (like the description of the twilight, when men coming from work stop in their yard a moment to play with their dogs).

10.2.29.

The Anglo-Saxon seems to have a talent for religion and none for saintliness.

[Ship-board: bound for Scotland] 12.2.29.

Talk with the Irishman from Texas. Left his home at age of thirty one Sunday morning dressed for church; so agitated he could not eat his breakfast, but shared it with the dog. He went to Belfast: had never been away before. Reached New York on a Friday and found work on Monday, and never went home for twenty years. An example of what Ernest writes—that it takes the puritan to colonize. He told me how he was put to run a hotel store with no experience at all. The manager, 'a hot baby', swore like a tap running. Told him "You're no more use to me than a blind woman." But he stuck to it and stayed four years, and ran up the hotel stairs with a naked butcher's knife after a nigger who had insulted him, and only just stopped himself at the dining-room door where the old ladies were trooping in to dinner: "With all those poor old dears, there'd have been an inquest." I told him about Jerusalem, and he quoted from Isaiah.

14.2.29.

Little elderly spinster with fluffy grey hair and beady eyes has an artistic temperament. She says that if she marries in the "evening of her days," he must be musical: "Because ye know, Miss Starrk, I'm ter'ble fond of music." And she belongs to a Franciscan order and

[50]

says her prayers on her knees twice a day, and is therefore glad to have the cabin to herself: "Because folk do not always understand, unless they happen to be well bred."

15.2.29.

Poor old Mrs. M, quite alone except for a niece in Scotland whom she is going to see after twenty years. She is old, and plain, and quite uncompromising—a nurse for small babies—and she has been eating her heart out with fury all these years over the vulgarity of her employers. "I cannot help it, Miss Stark, and after all these years living in America—but what I like is a *thoroughbred*"; and she still hopes to find a world all full of gentlefolk on this side of the ocean. She cannot live out of U.S.A. without losing the little pension which is all she has: but she is hoarding up every memory for this holiday: the snowdrops, the whins, the blue bells, "and oh, Miss Stark, if I should see a hedgehog by the roadside, I'll break down—I'll go and cry by myself on the moors—I'm not a one for whining," and she is nearly weeping. She is a fine old woman, so fierce and feeble. "If ye knew how little I care for position or money, but I do like a thoroughbred; and ye do still find them in Scotland, do ye not?" And she looks at me with a world of anxious inquiry.

16.2.29.

The little Roman Catholic spinster told me that her sister has a statue of the Madonna of Lourdes. It has a musical box inside it, which is turned on to play Gounod's *Ave Maria* every evening now while the returning wanderer is facing the perils of the sea.

Odyssey XVIII. "Nought feebler doth the earth nurture than man, of all the creatures that breathe and move upon the face of the earth. So, he thinks that he shall never suffer evil in time to come, while the Gods give him happiness, and his limbs move lightly. But when again the blessed Gods have wrought for him sorrow, even so he bears it, as he must, with a steadfast heart. For the spirit of man upon the earth is even as their day, that comes upon them from the father of Gods and men."

17.2.29.

Delight to arrive in Scotland again. How can one ever explain to the go-ahead west the charm of the shabby grey haphazard old land? It is partly the feeling that things just grow and are not made. Mr. Robertson, who came from Arran twenty years ago and had never been back, was an interesting study: all American on the voyage, one could watch him becoming more and more Scottish again as the hills came in sight—Mull of Kintyre, Arran, Pladda lighthouse, Whiting Bay, then Ailsa Craig. We talked of peat fires and the gaelic names. Yet the night before when I asked him whom he would fight for in case of war (he is naturalized American) he said it would have to be the U.S.A.

17.2.29.

Pen [Ker] and Nancy Graham to meet me, and all at Montgomery Crescent, and Car here with daffodils in my room and aconite, snow-drops and Christmas roses on the dining-table—'a wee February bouquet.' Good it all is.

18.2.29.

Skating to Menteith priory across the lake—silence and space. The thin snow parting under the skate—blackness of ice below. I think of the blue water round the Sporades—the same intensity of depth. Long clear spaces, like the track of currents, where the ice has no snow and is rough: a crack running deep along the middle of them.

Lovely to see the russet of the trees after all those straight Canadian pine stems, and Grahames of Glenny buried in the Priory: the Peninsula, Crimea, and Lucknow mentioned on one tombstone, father and son.

19.2.29.

With Pen to the Western Infirmary, the long cheerful wards to catch the sun all day, with the table down the centre full of yellow daffodils and red tulips. How pleasantly and easily the invalids accept a perfect stranger to talk to them. Possibly the long feeling of class bitterness is drawing to its close, and the sense of mutual obligation beginning to take its place in our country at any rate? It seems to me that there are a good many signs that this is so. It is certainly true that this is now the conscious aim of most educated statesmen. We do not notice it, but it is a new principle in the world, a feeling of *peaceful* nationalism: the question is whether we are sufficiently prosperous to carry it out—for it is an expensive experiment to make a crowded country comfortable for all.

20.2.29.

Pleasant walking home in the damp dusk, all greyness and trees dripping, the lighted train hurrying through the landscape with a sweep of smoke, pink underneath from the engine. The author of Hansel and Gretel and all its kind knew the charm of a light to those benighted outside. It is one of the earliest things I remember and has always kept its magic. The charm of coming home in the evening rain must be pure sentiment and association, for I have never known it shared by anyone of the South.

21.2.29.

Lord Burleigh's advice to his son Robert. To spend only three-quarters of his revenue and not more than one-third of that on house-keeping, "for the other two parts will do no more than defray extraordinaries, which always surmount the ordinary by much" and "gentility is nothing but ancient riches" and "live not in the country without corn and cattle about thee."

22.2.29.

Talking to Car [Ker] about days in Bologna and all the old things. My feelings always seem to be like the Kootenay river, no life on the surface: I do not even know that I am feeling anything at all. Then suddenly discover that the emotion has been working away all the time, and there am I—shattered, with not the wrinkle of an eyelid to show for it. Like poison gas you breathe up without any perceptible difference on the atmosphere. It is easier, if you can react more obviously.

[Wales] 23.2.29.

Penbedw in all its old beauty and Venetia so right in her setting—so like the spirit of the quiet lovely house. While I sit enjoying it, I think of Pips so far away. I feel that I should not be so happy to reach my own places and friends again. But what a rest to sit and talk of the things we care for, with no effort, moral and material, and life sliding, as smooth as a hedgehog when you stroke him in the direction of his prickles: I cannot forget that they may stick up again any moment, but it is pleasant meanwhile.

[53]

24.2.29.

Lady in the train yesterday, with a good Scottish accent, lived at Algeciras. Told me amusing stories. How Gibraltar dare not bring water from the mainland in pipes for fear the Spaniards poison it at the source. Terrible tales of Spanish brutality in the Moorish war and how to cure whooping-cough according to the Moors. You catch a flea, tie it by a thread and dangle it over a bowl full of grains of wheat. The poor beast will seize on a grain, which is to be put on one side. One flea is good to lift about twenty grains: you must then get hold of another victim. When enough grains are collected, they are strung on a thread round the child's neck, and the whooping-cough is cured.

The Druse Christians at Redeime cure pneumonia by branding a cross on the chest with a hot poker. Amatallatif at Damascus told me how, when she was ill, her mother covered her with the flat slabs of bread and the mullah came and exorcized the disease into the bread which was thrown away.

The little Frenchwoman on the boat (*"on en a pendu onze—après, ça a marché sur des roulettes"*) told me that a piece of sealing wax anywhere in pocket or bag, would preserve one from colds. And a hempen string under one's clothes round one's waist would cure lumbago.

[London] 26.2.29.

I had not realized what a lot of changes have taken place in me till I return here and find all so essentially the same. Like the return in a dream. Only that there are gaps—many people missing who belonged to this picture. It is a good thing to be conservative in one's house, not to renew and change too much, if only for this pleasant feeling of stability which seems so rare and precious.

11.3.29.

Day in British Museum reading room. Delightful repose. I come out filled with serenity, perhaps because, while one's brain works, one's own *self* practically ceases to exist. I seem part of the books I am reading and the quiet and silence do not bring constant turmoils of recollections and interruptions as one gets when studying elsewhere. Easy to work under such conditions. Only suddenly, after three *hours* or so, I discover I am tired, and have to stop: almost as sudden as a lid closing down.

14.3.29.

In British Museum reading about the old Roman roads in Moab and Edom. Disappointed to find that about fifty travellers have written about the Jebel Druse. I wonder if there is anywhere left not written about? The only thing that is not overdone is *thinking*.

11 *GROVE END ROAD*, 15 *March*, 1929.

Dearest Pips,

I am just on my way to Miss Doughty at Lowestoft. Will tell you all about it next week. Feeling rather nervous, but I have got a new hat which always is inspiriting.

I really do think that you are the most robust member of the family after all. All the infants down with 'flu, Mama ditto in Asolo, and Mario [Roascio] turned out of his motor and damaged (but doing well considering). Poor Roma Bonar was with him and also hurt, but also doing well now. I am waiting to hear whether I am to rush off to any bedside, and if so, which? Or whether to stay on here and let the doctors go on experimenting with my own insides. Now that they are not going to operate, I feel that their 'treatments' can be done any time and no particular hurry about it.

Last night I went with Viva [Jeyes] and H. Van der Weyden to the Royal Geographical to hear a man called Crawford who has been doing archaeology from the air. We saw the photographs of Babylon, and Ur and Nineveh with all the plans of the towns showing very clearly in faint straight lines. New York carries out the earliest principles of town planning: the idea of straight streets at right angles seems the most ancient of all. It got untidy in the Middle Ages. I think one might find an amusing connection between despotic government and neatly planned streets.

[Note-book] 17.3.29.

Music at the Temple, clear as falling water, thin and rare and fine: not luxuriant as the music of Santa Maria Maggiore. The eighty-eighth Psalm, filled with grandeur and terror and awe. As they sing, the great barren land lies before me, so pitiless, so utterly without refuge. In spite of all, our generations in Europe are too comfortable to produce literature like this.

In the lesson, Mark xiii, 18, the words "And pray ye that your flight be not in the winter", or to that effect, throws a very true light on the climate.

[55]

20.3.29.

We looked at the sixteen Germans buried at Theberton when the Zepp came down: their careful little gravestones, so well kept, and the text: "Let no man judge another man's servant, for in sight of his master he standeth or falleth." The tactful Germans chose for their Zeppelin pleasure flight the other day the very same route they had so often made on their offensive expedition: the monster seemed quite a familiar sight to the inhabitants of Lowestoft. They were shelled from the sea, but the only house destroyed was an empty one. A shell ran alongside one street through the top floor of one house (and the inhabitants were in the kitchen), then through the bottom story of the next (and the inhabitants were on the landing above), and finally settled, unexploded, somewhere in the third. Most of the shells did not explode because, being meant to impact against the hard steel of battleships, the walls of Lowestoft houses were too *soft* for them.

LOWESTOFT, 22 *March*, 1929.

Dearest B,

Such a nice time here. Miss Doughty is delightful, full of energy, character and fun, with the most charming smile, and an interest in all sorts of things. She lives all alone with a maid, and runs local politics. She is a magistrate and sitting on the bench now, after taking me to the fish market, which I enjoyed; looking at the yellow trawlers and the grey North Sea behind them, and the pretty brown backs of the fish slithering about all over the place.

Yesterday we drove out in a sea mist, which cleared before we reached the Doughty village of Theberton, the old house very deserted and lifeless among its park and trees: Italianate columns, bad taste but rather nice, speaking of leisure and comfort and the humanities, and the old church built of little flints (for this country has no stone) with a fine round tower, and the window to the young Doughty V.C. killed at Gallipoli. The family are all naval people, and Charles was heartbroken because his sight was not good enough for the Navy. Miss Doughty herself would make a splendid Admiral: she has the clear sensible gaze and the long upper lip and square chin of so many sailor types.

Her housekeeping most casual and one of those vigorous people who are always warm without fires: and as this is the easternmost point of our island, I feel half frozen.

[56]

Don't you think that Mario will *have* to marry Bonnie, now that he has thrown her out of the car? If they go to L'Arma I suppose I ought to go and look after them? Anyhow I will hear I hope and you will let me know *where* to go.

[Note-book] 22.3.29.

Through the flat country, Norwich to Cambridge by Ely. Very like the Norwich painters. Again feel as always how satisfying to the soul is space. Ely dominates; so do the windmills. When one thing stands above, the earth and sky centre round it.

26.3.29.

More and more it seems to me that the success of marriage lies with the woman: if she has the talent for it, she can make most men do, so long as she is sufficiently interested to make her feel it worth while. I don't think M is very interested. I like her, but V is quite fond of her, with that extraordinary passion for recognizing *only* the merits of second-rate people. I think I would go on my knees to true *excellence*: but why go into ecstacies over the moderate virtues merely because they might not have been there at all?

[Thornworthy] 30.3.29.

Never heard the beauty of the lark's song like to-day—the agony of sweetness in it, 'l'ultima dolcezza'—and to-day like the very voice of the moors, the pale grassy slopes and misty distance and the gentle horizons when spring seems to belong more to the sky than to earth. William chatting about horses, his bowler well tilted forward, and long lash curling from his hand like a sceptre: telling Whitesocks' virtues, as she steps along with pretty lady-like slimness and ears pricked forward. He will refer to her as 'he', though she has had one foal already.

1.4.29.

Riding this morning with the rain and the wind on our faces. The drifting showers sweeping over and around us, fierce and soft. The yellow dry grass all bent one way; the ground still hard with

[57]

drought, the water lies on it. The waterdrops on the new grass give silvery light like the sheen on velvet. The wind carries away our voices, but on the lee side of the slopes the tumult dies down into a delicious oasis of stillness.

3.4.29.

The real bliss of a morning on horseback is the delightful freedom from all conscious thought. It is like childhood, every minute full of incident and interest, and no consciousness of thinking about it. You come back with a feeling of satisfaction, with a mind swept clean, full of landscapes, and speed, and winds, and lights, which have settled in it unnoticed, while it rested. It *perceived*, but did not *think*: the thoughts slip through, meeting no obstacle of logic; not even reaching the stage of being articulate: and that is the real holiday.

4.4.29.

Lunch by the North Teign in the wood. Sunlight moving on the *under* side of mossy boughs, horizontal over the stream, the light reflected from the running water. All mossy boulders, and water with mossy stones below, or golden yellow pools: it shines blue in the distance through the soft feathery woods seen from above. The larch like green dewdrops along boughs. The pussy willows out, show up like blossom, which they are of course. An unending tangle of boughs, green and brown, where we sit by the stream. Lichen with long ragged edges, and ferns on the mossy trunks. And the russety carpet of dead leaves lets the spikes of the small daffodils come through: their heads, long and fine as a greyhound's, show everywhere.

7.4.29.

Philby took a fortnight to reach Riyadh from Bahrain: three weeks to reach Jedda from Riyadh, riding fairly fast. The temperature went down to about 41° in December.

9.4.29.

Note the different character of a continental and English gathering of acquaintances: both leave the real self equally untouched, but the former obtain the result by actively expressing sentiments which are not there; the latter merely do not express the sentiments which are

[58]

there and confine themselves to the non-committal—a system far duller than the Latin, but has the advantage that when a real sentiment does come along it has a clear road free of pretences before it and can make headway. It is the better system, though rather terrible in the hands of the really dull.

10.4.29.

No doubt that one of the purest most unadulterated of human joys is that of exercise. Thinking so while playing tennis, and perhaps the recognition of this is the reason why the Anglo-Saxon race alone still believes happiness to be an average attainment. Exercise, the attainment of knowledge, and the practice of affection: the three best in humanity—and beyond these a gift of the spirit, which is divine.

THORNWORTHY, CHAGFORD, 11 *April*, 1929.

Dearest Pips,

I am feeling almost immovable with stiffness to-day the hounds though never got a run except a tiny little one on that boggy hill above Teignhead. We were out, from the meet at 11.30 at Moortown gate, till 3, when William and I left them going up towards Grey Wethers and came home to save up for to-morrow when they meet at Chagford. We made a good round however, up by Canaan and then into Batworthy Mire where there is that sandy track on the Throwleigh side of Scorehill Circle. Then through the Mire (Jim Endecott leading), with Round Tor on our right, up to Wild Tor: over the ridge between Wild and Watern and then towards Steepleton and all round the Mire between that and Hanging Stone, till we crossed the Varacombe (going down to Teignhead) and came down into Teignhead Newtake. I had to jump a gap in the wall. Pony had never jumped and I am not great at it as you know—but got over somehow. Old Squire Dunning was out, very pleased to hear about you, and I stuck to him like a leech through the boggy country. He was very nice and waited for me at a little stream, trying to inveigle Whitesock across: she took a leap across finally, loosing both my stirrups, but I stuck on somehow, and the hounds found just then so we were off galloping all along that Teignhead ridge towards Watern —but the fox went to earth and the hounds were called off and we came home. Such fun it was all the same, and the Moor looking lovely with hail and rain storms sweeping over it.

[Note-book] 17.4.29.

People who have gone through sorrow are more sympathetic than others, not so much because of what they know about sorrow, but because they know more about happiness. They appreciate its value and its fragility, and welcome it wherever it may be. The Puritan attitude which grudges happiness belongs only to those who have never entered very deeply into life.

17.4.29.

Wonderful view from the point where you leave the N.W. passage and come out on the Fur Tor hill: long blue lines of hills and Tors: Langeford, Beardown, Crow, Great Mist Tor. So many beauties: the beauty of space on that horizon; the beauty of loneliness in the upper reaches of the Dart where no horse can travel; the beauty of age in the wrinkled granite of the Tor; the beauty of life in the larks with quick flickering wings, singing.

17.4.29.

Lost in the mist. Felt afraid: unreasonable, as there was no real possibility of avoiding a road sooner or later. But it is an eerie feeling—the silence, helplessness, and the white moving curtain round you: the heather under the horses' feet so plain and all outside the narrow circle, which moves as you go, so absolutely impenetrable.

3

To Baghdad, 1929

As early as October 1927 I mentioned in a letter to Venetia that Ja'far Pasha, then Prime Minister of Iraq, having been approached by friends, had invited me to go to Baghdad. This plan was interfered with by a change in the Iraq Government, and the Pasha and his wife were now representing their country in London—the Pasha, big, burly, and direct, exercised by the study of English law, and surrounded in a Kensington house by furniture that had twice made the desert journey from the Tottenham Court Road to the Tigris and back, without losing any of its gloss or self-assurance. Madame Ja'far, far less vigorous than either her husband or the furniture, stood a little in the background, with black-rimmed eyes, despondent. I was taken to lunch there, and went off to acquire a map of Baghdad and an Iraq visa on the strength of it.

These and my dreams I took with me on the summer's round in Italy—to Dronero and Asolo, to L'Arma with the children, to Macugnaga for an unexpected happy stay with Charles Ker and his family, from which I returned by Lecco and Brescia, for a three days' stay with Greta and Mrs. Robertson on the lake of Como. These were old themes, endeared by time— friendships and habits embedded in a mass of repetition and past days: the new thread was visible only here and there, quite small and unobtrusive among them, and yet it already made the sum of my world. I rested on the thought of it at night, and woke with it in the morning.

I read Al-Ghazzali (mostly in translation), and took a course of drawing by correspondence which has never passed beyond its

TO BAGHDAD, 1929

elementary stage, to help me on my journeys. I mounted my own maps for economy and continued to read Arabic in every spare moment. Surrounding all these pleasures and dreams was the usual swarm of troubles—the problem of letting or selling L'Arma so as to prevent its being an expense; the putting straight of the peasant's affairs, where—with disastrous consequences—my mother had asked Mario to interfere; the insoluble problem of the children's education in the face of his objection to any sort of school; and the news that my father might have to be operated on for hernia. This came a month before my departure. I suggested going out to him. The voyage to Canada cost twice as much as that to the East, and my bank account was more or less exhausted, but I was ready to disregard it. I have found that one can nearly always do what one sets out for, if it is only one thing at a time. I had half the fare, wrote to my father that it would be easy, and waited to the last possible moment to fix my journey eastward, when better news from Canada arrived.

I left at last on the 26th of September from Trieste, with a feeling which I was beginning to know, the opposite to the tearing up of roots—a feeling as if the body were pulling itself away, safe but lacerated, from numerous tentacles: if there had been only one it would probably have anchored me.

The explanation of my escape, when the majority of human beings stay and attend to duties, of which I had such a crowd to choose from—is, I am told, that I am wild by nature. Whether or no this is so I cannot tell. But the thought has made me wonder what the difference is between the wild and the tame, and I have come to the conclusion that one of the main differences is that of habitually making or not making up one's mind. Every wild animal lives in a state of danger, which means deciding all the time, while the very essence of tameness is the absence of any need for decision. The wild soul is perhaps conscious—as I certainly am always conscious—of the intrinsic danger of life, which is hidden from the domesticated, whether animal or human, by the fact that their necessities are provided

[62]

for them, and only a strong imagination or accident can make them realize the precarious nature of what they rely on.

It is hard to say which is the better of the two states of mind: but it does not do to assume the domestic alone to be laudable in a world where all the chances of survival are with wildness. On the other hand it would be unfair to assume that wildness alone is brave: there is a slow and steady noble courage needed to face, sustain and conquer domestic life. The wild are perhaps the more fearless as opposed to courageous; their minds are more mobile and their instincts more ready, by necessity, to face the unexpected when it comes; and whether they are bedawin, untamed birds and beasts, or eccentrics like ourselves, mere captivity is likely to kill them.

There is also a difference between the wild and the domestic in their ideas of travel. How often someone tells you that his or her chief pleasure is to see the world. You look, and lo, the most acclimatized product of a park—a creature scarce able to move without a railing round it. What it likes is to have the views of outside brought in to vary the sheltered panorama; and, though it may travel from the Crystal Palace to Timbuctoo, the park precincts will never be abandoned. The genuinely wild is not interested in 'seeing the world'; it is exclusively interested in *being*; it digests the world as a cow chews its cud not for what the grass looks like but for what it does inside. This hunger is insatiable, until the desire itself for being shall pass away; and these creatures travel, even if they are sitting motionless and chained. For this reason I can scarcely bear to look at the truly wild animals in cages, padding with their desperate patience to and fro; and particularly at eagles; those yellow eyes that see their own sights only, within whose unwinking flame, like pyres, their memories lie burning—it is surely no sight of sky or sun, but the *use* of the great pinions, their lift and their sweep in the air that they remember. I have long thought that one of the most touching things about wild animals is that they will not even take the comfort of love in captivity; they will mate—as we should all do—only in freedom; and when they condescend to breed in a cage, it is one of the most puny of the triumphs of men.

In my own escape, which had only the remotest resemblance to that of an eagle, I came for the first time fully face to face with the Zionists of Palestine. The S.S. *Carnaro* was full of them, and they happened to be unattractive, partly and unjustly because they were so plain, but also and chiefly because they gave an impression that they felt the world empty except for themselves. The English are often offensive for the same reason, but I could not help thinking that I would prefer a world all British rather than all S.E. European Israel, if one had to make such a lugubrious choice. One of them, anxious to get by, lifted me and my chair all together from behind and put us down in another place on deck, with no word or excuse, but in the mere *hurry to get on*, and looked surprised when I reacted in the most vicious German I could muster: he was pained with my want of sympathy with his efforts to reach his goal. At Jaffa they were all rowed ashore singing their national hymn, and again there was no particular sympathy from the outside world. The British troops were drawn up on the quayside to protect them; and the Arab boatmen could only show their feelings by their faces, and the muscular strength with which they hurled the Zionist mammas, their parcels and their offspring, among the thwarts, —taking a contrastingly tender care of a few descending British matrons, delicately passed from hand to hand.

The East affected me, on this second arrival, with a rapture such as I have never known except on my rediscovery of the Alps after the first World War. In both cases recognition and novelty were combined, and the reality so far richer, the air more light, the colours brighter, the human beings more fully living, the radiance more complete than I had remembered.

Fruits of the harvest-time were poured into the suqs of Beirut with a luscious richness of grapes, nectarines, figs and melons—and the same opulence burst out in the small patches terraced and watered on the sharp slopes of the Lebanese hills. There is I believe no country where the presence of the ancient world is more living and insistent than in Syria. The life of the Crusades goes on in the narrower streets of the cities with almost the same intercourse of East and West; and in the hills, as soon as you reach the stonier places, there is an atmosphere of awe, the feeling of a temple only just deserted that listens to echoes of voices only momently silent, all alien to us, yet filling the white and black rocky valleys with a sort of humanity to which we have lost the key.

From Brummana revisited I wandered in these high places, to Sannin and Afka, where the Adonis river breaks from its cliff by the earthquake-shattered temple, in a coolness of mint and shadow, out of a deep green pool: and then again to Damascus, walking with my friends of the year before in the gardens of the mosque in the twilight, and staying with them in the rich olive and plough-lands of Rihane, in the country house of a village they farmed.

It was the end of October before I crossed the desert by the cheaper way, with three other passengers and an Armenian driver, and reached Baghdad for the first time, with £10 and all the East before me. The whole of my expenses from Venice, and the month's living, had cost me £43.

*   *   *

PARIS TO DRONERO—ASOLO, 1 *May,* 1929.

Dearest Pips,

I left London rather worn out this morning, having had a perfect whirlwind of a week to get all done, including a little necessary reading in the British Museum: tea with my editor, Dr. Huxley, who was charming and talked of Alps; lunch with Ja'far Pasha and his wife who are giving me introductions in Baghdad; dinner with Sir Goscombe John, who very much wanted to be remembered to you; then an interview with a lady who runs a thing called the National Political Union, which is trying to keep Palestine out of the hands of the Jews: it seems it is a question of the Dead Sea potash which will

make whoever gets hold of it incredibly powerful; then all my shopping; toys for the kids, etc., and Herbert Olivier on the very last day
getting me to translate letters about his roads to the Ventimiglia
engineers, which will certainly get him into troubles. This is only
a selection.

I had great fun looking into old travels round Arabia, fifteenth to
seventeenth century. Apparently a man called James Pitt from
Exeter got to Mecca in 1680 or thereabouts. But the first European
to leave a record of it was a Bolognese, Lodovico Varthema, and he
enlisted with the Mamlukes and left a full description. If I can get
hold of it I will, and send it you, for it sounds very amusing.

I spent my last pound on a prismatic compass—a lovely toy: I
hope it may be useful. It shows the course by night too.

ASOLO, 25 May, 1929.

I have a good subject for the winter, if only it hasn't been exhaus-
tively done already—and that is to combine a sort of history with
travel notes to the fortresses of the Assassins, who were the followers
of the Old Man of the Mountain, and had a series of castles between
Aleppo and the Persian borders. I am very vague about it all, but
am trying to find out some more before going out. It seems to me
rather promising, although it may all have been done by some
thorough-going German already.

Heat has come along in a wave, and a new sort of rose opens out
every day. Teresa, very pretty yellowy pink; Simplicity, a lovely
white one; and all sorts and kinds. There is a copper-coloured single
rose called Austrian Briar which is a constant delight, like a flame
against the plain.

ASOLO, 2 June, 1929.

I have an amusing Arabic book—a traveller who wandered all over
the place as far as India in the eighteenth century. He was in Damascus
one day and saw a small servant-boy carrying a plate and drop it,
breaking it to smithereens. The poor little boy was very distressed,
and a sympathetic crowd gathered: one of the men there told him to
go to a certain place where a charity was instituted to give a new
piece of crockery for all the broken ones that were taken there: this
was a special charity to benefit servants. I wish someone would do
the same here.

[66]

The oleanders have three or four quite good-sized shoots, but their life is still doubtful. Beach's servant thinks it is only "*l'angonia della tisi*", but I hope they may recover. It is lovely out now, only too many thunderstorms.

We are up for a few days at S. Martino di Castrozza. I wonder if you know it? Feltre hills are below us to the south, and Fiera di Primicro, fourteen kilometres down the valley. There is a magnificent wall of lacy peaks on our east. I have been up the smallest of them, leaving at six, and getting to the top at nine, after an hour on the rope up very nice spiky rocks. I felt all right until after the first twenty minutes when I seemed paralysed with pure terror and thought I was going to faint or be giddy; however I set my teeth and by concentrating on the slab in front of me gradually lost the unpleasant sensation that I and all the hillside were going to topple over together. I felt fine while up there, but rather upset ever since: so no more this year; but I think I must give the climbing another chance and go at it more gradually next year, before deciding that I am 'past' it. Alas.

I found *white* soldanellas near the snow, and also a pretty yellow primula which I had not seen before. Lots of flowers everywhere now. Fields of columbines, yellow and white lilies, and what looks like an orchid, with a big yellow bay and brown petals. The alpine rose and gentians just out too; and the air is lovely, only coming up from Asolo we shiver with cold. I don't really like Dolomites as much as Alps because there is so much less water: I suppose the porous rock lets it all filter down to the valley bottoms, and you miss the little springs and fountains gurgling out everywhere.

At the top of this valley is the Passo di Rolle, and there are still the old trenches and shell holes. The whole place was blown to bits at the very beginning of the war and has been rebuilt more hideous than you could believe possible.

An American neighbour in Asolo was telling me that he drove an ambulance round about Grappa through the war. He was stationed at Bassano and was much impressed by the politeness of a British airman who fell into Brenta with his aeroplane and was fished out by an American as he was sinking for the last time: just before losing consciousness he managed to murmur: "Sorry you had to get wet for me."

This government is getting beyond anything. Our sale of

[67]

L'Arma hinges on some people living in France and the man who is doing the business cannot get a passport to go and consult them because he happens to be anti-fascist. I don't think any other people would sit down under it. Apparently Toscanini has got into trouble with Mussolini because he got tired and refused to play the fascist anthem whenever a prominent fascist came into the Scala in the middle of his operas. I don't know how it will all end.

Am having lots of trouble trying to get Mario to pay. It seems rather hopeless and makes one sick. Hope you can send that receipt (or power of attorney) and I will see what I can do when I have it. But I don't know that one can do anything by gentle means. He is a dreadfully dishonest little man, and I think he will end by being in serious difficulties all round.

L'ARMA, 15 August, 1929.

Dearest Venetia,[1]

I almost thought the other day that I should be looking in on you at Penbedw, for we had some anxious news of Papa, who developed hernia and seemed in danger of operations. However he is not to be operated on, and so far as I know the plan holds for Baghdad this year and Canada next. I feel a little jaded over it all, this has been such an exhausting time, or whether it is I getting old and easily tired I don't know. I had only a week to open up house and try to remedy all the usual disasters the winter produces, then had three days to train a new cook, and then Mama and Miss Doughty arrived here, and all our neighbours, the Beachs, up at Olivier's villa; Miss Doughty cannot eat eggs, meat, or farinaceous things of any kind; and altogether I long for the comparative peace of Mesopotamia. But the sky and sea are all they can be and do their very best to make the world look smooth and bright.

I have also had two presents, a new silk parasol with stripes, and Rutter's book about Mecca and Medina, which is really worth reading.

Otherwise I am reading about Assyria, and that has led me to look up Kings and Chronicles. These are all rather repulsive people when one comes to look into their characters.

Our latest effort in red tape is that if you want a large car to take you for a picnic to Baiardo, you have to get a permit from Genova: it takes five days to get.

[1] Venetia Buddicom.

[68]

Dearest Pips,

Just heard about the Schneider Cup—and glad we have got it. The papers here have been so horrid, what with Palestine and Snowden, that it will be good for the Italians to be beaten. I was listening to three young Italians at the table next mine in Venice discussing what they will do with Palestine when they get it, and felt so like butting in and saying that in that case the massacres won't be confined to Jews. However, I refrained.

I have got my visa and found that I can get a berth on the 26th from Trieste, and will wait till next week in case of news from you and then get it, hoping you are all right.

I came here by Como and Menaggio and broke the journey there instead of at Milan, with old Mrs. Robertson, in a hotel full of bishops and golfers. The Lombardy plain just sizzling in the heat.

I left Mary rather doleful at Dronero, but hope she may go on there for a while anyway; and Eva is as nice as she can be and makes it a little less trying for her. But her feelings on the place have become far more virulent than mine even, and I can't help being relieved that it is not an idiosyncrasy of mine to find it so unbearable, though it would be much more convenient if only she *could* like it and its master. She hasn't any authority over those infants, and they are getting very rampageous and badly in need of school, and everyone is trying to persuade Mario to send them, but I fear he won't. Paolo especially needs it.

12 *September*, 1929.

I had a delightful dream the night before last. I thought that I had a long, long tramp to get to you, and when finally I arrived and found you sitting at supper (or tea for it was still daylight) I strolled to the window and there to my surprise saw all the coast of Mentone below, with Villefranche and the Tête de Chien and all in the distance. I was so pleased over this remarkable discovery, and the thought that I could take a short cut and come up to you whenever I liked, that I woke up with this delightful feeling and took a few seconds to get my bearings again.

S.S. CARNARO, 29 *September*, 1929.

Darling B,

I am looking at Mt. Helicon, rising up out of the Gulf of Corinth, topped with clouds and snow. The gulf is dark blue, slightly ruffled, and the long shapes of the hills red like rust or bracken, with shadows marking steep valleys or travelling clouds. All just as lovely as I remembered it.

Three missionary women from Palestine are in my cabin, and lucky it was for me that they hit upon this boat or I should have been stranded quite alone among Germans and Jews. They are mostly from Central Europe, with sharp pinched faces and turn-up noses, and sit with their hats on at meals. Some ancient patriarchs with beards, who drone Hebrew prayers swinging to and fro with their shoulders swathed in black-and-white shawls and their little square phylacteries tied on their foreheads—all in what is supposed to be our lounge. Down below in the third class they sing their monotonous anthem, or dance in a circle three steps one way one step back, with a grunting cry, evidently next cousin to the Arab dance. On the Friday night they had candles on their table, and altogether we feel submerged by the chosen people.

That dour old lady in the train who objected to my saddle-bag being pushed at her like a battering ram turned out to be a charming woman, the mother of a Hungarian diplomat in Washington, and living in the country behind Trieste. She was interesting about things, and assured me that the Jewish massacre was financed by Italy. Anyway, from what these Palestine ladies say, there seems to be a great deal of work in this direction. I hope we keep the place long enough to make it independent of all the grabbers.

It was rather wonderful to go up across the Carso. Some of the old trenches still visible. A grim stony land without shelter. The hills were not clear so I couldn't see M. Nero and the bit of country I used to know.

2 October, 1929.

I tried to get ashore at Jaffa, but it is quite hopeless in the time. Such a confusion: the third class has to be got off first as they expect trouble and have a military escort waiting for it (and no wonder if you only could see them). The whole thing very untidily managed: thankful we had no shipwreck, or the passengers, crew, officers and stewards would all have lost their heads. A nice judge says all sympathize with the Arabs, but of course one can't give way to their energetic methods of expression. So lovely to see the nice lean Arabs and hear them, though rather deafening just now.

Saw Moslem woman in black with her veil thrown back in Beirut streets: first time.

BRUMMANA, 5 October, 1929.

Darling B,

It is so pleasant to be here, at home again as it were, and all so clean and fresh, including the air and the sky and the landscape. Beirut is a horrid place, and none of my friends were in it, so I need not have stayed over the night, except that Miss Audi had never received my letter and so was not expecting me. She made me very welcome and sent down a car yesterday.

I had an awful job getting off the boat. First, as we were landing off the little rowing-boat, a wretched young Frenchman pushing by made me catch hold of the side, when another boat promptly came and crushed my finger, which swelled up to twice its size in the twinkling of an eye: the young man was quite upset about it, but I didn't care about his feelings and kept my fingers to myself in the most unsympathetic British way.

Then the young Levantine who was also on the boat thought he might profit by my going to Baghdad and avoid paying duty on his luggage, mine being 'in transit'. The porter murmured some Arabic to this effect, and I would not really have minded annexing three more suitcases: but when a man's bicycle was added and I was asked if it belonged to me I said 'No', and also repudiated the young Levantine who apparently had described himself as travelling with me. What happened to him I don't know: I left him to his fate.

The next people to get hold of me were a native transport agency who promised to take me and all the luggage to Baghdad for £9 "because they like me". They have got my luggage. I hope it may be safe. I am to find it in Baghdad. The English Company, the Nairn, charge £19 without luggage, and I can't think the difference can be worth the £12. However I will tell you when I get there.

I found myself rather out of training for the noise and dust of Beirut and did not go out very much. I strolled through the Arab quarter, and bought a pamphlet of Arabic stories off the ground.

In five minutes the man told me he had been to America, had three sons there, a wife who had married someone else, and that and the fact that he was always sick on the ocean made him prefer Syria. Wise man.

13 *October*, 1929.

Dearest B,

I can't remember where I left off, or whether I told you I was taking Najm and a mule and going for four days up into the hills. Najm has turned gentleman now and refuses to look after mules, but came with me out of friendship, an arrangement I cannot put up with for it means I never can get rid of him, and I do hate going round with an escort: Najm, and Majid the muleteer, one of those plump flat-nosed faces off the Phoenician tombs. He was quite nice, though arak and cards seemed his chief amusements. Then two mules and a donkey; I couldn't get a horse or a proper saddle, so just sat like a sack, and there are advantages in this method over these stony lands, for you can sit on either side or astride, or indeed anyhow, and get a rest. I rode ten hours for three days with three hours' motor at the end, and climbed Sannin (nearly 3,000 metres) in the interval, and not really the worse: in fact it was heavenly to get up into the high air and among running water, and see little flowers, even though all the things we think of as nice harmless little plants seem to develop a thorn in this country.

The first day we went up a valley I had partly explored last year, through pine and fig trees all scented in the sun, up to the last of the tidy little red-roofed villages, then over a stony high land with the sea and the river, Dog river, and all its valleys spread below—till we got to the Khan Sannin where the water comes out of the stony side of the hill and runs down ridges of tilled land with white limestone cropping up very spiky here and there. We were not guided to the good hotel, and only discovered next day that it was still open at all: but two men in long overcoats and slippers welcomed us to a gramophone under the trees: we looked down to the sea, whose horizon seemed remarkably high as the sun dipped into it. There were only two bedrooms, one with six the other with two beds: one of the men in overcoats advised me which was the cleaner bed to choose. I asked for clean sheets, and he said sadly: "We are sorry: we have none. If only you had come at the beginning of the season."

Sannin is a terrific wall of a mountain, not rock, but all streaks of red stone and shale, and spread along like a great sleeping panther with long thin flanks. One climbs by going straight up and then comes over the crest into a waste land of pits and hollows, and then up till Hermon and all the northern ranges are in sight beyond and below.

Next morning we rode over the shoulder of Sannin, tilled country, with a few peasants, because it is now the time for sowing: but it is very lonely up there, and strange from the solitude to look down on all the inhabited land below. Luckily we met a man with a gun and a white cloth round his turban who told us to turn downward to look at what they call the Castle of Fakhra, or we should have missed it, an old Phoenician temple facing westward to the sea and leaning up against a labyrinth of strange cleft rocks where an army might be invisible. I went in among them; you never saw anything so strange. There are thousands of narrow passages where the sunlight never reaches, and except by climbing up on to the open flat top of it, you would never get out of the labyrinth. The peasant said there is an underground way from the temple, under those rocks, to the remains of the old tower. I don't know what time the tower belongs to; it has arrow slits, and a little square pit in the middle which they call the Well of Blood, but whether it is a crusaders' watch tower built with the old Phoenician stones, or whether it may be Phoenician I don't know: I should say the former, as a strange language was inscribed on the stone of one corner.

I wasn't allowed to linger, as Najm *hates* ruins and always finds a reason to hurry over them. We picked up the track again and went into what seemed the heart of desolation, a treeless land of shaly valleys full of thorns. The Nahr el Kelb here rushes out in two springs, the Spring of Milk and the Spring of Honey. I pictured green places with willows and grass, and was not prepared to find the first spring bursting out of this barrenness in a circle of grisly cliff spanned by a natural bridge of limestone.

We travelled some time in the barrenness, looking down now on the Wadi Salih, the last tributary of the Nahr el Kelb, and as we turned a corner we saw a lovely sight—about 200 sheep and goats with their shepherds sitting camped about the honey spring which rushes from the ground in a yellow mountain stream. It was lovely in that nakedness. These shepherds are quite a different type from the flat-faced townsfolk, they have fine profiles, burnt nearly black, but

[73]

their hair is not *very* dark. They milked a sheep and brought me a foaming bowl and we sat in a circle. The goats and sheep all made a happy family, and the river rushed by out of the ground with all its voices.

We only rested half an hour, then went up a valley just as desolate though a stream ran through, and a few alders marked its course. It was beautiful, as all the bottom of the valley was terraced with young green corn, but the hills round were quite pitilessly grim. Half-way up, with the poor mules sweltering and quivering, I became quite certain we *must* be wrong. I took out my compass and map, and tried to persuade Najm that Afka was east and we were making due west. All no good. We toiled up, and came at about 3 p.m. on to what looked like the top of the world: miles of barren ranges on every side: an impossible steep shale slope and flocks and a few fellah huts miles down below. Najm shouted, but it was too far to understand. Very uncomfortably we made our way down and found ourselves on the right side of the watershed, but with a weary way to go to Afka, which is the cave of Adonis, where people used to come in pilgrimage from the coast and hold strange rites in the groves around. We had to creep all round the range of hills instead of cutting through from the river side.

We went on, and it really was a dispensation of providence for we came in so beautiful a manner suddenly round a corner upon it. The huge walls of the hills rounded into a tiny bay, and the cave was opposite, a black hole in the immense wall; the place seemed to be shut in from every side.

From where we stood the ground sloped down, red and covered with small cypress trees, down to the lip of the cave. Wild fig trees and bushes hung from the cliffs: the half moon was shining white in the sunset over us: there was a strange feeling of all the ancient secrets, a feeling of awe and fear. It is an immense place: we went down and down, the sunset glowing far above us. At last as the twilight was falling we came to where the village of Afka used to stand: the sliding land has thrice destroyed it: the last time, sixteen years ago, the temple also fell, and the inhabitants fled definitely and settled in Baalbeck. Now there is one poor house, and heaps of stones, and a bit of the temple wall, half hidden under a wild fig whose branches still are covered with native rags, though a little cheap picture of Mary and the Child are hung up in place of the ancient

[74]

god. There was a great square boulder which had rolled down and looked like an altar. Below the cave, where the water flows and falls into a green pool, wild mint and maidenhair, and many fresh plants were growing: and it was brown water like a Devonshire stream. I drank in honour of Adonis and found it very light and sweet. I should have liked to stay and watch the moonlight creep down, but it would have been cruelty to the two men and the animals, and it had been good enough as it was. So we climbed up, where there is a little village called Muneitra close above, and the sheikh gave us lodging and a clean bed in a room with a huge wardrobe with three full-sized mirrors side by side. All the evening I still felt the influence of the ancient religion, for there was the sheikh's wife, with a profile that must once have belonged to the temple—a quite perfect profile, so lovely, flawless, and cruel, that I was unable to take my eyes off it all the evening. I wish I could draw it. It was not soulless, but it was not kind; the secret of it is lost to us, as the old worship is lost. It was wonderful to have that face to look at in the hills of Afka. The hair was plaited and loose over each ear, and the dingy European nondescript clothes seemed to make the wonderful face even more remote and secret to itself. We sat by the coffee hearth. The sheikh got into his bed after slipping off his overcoat: the lady remained smoking her narghile. I slept on an embroidered pillow under a yellow quilt and the white cliffs of Adonis shining opposite in the moon.

Next day we had ten hours ride to reach the sea. Part of it over the new road now being made. Next year Afka will have a road and hotel. I was just in time.

P.S. The lizards here all hold their tails right up when they run along: I suppose the stones might hurt them, but it must be very fatiguing.

DAMASCUS, 19 October, 1929.

I left Brummana quite sadly, all seeming so comfortable and familiar. A last affectionate visit all round, everyone really *so* nice to me. I had dinner with Najm and his family—six charming children, running round barefoot to wait, the *beautiful* Druse women sitting round, and a very good dinner on the floor with my host, who was however a bit subdued, having rolled down a valley side with his car the day before. I was also a little troubled, because there were small white animals running round; afterwards I was told they were lice by Mme Cortaz, who has also explained to me how to discover the habitations of bugs—useful knowledge.

I came down to Beirut by car early this morning, after a night of rain; the car ordered for five, the chauffeur came along at four, not having a watch. At Beirut I took the train, after waiting for an hour. We climbed up through the olives and vines, the engine hooting with joy at intervals; the country looking far more benevolent and mild than when I last saw it under snow. I wondered whether the edge of its loveliness would be wanting this second time, but no, it was the same unbelievable wonder, the far sweeping hills, the bare spaces, Hermon, and the villages in their poplar trees; the slow leaving of the West and red-roofed houses; the bare naked valley, and then the broad ranges of Anti-Lebanon; Zebdani in its orchards, every tree laden with apples or yellow quince, the poplars silver in the wind, the winding stream and thin air of these spaces, and the flat roofs and yellow mud walls, just embodiments of the land they grow from. Now there is a look of plenty: the olives are incredible with their weight of harvests; apples, melons, grapes; the yellow land has still the feeling of plenty over it, but a fierce sort of productiveness, quite different from ours. And then we plunged down between the walls of desert rock, and where I last travelled through the thin forest of blossoms there was now thick shade, woods along the stream, and glades and glades of plane and poplar and fruit trees. The country too looks much more settled than when last I was here.

I got to Damascus; my arabic now sufficient for porters and such, and pleasant to see the look of friendliness as soon as one speaks it.

I had barely got my things off when three black-veiled ladies were shown in, and turned out to be the two Azm sisters and a chaperone aunt—very pleasant, though their English and my Arabic have both deteriorated since last we saw each other. I gave them coffee in my room and we then made off to see the last day of the local arts and crafts exhibition. You would have liked that. Such stuffs: and really good pieces of the inlay work. The European imitations too awful of course, and I suppose increasing in number. Amatallatif heard that the embroidered dress she herself had sent got a gold medal, which is very pleasant. It was fun going round with the three ladies, the elder one strictly veiled; the two pretty girls only pulled their veil down when anyone began to stare. I think I shall adopt the convenient fashion. We came round into the pale gold sunset of Damascus, the electric illumination shining against it, the minarets very pearly and ethereal in that wonderful atmosphere. The twilight came down as we wandered through Suleiman's mosque with its lunettes of old blue tiles over the school doorways, and old graves among the flowers: the big square of splashing water full of light; the Moslems walking at the edge, and carrying their shoes to the mosque door: it was the evening prayer, we could not go in, but peered from the door at the row of figures rising and crouching. It seemed incredible to be here again and find it all better than before. I went home with the girls to call on Mme and made salutations for and answered enquiries about you; and had tea; and saw the Doctor who came in; and we were all very amiable in spite of my poor arabic. Then I came home and walked along the banks of Barada, feeling that it is indeed the Enchanted City. Amatallatif is coming to-morrow to take me a few days to their farm here in the country, and then possibly to Zebdani—and I feel I am in the real East again. I don't think I shall have time to call on the missionaries.

RIHANE, NR. DAMASCUS, 22 *October,* 1929.

Darling B,

I am sitting in a room furnished with rows of chairs in mother-of-pearl, and an immense tall wardrobe of the same, which glitters at one in the morning, when one wakes and looks up from one's mattress on the floor. It is a sort of country house with farm attached, at one corner of the village, and Amatallatif's uncle and aunt live here through the summer, looking after the property. The aunt is quite young, about twenty-four I should say, immensely fat and rosy, with bobbed hair, and a charming good-natured smile, and all sorts of evening dresses which she has been wearing for us. She lives here with her mother-in-law, an old lady with long nose and a nondescript gown of white and blue stripes, who smokes most of the time. The harem consists of two rooms on either side of the *dar,* or raised loggia open on one side to a delightful courtyard with a cistern and pump in the middle and masses of flowers coming out of the stone pavement, or so it looks. On the other side is the kitchen, dining-room, etc., with two maids with checked cotton veils over their heads and pink frilled trousers, running round. We can get out to the stables, but are careful to call out before doing so and ask if there is a man about.

I am getting to feel quite ashamed of my unveiled condition, and turn my back with the rest when we pass a peasant on the road: and I notice that the men are very careful to look straight ahead and pay no attention to us when we are near them. The two girls and the young wife are inclined to be careless about these matters, but the uncle, Najib Effendi, keeps them up to the mark. Mario would love to have been born to this sort of a household. To come home and find six women and two maids all waiting to be pleasant, must be a delightful feeling and is I am sure responsible for that sort of assured and reposeful dignity which the Moslem has. From the feminine standpoint, the life is easy enough too: I think the Western strenuousness and sense of responsibility would be very hard on them at first. · There is a sort of privacy with no privacy, for one can run about all over the place and know that there will be no men about; on the other hand, all the women wander about in all the rooms, so that even if one wanted to read or study it would be very difficult.

After lunch our host went off to the male part of the house and we sat on the floor of the mother-of-pearl room playing dice with six cowrie shells and a round embroidered cloth across which you move pawns: a simple game. They were all expert, collecting the shells with a sudden movement of the hand and jingle of all their bangles. About four we walked out and looked at the fields for sowing, dusty with the end of summer; the low ditches filled with iris leaves and lined with mint and yellow flowers; the groves of olives here and there (with fruit far bigger and better than ours); the lines of apricots and walnuts, and sown or harvested land in between; all very peaceful and almost Italian but for the red hills on the skyline and the clear wonderful light of Damascus skies. We came back in the twilight with the goats and sheep, and in the evening sat in the *dar* on cushions, the starlight over the walls of the court and a lamp in a glass lantern lighting up. I discovered that I could play chess with the uncle— a weird set of chessmen, which made it rather difficult to find oneself at first. We had the lute out, and the fat lady in her white evening gown and bunch of flowers on one shoulder, her bobbed hair and long black-pencilled eyes, played, while the uncle got his pipe out and accompanied her. Then Amatallatif's bed and mine were spread on the floor, and we all retired.

This is now my fourth day, and I feel quite accustomed to the harem, though not inclined for a lifetime of it. There is a deadly

boredom about it. The way of passing time is not really more monotonous than the way most of the girls at Dronero, say, spend their
time, and the talk—clothes, gossip, relatives, food is exactly the same:
the only difference is one of possibilities; someone very strong-
minded *can* get out of the rut at Dronero: here, I don't see how they
could.

The second day we took a long walk, the Effendi riding in a brown
'*abeiya*, a *kaffiya* and '*agal* on his head, and gun across his knees: we
women strolling on foot (he excused himself to me and said he
had been ill and couldn't walk, poor man). Abu'l Khair the peasant
trotted alongside the donkey with two big tins for water which comes
from a mineral spring out of the naked burnt hill to the north. It is
pleasant country here with its slow water ditches, the long stretches of
vineyard or olive, and the line of hills on the horizon. We reached
the spring and took snapshots—even the wife being taken while the
Effendi wasn't looking and great arrangements made to get the
snapshot to her unnoticed. We came back and sat under a walnut
tree, and fed the fish on crumbs, and ate fruit, and saw crabs, and
then on the way home I showed an immodest European desire to
look inside a mill, and the Effendi had to get off his horse and take me,
while the veiled ladies went on.

Yesterday we took another walk and talked to one of the herd
boys, a beduin lad hired from his tribe to look after the village goats.
They asked what he carried in his bundle. "Bread," said he, "will
you eat?" He earns 4s. a month, and yet his offer to share was
perfectly genuine and his manners those of an equal.

We had another afternoon with the gramophone, and another walk
in the evening, and a long talk with Amatallatif about herself and
things in general. It is all *very* like Italy only rather more so. She
has a cousin who wants to marry her, but she won't and is allowed
to say no; on the other hand a man she would have liked, has been
refused by her brother. She tells me the marriages are getting very
much later, twenty-three or twenty-four being now usual. She
is such a pretty girl, and her sister too, fresh and good-tempered
and lively—they seem very happy in their seclusion. It was rather a
shock when the mother told me about her uncle the Effendi, who has
no children, not even from the slave women he keeps in the village.

They are all amiable to me though we talk little, my arabic being
really very inadequate. In the evenings and afternoons the Effendi

[79]

spreads his carpet in the *dar* and intones the Qurân in a beautiful voice: the two older ladies, their heads swathed in white, spread their carpets behind him and pray in silence holding their two hands palm upwards for the blessing from heaven—I would like to watch and listen instead of having to go on playing dice close beside them with the young people who seem never to pray at all.

Amatallatif got into trouble for having wandered with me into the village houses. This morning we went out alone together and sat under the olives and then came back and were called by four old village women in the sun sewing at their old patchwork clothes, and quite as astonished over Amatallatif as over me—they asked her if she were Christian. I believe the upper class people know as little of the beduin and the peasants here as does the foreigner. It is a land of great gulfs. One of the women was doing some rather nice embroidery, like what I found in Hauran. One poor old thing asked me what to do for her leg which was hurting, and I thought it must be rheumatism and, having found that she had only one linen garment on, prescribed wool: but she says she is unable to procure any, being so poor. When we got back and told our hostess of this adventure she felt she must see the embroidery, and sent the little maid, and soon we had three peasant women looking round and listening to the gramophone. Zeinab's mother was there, a poor little animal who must have been married at twelve or so; she was staring at the mother-of-pearl room with eyes quite expressionless, holding her baby—so obviously a creature who had never known what it is to be *alive* that it was a pain to look at her.

You would be surprised to see me now, as I am sitting with the eternal gramophone and the ladies sewing, and my eyes are much beautified with a long black streak underneath them. Soon I shall go and have a bath. One is very clean here, only at odd times, nothing much being done night and morning, but a leisurely toilette in the course of the afternoon when the man is away.

ZIAD, HOTEL, BAGHDAD, 26 October, 1929.

Dearest Pips,

We had a great time strapping the luggage, and I was just able to insist on not having half of mine left behind. I thought we knew all about 'diligences', but the wooden atrocities which the poor pilgrims cram into for this long weary journey are quite beyond anything we

can remember. I saw one go off, packed so high it was *just* able not
to topple over if it took the corners slowly, with a good stout wooden
grating all round to prevent the human contents from bursting out.

We finally started at eight-twenty, out along the road which goes
east to Duma, then forks off for Palmyra, and becomes more and
more a track. One keeps the red hills on the left, and the land gradually turns from plough and olive to tufts of scrub and rush. The
lake I explored last year was visible, and the same tribe probably
grazing—about 2,000 camels I should say, like an army moving,
their colour exactly that of the hills behind them except for little
families of white ones here and there. It is always a lovely sight:
and the hills took on beautiful shapes and colour, almost like heather
in the distance where the plum-coloured light lay on them. After
about two hours we reached the last khan, with a garrison of French
Senegalese: passports here: and a general gathering of cars of the
various convoys. They all go together twice a week, and the desert
is alive with their rolling spirals of dust whirling along sometimes,
in fact often, so far apart that they are quite out of sight of each
other. It is not so much fear of raids now as that a car can get stuck
or lost: one driver alone two months ago went round and round in
the immense spaces till his petrol was finished, and he was found dead.
We had wonderful mirage as we went along: a great lake country
seemed to bound us on two sides: sometimes one would come up
to within a few hundred yards of the water—one could see the
shadow and reflections in it—even *knowing* that there is no water
at all in all this space, it seemed impossible to think it a deception;
and then one came near and the lake turned to a thin streak and
vanished.

Soon there were no more beduin, no camels, nothing: even the
hills sank away, and the desert lay in great heaving shallow waves.
I saw one rabbit or hare, and a few birds—some great big ones with
black-edged feathers and white patches on the wings, but long legs
not like eagles, and some also long-legged, tripping very quickly
with pointed heads and beaks and the wings sharply divided into
black and fawn when they flew.

It was quite comfortable, only there was an oppressive feeling of
the *ugliness* of the enormous waste, a cruel solitude: I think one would
lose it if one lived in the desert in the proper way and got to know it,
but it seemed a heartless flinty space.

The tracks are innumerable, every car leaving its mark, and leading one quite easily astray.

At about eight next morning we reached the first bridge and Iraq passport office: palm trees, flocks, the Arabs very much darker here than the Syrian and not so fine a type from what I could see: but the officials look much more attractive than the town Syrian, and all bright and quick and smiling and very efficient at their work—with an evident reminiscence of British training. I remember noticing the same thing on the Palestine railways and in Egypt.

I found here at this place, Ramadi, that I had omitted a visa: I got one there and then, I think because I casually mentioned having lunched with Ja'far Pasha. Anyway it was all right. Another two and a half hours over a dreadful road, between naked low sandstone, by Felluja, a miserable village over a bridge of boats across Euphrates; an hour's run over flat land with nothing on it but red earth and stones, between the two rivers, and then trees and fields, and Arabs and Negroes working at dykes, herds of loose donkeys, and a long line of palm groves hiding Baghdad. The last bit of road is asphalt. The suburbs horrid, with little mud boxes. The Customs office was redeemed by Kurd porters with red turbans, an extraordinary fine aquiline fierce-looking lot of men. And then I came across the Tigris, another long narrow clattering boat bridge, and Venetian view of buildings and water, to this hotel.

4

Into Persia, 1929–30

No medium has yet been devised for the translation of life into language, nor can any words recall the dazzling fluidity of days. Single yet fixed in sequence, they fall like the shaft of a cataract into time and through it. Letters give the most faithful picture, because they are fragmentary and concerned merely with the moments as they pass and are alive through intimacy, as are the funeral stele of the Greeks that choose the littlest and the easiest things of life by which to remember their dead. Of all the sights and sounds and feelings which my first winter in Baghdad brought me, three principal influences remained.

The first was the most obvious, the immediate enlargement of my world to include an East independent of the Mediterranean. A foretaste of this had been given by Damascus the year before, for the great valley behind the Lebanon, the Beka'a, is I think the boundary between the Levant and Asia. Where the tiled roofs end and the flat roofs become general, and the Christian churches have no bells, is the beginning; and it is roughly separated from the Mediterranean world by a curtain of wastelands, of which the Syrian–Iraqi desert is the easiest to cross.

To come suddenly upon Baghdad from Europe is a very big jump, and the winter of the year before now showed its usefulness; for I was already half acclimatized and prepared to fit the unexpected into its place. I am naturally disposed to take the unexpected easily, and therefore belong to that half of the human race whose enjoyment of life seems to annoy the other half. It is one of the things I have found most disconcerting and most unreasonable in my life.

I met this point of view *en bloc*, as it were, on my first introduction to the British Civil Service in Iraq. It was a far stranger world to me than that of the dilapidated East. Such people as had come within my range before were artists, writers, or other followers of the imagination; such as they were, they were all individuals; I cannot remember ever having felt that any human being could be classified as 'a man in the street'; it would have shocked me, naturally and without thinking about it, as much as it must shock a churchman who believes in immortal souls. The general official attitude in Baghdad seemed to be that everyone and everything (except a few things never to be mentioned), could be classified into a street of some sort, and an unhygienic one if Oriental. The Civil Service lived in a residential area, and thought it a poor sort of taste to enjoy anything outside: and if their 'man in the street' attitude towards the lovely and variegated world surprised me, it was as nothing to the astonishment with which I became aware of the British official attitude towards women.

Woman in the street is assumed to be more enterprising (though regrettably so) than man: the difference implied, though subtly complimentary to women, would fill the British official mind with consternation, and it may be assumed that, as opposed to men and ideas in general, the English woman in Iraq was never thought of as in a street at all, but as wife, mother or daughter attached to a 'man in the street' at a distance—in fact safely indoors. This double loss of individuality, inflicted on one-half of the human race, came to me with a shock of even greater surprise than that of the wholesale classification of men.

During the years that followed, some of my firmest friendships were made in Baghdad; I discovered many people who felt as I did, and I came gradually to realize what wide varieties of non-conformity lurk beneath the British orthodox exterior. Whether the uniform façade is useful or not is hard to say: conventions are like coins, an easy way of dealing with the commerce of relations, and a saving of trouble when used merely for convenience and kept rigidly subordinate. But like the golden calf, they easily take the place of the true and intangible essences they are supposed to represent; and then there is danger of that idolatry which has caused most of the miseries of history. For this reason I am disposed to stick to the conventions of my background in all small matters where the possibility of deification is remote; politeness, punctuality and dress seem to be improved by a formal touch: but great questions I should look into carefully to see whether their clothes are living garments or mere emblems of what was once living. Most human institutions would be strengthened by this search; they would no longer be taken as a blind wall in whose shelter the unkindnesses of men can hide. The ceremonies on which our life is founded, baptism, marriage, burial, the slowly-built scaffolding of human freedoms, emerge as living creatures when you examine them with care; the ritual of a wedding is not weakened by the discovery that to marry for money is equivalent to prostitution. Life-giving water, the earth we are made of, are foundations good to remember, and our sacraments are all based on things that are common to all. Like the skeletons of animals apart from their flesh, there is a similarity in the structure of all human ceremonial, so that insight will produce tolerance —which is but the recognition of sameness under an apparent diversity. And if this enquiring attitude towards our daily conventions were generally prevalent, there would never be a need for a reformer, and how restful that would be.

These ideas about the conventional, which I still consider moderate and reasonable, were implicit in me when I reached Baghdad; there they were hammered into a firm conviction by the extraordinary henlike reactions of the British community to everything I did. The unattractiveness of the local hotels was notorious at that time, and I was too poor to live in even the most squalid of the respectable among them: the alternative suggested was the British Club, from which Arabs were excluded: it seemed a poor terminus for someone who had travelled so far to learn Arabic. I was soon considered a rebel, a dangerous eccentric, or a spy, and my lodging with a shoemaker's family, with a wide room on the Tigris bank, a flouting of national prestige. There was a *Passage to India* feeling for which I had been quite unprepared; and half a dozen women told me in a marked way that they had lived in Iraq for a varying number of years "and never had a *wog*" across their doorstep.

I would now sail serenely through all such froth and foam. Even then, in a few months' time, I discovered my own friends and made myself a refuge: but the first impact was like a cold shower on someone who is not expecting it. It was my first meeting with one of our worst English characteristics—the absence of any human curiosity, a result of the degraded habit of classifying human beings in sets: and this offended me in an abstract way, quite apart from the fact that I was classified among the 'lesser breeds without the law' myself. I also came up against a disconcerting novelty in the official attitude to conversation: even at a Baghdad dinner-party, where goodness knows one would not gather for the sake of the food, the idea of conversation seemed to be viewed with distaste, and as soon as the meal was over, some game, *any* game, was provided like a cake to Cerberus, to keep our mouths as far as possible shut.

Meanwhile I met people: Stefana, now Lady Drower, and the Caparns, Vyvyan Holt, Lionel Smith, Mr. Cooke became familiar at once, and Evan Guest and his father and the Hubert Youngs came into my life in the spring. Lady Humphrys was immediately kind, and at my first party at the Residency came up to me as I was leaving, with one of the home-made cakes from the table wrapped in paper in her hand to give me— a most gentle present to anyone cooked for by a Syrian shoemaker's wife at a primus on the floor.

With Lionel Smith I soon spent all my Sundays. We lunched in my controversial lodging or in suburban comfort at Alwiyah. Here we were surrounded by a green garden (Baghdad being one of the few Arabian cities where lawns exist), and sat amid furniture which in its contrasts showed the difference be-

[86]

tween Lionel and his friend Major Gumley, who shared his house:
the two sets of belongings gave one a feeling of schizophrenia, and
Lionel never failed to begin our day by eliminating Major Gumley's possessions through some appropriate but guarded adjective.
Judge Prichard, one of the nicest of my friends, also shared the
house, with no furniture that I remember.

We spent the whole afternoon talking and then walked
to the now vanished church at South Gate for evening service.
It has become a suburb with boulevards and rows of lamps and
oleanders, but in 1930 it was open country, lonely and sad,
with tufted grass and dykes, darkened by red bands of the sunset
—and Lionel strode across with his long legs, oblivious of my
difficulties with water channels. He was a friend of W. P. Ker,
so that we had a background in common, but we had never met
till I walked into his office in the Ministry. It was surprising to
see anyone so vivid, with such an eagle look, a shock of ruffled
hair, and head so finely poised, with that rare youthfulness
which has nothing to do with years—all sitting at a government
desk. Lionel took me home that first day by the narrow towpath
and high dark suqs of the west Tigris bank, and supported me,
with a front of official disapproval which he tried and failed to
maintain, through all the disturbance my first activities seemed
to cause.

He had been a friend of Gertrude Bell, who died two years
before my arrival in Baghdad. The Iraq she had helped to
make had almost passed away. The country was still divided
by the deep racial division of Sunni and Shi'a, and by the three
divisions of north, centre and south: but the reins were held by
King Faisal with a genius for diplomacy, and a small competent
band of British advisers and officials whose experience had been
won in the country itself during the war, were building it up for
its independence. Nationalism, as catching in the Middle East
as measles, clamoured in a newspaper racket that gave public
life the feeling of a hornet's nest; and it surprised me to see how
often the good men of both sides found and liked each other
through the torrent that washed about them. Between 1929

and 1932, when her independence and entry into the League of Nations were achieved, Iraq reached a climax of invective and inaccuracy only equalled in Egypt and in India. It was not deep-seated, but was irritating like a nettle rash, and was carried on in an outer frame of older, more sporadic but more perennial troubles, of tribes, floods, Kurds and Assyrians, which harassed the districts where the political officers lived relying on personal relations, far from the towns.

I was shown Gertrude Bell's small house and garden, in the part called the Sanak, on a street so muddy in wet weather that I once saw an American visitor looking there for one of his goloshes, which the mud had prised off his shoe and caused to disappear. From what I could gather, Gertrude Bell might not have been kind to me if she had been alive—she was said not to have been fond of female Arabists—but I regretted not having known her. The Oriental Secretary who followed her at the Residency was Vyvyan Holt. He sat next me at my first dinner-party and added to my shyness by remaining completely silent till the coffee came, when he told me that he had had that day to sack a Kurdish house-boy for pursuing his cook with a knife under the dining-room table at dinner. I met him often at Lionel's on Sundays, and he too—with the same reluctant weakening of disapproval—supported me through the winter and spring. It was worse for him than for Lionel, who cared nothing for what people thought, never went to parties, and walked up the Residency steps on some official occasion with his socks tied with red tape. But Vyvyan, though eccentric enough in his own way, was a cherisher and collector of conventions, and my existence on the other side of the fence filled him with a mixture of impatience, envy, and perhaps awe. He and Lionel became my friends and came to Asolo, and I rode with Vyvyan on his ponies off and on for years whenever I was in Baghdad. He was the most modest man I have ever known, with a fund of natural and unselfish goodness, a readiness to give devotion to anyone he could admire, which should have brought him contentment if he had not been so complicated with inhibitions:

for he was too brilliant not to see through many shibboleths which a certain timidity, a humility rather, made him reluctant to relinquish: hence the mixed exasperation and liking with which he regarded me.

Stefana Drower on the other hand was singularly happy, moving through life with a peaceful vagueness, gentle to her family though absent-minded, and passionate only about folklore and the Mandean gnostics, who sit in their shops in River Street and beat out little landscapes in black antimony on silver, and whose religion I imagine Stefana now knows more about than they do themselves. She was friendly and kind and went about with me in that first winter and spring, and I noticed in her the patience, the apparent absence of reaction to accidents and delays which the West finds exasperating—the sure sign of an habitué in the East. I have seen little of her and the hospitable Caparns in these last years, though the kindness remains.

Mr. Cooke also had been a friend of Gertrude Bell, and took me on as one in the same tradition, giving me credit for what I had as yet done nothing to deserve. He was a generous, self-educated, imaginative man, a small and stocky Scotsman with a round head, and an amused and interested way of looking at life which made him liked by the Iraqis. It was a pleasure to go about with him because of the cordial atmosphere which greeted him wherever he went. He was Adviser to the Ministry of Auqaf, the religious endowments of the country, and this and his interest in antiquities opened to him all the most interesting places. He first took me to the Holy Cities, and with him I went into Baghdad mosques closed to most travellers. "Ooh, ye'd make a fine spy, Miss Starrk," he would say at intervals: and I never knew whether or no he believed this absurdity, which was irritating me and perturbing several of my compatriots at that time. What most annoyed me was that if I were a secret agent and suspected of being so, I was evidently taken to be very inefficient; and I used to explain to Mr. Cooke, to his amusement, that if I were a spy I would be playing bridge all day long and living at the club.

I met many other people during that first winter, and among them Kinahan Cornwallis who afterwards became a friend; but at that time I saw him and the other British in Baghdad only occasionally, being absorbed with my Arabic and my school, and also unduly sensitive to disapproval. It is surprising to me now how much I minded; and I can only explain it by the facts of my childhood, which had made me suffer from criticisms at one time, and had given me a feeling of inferiority and a natural tendency to think other people better than myself, which is still there, though obstinacy, optimism, and a sense of the ridiculous have managed to overcome it in great part. My feeling of inferiority was not I believe modesty so much as a natural inclination to agree with people; if they thought themselves right and me wrong, I was made unhappy by the necessity of differing, and it was an immense support to find anyone who thought as I did about things in general. Yet even when I felt most alone, I cannot ever remember wavering about my own path; I felt that other people might know what was good, but not that they knew better than I did what was good for *me*. Standards have been given through the ages, for each to interpret in his way; and my objection to philanthropy is based on its encouragement of interference, which I dislike inflicting on others as I dislike receiving it myself. I believe it is a modern impertinence, and I prefer the Islamic and the medieval way, where you do good for the good of your own soul, which is as much as one single human being can attend to.

It was a comfort when new friends came into my life, not in spite but because of these ideas. I met Evan Guest and the Hubert Youngs in 1930. Evan ran agriculture at Rustumiya on the banks of the Dyala, among sunny sunk lanes with cultivation behind them, and trees filled with light warm shadows, and birds. There in a little mud house he thought out his universe in a conscientious masculine way, which surprised me who generated these conclusions only too rapidly and spontaneously by intuition. His father was a fine Arabic scholar and one of the dearest, most generous and unselfish of human beings. He had been in the navy; this discipline with the later one of scholarship added to it made one of the best mixtures there can be. He came out that year, and my friendship with him lasted till his death. He and I urged and eventually obtained the addition of an Islamic room to the museum in Baghdad, which had hitherto neglected anything later than the Babylonians.

Hubert Young was Counsellor to the High Commissioner. His wife, Rose, was like a wild rose herself, unambitious, unselfconscious, graceful and remote, a painter and a maker of gardens. Hubert had the talents and versatility of the Youngs; he was much more intelligent than most people. The best like him; and with all his gifts, I think that the riches of his life, the thing that most made and endeared him and mellowed him to the gentleness of his last years, was his faithful, unquestioning, uninterrupted devotion to Rose. These two became and remained my friends, but I saw little of them at first, for when they appeared I was already studying Persian and my mind was set on Alamut.

I cannot remember when the idea of this journey first began. I brought it with me to Baghdad, for in England I had already studied von Hammer Purgstall and one or two books on the Ismaili sect: the actual learning of Persian was furthered by Vyvyan Holt, who knew ten languages himself and could never resist helping me to a new one, though deploring the inevitably resulting expeditions. He sent me an old mirza so overburdened with poverty, children, and an obviously dreary wife that he had no energy left for the abstract, and I soon dismissed him: my finances were so extremely meagre that I could not afford bad lessons. The seed however was now sown; I went on alone with my grammar and decided to practise conversation in Persia itself: on April 13th I left for Hamadan.

There are some countries in which, at every visit, one recaptures the magic of a first arrival; Greece, Italy and Persia are such to me. However often, misted with sand, I leave the hot borders of Iraq and climb the Paitak pass and, through the cliff-gate of Sar-i-Pul, come on to plains where the larks sing over nests hidden in flowers; and see slow clear rivers under bridges bent like bows; the tumbled mountains of Kermenshah and poppy fields of Kangevar; the Asadabad pass and its grassy shoulders where the sun seems to lay a separate mantle of gold on top of the green; and the high gentle wave of Elvand south from Hamadan—however often I may see them, I think there will always be that tightening at the heart which comes with the remoteness of beauty, just beyond the possible footsteps of men.

The great carts with their strutted roofs of canvas built like tunnels and four horses abreast (I have seen eight abreast on the Paitak) are no longer on the road; and the old costumes have disappeared leaving no worthy substitutes; but the beauty of that land is beyond the accidental, a part of its very bones, and the merest trifle—a man on a donkey trotting into the solitude of the *dasht* and its flowers, or a ragged group squatting by a *chaikhana* in the sun—are enough to call echoes like the wind in a lyre, speaking music from distances we love but cannot know.

Hajji Mirza Hasan in Hamadan, and the Hôtel de France with its casual garden and long balconies, its scented honey and spiced Shirazi wine, were quieter than Baghdad. John Chapman with his new wife was there as interested in the East as I was and with knowledge behind him; and otherwise there were few foreigners and all friendly. Nearby, a tumbling stream accompanied the main street to the suqs of the town. The grave of Avicenna was on its bank, with a small dusty library beside it, a place of resort for veiled townswomen who strolled and sat on tombstones under flowering almond trees in the sunset. It has become difficult to recognize the charming old shabby town now flattened out with boulevards. My stay there and the way to Alamut in May, I have described; but the continuation of my journey to the Caspian, left out of *The Valleys of the Assassins*, is here given in letters. I returned to Baghdad at the beginning of June—to the fullness of summer, and the Residency garden party, and a general kindness and cordiality, the eccentric tribute of British public opinion to those who treat it with indifference —extremely pleasant to me and surprising.

I left for Italy soon after, in an orthodox manner by the Nairn six-wheeler bus across the desert, and found my ship at Haifa full of friends and acquaintance going on leave. The week at sea was, I think, the only one I have ever enjoyed in a ship, through water blue and deep and smooth as a gem and studded with islands. Summer passed as usual—Asolo, Dolomites at S. Martino, Venice and fireworks of the Redentore, L'Arma, Dronero, some sickness, writing of Persian legends for *The Cornhill*, a month in England, and departure on September 19th from Glasgow for Quebec. I found my father better and stronger than the year before; in fact it was my own health that gave way. Tom and Alice rather naturally objected to turning out of their room every year to sleep in the cottage at the bottom of the hill: I could have done this myself, but my father would not hear of it and threatened to go down there to sleep alone: so I made up a bed on the veranda, to the pleasure of all his pigeons, who liked the warmth of my body and came to settle on it in the icy hour of the dawn. We planned to build a little apartment in the cottage for the next year, so that I might spend my time in Canada in comfort. The time never came; I left in December, with the same heartache and the perplexed feeling that it was wrong to go, and the pain of the last sight of him on the platform as he stood to say good-bye; and he died suddenly the next August, and left me always with the remorse that I did not stay.

I have said that in Baghdad three new things came into my life; the third was a strange, unwanted falling into love, unprovoked and unexpected, inspired by the most conventional person who, for his part, hovered on the edge but never fell in, and yet held me with no active effort of his own so that for seven years I never felt quite free: then it all dropped, as a shutter might drop, and I awoke with an immense delight of liberation, though friendship and tenderness remained. I am not often disposed to regret what happens, whether my own doing or that of others, and feel life rich on almost any path; it is a lean employment of time to brood on what might have happened along some other turning. But I do regret the time wasted on unrequited affection. It is like a duet played solo, or those silly bouts at tennis, for exercise, with no one to send back the ball: there must be something that can at least be imagined to be alive at the receiving end. The natural heart loves as it beats, and the sooner it can turn from a sterile expense the better; and for this reason I regret walking so long down a one-way lane with only a blank wall at its end. Meanwhile this magnet, also, held me in the East, and drew me away from Canada and Italy and all my old thoughts; and in Baghdad kept me constantly torn between the things I had travelled for, and the wish to conform to someone whose ideas were so different. The poverty of his affection saved me, and I kept my own way, but it was with stress and trouble, like a dominant melody pressed as it were from a full orchestra alive with other songs.

* * *

BAGHDAD, October, 1929.

Dearest Venetia,

It is very remarkable—here I am in Baghdad. I sometimes wonder how it comes about. It is a long flat city in a flat land, and all you see as you come from the West is a fringe of palms and a mosque. The bridge of boats is not nearly as beautiful as it sounds, and there is a faintly English flavour of the 'High Street' about the one tarred road which runs down the length of the town. There are no beautiful bazaars like Damascus, and the mosques with their gaudy domes do not seem beautiful from what I have seen (but I haven't yet examined). But the people are there, and I shall be very happy I do believe. That is after all the real interest: buildings and the beauties of nature I do think are subsidiary; and the people here are of all fascinating sorts, the beautiful ones being Kurds.[1] Never have I seen more fine-looking men, so agile and strong with legs bare to the thigh and red turbans, and long hair under, and a wild aquiline handsomeness that is quite intoxicating and I only wish I could paint it.

[1] I meant the Luristan porters.

[94]

28 *October*, 1929.

Darling B,

I went round to the museum this morning. The Ur collection is really amazing—the sheer beauty of the gold work so remarkable, and very wonderful to find the filigree jewellery, the mosaic, and inlaid ivory of the Italians here in Mesopotamia nearly six thousand years ago. These old Sumerians appear to be the people who brought its civilization to Egypt. But where they in their turn came from is yet unknown.

I was surprised to see quite a number of Arabs, in turbans and flowing abbas, and women with infants, wandering round the museum. What obviously impressed the group next me more than anything was that every object should have a ticket. It is an attractive museum, evidently done and arranged by the men at the job, and not by experts for the public—for they hardly ever condescend to write a date. When they describe something as a "stone *object* found at Ur" I think the public has a right to be annoyed, as even the least intelligent can recognize an 'object' as such.

To-day I discovered the bazaars, all vaulted brick arches with more light than Damascus, and even more fascinating from the varied types, though the European mixture of goods is rather more evident. There seem to be two distinct Iraqi types, one full round face, with thickish underlip, one long very narrow face with pleasant quick eyes and rather high heads. Then there are the magnificent Kurds, and the Christians, Assyrians, Jews, Greeks, Turks, Persians, and who knows what beside the real Arabs from the desert outside. The Christian women wear the lovely silk wraps like my white and silver one, all beautiful colours, a joy to watch as they go about the streets among the black veils of the Moslems, who wear their 'abbas' over the tops of their heads in an absurd but graceful way with the sleeves hanging down over the shoulders.

I stayed in all the afternoon waiting for Munir Wakil and also feeling sleepy, still from that desert journey I believe. I wish I didn't need so much sleep. I went through agonies trying to keep awake in Amatallatif's harem, and when we started from Rutba I found that I was sleeping while my head was bumping up and down against the hard edge of the car, an awful danger to all my teeth.

It is very pleasant to be in a free country again. What a difference it makes, and why, is hard to say but one feels it everywhere. And the people may not like foreigners, but there is none of that sense of fear: they behave as if they *know* they will be fairly treated—it is the same sort of pleasant feeling a dog gives when he comes up to you instead of crouching his head when you move your hand, which is what you always feel in Syria.

The shi'as are fanatic here and one cannot enter their mosques. I should like to get into touch with them, but it is a toss up as one cannot very well combine shi'a and sunni and I don't know which my fate is to be.

1 *November*, 1929.

I have been to see the big girls' school and Mrs. Kerr the nice American at the head of it, and next Monday I shall begin and go to classes there; the twelve-year-old seem to be my standard. My first experience of any school, as I told Mrs. Kerr, will be rather alarming. It is a pleasant place tucked away where the Moslem and Jewish quarters seem to join.

Mrs. Drower has given me a letter to the bank manager, but even that does not enable my cheque to turn into money before the 11th, which may leave a hiatus. However, I am not really bothering.

[Note-book] 1.11.29.

Lovely to see the yellow sunset sky from Mrs. Drower's terrace on the Tigris. The old Babylonian deluge legend says that the dove, the swallow, and the crow were sent to seek for the dry land: and there as I looked was the dove below me, and the grey-backed crow higher up-stream, and a little bird I thought to be a swallow, only it turned out to be a bat.

This morning was again old Baghdad of *The Arabian Nights*—the hanging painted balconies, the streets opening and narrowing in surprising sudden ways, the flapping white gown with bare leg showing through its slit side, the turban with bit of fringe falling on the neck, the shadows which are still pervaded by the intense sunlight above. Dust everywhere, scarcely worse when the white donkeys, with their dab of henna on the forehead and a raucous driver shouting from behind, pass along at a canter, filling the space from wall to wall. I was in the Jewish quarter. A bright neat small boy took me to the big girls' school, talking charmingly: he told me the Jewish school is better, and that his uncle travelled in all the world; and he refused my

[96]

two annas. Then, leaving the old mullas with children round the Qurân under trees, I walked into the modernity of Mrs. Kerr's school, all clean—and yet neither East nor West, and though change must come, and our British variety seems better than the French, one can but wonder what these Western waves are really bringing —no one quite knows. I watched the second class at work, and was a source of distraction. The teachers all young, and pleasant looking. The Iraqi has not the haughty beauty of the Syrian: more the sort of pleasantness of the Venetian compared to Rome or Tuscany. Nose wide at nostril and slightly tilted: eyebrows inclined to meet: three-cornered face: lovely dark brown hair with wave in it seems typical.

Home by the coppersmith's suq. Hardly ever see British off the main road, and more stared at than in Damascus.

BAGHDAD, 2 November, 1929.

Dearest Pips,

On Monday I go to stay a few days with Mrs. Drower whose husband is legal adviser to the Government, and so see the leading side of Baghdad. She is very charming, and so kind and interested in the people and knows a lot about them, though she did not know or believe that anyone could get a lodging for 1s. a day or near it. But I think the nicest way to know people is *not* to be important or wealthy and so come upon their genuine kindness: if you have a position here, it is always that which counts, and many tales are told of the way the native turns from you if anything goes wrong; but I find that they are as kind as can be to me who have nothing to profit them by. It was rather a sad shock the other day when mentioning Lawrence to hear my friend in Damascus talk of him as *mal'un*, 'accursed' and to hear that he passes now as one of the chief British spies, sent to betray the Arabs. Mrs. Drower thinks he did far more harm than good, and is very down on him, but it seems hard that the people he tried to help should also share this view.

This is a city of wicked dust. Every scratch turns septic if you are not careful, and both I and a woman in the hotel just out from home are laid up with what they call a 'Baghdad tummy'—unassimilated dust it seems. We hope to get acclimatized in a few days. Meanwhile even the things inside one's wardrobe get coated.

5 *November*, 1929.

My dearest Viva [Jeyes],

I am here in the lap of luxury at the Drowers, in a spacious house with two courtyards, on the Tigris. We have breakfast on a little terrace over the Tigris watching the water buffaloes with only their horns and backs showing and the water rippling gently round them. The old old round boats, made of wicker-work with a coating of pitch, are punted slowly across swinging round and round, with the boatman like a busy spider in the middle. On the opposite bank the whole length of the river as we see it is fringed with palm groves. It is great bliss, after the hotel where I just *ate* dust, to be in a spotless house with a Gulf Arab in nice white gown and red headcloth to wait at table, and an Iraqi to keep one's room immaculate, and an Indian cook to send up delicious meals. It is all rather providential as I picked up a microbe *instantly*, but took drastic measures and now only have a cold and disinclination for any sort of work.

Dearest Venetia,

It is very pleasant here with Mrs. Drower, who is delightful and so kind, and interested in the people and things of the East. She has been out ten years and speaks Arabic and sees the ladies of Baghdad and one feels that if only all our women were like her in this we should be the most popular nation in the East, with very little trouble. We had a dinner-party last night, and talked of polo and tennis and people, but while the men are, I rather think, usually interested in their work here and only keep it dark, the women I imagine are very much apart from it all and Mrs. Drower is quite peculiar in her cultivation of Arab ladies. She has them to tea on Wednesdays, when men are excluded; such a pretty little woman from Damascus came last week, just married to an elderly man whose first wife was provided by his mother. He found this one to please himself, and though he presented the first lady with a complete new set of furniture and goes to see her dutifully once a week, it is a great tragedy and life has not been made so very easy for the old wife either. She gave him an embroidered coat which he wore constantly for years and was much attached to and the young bride has turned it into a wrap for herself and rent the heart of the rival rejected wife every time she wears it.

My arabic is very little good in Iraq so far, but as soon as I get settled I shall find a teacher and get down to it.

[98]

[Note-book] 8.11.29.

Walk with Mrs. Alexander along the bund, the brick kilns like fortresses behind us, and listen to the tale of the flood: how the dyke was patrolled by the men at Alwiyah, walking along it in shifts, with a gang of labourers ready with sand-bags to rush to any spot where water oozed through. The Maude bridge went, but the old and feeble one held good.

BAGHDAD, 10 *November*, 1929.

Dearest Car [Ker],

Just to think what I have done to-day. I have been threading little blue lapis lazuli beads from Ur on a pink thread for the museum. Mrs. Drower brought them home in a cardboard box, all mixed up with bits of bones of ladies who attended the queen's funeral and were then knocked on the head. They are nearly four thousand years old, and just like what you find in Venice now, except for the value of the stone they are made of, and it is marvellous to think what instrument was small enough to pierce those tiny holes.

My new house is smaller than anything I have yet seen in Baghdad, and cheaper than anything anyone British has ever heard of here, and the only drawback seems to be that the water supply comes from the mosque opposite, so that Suleiman is sure to dip his pail into the ablution tank instead of putting it under the tap, and Mr. Longrigg, the receiver of Revenues here (though they all say there aren't any) tells me I shall certainly die unless every drop is boiled. I think I should rather not drink even the boiled water the Moslems have been washing in, and shall get a tap laid into my kitchen. If it comes direct from the main, the water is unpleasantly chlorinated but innocuous.

11/186 *AMARA QUARTER, BAGHDAD*, 14 *November*, 1929.

Dearest Pips,

I have just got into my house. A woman at dinner last night asked me if it is "fit for an Englishwoman to live in", and I'm sure I don't know, but it looks quite nice once you climb through my dank little well and up the incredible steepness of the stairs (of which only the narrowness keeps you from falling down headlong every time, so that you are like Pickwick's cab horse, supported by the shafts).

An awful tragedy has just taken everyone by surprise: the Prime Minister, who seemed quite happy when sitting next Mrs. Drower at dinner on Tuesday, came home from the club on Wednesday night and shot himself dead through the heart. He was the most if not only honest man in the cabinet, and comparatively a friend to the British. He wrote a letter to his son, a boy of nineteen now studying engineering in Birmingham, and went out on to a veranda over the river, and shot himself, his wife holding his arm and begging him to shoot her instead, and his daughter looking on. It was just that these filthy politics were too much for him and he was so badgered by every party that he could stand it no longer. It seems that his colleagues in the cabinet got hold of the letter and cut the bits out with which they were concerned, but left all that tends to show him as a martyr to the British in Iraq. Mrs. Drower and I watched the funeral as it passed our window: first the Iraq mounted police, a fine-looking body of men with beautiful horses very well kept: then the Iraq army, not so smart, its shoes and harness not bright and the horses rather badly groomed, and most of them having difficulties to keep them at their slow pace. There was a huge crowd, very silent, but no hostility visible. It was fascinating to sit above and watch the different faces; the costumes are scarce worth watching, they are so drab and mixed with European here. Then the coffin came along with the Iraqi flag wrapped round, the band before, and a crowd of relatives bearing it along from the back. Then the king's vizir walking along stiffly in blue and red uniform, and a row of all the ministers also in blue and red uniforms mostly, in a long line behind. Then a crowd of people, all the official British in top hats mixed among the flowing gowns, the green turbans of the sayyids or members of Muhammad's family, the white ones of the 'ulema and hajjis, the little khaki highlander caps which King Faisal has chosen as the national head-gear, the tarbushes, or the white and black check keffiahs of the shi'a. The head always seems the distinctive part of them: the sunnis often wear red kaffiahs, the shia never. A Kurd in the market to-day was wearing a lovely embroidered cap with big silk affair wrapped round: he was so handsome, like a bad cinquecento Italian, with small features and his eyes blackened with kohl all round: but he had a charming smile and was very pleased to be spoken to, and told Mrs. Drower that he came from Rawenduz, far away in the Kurdish-Persian hills, and was delighted to see his cap admired.

I am just reflecting what an awful place one of these flat-roofed towns must be in times of massacres. There is *no* way of defending your house, for anyone can walk over from the next roof and find himself at once and with no barrier in the heart of your house. To-morrow I am going to have the Armenian woman to sleep here with me, but to-night 'Abbas has just gone, begging me to take away the key from inside the lock in case anyone comes walking downstairs. I have not done so, as—if they *do* walk down my stairs, I would much rather they were able to get out. But I have put a pot of paint just in anyone's way coming down from the roof to my bedroom, and if a cat comes along and overturns it in the middle of the night I shall get a most awful fright for nothing.

I was actually dancing a few nights ago the first time since Creston, or rather on the boat home. I went to dinner—very distinguished: Mrs. Kerr, the head of the school, gave the party. Major Edmonds, an authority on Kurds, and Sir Kinahan Cornwallis who looks like a sailor but is really adviser to the Home Office here, and so tall that I really thought I couldn't dance with him and asked him to be careful and not drop me. We were just comfortably settled at the Alwiyah club when he was telephoned for by Major Young the Acting High Commissioner, because of the Prime Minister's suicide—and so the party broke up.

[Note-book] 17.11.29.

Sore throat and temperature. Hope not diphtheria, but I think it is the smell. Yesterday I rode to Hinaidi and Tell Muhammed with Mrs. Caparn's *saiss*, and all the symptoms seemed to vanish though the one and a half hours' ride left me tired. Wish I had a better body.

The newspaper the other day published the corrected version of the Prime Minister's letter—only it was not correct, and was not printed in arabic. Corrected statements are little good anyway: Marie told me that the Prime Minister shot himself because he was against the English: my mention of the letter only made her say that that is the 'official' English statement: and that is what will be thought.

19.11.29.

Fortune-teller came in to-day: fine figure of a woman with two black curls over her ears, tattooed hands, bracelets, all in moslem black,

[101]

with the buxom silhouette very unusual among these poor women
—product no doubt of an optimistic and artistic temperament, for she
had all the manner of the gipsy. Told fortune out of a mirror on to
which my right hand had been pressed. All wrong, but plausible.

22.11.29.

My new teacher whose name I don't know, tells me he has *seen* a
Dervish take a red-hot plate between his teeth and walk about the
room with it: and stick a bodkin through his jaw and pull it out
leaving no trace.

24.11.29.

Munir told me of his journey from Damascus here ten years ago
before motors: eighteen days across the desert in July; four hours
sleep at night. There were two wells before Rutba and one after.
Large caravan of about four hundred people, mostly Nejdi, for Hasa
and Basra.

BAGHDAD, 25 November, 1929.

Darling B,
    Your letters, and to tell the candid truth the two enclosed cheques,
came as manna in the desert yesterday. I found them at Mrs. Drower's
when I went to get her advice before plunging into the next housekeeping adventure. I had seen a dear little house with Mrs. Kerr in the
morning in a clean and respectable part of the moslem quarter—
really a dear little house for £20 for six months, with most satisfactory
sanitation and a court painted yellow and not smelly, and a nice
roof, and a sitting-room with one side all window although decently
shrouded in lattice work (which makes it impossible to clean it from
the outside where the dust is). Well, I would have settled on this if I
had not seen the room on the river, and yesterday Mrs. Drower gave
me tea and we went across, and when she saw the lovely view, and
big court with shrubs growing in it and a view of palm trees behind
and nice wide balcony over the Tigris she said I could not do better
and that the distance wouldn't really matter. So I have taken it from
Wednesday and do hope to be really settled by the end of the week.
My *bahai* has just been and is arranging for my leaving this house;
I am sure it is high time, and everyone else has been sure of it even
before I came here.
    This morning I had an awful time at school doing dictation—

[102]

quite hopeless as I can't understand the meaning at the first go off, and to write Arabic words without knowing their meaning is impossible: however it should teach me to distinguish the niceties of pronunciation. I went from school to Dr. Raghib's family and took the two ladies to look at the museum: the director, Mr. Sydney Smith, would have been rather pained, for their only comment on the treasures was that they should have been dusted more carefully. They have lived two years just opposite the museum and never knew of its existence. Their idea of pleasure is to drive in an open car round the suburban roads of Alwiyah and "look at the English", a sort of substitute for a zoo. I was taken and found it quite amusing to watch the curious spectacle of my compatriots, playing golf, etc., from this new angle.

It is nice to meet these friendly genuine moslem elements again, with no thought of politics among them—which seems to be the disease of Iraq: and it seems that the feeling is not really so friendly at all. What the people want is not very clear, for the demand for independence is just made by a few politicians who know that they are asking for what has already been agreed upon. I think it is much more a sort of psychological problem—a feeling of resentment which our aloofness gives; a feeling of superiority which is, I believe, quite real but which we do not trouble to hide, nor notice that it is a barrier. My *bahai* and his family are doing all things for me for nothing, and the teacher brought by the greengrocer is teaching me for nothing: if I were a proper Britisher I should not allow this. I should insist on paying, they would charge too much, and neither would like each other. As it is I shall have to find nice presents for them, and they will have the two pleasures of being kind and getting a present, and there will be a really pleasant relationship.

My teacher on the other hand will follow me across the river. He is a pleasant little fat man with curly features if you know what I mean and sits on his own stomach in an upright manner and tries to be polite while I read the rude things about the English in the paper. He doesn't believe the Qurân himself but is pleased that I should like it. He has been among the beduin and at Stamboul, and is a very fair type of the modern civilized Arab.

[Note-book] 26.11.29.

I notice my arabic gains me a genuine regard because, though so poor, it is grammatical: I think there is a good deal of value in knowing *good* arabic, well worth the extra trouble, which is not so *very* great.

Our good qualities are appreciated by *reasoning* and all the *emotions* are against us, and it is quite on the cards that the Latin will act selfishly and succeed while we do our best and fail.

BAGHDAD, 27 November, 1929.

Dearest Pips,

I paid a call on my teacher, who was wandering about in a long yellow shirt and the rest of his costume European and showed me up into his untidy room full of carpets and Baghdad silver work and Birmingham damasks. There were three large silver boxes made in the form of ducks and presented at weddings: I feel sure it comes from an old Sumerian goddess whose name was Ban and whose sign was a duck: she is sitting carved in marble in the museum, in a frilly dress with a duck on each side and two under her feet.

Apropos of heredity, I find that there was a man called Stark in the eighteenth century who was a very distinguished Orientalist and held posts at Weimar and (I think) Göttingen: so that must be where it comes from.

Mrs. Caparn, the wife of the Adviser for the Ministry of Works here, gives me a mount and I get out into the desert twice a week and get the good air into my nostrils. The ground is lovely, of course, because one can go where one likes, but very hard now and with troublesome shallow holes. They play polo and as soon as the first rain has laid the dust I am going to look at a match. But I find that my time is getting desperately full.

My school is off the main street at the far end among the little narrow ways: every day I turn off at the blue and yellow tiled gate of Haidar Khaneh mosque and go up past half a dozen beduin women crouching over baskets of their flat bread, past a group of Kurd porters with red-striped cotton turbans and thick felt waistcoats, by a sweet shop and a mattress carder's and a corner where an old one-eyed man sits in the dust with a tray of dusty pink and white poisons for innocent children, through a district of private houses with studded doors and latticed balconies almost meeting overhead, till I reach the school. It is quite an ordeal to read aloud in class, but very good for the arabic, and I know really more of the grammar than most of the children, though less of the spoken language.

[Note-book] 4.12.29.

Mu'allim tells me that Justice is the best department in Baghdad, and quite fair except when the British "force the Iraq judges to give a false verdict" to help someone important. I believe the man is quite convinced of what he says.

6.12.29.

Mu'allim takes me to visit his brothers—wild day, sticky descent into the motor boat, and had to jump quickly to avoid sinking over my shoes in the soft bank: Tigris all small mud waves, splashes of water over us from the bows, and gleams of sun and a rainbow on the left. Pretty going down the banks, and Karada has a good front of nice houses with not much untidiness between one and the other. Find the brothers not in the guest room, but two Arab and one European-dressed guest sitting smoking. Man from Hillah: black silk 'abba and 'aghal. Tells me that the men like to wear silk wound round their body when they fight because it strengthens them. Told that they had a Syrian girl in their house: had been a guest there for four years and he had never seen her nor heard her voice.

Painful silence whenever British are mentioned as such. The brothers came in: elder one 'Abd al 'Aziz the advocate and the younger brother 'Abd al Qadir: the advocate very anti-British I should say, and rather a nice face but sulky. Tired after going to Kut and back, having been prevented by mud from actually reaching the town. Woke up when we began to trace Arab derivations in English

Great disadvantage it is to us that we call ourselves Christian: puts us in the wrong from the first, for we are not only *non*, we are really *anti*-Christian: that is to say that if Christ were living now and were proposed for the Alwiyah club say—not only would he not be elected, but the proposal would be generally considered absolutely bad from every point of view. Muhammadans may neglect their religion, but there would be none of this fundamental *antagonism* to Muhammad if he were to appear to-day. Our whole position is a lie in this most important point, and we have no business to feel so very superior to the people who think nothing of their everyday lies, but yet have so far more truthful a standpoint essentially.

[105]

Dearest Herbert,

A very happy Christmas to you, and may the Telefunken behave on that day so as to do you credit. I feel quite glad you got it just when I left so that I shall have all the benefits of a *well-educated* instrument to come back to.

I never can remember when I wrote last so as to know what news to give. I have had a week-end at Alwiyah, being thoroughly British, with a dinner-party of ten people (which terrifies me) and general luxury. Came back yesterday and called on a lady of Turkish origin with a completely globular small husband who complained to me that his wife insists on trying discipline on their one little girl, which he thinks is bad for her character: it has not the slightest effect on her but I didn't reassure him by saying so. The little girl has chicken-pox, and we were being received in her nursery: I arrived early, and having just held the little darling's hand, heard the news with a slight (inward) shock: the next American lady who arrived— it was an 'at home'—got half across the floor and made a scene before she realized (and said) that the harm was done. There was a painful pause in which the room divided mentally into East and West and each thought things about the other: a young Moslem and I then tried to lighten the atmosphere by enumerating the arabic names of all the diseases we knew, and then lots of people arrived: the German consul who edits Persian plays, the British Officer who has married a lady with an appearance as picturesque as (they say) her past: the pretty American with a rich bored-looking Syrian husband: one or two serious young schoolmistresses looking so much more dignified than anyone else, and so on.

Last night I got home after dark—you can't think how lovely to be rowed across the dim waters of the Tigris, with the outline of palms against the sky and the few lights of the houses on the banks.

My room is beautifully warm now with the stove burning paraffin recklessly.

[Note-book] 10.12.29.

The new High Commissioner arrived this afternoon—nine aero-planes very loud in the sky over the palm groves. "I hope he will be loved," said I to Salih the *bellamchi*. "I hope he will be good and beloved," said Salih. I wonder if there is one Iraqi in the country who really wants us: and the poor people like the boatmen are really those who benefit by our presence.

Dearest Venetia,

This afternoon, in a clear blue sky with a few shining white clouds floating about in it, I was watching the nine aeroplanes which brought the new High Commissioner; three of them headed the flight and turning separate ways came slowly down in great circular sweeps to the palm groves, while the escorting six flew away. No one is too hopeful, for the difficulties are beyond any High Commissioner, but they are specially hard for anyone with no experience except Indian.

While the arrival was taking place Mrs Drower and I went to a big Jewish wedding in a house outside the town on the N.W., on the loveliest reach of the river I have seen, where it bends into a broad sheet of smooth brown water with brown boats and the waving palm gardens and the four minarets of Kadhimain and the blue dome where Abu Hanifa is buried, shining up among the tree tops. One never gets accustomed to the sudden alternation of beauty and squalor, kindness and cruelty, every contrast jostling about in this chaos of a world.

My room on the Tigris looks very nice now: a square curtained place like the Kaaba hides my dressing arrangements, I have my camp-bed and have bought a rug, covers, cushions, a chair, table, lamp and stove. Kind people have lent sofa and curtains and I have bought four ornamental candlesticks and two gazelles (metal) and feel that I live in elegant and refined surroundings and I pay 4s. 6d. a day to be fed and bathed and generally looked after by my landlady. She is a pretty woman and looks really lovely when I can ever see her tidily dressed. I vary in the most inconstant way between liking the friendliness and charm of the people and being exasperated by their hopelessness, and the same with the British—they are such splendid people and doing such magnificent work, then just our insular stupid way of hurting everyone's vanities makes us hated all round and one's feelings just torn all ways. This is a very poor letter, but I wanted to be in time for Christmas and am *so* sleepy.

On the river bank southward are flat mud hovels where the peasants live: a little pale maid in her dark blue gown and with her slim little figure and silent bare feet comes every morning with a bottle of milk: she has a gold circle with turquoise and little gold discs hanging from it sticking in one nostril, and her name is Jamila. I am glad I have no such obstacle for my handkerchief just now.

10 *December*, 1929.

Darling Pips,

I have been to a Jewish wedding. A huge house with as many people as it would hold—mostly Moslem ladies in black who come uninvited to look at the bride, who was sitting in white and silver, a diamond ring over her white kid gloves and a bouquet sent by King Faisal on a table beside her. It was mostly European. A few old ladies wore the little band of blue satin embroidered with pearls on their head and one had the proper gold sort of turret arrangement in the middle of it, but it was mostly fashionable Parisian. We came late, and did not see the actual ceremony, when the bride and groom drink out of the same cup and then dash it to bits on the ground[1] (which seems a tempestuous opening for family life).

I had a visit yesterday from an elegant young man, the king's chamberlain, a friend of my Damascus friends. He has been to New York and Columbia University, and thinks the Syrians are happier than the Americans on the whole. I wonder whether we shall ever give the East anything quite equivalent to the leisure we are trying to deprive them of.

I am going to give a dinner-party to two Arab ladies and Mrs. Drower. I feel rather nervous and hope it may be a success. Husbands will be allowed in after: I could not face the problem of feeding them.

My teacher has been telling me of his experiences as a Turkish officer against the British. Every morning four or five deserters used to be shot here in the citadel while the British were fighting at Kut: my poor man felt ill one day, and strolled along to get a 'tisane' from a friend nearby, and returned to find a sentry at his door and himself court-martialled, and was only saved by the efforts of the German general on his behalf. He says the Turks were wonderful soldiers: with no trenches, they would stand up to our charges and not retreat an inch: and my poor teacher who was longing to run away, couldn't, because there was no one to run with him.

[1]The glass is then trampled to bits by the bridegroom.

12 *December*, 1929.

Dearest Pen [Ker],

I have seen Lionel Smith and liked him so much, and hope to see more of him sometimes, though he lives out in Alwiyah, the English suburb, far from all our dusts and noises. My home at present is rather lovely, with one whole wall of my room just a window on the Tigris, a lovely place in these beautiful twilights and moonlit nights. I look down on the wide bay of the river and can see the ancient boats go up and down it just as if they came out of text books of Assyrian history.

This morning I went to Ctesiphon—a cold clear desert day, with the sun bright over a yellow earth and the low far cliffs and little tiny knolls and creases of the earth all caught up into a blue sky by the mirage. And we had to make a great detour to reach the arch and saw it like a huge temple with minarets in the distance, its façade end-on looking like columns—getting bigger and bigger and more lovely as we drew near till we could come close enough to see it in all its majestic desolation. There is just one façade and the great arch of the central hall left, and that is nearly (or quite) 400 feet high.[1] I climbed up behind an Arab going like a cat barefoot: thought for a moment I was going to feel giddy, but that humiliation was spared, and it was very like good rock-climbing. And, below, all the flat land lay from Hillah south-west to Karrada north, fields and desert and the shining curve of the river half hidden: the little mud village, its dome and palm gardens, and untidy neglected graves, and Seleucia the old dead city across the stream looking also like a new graveyard, for Americans are digging there. We went round afterwards looking among archaeological heaps for some treasure, but nothing worth while turned up although there were chips of marble and glass— blue stones or chips of mother-of-pearl in plenty.

I am trying to think of a Christmas treat for my class at school— rather difficult as they average from twenty-five to nine years old. A woman in Alwiyah just asked whether I don't think it is lowering British prestige to go and learn with the school children. I did feel so annoyed with her.

[1] It is actually 95 feet I am sorry to say.

17 *December*, 1929.

Dearest Pips,

I had my first experience of Iraq mud on Monday. We were going to a dance and dinner at Hinaidi (five miles away across desert fields) and the rain set in in torrents about 4 p.m. Telephone message through however said the road was possible and so we started—Mr. Caparn and four ladies. I find ignorance is bliss in regard to cars. I asked what the funny manœuvre was that we were doing, and was told it was a skid and found both women near me were really frightened. When we got to the last two miles the decent road is closed with barriers, as it is that delicate sort of tar which spoils if used in rain, and one is supposed to go along a rough side track. Here two cars and a bus were embedded in the mud, the cars having gone down into a hole with a pond in it by mistake. The landscape looked just like pictures of the Western Front, with no vegetation, but mud and water holes and the abandoned cars.

Mr. Caparn got out to find a way round and was sliding about in gum boots as if he were drunk: it is really incredibly slippery. He came back saying one could get off the road further back. Chorus of two ladies begged him to go home and leave it, while he sat quite stolid at the wheel, saying "I think we can do it" at intervals, and suitably ignoring the feminine clamour. We got on to what could really not be called a road; we bumped the ceiling with our heads and went wobble wobble with a skidding feeling, just like a horse wanting to shy at all it sees and not actually doing it. We had to pass a few cars and that was the most difficult, as one couldn't be sure of not skidding into them and couldn't stop or the wheels would never grip again in that soup of mud. Mrs. Caparn gave the finishing touch to the agony of the young woman next me by saying that she had left all her ambulance things at home. We arrived however and our four ladies made half of the women at the dance that evening— and they had prepared for seventy-six guests.

I have been doing a little sightseeing, the tomb of Zobeidah to-day, very ugly in a tidy but not cheerful graveyard with palms and yellow earth. But the view from the roof of the shrine is fine. The whole of Baghdad spread before you.

Darling B,

I have put my foot in it most dreadfully by accepting the mu'allim's invitation for a visit to the beduin sheikh: I am surrounded by a kind of frost, and Mrs. Drower tells me that *all* the men disapprove of me. It makes me feel like a kind of pariah from my own kind and awfully disgusted, because after all I really have done nothing, beyond wishing to talk as much arabic as I can, and regretting that we can't be less superior and more polite. I am not even pro-native, certainly as much of an imperialist as any of the people here. But Mrs. Sturges told me to-day that one can't be friends with the natives and British both, and so what is to be done. It seems to me an almost unbelievable idiocy and I shall have to put up with being out of it all and getting on steadily with my grammar—and I suppose it is good for one's character. Mrs. Kerr gave out at the last moment and told me that Lionel Smith didn't want her to go with me; so I should have had to go alone if dear Mrs. Drower hadn't come nobly up to the scratch: she hasn't yet told 'Teddy' that she is coming. It is only for one night, with a tame sheikh who is a friend of most of the people here. So this fuss is too ridiculous. The sheikh came to-day to call, looking so nice with his flowing 'abba and fine head, so infinitely better and more dignified than the degenerate townsfolk who have lost their own virtues and not taken ours. And it was a joy to listen to the good arabic of the tents. We are to go on Friday, and the Sheikh Habib has gone on to see that the falcons are being starved so that they may be ready to hunt for us. It will be great fun, and we will pay the Devil when we come home. I have written a note to Lionel Smith asking if he is really responsible and whether it is I or the beduin who are bad for Mrs. Kerr (in a polite way). I reminded him that even a dog is allowed one bite before being suppressed: and I really haven't yet had my bite.

It seems as if the Air Force is to be my comfort in life, as I am practically ostracized by the Civil Service. The trouble is that a sort of gleam of adventure comes into the eyes of the nicest wives here, and that of course adds to my unpopularity with the husbands. Mrs. Sturges would have loved to come and hunt with the sheikh, but Mr. S said he thought "it would be cold for her" with the tones of an iceberg. She now wants to come and study in school with me, but I bet anything that will be squashed, before the first lesson even starts. Mrs. Kerr this morning explained that Lionel was not so violently disapproving after all, but thought we ought to take a man: it was really she who let me down, and she was rather upset at my having written to him and blurted it all out. Poor man. He is so nice and genuinely conscientious and kind: I think he would give anything if only I would go back to a nice safe country. The truth is that the people here don't want any English in the land except themselves: they feel responsible, and yet can't actually order you about if you are an independent traveller. In fact it really *is* the attitude of *A Passage to India*, though I would never have believed it before, and it does make one rather sad.

I have had my *bahais* to tea to-day—the whole family—very nice and friendly. I do find that they are all quite different and more comfortable when I am alone with them.

Heard a new superstition to-day: that you nail an old shoe over the door, or somewhere near in a new house. I also stayed on at school and listened to the history class. It was supposed to be the early Caliphs, but the teacher, by making comparisons at every moment with the modern world, turned it into a history of modern politics. She is one of those who keep in with the British, but I am sure would turn on them at any moment and I believe when I am not present she instils anti-British feeling into the class—because one of the children made a remark about the British advisers here which was promptly checked—evidently in my honour.

26 December, 1929.

Darling B,

I have had three of the Syrian mistresses to tea—nice young girls: it is plucky of them to be teaching away in a strange country. I don't think they are brilliant educationalists, but they made a jolly party and I lent them a frock to copy and we played card games, and it was altogether quite successful.

Before this I had a real surprise. First Michael (the shoemaker) peering over the balcony came on tiptoe to my window with a conspirator's whisper to say that a guest was approaching. Then Jamila, particularly dishevelled, corroborated the interesting news and added that the apparition was English. And presently up came Mrs. Young, who is the wife of the Vice High-Commissioner, pretty and charming and a cousin of Geoffrey Young and a friend of the Trevelyans: she asked me not to call on her, but that she would let me know a day so that she might be in. And she had heard all about my "bravery" (in going to school: this seems to be what causes all the emotion). She is going to learn arabic too in a special class which Mrs. Kerr is to organize. Isn't this all rather amusing?

Mrs. T came to school with me (but I don't think understood much), and all together I seem to have set a spark going, round which the enthusiastic can gather. I believe there are really quite a lot of the women who would like to take an interest, only they couldn't start in face of the general attitude. It now remains to be seen whether the interest is strong enough to carry them along.

27 December, 1929.

Darling B,

I went and called on the O's to-day and found only Mrs. O, he having gone with Lionel Smith and the High Commissioner to Babylon for the day. She had a lovely fire and sat in a high-necked red knitted dress telling me in a dreary voice anecdotes of Gertrude Bell, who was a great friend of theirs, and of Lionel Smith, and one gets quite a different picture from that drawn by the people she did *not* like. She was quite elderly of course when she died, but even that year would go striding across the fields with Lionel Smith. The last day of all she bathed in the river and came home feeling too tired to sleep on the roof, and so had her bed made downstairs and died there in the night.

Mrs. O tells me that Lionel Smith is like Gertrude in not liking many people and in showing which he does and which he doesn't. I do hope he won't show me the latter. I am feeling rather in want of a little human kindness just now or rather of someone who is *not* kind but likes me: the atmosphere of "here is this freak: we must look after her, but why didn't she stay at home"—has been rather trying and would have been really difficult to bear if it hadn't been for Mrs. Drower and Mrs. Caparn who are so genuinely nice to me. What is rather sad is that a worse form of our own snobbery has infected the natives here and they watch anxiously to see exactly how one stands with the powers before being nice or not according: this is I believe quite foriegn to the proper feeling of the East and one of the bad things we have brought (Europe generally I mean).

[113]

I saw two pilgrim boats going upstream to-day to Kadhimain : flat barges packed from bow to stern with dark figures and three huge banners, two black, one green, flapping in the wind, upstream : and from the packed decks came the monotonous chant of the shi'a, fierce and repeated over and over with no variation : I could not catch the words.

1 January, 1930.

Dearest Pips,

Saïd Mustapha is the Cabbage King: "father of cabbages" it goes here. He has acres of them, surrounded and interspersed with palm trees, and irrigated by two oil pumps from the Tigris; and they looked very beautiful, blue and green like a sea with waves, as we sat on a divan among them and had a tin table and white cloth with all sorts of tea things before us.   Mr. Cooke and Lionel Smith left me to do the best I could with my arabic and Saïd Mustapha, and he explained the difference between Belgian and Roumanian varieties, and showed us the prize specimens, which were really too heavy for me to lift. He told me that before the war a man and his wife would work sixteen hours a day for $7\frac{1}{2}$ rupees a month : now they get 30 rupees a month for a twelve-hour day and the wife is no longer thrown in to the bargain.

While we sat at tea a dignified man with neat white turban and black gown and a grizzled beard came along : he is Hamdi something or other and drafts the laws for the Iraq Cabinet and speaks a beautiful arabic.   I gather he is against the present ministers, for Lionel Smith, in talking of the minister who committed suicide some time ago and one still alive who has a most horrid foxy sort of face, coupled them with a "May Allah have mercy upon them" which is usually kept for the departed and was a delicate and I thought rather rash way of wishing his present Excellency somewhere else : and the old boy enjoyed the *bon mot* immensely too.   He looked so much nicer than Mustapha, who was all in drab-coloured European clothes with the awful *Sidàra* which is the Iraq bonnet, and glasses.

I have just found out that the Baghdad Christians believe in an evil spirit called "deu" which kills people : obviously the old Arian word God turned into devil.   I believe the gods of the conquered are usually turned into the demons of the conquerors, but it is an interesting old survival.

[114]

Darling B,

I had a pleasant ride yesterday by the north of Baghdad, the Middle Gate which is the only one of the old gates still left, a melancholy round bastion and bit of wall in the midst of an untidy depression filled with tombs and railway shuntings and children and buffaloes where the suburbs and the Assyrian refugee camp begin. You get a good view of Baghdad as you approach the Ghilani mosque, with its blue dome and minarets and palm trees before it.

Did I tell you about the Csarevitch? It seems a poor young refugee got here across the Russian border through Persia and announced himself to be the Csarevitch: no one could make out if the story was true or no—but they have now tried a medical test to see if the peculiar disease which prevented any scratch to close up and heal, affected this young man: and apparently the test is in favour of his really being the Csarevitch: they are writing for news to know what to do with him and meanwhile he is amusing himself with the rather less respectable Russians here, and *voilà* all the gossip.

What was more exciting was my Persian lesson. The old teacher was a judge it seems, though he looks far more like a buddhist beggar carved in ivory; and he came with an ancient ulster filled with pockets out of which he drew all the most worthless curios for which he asked preposterous sums. Poor man, his children have typhoid and the woman won't send them to hospital as that would be a pollution. He is going to come three times a week for sixty rupees a month, which is rather ruinous!

To-morrow is the 'feast of the baptism', Jamila says. They put a bowl of holy water before the altar, and dip the cross in and leave it at the chancel rail and anyone can come and dip a cup in and drink, and get their wish or healing. And after to-morrow is St. John the Baptist's feast.

Mrs. Young is taking four arabic lessons a week from my Mistress Sabiha, who now nearly falls on my neck as she believes me responsible. The other ladies have one lesson a week all together, but I imagine they will not last long.

6 *January*, 1930.

Dearest Venetia,

I had a pleasant morning listening to an old story-teller woman, a Christian Assyrian, on Mrs. Drower's terrace. The story was a jumble. Androcles and the lion, Jinns and princesses, the young woman dressed as a man who wins people's money at chess, the sort of medley of *The Arabian Nights*, procured by centuries of stories handed on by word of mouth: and the old woman with a charming puckered old face and one very bright eye, and the other blind, got so excited over her adventures, seized our coats to impress the climaxes on to us and was altogether the best part of the performance. She also told us how one can make oneself bullet-proof by boiling a hoopoe at night by the Bab Wustani or the Talisman gate of Baghdad: you must never turn round though the Jinns come and pluck at your clothes, but when the breast bone of the hoopoe has boiled so long that it floats to the surface, you take it and tie it on your arm, and you are bullet-proof while you wear it.

To-day the Tigris is like a small sea, the waves all going upstream and the east wind and rain beating like hurricanes—turning the palm trees nearly inside out. And I won't be able to ride to-morrow.

I am reading Layard's early travels—early adventures he calls it—a splendid book—he must have been very strong.

9 *January*, 1930.

Dearest B,

We are all off to Kadhimain, which is only about four miles off and one of the shi'a holy cities, where the Imam Musa is buried. We were to have gone the desert way on the west bank and stopped at some tombs en route, but the ground was far too sticky and even by the good road we were often nearly a foot deep in mud and wriggling and skidding. It is a lovely way out of Baghdad running past the King's palace through palm groves which now have already a bright green flooring of plants and grass: and above the metallic shimmering palm leaves appears first the Blue Dome of Mu'addham and one of the spires; then when we leave that and cross the river, the long sun-baked walls and drab bazaar opening of the holy city itself, and its double gilt dome and four golden minarets shining surprisingly over the dingy colour of the rest.

The police had been telephoned by Mrs. Drower: they are always obliging, but now more than ever, and took us first to look at (I think) the north door from the roof of a bath opposite; one can see the lovely gold domes and minarets at close quarters and the tiles of the great archway like a garden of flowers, chiefly rose and blue with delicate flower borders and a band of writing in white on blue majolica. A crowd going in and out touching the heavy brass chain which hangs across the door at the height of a man's shoulder, and which is so holy that the metal in the middle tracts of it has got bright with touches! An old man with baskets of oranges piled in the corner completed the picture, and the crowd of people moving in and out incessantly varied it. They had no objection even to our cameras but when my foot nearly touched the sacred threshold the policeman drew me back in the most alarmed manner. The inner building appears through the doorway, more high arches, with stalactite work of mirrors that glitter towards you, in the middle of a wide flagged court. (Dear B, I just dropped fast asleep—must go to bed and finish this to-morrow.)

What one misses here is that the beautiful things are so rarely in beautiful settings: it is almost impossible to feel *satisfied*, as one does in Italy: always there is a jarring or sordid or cruel touch somewhere. And yet it is indescribably fascinating.

I believe A's family, whom we called on after tea, were none too pleased to shake hands—three little girls with very gaudy Qurân cases slung round their necks and equally bright gold teeth, and an extremely dull lady with a few spots of tattoo whom we thought his wife. Captain Holt tells me she can't be however as he happens to have special information on the subject. When Lady Clayton wanted to paint the domes from A's roof, there was some misunderstanding, and the poor man came to Captain Holt in great perturbation and said that he had heard Lady Clayton wanted "to paint his wife" but there must be some mistake, for "his wife was black and had only one leg"—and he was much comforted when told that it was only the golden domes that were wanted. He is a charming old man with a very red nose and a twinkle and the dignity which a beard and broad belt and flowing garments seems to give in spite of all. And the tea was wonderful—a huge table completely covered with small dishes of eastern sweetmeats and Peek Frean's biscuits mixed. I was very popular because, having

[117]

my plate heaped with 'manna' and being quite unable to eat it, I asked if I could take it home with me.

We wandered a little in the bazaar, and I bought painted wooden combs—the kind that were first no doubt invented by the Sumerians. Walking-sticks also they made, but I felt poor.

16 January, 1930.

My dearest Herbert,

I have just been to a lecture on Kish, watching the slides of the Deluge and the graves of the people who were buried before that, and the marks of their chariot wheels studded with big copper nails on the leather tyres: of course neither tyre nor wheel exists, only the copper nails and the place in the earth where the rest should be, but the clever archaeologist can supply more difficult objects than these out of his inventiveness.

To-night is the night of 'Qadr' for the shi'as (last night was that of the Sunnis): during it, God apportions the year's fortunes to all and sundry, and the shrines are full of people praying for a good lot. May yours be of the best. The little boys are celebrating it by dancing about in the moonlight of the river bank and banging tambourines and asking for peace, or letting off petards which are disturbing to the nerves in this country where shooting is such a common art. A Jew was shot in the bazaar the other day for asking to have his bill paid: he wasn't killed, but no doubt he will give longer credit next time.

My wall is not yet well from its attack of humidity and its spots are only disappearing slowly. These bricks are so porous that, when they are too big for building with, people take a saw to them and saw them in half: I watched a stack of them to-day being treated in this way.

17 January, 1930.

Such a truly oriental tale has just been told me by Jamila about our neighbours who own a little mud peasant house and palm garden beside our court. The old man is a wealthy old miser who has a nephew whom he keeps short of money: the Prime Minister, or one of his family, wanted this garden and ground and his factor arranged matters with the nephew. They found an old man to impersonate the owner of the garden, brought him before the judge, got the owner's seal and had a deed of sale drawn up and ratified—and now the owner finds himself deprived of his land and no money for it—and having been rather violent in his protests, was put in prison for a few days as well. Whether the Prime Minister, or more probably his agent, is responsible, is not known.

20 *January*, 1930.

Dearest Venetia,

I do *wish* you were here. Partly also because I have been so depressed by the sort of general dubiousness about my character and aims, I badly feel the need of someone to help combat the general disapproval. Did you ever read the *Passage to India*? Some have been like that, other people the very extreme of niceness but all finding it very peculiar that I am here at all, and this is what I find so tiring. The *orgy* of politics they indulge in has got on the nerves of Iraqis and British alike, so that they really have lost the perspective. I don't think the Iraqis have any real grievance, on the other hand I don't think our people, and they really are a splendid lot of people, realize how *much* more influential the unreal grievances are with all races, even our own, but much more so with people made up of variety like these. We don't go to their houses, and we ask them to be grateful for things like police and bridges, and they would probably much rather be without these latter and not feel inferior. Do you remember in Colonel Bramble where Major Parker tries to explain the Irish question to Aurelle:

"C'est un pays impossible," he says; "ils vont à la chasse en culottes marrons!" And Aurelle says: "Alors j'ai commencé à' comprendre la question Irlandaise." I think here it really is a 'peuple impossible'. But if we had had a few less theories and a little more of the real democracy that doesn't cut people up into layers and cliques, I think we might have done better. I can't help thinking that a multi-millionaire, with two hundred picked people to help, could yet turn the country pro-British—if it is worth doing, for it could only be rather temporary.

Well, I wish we could talk. I wish I were younger, and with a better inside too, though it is not too bad considering. My windows on a moonlight night are a joy—the Tigris a noble yellow stream.

20 *January*, 1930

Dearest Pips,

On Saturday they had the unveiling of the memorial to Miss Bell. The King had promised to make a speech, but apparently had not prepared anything, and got up with just a few mumbled words. However no one complained of the shortness of speeches. I did not go, but had eight Moslem ladies to tea—rather overpowering, but quite pleasant, they were mostly officers' wives, and one of them told me how her father, when serving with the Turkish Army against the Muntafiq tribe south of Baghdad, got taken prisoner after wounding the sheikh. They told him that they would see how the sheikh did, and if he died they must kill him, and after three days the sheikh died and the officer was killed.

My Persian is getting on finely. I can say quite a number of things but it is hard work. It is extraordinary how many Persian words I find in common Baghdad use.

Last night I went to dine at the Cookes, and heard about excavations, and the earliest of all skulls found, which are Armenoid and seem to have come down from the north-east. How I wish I could get some archaeological work out here. You would like the Sumerian fork I saw the other day—a really lovely object—two-pronged with some winged animal on the handle. I am going to indulge myself and spend £3 on an Assyrian cylinder seal.

24 *January*, 1930.

Darling B,

I have lost trace of dates of letters and yours are late this week because of the mud in the desert. Everything is damp and dirty and it is still raining off and on, and the streets unspeakable, and the returning in the dark to my house seems wonderful to everyone, though it is ever so much easier than the old path down to L'Arma. But the hotel-keeper's son on our side of the river has been found murdered away by the Diyala: the hotel clerk, whose job he had been given, took him away in a motor and strangled him and then put both his eyes out, because it is supposed that the picture of the murderer shows in the pupils if you are strangled. It's a horrid story, and the Chaldeans, among whom the tragedy occurred, are much upset at the discredit.

I went this afternoon to see the charming Ghilani family, the hereditary keepers of the old mosque whose turquoise dome is just opposite their house. I spent an hour there very happily getting on in quite good arabic, and when I went I was taken to the lady's sister-in-law, an ugly but attractive old woman who is given over to devotion and sits on a mattress in one corner of a room which one does not profane. If one goes in the whole place has to be spring-cleaned. I did not know and was just going in when horrified exclamations stopped me and I stood on the little mat at the threshold and talked to the old lady. They are among the nicest of the Moslems here and have not very much to do with the foreigners—a rather old-fashioned family very like old-fashioned Piedmontese—and I should say far more reliable than others I have met about.

I went in to Lionel Smith the other day and told him I was rather fed up with being considered a Russian spy (that's the last I have heard of): I think it is so incompetent: if people have these picturesque ideas, why not verify? They might find out I had been in the Censor's office and ask questions of either Maurice or George who vouched for me then, and the matter would be settled. The only other sort of suspicion is that one comes here to look for a husband, but arabic grammar and native housekeeping seem such a laborious way of doing this that I believe I have been spared that supposition.

3 February, 1930.

Darling B,

The dress has come—too lovely it looks, though I will tell you more when I take it somewhere where there is a glass big enough to see it. It is a lovely colour. I am writing to Minnie to-day. Thanks ever, *ever* so. And the fancy dress has *also* arrived and in fact was there a long time ago only the Airway people were too slack to find me out. I have mentioned what I think of them. They said that if I had come over by Nairn they would have known where I was. This must be the disintegrating effect of life in the East. The only trouble about parcels is that one has to pay 20 per cent on the declared value, whether used or not—so for goodness' sake declare everything at twopence, or, if you have *not* yet sent, perhaps better leave me clothesless: I shall be in the Persian wilds anyway after the next two months.

I had an amusing dinner and dance on Saturday. The B's and the L's—both still polite but defensive: Mr. Anderson, a new arrival, who electrified Alwiyah by appearing with an opera hat and yellow gloves, and liked me: and Mr. M who is in the Embassy and to whom Lionel Smith wrote when I really got fed up with the spy story and said what I thought about them all. The effect seems to have been quite salutary, for he was much less unnatural than before only a little nervous as to how much of his letter Lionel Smith had shown me: he hasn't shown me any as a matter of fact, but I did not mention this and left him uncomfortably vague—and told him about travels among Druses which makes them only a little less unhappy than talk about Iraq politics. Mrs. Caparn says the whole fuss is just because I am the first Englishwoman to have settled in a native house. Mrs. Drower also says it requires time to live down anything so shady, and I made her rather unhappy by telling her what I thought of the Civil Service in this regard.

Last night Mrs. Caparn took Mrs. Harvey and me to see the Queen. It was after dinner because of Ramadhan, and I wore my Asolo dress. We went up by a police sentry through miles of what might have been hospital corridors with very inferior coir matting spread along, and, instead of the Nubian slaves, little girls in high heels and knitted jumpers and an apron tied over them, who took our coats off. Then we went into a big room, rather bare walls, and crimson furniture—quite dignified in its bareness, and the little figure of the Queen, with an ermine wrap and gilt shoes, standing up very straight, and with a charming smile, in front of her crimson throne. We managed our curtsies nicely and then sat at some distance and as Her Majesty didn't help at all but merely turned with her beaming smile and brilliant black beautiful kohl-rimmed eyes whenever you spoke, it was rather difficult to plunge into conversation. Mrs. Caparn can get along in arabic but I was supposed to do the talking, and got through somehow. The two princesses presently came in, slim, rather plain, with their mother's big eyes, and something very young and pathetic about them. They both talk English but were happier talking arabic I thought. A white fluffy cat sat under the throne and the white ermine. The Queen's face was ugly and charming—a huge mouth and henna'd hair which she has bobbed, but the only things noticeable are the vivid eyes so brimming with life that it seems a miracle she should say nothing. She complimented my arabic and had heard all about me. Presently the little girls in aprons came along with coffee; and then in ten minutes or so with tea; and then in another ten minutes or so, with huge slabs of cake; and then Mrs. Caparn said we must be going—which seemed the wrong way round when sitting round a throne: and we got up and curtsied again and got all down the length of the room without turning our backs The princesses just outside the door told us that dozens of Arab ladies were being kept waiting till our audience was over. I rather wished they had been let in before we left.

I have done with my Persian teacher. I didn't like anything about him—but now, after his son has had a bout of some unknown disease which seems to hesitate between typhoid and pneumonia, his wife is down with it too; and I feel he isn't worth the risk of contagion. So I must get another.

The Air Force are shepherding Ibn Saud's rebels and preventing their melting away before they are handed back. I am glad they are handing them over, as there was not much to be said for them and Ibn Saud ought to be allowed to keep order in his own country— though I rather expect the two heads of the revolt, who are to be "well treated" by him, may catch a chill or something and die one of these days.

Such a horrid sight as I came by the bridge the other day: a dead body washed up by the side.

13 *February*, 1930.

Dearest Olivia,[1]

Yesterday I went over one of the few old things in Baghdad, the old palace of the Abbassids which is shut away in the wide enclosure of the citadel and now littered with rubbish, but its beautiful brick-work is still a joy to look on and the carved brick decoration of the gate and great hall. It is all Persian work cut in sharp deep chiselling out of the yellow brick, with patterns of leaves and hieroglyphics arranged, where the vaults spring from the walls, in a series of over-hanging niches and jutting corners that give a charming sense of lightness. The rooms must have been immensely high, like deep wells with a small hole in the middle of the roof for light to come in by, and a few small windows, so high that there was no looking in or out. Once upon a time a cloister ran out from the central hall, but this the Turks bricked up or destroyed and only the narrow passage behind it remains, very high and severe, the mortar running in long

[1] Mrs., now Lady, Barker.

[123]

straight lines all along till the eye loses it—for the Abbassids seem never to have put any mortar vertically between their bricks, and this effect of straight severity is all the decoration their walls seem to have had except for rounded corners of their passages where the slaves used to hustle along no doubt, and be saved from hitting a sharp edge by the scientific treatment of the corners.

Everything is old here when you come to look beneath the surface. I was shown a girl's bracelet, pearls and gold, made on the *exact* pattern of what is dug out of the Babylonian tombs. And all my native Christian friends these three days have been keeping the 'fast of Nineveh', to expiate that city's ancient sins.

14 *February*, 1930.

Darling Pips,

We went to a rather attractive place last Saturday, not more than forty minutes car ride from Baghdad and with cultivation close by, but actually in the desert with the black flocks and tents about in the distance among the grass just sprouting invisibly to all but Iraqi sheep, and with the yellow mounds and low ridges of old cities and canals spread round us. It is Aqqar Kuf, a corner of an old Ziggurat built up like a Dartmoor tor with ridges of three feet or so of solid raw brick like the earth around, and layers of reeds—still doing their work—appearing with rough edges just like the crystal ridges that run along the granite of the Tors. It is a shapeless block, very tall on a sloping mound once built up to support the temple; and is the home of wolves and hyenas and such who live in its crannies and scatter the whole surface of the mound with bones. You see it between the shallow undulations of the desert earth as if at the end of a vista, and very impressive. Far away Baghdad palm trees and the golden dome and four minarets of Kadhimain: and the good desert air, inexpressibly light and unlike any other. On the ground we picked up a few shards of old blue potteries, and shreds of mother-of-pearl, but no real treasure.

Mr. Caparn has been telling me amusing stories. It seems that some years ago they were so hard up for a Prime Minister here that they finally asked a successful dentist, who however did not think it worth while to leave his shop in New Street. In the early days, frock coats and such were unknown among the Ministers: when the British delegates for the Persian Oil Company came along to treat, King

Faisal ordered a reception with full evening dress (European): the Ministers grew pale: the Persian Oil man saw his chance, collected all the scratch suits he could among his acquaintance and sent them round to the various members of government and *all* his demands were complied with.

20 *February*, 1930.

In spite of not being ready for it by any means, I believe Iraq will have to have its independence—if only nominal, the current that way is too general all over the East; and we help it by educating more and more in this direction so that we pull them back with one hand and push them on with the other. We might at most delay the matter for a generation or two at great cost—and on the condition of making things more difficult when they come to a head.

As a matter of fact the plea that Iraq is unfit to govern itself seems to me rather feeble: one might say that of dozens of countries in Europe. The real argument is that we cannot risk a bad government in Iraq, interfering with several vital interests of ours: oil, and the Indian route and such: if we could keep these safe, it seems to me that the Iraqis might enjoy their bad governing if they wish without doing us any harm.

What I do feel is that our English love of conformity loses most of its advantages when you come to the few people who have the actual framing of policies in their hands: they *ought* to have all the creative virtues which are not encouraged in the official just as the material which makes the best rudders is not what is most suitable for the inside of the steersman's head. And one does feel a rather terrible want of a steersman here just now. It is the unpleasant feeling of walking down a cul-de-sac.

25 *February*, 1930.

My darling Pen,

This morning I had a rather sad experience. I was taken to call on Queen 'Ali, the wife of the deposed King of Hejaz. She is kept in a big house lower down on the river, and the house and its yard, and a rare outing to visit her 'in laws' at King Faisal's palace, are all the range of these poor ladies' lives. We banged on the door, and then answering bangs came from inside; the doorkeeper was away somewhere and our chauffeur went to find him: at last a little black boy with a long red gown and turban came running along, opened the door and let us into a yard. A big board, like a scoring-board for cricket, was just about six feet inside the door, so that even when open no one could look into the courtyard. If the house caught fire, all those females inside would be burned. A beautiful white seluki came bounding down the steps to meet us. But the house was old and squalid, with its earthen filter for water in one corner under painted capitals of light blue wooden pillars picked out with yellow. Upstairs, we went into a long room all upholstered with embossed yellow velvet, and purple cushions and enlargements of royal photographs on the walls. Faisal, and Hussein, 'Ali, and his son the young Emir who is learning to play tennis in a British school in Alexandria, while his mother lives this life of ten centuries ago here. A lady-in-waiting with untidy hair and a shabby old flannel coat entertained us, till Her Majesty came in, in a little green ready-made house dress, very simple, with bobbed hair and the most unhappy eyes you ever saw. She is still quite young, and had been used to a pleasanter life in Constantinople (where she belongs) and even in Mecca: people hate to visit her for she hardly speaks or even answers, but sits in her yellow chair on the opposite side of the room with her fierce unhappy eyes and rather pale plain little face, saying 'ay' to all efforts that are made to entertain her. To-day she was more talkative than usual, and at times looked pretty and gentle when she smiled. The black slaves came in, with very heavy steps, because they had been made to put on high-heeled shoes, and gave us coffee out of black and gold cups, and we then came away feeling quite saddened in the lovely sunshine. The man outside who sat in the mud skewering a huge fish to roast over a fire on the ground, was a much happier sight.

25 February, 1930.

Darling B,

Jamila has just been telling me that once, when King 'Ali was away, the Queen did get out, with a black slave to chaperone, and went to look at a house that it had been planned for them to buy. Jamila was with friends on the terrace of the next house and spoke to them from roof to roof with the pleasant democracy that still exists beneath our snobbish Western surface.

I had a nice quiet Sunday pulling up weeds with Lionel Smith in the garden and then watching squash racquets, which he plays very well in the most disreputable clothes you *ever* saw: and he seemed rather pained when I pointed out the different streaks of fading on his coat!

Captain Holt told me I had better go home from North Persia by way of Moscow (where he is to be): and I had to remind him that I am a Bolshevic spy.

There is another cabinet crisis on and probably a change of government coming: it can't be worse than the present and is not likely to be better. All the ministers, being in the throes of their disagreements during the three days' festival which is just over, gave out that they meant to mourn for the man who shot himself in November and whom they have ingeniously turned into a patriotic victim, and have refused to receive the usual calls.

6 March, 1930.

Dear Henry,[1]

I was awfully disappointed when I first came out, expecting to find that we were popular out here. Instead of this, we seem to be only one degree less disliked than the French in Syria—or perhaps two degrees, for there is a difference. The strained position makes you a source of pain and discomfort to all your friends if you go about with an enquiring mind. I should have liked to have made much more of the introductions: they were so anti-British that I did not feel it was fair to have too much to do with them now that things seem so very uncomfortable. This self-restraint I may tell you has not been really appreciated—I suppose I am considered so bad already that no one takes account how much worse I might be if I tried.

The nationalism is as vague and academic as it was in Europe a century ago; and not so disinterested by any means—which might make it fairly manageable if it were left alone. But there are too many people in the world anxious to help it along, so that we no longer have a clear field for the disentangling of our muddles.

The whole show here is run by a few rather disgusting local politicians: they don't represent anything except themselves (which is neither here nor there, for it is always the minorities that do the damage). And they really have not many grievances. I think

[1] Sir Henry Lawrence.

genuine grievances have a much smaller influence in revolutions than is usually supposed. Clever agitators make use of them, but they are hardly ever causes in themselves. What happens is that new classes of people grow up through trade, or education, or some economic reason, and suddenly discover that they are living in a world arranged and organized long before they ever came into being at all, so that there is no scope for them: an outlet they feel they must have, and there is trouble till they get it. Any real hardship will, of course, be made use of: but if there is none, the new energy will find its outlet just the same, and *invent* some pretext or other. This seems an ordinary law of growth and as useless to complain about as it is to complain of the injustice of measles. We are creating this sort of position here all the time. Every new batch of students is so much stuff which has no place in the old scheme of things and whose *only* possible energy is nationalism and agitation. It is bound to go on too. If we don't educate and westernize them, they can now do it themselves. So that the very root of the trouble is constantly on the increase, and it is absurd to expect the effects to diminish.

Everyone agrees that Iraq is not fit to govern itself (might be said of lots of countries in Europe too). I think the Iraqis themselves agree in this: the difference is that they don't care so frightfully much about being well governed. It is rather peculiar of us to be so particular about it, don't you think? And a mistake to assume that other nations are the same. I am sure that Italians prefer good opera to good laws; and these people, who suffer dreadfully from an inferiority complex, would much rather do without police and roads and bridges and not have constantly to admit themselves inferior by being brought up against us. One can see how it works with the servants here: our people treat them well and have trouble, or have to pay enormously for avoiding it. The Iraqis treat and pay them badly, but let them sit about and talk in their drawing-rooms, and have hardly any trouble at all. I find the same thing over and over again in all sorts of unexpected ways. I have been living more or less as they do (the only way in which I can afford to do it out here) and it has been quite worth while for the kindness and real affection I have found. I think it is rather fatuous to worry over such things when once one is middle aged, but Englishwomen here—quite as old as I am and some more so—seem to expect to be assaulted if they walk ten yards alone in the evening: as a matter of fact, I have never had a rude or familiar remark from anyone, and the people I have actually had anything to do with have all been as respectful and really chivalrous as can be : and I think it is just because, knowing me to be comparatively poor and living as they do, they need not feel inferior all the time. Anyway I have come to the conclusion that they value politeness more than philanthropy (grace and works), and no amount of solid good balances the hurt vanity.

I don't know why one should bother so much about how Iraq is governed. The matter of importance to us is to safeguard our own affairs. It is only because we assume that the two are bound up together that we give so much weight to the local politics. It seems to me that the one *only* vital problem is to find out how the things we are interested in can be made safe *independently* of native politics. If this were solved, all the rest would follow—including as much Arab freedom as their geography allows : for I imagine no one would wish to stay here for the mere pleasure of doing good to people who don't want it.

The position at present is so uncomfortable that everyone knows in their heart that it cannot get any better without some radical change. There seems to be no constructive vision behind it. But until some Idea emerges, the present groping sort of system continues because it is not safe to let it go. The danger is that it might continue so long, that we might *have* to let go before any alternative is solidly established.

It is fairly easy to feel convinced of all these negative conclusions, but of course it is absurd for anyone as ignorant as I am to try to think what the alternative might be—except that when one is out here, seeing it all so wavering and moving so uncertainly—'nave senza nocchiero in gran tempesta'—one cannot help speculating. If I were like Miss Farquharson, and had the Arab League in my hands and all the elements at my disposal, I should really go into the matter, taking my time, gathering information, talking not only to political people but to business men and all sorts, and keeping an open mind till someone comes along who is able to use it all. I believe it might be useful : real *thinking* should be, and the number who employ themselves that way is not very great : most people, after accomplishing something, use it over and over again like a gramophone record till it cracks, forgetting that the past is just the stuff with which to make more future.

She is very free too if she is not tied to any particular party : and if she were really able to gather materials together, I believe the labour people might possibly use them to some purpose. They have the prestige out here at present and really great power for good or evil in their hands—all the effendi editors reading Ramsay MacDonald. Anyway it would be more useful than agitating for Arabs without knowing exactly where it is all leading to.

I don't mean to disparage her League : because it seems to me that any sort of machinery in friendly relation with these people will be very useful later on. All I mean is that, as she has all the facilities to hand, she might, without interfering with her other work, use them to collect really valuable data which might help in the shaping of whatever the policy out here will be. The time when all was done by the man on the spot, who knew something about it, seems to be over ; it is now almost bound to be done from London as part of a general scheme : and the danger is that a whole line of action may be evolved quite out of relation with the real facts.

One of the most serious things out here is that the commercial people have no confidence so that there is nothing like a sufficient financial development. Our best hope would be to have big enough local concerns to make people unwilling to risk political changes. At present there is very little of this sort.

I think out theories now and then, to amuse myself when Persian verbs grow monotonous (they are most amusing imaginative verbs by the way).

It seems to me that we might, given a period of years and a strong man to carry it through, shift our weight here entirely from politics to commerce.

Governments are after all nothing but symbols in normal times : a handful of troops, a few officials, standing for something much more powerful than their actual selves : their power depends not only on what they really represent, but, almost more so, on how much they are *known* to represent it. (I mean that they would have no power in a place where their country is not known or where it is not realized that they can command its support at any time.)

But there is no reason to take it for granted that only armies or politicians may represent one. Any set of people can become the symbol through which a government acts, provided that they are *recognized* as such. The old Italian republics acted through their merchants for a long time. Canada is run unofficially by its big railway companies. I don't see why a powerful irrigation company, or oil, or whatever it might be, should not do the same here provided that our support were sufficiently certain first of all to give it the confidence to start, and then to give it the prestige really to represent us (though not necessarily nominally).

There would be some great advantages. If our people were strong enough to insist on what concerned their own affairs, they could leave all the odium of local politics to the locals here. A commercial enterprise important enough to make home governments afraid of interfering, would have a far more stable policy than the present, which, though it may not actually change, does so *potentially* at every election, and that is almost as bad in its effects out here. It should also pay its own way in time and turn the British taxpayer into a shareholder and supporter. Security need not be less. The Air Force would protect our commerce instead of our politics and much of the unpopularity be removed. Possibly there would be not much more than a change of name—and that is what the biggest historical changes often are.

I don't think we tried this policy even in East India Company days, being always wedded to the theory that commerce should be independent. But there is a tendency for governments to link themselves up more and more with their financial ventures, and I believe it would be leading in a direction which the world is going to follow quite soon.

Everything would depend on how much power the thing could really command. A trading company struggling for its life against odds and only spasmodically helped from home is no use at all politically. But if it were really a deliberate policy, with a certainty of support from home, I believe there might be something in it. It would not be more difficult to carry through than the Jewish business in Palestine, and for the benefit of our own people, and could be started unobtrusively with no visible change out here till it were fairly established. These are just speculations. But here we have the best men, and most experience, and money if there were confidence to bring it out: we should be at the head of things.

Some alternative will force itself upon us fairly soon, and the passing of time is dreadfully to our disadvantage. I don't think Miss Farquharson can hope for Arab kingdoms till the alternative is found: Iraq would be swallowed up in no time if left to herself. But I believe that, if they find a way out of these politics to keep safe all the things we have at heart here, the local people will be given full freedom to make their own muddles and no one mind if they are badly governed or not: everyone thankful to get out of it.

I am going to Persia in a few weeks. One's dreams come true—only not quite, for Venetia is not well enough to join and I am troubled about her. It is trying too, for it seems to upset people if one travels alone, even after thirty—and after all one can't wait to be quite decrepit to enjoy life. I always think it a reflection on human nature that you must be old or ugly or disagreeable so as to appear virtuous.

Baghdad colony has not been as bad as you prophesied: rather like a cathedral town involved in Edgar Wallace. They put me down as Edgar Wallace undiluted and the cathedral part has been disapproving, but recovering slowly: what they thought I don't know, but it was probably bad.

7 *March*, 1930.

My dearest Viva,

I must tell you about Kerbela and Nejf yesterday and all our doings. Mr. Cooke who knows all about this land and its antiquities, the Harveys (two flying people) and a Mr. Guest shared a car and we left at six-thirty on a lovely spring day with the Eastern chill still in it —which cuts you in two like a knife so that we wrapped our heads in woollies and padded our fronts with pillows and quite glad when about two hours across the flat half-desert fields brought us to the Hindiyah barrage. There the Euphrates is dammed and swishes down over a weir into a peaceful flat landscape: on the river below you can still see, half under water, the breakwater which the Turks built and kept in repair with the ancient bricks from Babylon. We went out into the desert after Hindiyah with gardens on our left— palms and a thin veil of blossom below them: then into gardens, glades and glades of palm and narrow reaches of water: magpies and kingfishers: traffic of donkeys chiefly: and suddenly a few ram- shackle houses, and this is Kerbela.

Mecca and Medina are, of course, the holiest of all, but for the shi'a Moslems (and they cover half Iraq, all Persia, and much of Central Asia and India) Kadhimain, Kerbela, and Nejf are almost the more sacred. Along the stretches of desert as we went it was strangely touching to see here and there some gaunt figures of the Persian pilgrims, walking months on end over that unending blistering freezing flat land: sitting two together by the roadside, or walking with a woman and child plodding behind, or lying stretched flat on their faces on the sand with the yellow desert flowers and purple irises springing up around. Nejf is right out in the desert and springs like a vision on their weary sight—a town inside a buttressed wall with its golden dome and minarets rising from the centre of it—the very embodiment of the promised city. But Kerbela is hidden in its palm groves, you come in through mean and dirty suburbs, and then gradually through streets porticoed in a miserable way by crazy palm-stem pillars, by cafés full of dingy seats and pale malarial faces, in to the centre where the suqs run in a shadowy circle round the mosque where the body of Hussein lies. There is not a European in Kerbela, or in Nejf, but the police welcomed us politely and Mr. Cooke knew Sayyid Abu' l'Hussein, who wears a green turban and is respected—he is a nice man and helped the British when we were glad of help. He had the sleepy eyes half hidden under their lids and the full-lipped large mouth and long sallow face of many of these Persians who live in the holy cities. We expected to be followed about by looks of black hatred, but as a matter of fact many of the people seemed friendly enough, and a coffee keeper allowed me to pollute one of his seats by standing on it to photograph the great door and two black flags which show the way in to the Mosque of Abbas.

In all the shops of Kerbela you see booths where small grey tablets rather like soap are sold: these are pieces of the sacred earth which only a true believer can buy, he puts his forehead on it when he prays.

You go straight into the open desert from Kerbela, skirting the palms far away on your left, and with a clear horizon on every other side. It used to take two days, and there are three old khans, deserted now, which once used to swarm with pilgrims; a few bedu, and the police, are all the inhabitants, but the yellow walls and sound buttresses, and the arched gateways, still look very fine on the landscape. Then as I said, Nejf comes to you like a vision—blank walls, gold dome and its graves strewn round it the colour of desert sand, with here and there the blue glazed domes of richer graves. Coffins come rattling along in Ford cars to be buried here from many distant lands. If you die of plague or anything contagious, you have to travel 'dry'—that is to say you are buried for six months first and then dug up and brought here. For £50 you can be buried in the sacred enclosure itself: there is a limited number of graves available, and it never diminishes. The people who are not buried 'dry', are, of course, rather unsanitary travellers, but less so now that the motor gets the journey over more quickly. Right across the bit of desert between Nejf and Kufa you can see a funny little tram on wheels being drawn by horses; that is the Nejf water supply, and you can buy a fat skinful of water for half an anna.

The desert air is all in and out of Nejf's narrow streets. It is up on a height, and where you get an outlook at all, you look into the lovely tawny distances—and the people are freer and healthier and have the good walk of the desert people, but even more fanatical than Kerbela, for Ali is buried in Nejf and it is the holiest place of all, and though we went with the sons of the Killidar, they themselves kept us as far as they could from the door of the mosque and pressed in between us so that they might prevent the pollution as much as they could. There is a beautiful great door to the Nejf mosque, done far more simply than most with coloured glazed medallions in good plain brickwork and the golden gateways of the sanctuary itself showing behind across the court. The Killidar was away. His son, a young boy scented heavily with some sort of incense, gave us the bitterest coffee I have ever drunk in a room lined with *lovely* rugs. I should like to stay in Nejf for a month or so. Mr. Cooke says it would be perfectly feasible as the Killidar's guest, but of course the government people here would make a fuss. Mr. Cooke quite sensibly thinks it is a mistake to try to make these places safe by never letting people go there, the best way is to make them safe by getting as much traffic through them as they possibly can. As far as exploiting the tourist side of Iraq goes, we compare very poorly with the French in Syria: I do think that the average Englishman is naturally antagonistic to ideas as such: he sniffs and sniffs at them like a pony at a bog, while everyone else has long been getting to the other side.

Having escaped the Killidar and his lunch, we left the pilgrims' city and went again across desert to the cultivated land and Kufa on its edge—a tiny little town with a huge empty khan and half-dead little suq and the great mosque buttressed like a fortress, with a good door of Abbassid carving and a pleasant friendly old gentleman with a yellow kaffieh on his head to welcome us. It had all the charm of a place that had once been flourishing and then died suddenly without any dingy transformation in the process and here again the clean desert air, like freedom after the stuffy narrow ways of the inland towns. Ali was murdered in Kufa, as he was praying in this very mosque. His body at his request was loaded on a camel and was to be buried where the camel kneeled down; and so as it wandered out browsing into the desert, and rested on the little rise, the city of Nejf was born. That is the legend.

I must really finish this letter and hurry you past Ezekiel's tomb at Qifl. He is bunched together with the 'friends of the prophet' who are kept in a back room as it were with a few polished stones which take away whatever pain they are rubbed against. Ezekiel belongs to the Jews, and one can see at once the more artistic race by the decoration, and the beauty of the rugs. An old Jew went round with us, blue-eyed with heavy lids—quite different type and I don't like it much. His young helpers were all Moslem however, and all the faiths come to visit Ezekiel, and the hands printed in henna on the walls are all Moslem. This also is a little half-dead village with small dingy suq among fields and palms, and lives by its tomb and pilgrims: a little court, and minaret of Abbassid worked brick crumbling and tottering—the holes loud and busy with pigeons, and a stork on the very top. Outside the village is a little colony of weavers, their bodies half buried in the ground which is thus brought to a convenient height for managing the shuttle. It was too late in the day for snapshots, and we hurried on, and in the last sunlight saw what is left of the tower of Babel on its mound, a very impressive hill built by the hand of man. Then to sleep in the rest house at Babylon.

8 *March*, 1930.

Dearest Venetia,

Just back after a glorious tour. I am going to begin at the end and tell you about Babylon and Kish, for I shall not have time for more and that is what you would have enjoyed most, especially as Mr. Cooke made us see it all as it once was and stole a brick of Nebuchadnezzar for me into the bargain (so good for my luggage). We saw Birs Nimrud, which was once Borsippa, and the tower of Babel, in the evening with the last of the sun behind it—an impressive mound like the Pyramid with its bit of solid brick tower on the summit. There is a mystery for the whole top is covered with great blocks of brick

coagulated by fire: they must have been incandescent once and explain
the 'fire from Heaven', but how blocks of brick can become incandescent of their own accord is hard to explain: no human agency
could do it without very powerful furnaces. Mr. Cooke's theory
is that the weight and friction of the brick tower above them must have
melted them as the whole thing came crashing down. Anyway
there they are, a mystery, and symbol of the old legend. The river
has long left the land, and it is now desert or desert-like fields, rising
into mounds where the dead cities are strewn. Every year in the old
days, the gods of Babylon were brought downstream to visit the
gods of Borsippa, and one can picture the river procession from where
the Ziggurat of Marduk by Babylon stood up as a landmark—seven
miles away. We got to Babylon at nightfall and settled in the
German rest house, to a supper of Bovril and sandwiches and an
entertainment after from the small village boys who sang and danced:
"Oh, Father of the railway, curses upon you who carry my love so
swiftly away" or: "Her beauty shines as far as Basra and Baghdad
and Damascus and turns the Moslems into Unbelievers": or "She
thinks that I love her as she stands by the sideboard and combs her
hair . . . but she is quite mistaken," the little wizard of a boy wagging
his whole body as he danced and snapped his fingers with an expression
of astonishing wickedness.

Our first day was cloudless blue and sun, but next morning the
clouds came up in great bands over the desert and suited that old
melancholy land, though we grew anxious: the last archaeological
visitor having been imprisoned for five days by weather. We walked
for nearly three hours over the mounds and pits of Babylon. Nebuchadnezzar was really *worse* than Herbert and when one sees
the scale of his buildings one can quite understand the decay of the
empire after—it must have completely exhausted his own resources
and his subjects' patience, for he built three times, always widening
the circuit of his palace quarter, and raising the level of the town
bodily, burying all he had built before, including the beautiful Ishtar
gate with its carved animals. The city rose on great solid walls 80 feet
thick in one place, 57 in another. Lapping it on one side was the river,
and a great bridge, and the Ziggurat of Marduk and other temples on
the far side. The sacred way, flagged with great blocks, with a
parapet of more blocks and two rows of glazed lion figures to line
it, ran alongside one of the walls, through the Ishtar gate to the temple

of Ishtar at one corner and the King's palace. The blocks are left, and plans of the rooms and courts, and shells of great walls, hollowed out as if they were rooms by Turkish looters of bricks. They used to leave the outer shell to prevent the debris falling in on them, and they looted enormous amounts, so that Hillah is almost all built of Nebuchadnezzar's bricks with inscriptions here and there. The great hall of Belshazzar is approached through two courts, where the offices and officials' houses were and the hanging gardens on the left near the Sacred Way and the river. We did not linger here, for the weather grew darker and darker. We hastened across the obliterated river bed to the Parthian city opposite, which was inhabited down to the thirteenth century: then back again to the Greek theatre; in the distance the pile of debris where Alexander brought Marduk's Ziggurat bricks to build a second tower of Babel: and the flat sort of small hill where his friend Hephaestion was burned: the charred pieces of wood were still found there. Then—greatly daring—we decided to risk Kish after all, chiefly because Mrs. Cooke was to meet us there. We went across open desert, *strewn* with dead cities like dunes in the sand: ridges of old canals—all dead: we passed camels and saw then trying to jump the ditch, a ridiculous clumsy sight: one collapsed, and its load of two small infants came rolling down in perfect silence and with great composure over its tail while it lay helpless astride the ridge.

At Kish, a little low mud house with a small square of barley enclosed on three sides by the building: there is nothing else visible, and here the mission lives, Mr. Watelin and Mr. Martel—two charming Frenchmen. What a relief to be with people so interested in ideas that they do not take you for an unnatural phenomenon whenever you express one. They assured me that with one exception I am the only woman in Baghdad with a soul of any sort. Whatever it is, I know it is unique here and a most inconvenient commodity: but it was charming to sit and talk French and be liked and have a delicious lunch with one's *tumbler* refilled with champagne at intervals: and our hosts asking when could they see us again.

Kish is older than Ur I believe; anyway the streak of earth which represents the deluge is quite a good way up and all sorts of pottery found below it—besides round skulls and flints and crystal pebbles used to count with (probably). After the deluge the round skulls go and a new layer, long skulls and different sorts of pots, are found. But the exciting thing is that these earliest pots were beautifully painted and decorated and all in an age long before the discovery of metals. The ages come up gradually layer by layer —from the flints to a lovelier terra-cotta relief of Ishtar than I have seen anywhere except among Greek things. The treasures were all laid out, ready for Mr. Smith to come and divide: what is due to Iraq and its museum is much grudged, rather naturally for goodness knows what will happen to it in years to come. But anyway they have to get half of everything. *We* however got an ancient pot each and came home rejoicing, trying to roll ourselves round the treasures so as to preserve them from the bumps of the road. Kish is really more impressive than Babylon to the naked eye, for its temple walls still stand with their broken surfaces to catch the light and shade, like the newest skyscrapers in New York. It was another of Nebuchadnezzar's palaces and never finished: and next year it is going to be blown to bits with dynamite so that the next, older palace down below may be investigated: so that we saw it at its last. Next year I hope you will be out here to see the next.

13 *March*, 1930.

Darling B,

As I went down in the 'bellum' to go out to dinner last night, I put my foot down and slipped bang into the mud, and was much annoyed with the boatman, who had shown me the wrong place. "But your head is safe," said he, and of course that is a disarming way of putting a damage to one's shoe. He told me as he rowed me up that a purse and five rupees had that day fallen through a hole in his pocket and been lost: "This is destiny," says he; "it is the power of Allah"—and I didn't like to say that a stitch in time was what was needed to make the power work differently.

MOSUL, 15 March, 1930.

It is good to be up here at last. Mrs. Drower and I came by train to Baiji: a night in the train and wake up with early sun shining on a flat green country with a sort of backbone ridge of low hills, Jebel Hamrin, on our right. Car waiting. Breakfast in the train, made by Mubarak, Mrs. Drower's good Bahrein Arab, with the effect of his red kaffiya and the immense woollen fluffy ''agal' he always wears like a crown, rather spoilt by a very bulky Burberry. We had six hours by car, most of it delightful over the short desert grass with blue patches or white of anemones, and pink patches of tiny wild geranium—red tulips or anemones here and there, and wild mignonette and marigolds growing over the ruins of Asshur. This is still a wonderful ghost of a fortified city, seen from the north where its buttresses face the Tigris valley, and the opal-coloured sands and water of the broad river bed sweep beneath the ancient ziggurat and the quay. It is buried under earth and grass and later cities and graves: and no habitation is there now except the empty rest-house of German diggers before the war: but one can still feel it under the blanket of all those ages, a fine place for a young nation to grow up in, the hills in small shallow ridges behind it and the rich lands and river before, and many further ranges visible far off in the north and east. Here the Assyrian power grew and spread and gradually left its old home. We scrambled over it and then sped along, and sat to lunch in the sun and wind with endless dipping horizons of various green around us, and camels and tents, grazing homes of the beduin everywhere in the distance. Then we came to stone in the landscape—the first after the stoneless southern plain: arched doorways, milestones, stone bridges: outcrops of limestone: sloping roofs here and there with storks building on every one of them. Hills on the horizon, and here and there lonely round mounds where cities are probably buried.

By the time we reached Mosul the sky had clouded over and last night it rained, which may put a stop to our expedition for some days. But Mosul itself is full of charm though dirty: not the *sodden* sort of dirtiness of Baghdad however. The bazaars are full of colour: good costumes: Kurds in baggy trousers and long bands of cloth tied in voluminous knots to make a padded waistcoat round their middles: Tiaris, with small pagoda felt hats and shrewd mountaineers' faces: Christians, with bright colours, and baggier trousers than the Kurds. The stone gives more variety to the building and lets it fall to bits more picturesquely than Baghdad, and the town is on a shallow mound which gives it a little up and down in its streets. These towns all rise 'on stepping stones of their dead selves'. Across the old bridge— which begins on wooden boats studded with great nails and looks very Viking-like, and goes on, when it reaches the bank, in a series of stone arches, and has women washing on stones like Italy—is Nineveh, with a little clustered town built on its mound so that no one can dig it up.

17 *March*, 1930.

Dearest Car,

I spent a lovely peaceful morning yesterday in what was once Nineveh—a low very wide saucer of downs and wheatland, with a shallow rise holding it like a rim where the old ramparts lie buried. There is nothing much to see, only this consciousness of great peace over what was once so tumultuous. The mound where the palace must have been, still stands high like the old hulk of a ship: and over against it, the other mound of Jonah which cannot be dug into as the Moslems have a very holy mosque on it. I wandered over it and they all became very friendly, and we discussed carpets of which a special red kind are woven here. They are sunni Moslems and showed me one Persian rug where the shi'a Persians had woven the name of 'Omar so that he might be trodden underfoot: and these people had hung it carefully on one of the walls out of danger. I was just hearing the other day of a little schoolgirl in Spain—so ardent a republican that she stuck the soles of her shoes full of stamps so as to tread on the King's head—evidently the same sort of attitude.

(20th, continued after interruptions.)

Mrs. Drower and I are now well out in the desert, a marvellous grassy world, and we are staying with the chief sheikh of the Shammar. We have a big tent to ourselves, with white mattresses and purple cushions spread in it, and all the tents of the sheik's family and slaves spread around, with horses, donkeys, camels, and small foals and children all out enjoying the short delicious season. I can't tell you what a scene of peace and loveliness it is: the women sit out with their tents open on the sunny or shady side according to the time of day, and show us their old barbaric jewels and magic beads. The daughters of the Jinn were once battling when some wolves rushed out and frightened them and they all turned themselves into stones: and there they still are, and the beduin find them—often old cornelians and agates or Assyrian seals from the mounds that are scattered like green islands over the buried cities all around us: and they wear them in strings at their belt with a silver thing with bells or tassels to dangle at the end, and have a meaning for every stone; some bring children, or cure serpent bites, or, if they touch a man's cloak, will make him instantly love you: and one, which was offered to me as a present

[140]

yesterday, is to be rolled on the carpet and any woman you happen to dislike is brushed out of existence on the instant: this is called the 'carpet stone'.

SHAMMAR TENTS, 20 *March*, 1930.

Dearest Herbert,

We spent this morning hunting the lesser bustard (I think that's his name). Anyway it's a silly bird with a confiding nature which should have destroyed it long ago, and will too, now that it comes into contact with civilization. It is about as big as a large turkey, with a flat light-brown back and long legs: the motor goes round and round it in narrowing circles, and though it raises its head with a foolish sort of look like that of a distressed woman in the midst of traffic, it doesn't seem to think of flying away till one is near enough to shoot. We got three, to my sorrow, for I do hate to see things die. However the feathers will look lovely on a hat and the lunch was excellent. But what was really pleasant was to wander for hours over the soft grass with the hills all round in blue-white edges on the horizon.

I have got two old Assyrian seals, but I am always being harrowed by seeing most lovely valuable ones on the girdle chains of these beduin women who keep them as talismans: they get worn with use till the engravings disappear and they lose their value, and one cannot get them to part with them as they have a great opinion of the magic in them. The sheikh's daughters here are wonderful to look at with their jewels, their heads jingling with gold as if it were a harness.

SHAMMAR TENTS NEAR MOSUL, 21 *March*, 1930.

Dearest Pips,

I am writing from the guest tent of the big Shammar sheikh of north Iraq, and Mrs. Drower, who has brought me, is writing down stories about Jinns which his slaves are telling her, squatting round in a circle. It adds a great charm because they really believe in them —and some are most delightful stories. You would so love it here —the lovely free life of the tents, and pleasant family feeling of the tribe. I feel I should like to belong to a tribe, something so big and comfortable, and if you do come to grief you do it all together: and there is none of the horrid petty bickering feeling of the towns.

[141]

I had three wonderful days in Mosul before coming on here and can't tell you about all of them they were so glorious and crowded. One of the nicest was among the old Christian villages: you would have liked it best because of the marvellous costumes: you can't ever have seen anything like it; I felt I was being almost knocked over with the wonder of it. There were two villages, one Syriac and one Chaldean, and not a woman in European clothing there, and all dressed up with long gowns of pink or red or blue stamped stuff like the old bed-covers we get at Dronero: and over this a cloak tied on one shoulder of the brightest embroidered yellow and orange: it was like the Middle Ages come to life. On their heads they had veils and beads over a sort of small turban, and under it a band of gold coins: and their necks swathed in a wimple with gold beads under the chin. These visions were all out picnicking and playing in groups on the green grass outside the mud walls of the village. The men wear immense baggy trousers woven in designs; but they were not so universal and altogether the Christian superiority of the feminine was rather apparent, the men being a poor lot. Karakosh, the Syriac village, was specially fascinating in itself, because of its old churches dotted round, and the millstone for grinding corn standing in the foreground. I was all alone and went about with most of the population, looking at the very primitive churches which had to be opened with huge keys: one had only a woman left as guardian, and after refusing to get into my car as if it had been a demon, she opened the outer door, then lost heart altogether and fled out from the village to her husband for protection. It was getting dusk already, and a good hour from Mosul, and a police rule that one must not be on the road in the dark: I had finally to look over the old tiles (lovely Persian all in bits) by match light, and then have a short but firm argument to refuse a police escort, and got home only twenty minutes after dark. The old churches were not very beautiful at Karakosh, but there was another, which I saw before, called Mar Behnam, which had very lovely sculptured doors and interesting arches, one stone fitting into the other with perfect neatness. Behnam, with one sister and forty other martyrs apparently came from Persia and was murdered here: one climbs down into the middle of the ground in a horrid little modern building outside, and there is a round crypt where they are all buried: and however it may be, it is certain that this is the best stone work I have seen here (except a little

[142]

in the great mosque in Mosul), and it may be Persian like nearly everything artistic in Iraq.

I began this day at Nimrud, where nothing is left but the great grassy mound, the lovely view over rolling green country (like Dartmoor in the distance), and a few winged monsters half buried in the ground. But there is something extraordinarily poignant in this solitude of the old Assyrian cities: just a beduin and his flock, and an old bit of brick with the wedgelike writing I picked up in the ploughed land as I got out of the car. I have seen Asshur, and Nimrud, Nineveh, and Khorsabad—all nearly in sight of each other, and it seems incredible that this small kingdom could spread its armies all the way from the Persian Gulf to Egypt. All the beduin here wear Assyrian seals among the bead strings they keep for talismans: against snake or scorpion bites, for milk or children, to make their husbands love them or to kill their enemies, or one to shut up anyone who contradicts you.

Our host himself, Sheikh 'Agil, looks just like an Assyrian king. He is enormously tall and broad (not fat), and when he and his tribesmen stand up to welcome us in the supper tent (about 80 yds. long) it is really an impressive sight.

My name, being welcomed as Arabic, is most useful and 'Faraya' is asked to come and sit near the sheikh at meals.

Just heard a nice Arabian proverb: "If you spit against the wind, it will blow into your face."

The big mosque is a wonderful place. All its original pillars have fallen about and are slanting at absurd angles and they have stuck in other supports: but there is a lovely window and praying niche of stone tracery. The mullah, whose politics are bad I heard, though his manners charming, told me that Mosul is the only town Saladin failed to take. The people thought they could not hold out against him and sent the Queen's daughter to beg him to spare the town: but he said: "Mosul cannot be given for a woman's prayer," and sent her back; which so annoyed the Mosul people that they pulled themselves together and kept Saladin at bay. There are still bits of old walls and the moat ditch, and a fine old piece of medieval bastion, the Sinjar Gate, at one corner. The Tigris flows down one side of the town, a slow yellow stream under a bridge of old wooden boats with big nails, and then a flat piece of gravel with the arches of an old stone bridge and women washing on the stones, beating the clothes with wooden bats. You never go near without hearing this constant sound of dull thudding. Rafts come down, and people cross swimming on skins filled with air as they did in the old reliefs; and you go up from the river into the most fascinating bazaars you ever saw.

MOSUL, 23 March, 1930.

Dearest B,

We heard about the wolf—more legends: how you hush your baby, by saying 'In the name of Allah', 'In the name of the wolf' (*Bismillah b'-ism ed-dib*) and he won't cry, and Sheikh 'Agil explained the reason by saying that the wolf is to be the last creature left alive on earth before the day of judgement.

We are back in Mosul now and find all sorts of things have been going on in our absence: anti-British demonstrations: the new government (all the decent people weeded out of it) settled upon; and the Woolleys here on their way home.

BAGHDAD, 31 March, 1930.

Darling Pips,

How I wish I could send you a little of this gloriousness: the nights just pleasantly cool with all the windows open; the days dazzling and not too hot; and everywhere, from every court and garden, the scent of orange blossom. Certainly from November to April with the exception of the few dust storm days, Baghdad is the perfect climate.

To-day I showed Mr. Cooke my flints and obsidian and shards of pottery found on our own 'tells' north of Mosul, and both he and the head of the museum here say it is a most interesting collection: all the painted shards and the stone implements are pre-deluge, long before Noah. It seems almost incredible that one should go picking them up casually out of the grass. The extraordinary thing is the fineness of some of this ware: I have a little bit of a rim which might almost be porcelain.

Lionel Smith took the King of the Belgians to Ctesiphon, and he was immediately for tracing the way up to climb; only he was planning it on the side opposite the one I went up. I suppose it is feasible either way.

To-day I wandered over the sites of Baghdad with Mr. Cooke and the Americans, looking out bits of fine brick carving hidden

[144]

away among its untidy corners. There is not much; but what there is is very fine in design and workmanship of the twelfth and thirteenth centuries, and the new bricks look dreadful beside these clean-cut old ones. There is some hope of the palace ruin in the citadel being restored and possibly turned into a museum. It has some lovely carved vaulting and so has the old school of the Mustansiriyyah; what lovely use they all make of the good arabic lettering. We went into the back streets of the town, and found a beautiful carved wooden tomb in one mosque ('Aquliya): and then we went out to the old city gate at the back, where nothing is left but the round gatehouse and a sort of ramp that went up to it, and a bit of water and rushes where the moat once was. All around are tombstones in a sunny dusty desolation, and the blue domes and minarets of Baghdad rising out of its honeycomb of houses.

I leave for Persia on the 10th. I have got my route mapped out for me by M. Watelin, the French archaeologist of Kish, who is one of the few people who have ever been near Alamut. He says it is a most peaceful population—no danger of any kind except mosquitoes, for which one takes a net. So my next will be from Hamadan.

2 *April*, 1930.

Darling B,

I leave on the 10th with some Americans who are nice though cultured in a laborious way—always miles behind, discovering things long ago taken for granted, and I believe that is why they are so fatiguing: as if someone were expecting you to share all the time in his enthusiasm over the alphabet, which you have long ago ceased to consider as a subject thrilling in itself. However I shall be respectable which is something, and even the most fastidious will "deem me to be accompanied": I am really submitting to this discipline entirely to please Lionel Smith, who, after suffering visibly but in silence all this time, when he saw me hovering between respectability and the charms of independence, actually said that he thought I had better go with these people: I felt that he must really be concerned about it, as he is so very reticent about expressing opinions, and so I gave in with a feeling of virtue which alas, passes quite *inaperçu* among my many misdemeanours.

I am now going to be inoculated for plague—a horrid business.

10 *April*, 1930.

My dearest Viva,

Your letter of March 27th just this minute come as I was setting about the writing of one to you—and most opportune, for here I am in a dingy hotel (paying 16 rupees a day instead of 4 and far less comfortable) with a dust storm from the south and all the windows closed to keep it out, and incapacitated for the time with a broken muscle (at least the doctor said broken, but I think he meant strained, for it is to be well in three weeks). It was a foolish accident, due to the susceptible temperament of my pony, two or three mares being about while I was standing him near the polo ground and watching the play, he suddenly reared, pirouetted and had me off among the Iraq policemen. Luckily the drama passed unperceived by the audience, and the pony was caught before dashing itself at the grand-stand. A kind Iraqi hoisted me into the saddle as I couldn't use any strength and I rode home slowly over the two miles or so of desert ground with the sais lamenting behind "that this should have happened to him before all the gathering". However, the doctor says I can travel if I tie myself round with a bandage, and I have a charming young man to help me upstairs.

I am sad at saying good-byes here. I feel I have good friends, Lionel Smith, Mrs. Drower, Mr. Cooke, and they all think kindly of me and far more of my capacities than I ever thought or imagined. And I believe my chance will come and a good one in its time, and if I can have the time to give to it I may do really good work yet. Everyone *now* says: "What a waste if I don't come back"; such a different note to six months ago; and even Captain Holt who is oriental secretary and does the work Gertrude Bell used to do and tells me that I am quite mad, takes it as a matter of course that I am to reappear among his archives where all the troublesome characters are docketed.

I was most deeply touched when I left my lodging—so much affection and really disinterested affection, for I could hardly get the people to accept their rent or the little milk girl to take a present.

11 *April*, 1930.

Darling B,

My broken ligament is still very troublesome, but I shall be able to go on Sunday morning, well bandaged like a mummy—and

it seems a special attention of Providence that the matron of the
hospital should be travelling with me.

Captain Holt came in to lunch to-day much amused. He received
a confidential report this morning to announce that I had moved
from my lodging to the Maude Hotel where we have been lunching
together daily these last four days. Fifteen rupees I have cost the
British Intelligence service for this thrilling bit of news. I told him
he had better rope me into the government service—on the principle
of setting a thief to catch a thief as he politely suggested. He told
me most amusing stories about spying and counter-spying in Afghan-
istan. I really would never have believed that this 'best seller' type
of life really exists—but it does, and just as colourful or rather more
so than what you buy on the bookstall. It is rather fun to think
that here it all is, ready to provide entertainment for anyone who
finds his way into it, though of course it does also provide complica-
tions and interferes with one's most innocent pleasures. I made some
remark about not having burst into tears in anybody's office (as when
I first came Lionel Smith gave me a long list of all the independent
ladies whose ventures apparently always end this way) and Captain
Holt said he did not know how I had managed to stick it: that I
must have an extraordinary fund of natural philosophy.

Rather glad I didn't stay late at the Sheikh Ahmed's the other day
to meet the great Egyptian actress Fatima Rushti again: when she
came all the Arab ladies got up and offered her gold bracelets, and the
English women felt rather embarrassed, having come to the party
unprovided.

HOTEL DE FRANCE, HAMADAN, 17 *April,* 1930.
Dearest Pips,

Your note came just as I was leaving Baghdad, and I must begin
by answering as to your selling out. It isn't a thing I would like to
advise about, as it is just entirely depending on your own feeling
about it. You know that Asolo and L'Arma are both ready waiting,
and that it would be lovely to have you a bit nearer at hand, especially
as I don't see any prospect for a long time of being able to manage
the financial part of the voyage out to you more than once in two years.
That seems a long time apart. On the other hand you must think
whether you would mind leaving all your surroundings and settling
back into the life in Italy. I am sure I *can't* make any suggestion,

except to recommend as strongly as I can that you don't worry over anything except your own feeling in the matter. We shall have enough to live on anyway if you come along, so that this need not enter into the matter at all. And if I can go on a few years with my languages here, I think I shall be able to get a really good position and make everything comfortable financially too, enough to do nice things like trips to Rhodes or Rome when we want to. The thing is to think out the two sorts of life and think of *yourself*, dearest Pips. Of course I would rather have you in Asolo, because I should see you more—but not if you are not to be happy there. Otherwise it is very easy. We will furnish the house next door, so that we can be independent if Herbert finds us too much, and you and he can collaborate in the cultivation of bulbs: I may bring you all sorts of rare kinds from the wilds of Persia. But I don't want to influence you either way. I shall try to be out by end of August. I have had to change some War Loan and it has upset the year's budget, so that I won't have enough balance to come out before, but I shall hope to be there for the apple picking, and of course it would be like a dream to fetch you away before the winter and not have that constant ache of knowing you out there in the cold weather. And if you managed to sell for anything that gave you an income, we could go to Rhodes for the spring and enjoy ourselves. But if not, I will just come out as often as I can; I do want you to feel that you are doing what you *like*. What an awful pity I am not a man, to be of some use in working there with you.

Now I must tell you about Persia, though I have not yet begun examining more than this hotel garden, as I am rather sorry for myself with a strained side-muscle I got when my pony reared and threw me down by the polo ground, did I tell you about it? Anyway it is nothing serious, but was very excruciating over the bumps of the road, and will take a fortnight to get right again. I had moved to the hotel in Baghdad and was doing no good and spending too much, so I just came on *coûte que coûte*, and shared a car with the matron of the hospital and a young daughter of the bank manager just out of school. We had the usual affair in getting off: it was to be 5 a.m.: to make sure, the car came at three-thirty and, being now philosophical over these things, I told it that it could go to blazes for another hour and turned on to my other side. When finally we were all gathered and packed in, it turned out that the driver was not the owner, and the owner wouldn't trust him alone with his car in a country where there is no extradition—at least this is what we delicately gathered. We got off at five-forty-five; Baghdad looking comparatively clean and empty except for lorry-loads of pilgrims: they travel in sort of cages with wire-netting sides on which the water skins and jars are hung, so that the view from inside is completely hidden. It is dull and flat as far as the frontier, except for the long, red bare backbone of the Hamrin range, which I believe does not own a tree. And the flowers seemed over: but we had a crowd of green sunbirds flashing round us on the way, sitting in rows on the telegraph wires, and catching the sun like jewels.

At Khaniqin the railway rest-house provides breakfast in a lugubriously neat room, enough to take the oriental flavour out of anything: even the genial man with the tall black curl over a bald forehead, and exciting tie, who told us he was British born—couldn't make the atmosphere gay.

It is an awful business to pass an oriental frontier, as it means drinking tea with every official, who is probably hurt if you don't. We spent an hour, mostly drinking tea, but partly spreading our things out on the road. We are supposed to be very unpopular here just now, and English doesn't carry anywhere: it is all Persian or French. I find I can only just get about with monosyllables, and lose the replies completely, but I hope to start with a teacher tomorrow—two hours a day for 1s. 1d. The hotel pension is two tomans—about 6s. 3d. a day—and it is a lovely old Persian house in a walled garden full of blossoming trees, with a tank and geranium pots round it in the middle, and little channels of water running over stone troughs of carved stones. The bedrooms are in a long row on the first floor with a wide bricked veranda before it, and the dining- and sitting-room in a little pavilion all by itself. Outside the walls are thickets of poplar trees just coming into leaf, and the snow ridges behind—13,000 feet is the high peak—and we are 6,000 here, and nearly dead with cold after 93° and a dust storm in Baghdad.

Well, we got into a wonderful wild, waste country as soon as we were in Persia: tumbled seas of mountains, with pale green valleys, very shallow, and blue and red ridges, and no sign of humanity except the white road and a police post here and there: little mud villages, very miserable, and then a mud town on a rise, Qasr Shirin, with old walls and ruins on a hill nearby, but all sunk into the earth.

It all felt untidy and poor, and ugly bits of modern motor-car life all about, and the unspeakable Persian hat like a Cook's tourist agent's who has long forgotten to shave. But in some subtle way there was a pleasant sense of freedom after the efficient machinery of Iraq, and I feel there is something to be said for these people who prefer to be poor and keep us out of their way.

A Lady of Luristan

You can't imagine the loneliness: you feel, as you go from plateau to plateau, with more rocky ridges, with immense vistas and no human house in sight, that you have climbed into some moon landscape, only with a clear light and thin veil of growing things flung over it, and pure thin air. And then we turned by a little village with a bridge—Sar-i-Pul—into the valley that runs to the Paitak Pass:

A Gentleman of Luristan

and there it was the real mountain again, as it might have been Simplon or Gotthard when the road was still used. Long strings of immense covered carts with a carpet spread high above the horses and the strong Kurds or Lurs or anyway hill people: their faces obviously belonging to our own family, only wild because of the strange felt hats and black locks sticking out on either side.

After the pass, you come down into a lovely open valley —Karind—where the English women from Iraq were camped out during the 1920 revolt: and a lovely place for tents too, with a thin veil of blossom and poplar leaves over the village against the rocky valley sides. Here there was a long confab with the police—not official we afterwards heard, but our driver had brought up a watch as a present some time before, and it had been lost, and a hunt was now being politely made for another, and tactfully received: the result of this judiciousness was very visible, for we were beautifully treated all along, and it is worth making friends with police in a country where they look at your pass as you go in and out of every town.

We got to Kermanshah late at night and spent next day there in pouring rain. I was really as tired as could be, as each bump gave me a twist. Next day, however, was lovely, the ranges round Kermanshah shining in snow, and again we went through seven hours of the great tablelands: sometimes with a slow river, sometimes with just rolling downs for infinite miles; once through a great plain where the road breaks off for Ispahan and a lonely mountain with a flat top made me think of Soracte as you see it from the Viterbo road. We climbed up and up to the Asadabad pass into the snow: six weeks ago our driver and fifty other cars had to spend eleven days blocked in the little low *grangia* at the top. The people here in Hamadan sometimes get cut off from the world, no cars, no aeroplanes, nothing!

HAMADAN, 19 April, 1930.

Darling B,

Here there are not many British, and the houses we have called on, the Consul's (Summerhayes), and some oil people called Williams, are charming. It is a simpler life altogether, more walking in the country and less entertaining, and not so much dashing round with motor cars. The people are a very sombre crowd, with black or dark 'redingotes' and trousers, and a peaked cap. The little cabs are far more gorgeous than in Baghdad, with bright velvet flowered seats and the arms of Persia stamped on the woodwork, and on Fridays they all go heaving over the cobbles with unshaven Persians whom they deposit in rows on carpets by the river or here and there on boulders and tombstones, where they sit apparently in silent enjoyment. Some smoke enormous pipes with thick stems. The ladies, very highly painted, have far less pretence of covering their faces than in Iraq. They all look much more European: a rather degenerate Mediterranean race in the towns, and good hill types in the country.

[151]

23 *April*, 1930.

Dearest Car,

It is wonderful to be writing from Persia. Have I been saying this before? I wake up with that feeling every morning, and then feel how very like one's own country it is—not so much Scotland as North Italy, if one looks beyond the poplars to the snowy ridges: but if one looks out over the naked plain and the far bare ranges, it is just Persia, some high land in the centre of the world, getting near the very central tableland where all history began.

The tomb of Esther is here: a neglected dome in one corner of an untidy square where a few Persians slouch about in their absurd long frock coats and peaked caps, looking like people in a mid-Victorian farce. The tomb has a large stone door like those of the Jebel Druze, with a hole where the rabbi's arm goes through. We had an appointment with the rabbi at five o'clock and were waiting for him on the steps of the tomb when a venerable Being with a Beard came up and took our proffered hands in both of his, pressing them gently between his grey cotton gloves: we were deeply impressed, till the real rabbi came, with a longer and broader beard, and we found the other to be merely a dervish of no importance. Inside the little vaulted room are the two carved wooden coffins, all swathed in damasks and brocades. Esther and Mordecai, side by side, and in a little room close by, a beautiful case with the rolls of the Old Testament written on parchment in lovely lettering. And every Friday night the Jews of Hamadan (there are five thousand) gather here, and the book of Esther is read out to them. They seem to be on friendly terms now with the Moslems, but it is only quite recently. In fact as far as one can see everything is beautifully peaceful, and all the population intent only on picnics and motor cars, or little drives over the cobbly streets in a small 'fiacre' vividly upholstered with crimson velvets and flowers, and a hand for luck stamped in henna on the horse's back if it happens to be a white one.

Lionel Smith persuaded me to come up here with Miss Eyles, the matron of the hospital in Baghdad—and this has made me be welcomed as a respectable member of society by the British of Hamadan, though it was about twice as expensive as my own ideas of native travelling. Anyway it could not be pleasanter: the hotel garden has hoopoes and blackbirds and blossom of every kind, and the most amusing lot of nondescript passers-by, as Hamadan is a necessary stopping-place on the road. Very few English, and it is rather a pleasant feeling to be in a country which is living its own life, however it may be mismanaging it.

My Persian is getting on: I can go about the bazaars and shop, and yesterday we went up into the hills among the orchards, where the grass is covered with little grape hyacinths, and the village women invited us to sit in their 'bath'—a dark arcaded dome with tank of very brown water in the middle: and we talked as well as my few words allowed. The women looked very fine with the half light from above and dark shadows of the arches, and their bright-coloured cotton veils swathed over their heads and figures. I have a nice old scamp of a teacher with a beard dyed in henna and a twinkle in his eye which doesn't quite disappear even when he tells me that he has twice seen the Hidden Imam. He got rather annoyed with me for asking for details of his costume and appearance—which appear to have been ordinary coat and trousers. Anyway he is an excellent teacher and comes two hours a day and promises to make me ready for talk with the assassins by the middle of next month.

26 April, 1930.

Darling B,

I had a most interesting evening last night, being taken by the Chapmans to dine with the Governor, a nervous thin elderly man with the nose and quick movements of a bird and most charming manners. We sat for over an hour in a long room, hideously carpeted, with cakes and the little glasses of pale tea beside us, and I found I could follow the Persian and join in a feeble way, enough to enjoy the conversation. In fact Mr. Chapman says my progress is remarkable. The head of Hamadan sanitation, a little old doctor with very gentle manners and speaking English, came in, and we presently went to a charming dinner-table over which pansies and almond blossoms had been scattered, with a tall sort of crown-imperial which grows wild here standing in the middle. The dinner was excellent: mayonnaise chicken, soup, chicken, then pilau with some bitter vegetable (most delicious), cutlets, and stewed fruit; the best cherries, preserved in sugar and brought from Lake Urmiah, that I have ever tasted; and delicious spiced wine (I am feeling rather ill to-day). We talked about hunting, food, politics: the sort of talk one would have with any country gentleman in a quiet district. What

[153]

was so pleasant was to feel that here were no axes to grind, no one thinking what was to come of the interview: it really is pleasant to be in a country that is managing its own affairs and where we can just travel about on our own merits. Everyone speaks wonders of this Shah, and the immense changes he has made, the safety of the country and its general prosperity. He has a good head, and his little son looks very like him in the photographs. A large sum is being devoted to Hamadan, to a new boulevard and a reservoir of water: in these towns the old costumes and picturesqueness have gone so much that one does not regret the innovations: they had better get them over and done with. I don't know what it may be like in the hills.

The Governor had a setter who sat near us at dinner, while he told us how he used to race in point-to-points at Teheran: and how his son is a great footballer (they play quite a lot here), and is studying aviation with the Russians. He gives a very miserable picture of the life in Russia, everyone in abject poverty except the Commissars who, says he, are mostly Jews.

30 April, 1930.

Last night I went to dine with the Williams'—nice Irish people and so friendly. I am going to ride their horse to-morrow and see how I feel. Mr. Williams told me how he could have made a large fortune: he and his friend rented five or six villages—about 180 square miles—and were getting wonderful results; only as soon as the government heard, down came the taxes, and made further progress impossible—and they had to give it up. At present there is a coinage crisis: the government won't let any money out by way of the banks so that lots of perfectly wealthy merchants can't pay their debts in London, because they can't transfer their money out of the country.

There was a Mr. A, a rather nice man but just a wee bit flashy and too fond of various drinks: I think men out here are better with wives, or else they should be strictly teetotal—because they seem to lose the sense of proportion very easily. My 'droshky' never turned up at ten-thirty as I had ordered, so he sent me home in his lovely car: just as it was starting, up came the droshky, and was left stranded in the dark without a fare and much abuse, which of course it deserved: however I have given the man two krans to-day—I can't help feeling that it is rather hard to expect punctuality when people have no watches.

At present I am sitting in the hotel drawing-room over a fire that is being politely left to me while the other end of the room is occupied by an odd international mixture—Swiss, French, the Chaldean priest, two Syrians, the landlord (rather too much wine) and a German-Persian couple whom I cannot make out at all.

30 *April*, 1930.

My dearest Venetia,

I can't remember how long ago I wrote, or where I left off. Had I reached Hamadan? It is a poor little mud and brick town of houses and cobbled streets with a brawling stream tumbling downhill through the length of it, and little bridges across that remind one of willow-pattern plates: but it has a glorious setting—the Elvand range behind, still white with snow, and the plain and the Kurdish hills. I have settled down into it and to a quiet life of Persian grammar. I have rather a treasure of an old shi'a teacher in a turban. He has spent forty years teaching American missionaries, and now that he has found that I like old Moslem traditions better, all his shi'a fanaticism is coming to the top and he spends two hours a day interspersing texts from the Qurân with all sorts of odd bits of superstition and tradition. How the wives of Hamadan poison their husbands with wolf-fat; and the 121,000 prophets that have tried to improve the world since it began, and the wickedness of the present generation.

My Baghdad friends gave me letters to the Bahais here and they have been taking me to look at their two schools this morning. It is rather touching and pathetic to see them doing it all on their own, with very scanty means. The teachers get from 30s. to £6 a month. They have 300 boys and 200 girls, and the boys are prepared for college (Beyrout is the nearest university), and the girls get only primary education. Their headmistress was a beautiful young Bahai in her long black veil which she held over her mouth while the head of the boys' school took me round and spoke to her. He told me they get quite a lot of Moslems to teach, and they are forging ahead now and have Bahais in every Ministry (very useful in this country) though they often have people who are not nominally converts. The Mission here has nothing to do with these people—and this just shows how silly the missionaries are: the Bahai teaching is so near the Christian in its results, and it has a real chance of spreading and improving the whole country—is in fact a vital and growing force. And they are the only really tolerant sect in the East.

I can't make out whether this new Persian regime is really doing very well or very badly. The British business people here are very down on it. It is playing about with the currency and lowering the price of bread arbitrarily, so that all business with the outside world seems at a standstill. The people on the other hand seem enthusiastic and there is perfect safety and a real look of national feeling. From just a casual traveller's point of view it is much better to see the work being done even badly, in this natural and wholehearted way, than with all the friction of Iraq. It makes one realize more than ever that people *prefer* their own muddles to other people's efficiency. They are getting westernized, but in a happy-go-lucky way of their own—playing football and bribing the police, the old and new all jumbled side by side. I, by the way, am busy making friends with the Chief of Police, who is the most amiable plump-looking scamp who evidently takes life easily and now lives in this hotel while his wife is in Teheran. Such an odd mixture comes through here. The distance between towns is so great and nothing in between that everyone has to stop in these places. Dutch diplomats, the Consul from Iraq, Russians with peculiar manners, all sorts of weird commercial people with a few weirder ladies, young Englishmen with their luggage piled behind them on a Ford lorry—and every shade of Persian and Arabic on its way to and fro.

3 *May*, 1930.

My dear Mrs. Drower,

Thanks ever so much for sending on my Mother's cheque: they are always like manna in the desert and I *was* just wondering how, having got into Persia, I could ever afford to get out of it again. I have bought *emerald beads* (so they swear they are) for fifteen tomans and was wondering how to pay my hotel—I know you will sympathize.

I love the place, and begin to walk about. Mrs. Williams lends me a little gem of an Arab pony to ride, but my side still prevents a gallop.

I leave for Qazvin on the 15th—and no one seems to know how one is to find a guide: but I am, as you know, an optimist, and my old Mulla says he will introduce me to the '*ulema* of Qazvin. It is all such fun.

I had a pleasant day yesterday, walking up among the orchards: a little peasant woman joined me and we jogged along together till we came to her vineyard: and then we sat down and made a fire and took a forked stick to use as a pair of tongs to pick out the embers for the samovar, and made tea and stirred it with a branch pulled off the almond tree, and talked about life in Hamadan, and how her husband, who is a policeman, gets fourteen tomans a month and his clothes and a horse—which doesn't seem enormous pay.

4 *May*, 1930.

Darling B,

Mrs. Drower writes that Sydney Smith has collared all her lot of potteries and flints from our Tell for the museum and wants to put people on there to dig, the finds are so interesting. Isn't it thrilling to think that our wanderings with the beduin there may probably result in the opening up of another old city? There was a big canal near it: one can still trace its sunken line in the grass: I feel sure it was a place of some importance.

The only other piece of amusing gossip she gives me is that Captain Holt, while inviting the ladies for Lady Humphrys' Arab party, invited one who has been dead some time, and so caused dissatisfaction.

I had lunch with missionaries to-day and then they took me to drive out, a lovely road with the snow mountains and their poplar fringe on one side, and the wide rolling plains and hills on the other, till we came to a little stony river and a bridge, and turned aside down a poplar avenue to an old baroque house, all peeling stucco, looking down its terrace and across the walled garden to the trees and hills. Once a lovely place. There was a channel for water to tumble over steps, and stone stairways either side, and the water ran in a straight paved channel down to a square tank in the middle of the garden: now all dry. The bridges have been replaced by ramshackle wooden planks, the stucco has left the shoddy brick and wood bare: only the Corinthian pillars and garlanded balconies and windows show what it must have been. Opium, or civilization drawing them to Teheran, has probably accounted for the landlord's absence; there are many such lovely places round about. Outside was a great square 'piazza' which used to be the stables: over a hundred horses could feed at once, for all round the outside are little niches where the feed could be put into a small trough, all in mud bricks. We

[157]

got home and went to church and had a terrible sermon on prayer and the radio—the Lord being compared to the Receiving Station.

Yesterday I called on the mother of my Bahai friend. He is a modern young man with a butterfly tie and eyes exactly like Achille. But she has a most beautiful old gentle face, with her lace pinned under the chin as the fashion here is and her cotton *chadur* draping her whole figure from the head. About eighteen ladies came to see me, and we sat and had sweets and salad dipped in a strange bitter seasoning: quite nice—only I was wondering all the time whether my typhoid inoculation would be really effective. I can't follow anything like a general conversation yet and I only look at the faces, always interesting enough.

Miss Eyles fell out with the Bahai who took her to Teheran. I was amused: he came to fetch me yesterday and after enquiring to see how much Miss E had told me, and thinking she had said nothing (I being discreet) began to tell me how happy he had made her and how delighted she had been to be with him. He apparently tried to fleece her badly. But as for me, I could not get him to let me pay for my own cab.

5 *May*, 1930.

Darling B,

This evening I had my Bahai garage owner to call. He married a wife whom he had not seen, ten years old, and sent her for four years to school: and she is not his ideal, so he says. "Few wives are," says I consolingly—"and hardly any husbands." He wants to take me to Qazvin and get me my muleteer, and it would be rather a godsend though I feel sure he will make love to me on the way, and it will give a fit to the British here who all think me so nice: on the other hand he assures me I may be murdered if I don't get someone to help me to a guide.

6 *May*, 1930.

Don't know why, but I am so very depressed this evening—feeling so old, and as if my whole life were wasted and now it were too late to do anything with it: such an uphill work, with so much less health and strength and power than most and already half-way through and nothing done. And as if what I *do* do were not worth doing: no one seems to think it is, but just wonder at me and are sorry for me

[158]

if they are nice, and disapprove if they are not. To be just middle-aged with no particular charm or beauty and no position is a dreary business. In fact I feel as if I had been going uphill all the time to nowhere in particular, and feel like poor E, most dreadfully lonely, envying all these women with their nice clean husbands whose tradition is their tradition, and their nice flaxen children who will carry it on in the same simple and steady way. And though it *is* my tradition too, no one thinks it is, because of a silly difference of form and speech and fashion—so that I feel as if I *had* no people of my own. If only I could eventually find some work that would make me feel settled and interested; I hope it may be: but no one seems to want women very much, and I don't quite know that I am fit for anything but philanthropy, and that would not really thrill me. Well, I mustn't go on in this dreary vein. I think it must be because no one any longer makes love to me except when they are drunk.

A dreadful tragedy happened yesterday: a huge petrol lamp disappeared from the drawing-room—stolen in the middle of the afternoon. The lampshade remained, but disappeared while the lamp was being searched for and was eventually found buried in a tank in the cellar, so that it became clear that one of the domestics was to blame, and two were sacked to-day. Gloom and excitement all over the household. Also a man has been found murdered in the desert outside Hamadan: all the crows gathered round him and so drew the attention of the peasants.

I went yesterday with Mrs. Summerhayes to call on the Governor's wife and two daughters. It was pleasant; their manners very agreeable, and our Persian just enough to be able to talk about pilgrimages, curios, and silver work: they had some really lovely specimens of the Isfahan work which is so hideous when not very good. We sat round the walls and sipped little glasses of tea, and had about half a dozen silver dishes of biscuits, cake, sweets, preserved cherries, all placed within reach. It is rude to go away before one has had two glasses of tea. Then you say: "Will you command our excuse. We have given much trouble," and go.

The villagers here wear good costumes, loose blue cotton coat, and trousers baggy at the bottom like a sailor's only short above the ankle, and the old felt cap.

Greenboy, the little white arab (when the sais tried to tell me the name, it was 'Gurumbor' which sounds much better) is a little gentleman to ride except that he stumbles badly when walking and one has to be careful. I am trying to get 'hard' for my trip, but my fall and the chills up here have pulled me down a bit. Anyway I don't imagine I need take very long days and I shall have my tent so as to be independent of villages. Mrs. Williams is lending me a mosquito net, and I shall take a daily dose of quinine as a precaution.

I have collected a lovely lot of stories from my Mirza—and am very sorry to have to leave him. Again I was right and the experts wrong; they told me the Qurân was *no* use now for getting into touch with people. If I had not known the Qurân and been able to talk to the old man from his own standpoint, he would never have started all these tales. The Qurân has been their one source of inspiration for centuries: it is their background—and however Europeanized they may be, one is sure to get nearer to them *really* if one comes at them from behind as it were, through the things they knew as children, or that their parents and nurses knew, than if one comes through the medium of a new civilization which means something quite different to them from what it means to us. When I take the old Mulla's standpoint, I know where I am and what to expect: when I take a European standpoint with a 'civilized' oriental, I can never know where I am, for I have no means of judging what 'European' means to him: it is certainly not what it means to us.

I feel that I really may end by doing something; only it is not a thing that can be hurried. But in three years' time I could know enough Persian, Turkish, Kurdish, and Arabic to get about, and I believe I would be the only Englishwoman in the Near East to do so: and then something amusing is bound to turn up. As it is, another six months here will give me Persian: it is most comforting to find how easy these languages are after arabic. It is merely a matter of learning the words. If only I had a better memory it would be such a blessing.

7 *May*, 1930.

Just got your letter before leaving for Qazvin to-morrow and so very glad to have it. I sent you such a depressed one—I'm so sorry. I meant to tear it up and forgot; but I was just feeling that I really had bitten more off than I could chew and was down in the mouth. However my natural buoyancy has now reasserted itself and I am looking forward with pleasure to the Assassins, though my boots do rub at the heel and I have no money and *no* balance. Viva writes to say that my dividend can't be put into the bank as it needs my signature. So I only hope my bank will play up and pay on trust.

Well, I have been round to Mr. Williams to say good-bye and am going to stay there on my way through: so nice they are, and being Irish really don't mind showing that they are friendly, and one feels it doesn't matter if one drops in at an unofficial hour. My Persian was sufficient to explain to the carpenter how I wanted the support for my mosquito net made, and I have a wonderful arrangement now on which I lie, and I hope it will work, for the map looks like nothing but large white empty spaces with little wiggles for the different altitudes: my own small-scale map had only a tiny brown bit of emptiness which looked quite friendly and easy. I have got a place in a native car for 12s. for seven hours' drive, and a letter to an Armenian A P O C man: he got the muleteers for the people who went up in 1928, so will know all about it. I believe also that Mr. Summerhayes will get me a letter to the Governor of Qazvin. It is going to be a real Adventure.

Here is what I am told is a typically Persian story. A merchant was doing very well in the bazaar. When his son grew up he took him into partnership. The son cheated the father till he reduced him to bankruptcy. Mr. M, who told me, says he went some time after to visit the old man, now reduced to great poverty, and was told the whole story—only the old man was just bursting with pride over the intelligence of his son.

The bank manager was telling me some of their idiotic financial doings yesterday, and says that all the royalties from the Anglo-Persian Oil Company, *millions* of pounds, instead of being used to benefit the country, are being poured into a bank in London for the Shah. One would be very sad if one were a Persian, but there is a nice spacious careless feeling in the land all the same, and such a relief after all the looking after one gets in Iraq.

9 May, 1930.

My darling Venetia,

I miss you more than I can say and think of you so much that sometimes it almost seems as if you were with me. My trek will be very lonely. I go to Qazvin on Monday and make NE. for the Caspian which I should hit at Khurramabad: but I don't know if I

[161]

shall reach it: you will see there is a large uninhabited patch to cross over very rough passes. If I get to Alamut (this side the pass) my main object is gained and I may come back the same way. The main trouble I expect will be swollen streams as there has been lots of rain and snow, and it is still early in the year. Also, my dear, I am going most absurdly unprovided with money owing to a hitch in the getting it in time: I shall have only about £2 to start with from Qazvin when I pay up here: the only comfort is that there will be the less to rob.

I can get along in Persian now, though *very* badly: but enough to read the newspaper headlines and pass the time of day with the peasants. I took a long walk to-day (five hours) up the valley which ends in the gentle white cone of Elvand. Up there the blossom was still out, and I walked through woods of baby apricot trees; you could see *nothing* but blossom and every breeze shook it down like a heavy shower. The trees were just a few feet taller than I, so that I was on a level with that sea of white flowers; the grass very green below it, and studded with little grape hyacinths. The whole valley was one green wood of trees of every kind and a white torrent foaming through, and I walked on till the trees got sparse, beyond the last village—then only willows and the little thin blades of corn, and sheep grazing in stony patches, with boys in wide blue cotton trousers and little black felt caps like a bowler with no brim, and bold brown faces. I sat down with a woman and two little girls and had lunch —some mess of a sort of bean they grow here (*ceci* the Italians call it) and very good. The two little girls were called Balkis and Tuti, and had bright henna'd hair, and were a disappointment to their mother owing to their unfortunate sex. None of the men you meet here on the road say good day to so inferior an object as a woman, but they all speak politely to my sais if he rides behind me.

I have been riding a good deal, and it is very lovely in the orchards and along these winding streams. But the truth is, I am lonely and feel worn out with the strain of being considered a phenomenon all this time. It is restful here: the few British nice and simple and sympathetic.

The Persian, so far as I have seen him, I don't like as much as the Arab. The Arab really is *free*, in himself: here it is feudalism at its worst—the miserable villager downtrodden and ready to take kicks from his landlord, who grinds him down without mercy. The Arab

woman may live hardily, but the poorest have gold and silver trinkets
to wear; and feel at home in the tent of the sheikh; here there is hardly
a jewel—the people are miserably poor. Though they look healthy
and much better than the townsfolk. I believe nearly everyone
smokes opium: a little peasant woman the other day pulled a piece
out of her brother's pocket to show me, and complained of its price.
They say fortunes are wasted on it all the time, and there are poppy
fields all roundabout.

There are so many birds here. All the landscape is like Persian
embroideries and pictures: absurdly big birds perched about (hoopoes
for instance) and intricate patterns of branches and flowers where all
the different fruit trees grow together.

QAZVIN, 13 *May*, 1930.

Dearest Pips,

The adventure is starting: it is all being set going and now
promises well: at least the Armenian head of local A P O C is finding
me a reliable guide with mules. A Bahai letter I have is to a doctor
who owns several of the villages en route, and I have already separated
myself from civilization by leaving all my respectable clothes behind
and am here with only my tent, bed and saddle-bags full of woollies
and things. The tragedy is that my boots rub: I am going to get some
of the native things with cotton top and soles made of cotton in close
layers put on perpendicularly, cut to the required thickness and kept
together by camel's hide. If I can I will bring you out a pair. I'm
sure you would like them.

I got a seat in a native car for four tomans yesterday, and was to
start at eight o'clock. By ten I was still waiting and having a second
breakfast with some Irish called Warren from Baghdad, who have
come up for a holiday. They were wondering how far they could
afford to go, as the drivers are all robbers, and I believe they looked
at me with some envy, climbing up over the saddle-bags on the
mudguard, into a little niche beside the driver and a Persian traveller, with one man, three children and two women in black
chadurs behind (12s. for 210 kilometres isn't bad is it?). It took us
eight and a half hours over great plains bordered with bare hills and
then another great plain, till one thought it would go on for ever
and ever. In all this distance there is not a single town and not many
villages: just the road and perhaps twenty to thirty cars and lorries in

[163]

the course of the day. One or two strings of carts on their squat wheels with bodies like the ark, and the driver sitting on bright carpets high up above the horses. By the roadside one would come upon little temporary camps—the donkeys turned anywhere to graze, the sacks of merchandise dumped among the desert flowers, and the drivers sitting round in a group making tea. The whole desert was full of flowers. I couldn't even see them clearly much less collect any, but they lay like a carpet, a little blue lily, a sort of borage with pink bud and blue flower—at least it may not have been borage but it had that sort of prickly leaf—a deep purple thing with lots of little blossoms on one stem, and a brilliant crimson vetch. I hope to get some and send seeds from the hills.

A horrid new street leads all down the length of Qazvin: a local doctor has been given *carte blanche* by the Shah and has laid out the whole place in boulevards and electric lights, the roads are cut quite ruthlessly (the Shah told him he could cut the royal hand off if it happened to be in the way); no compensation is given and the Persians are all fearfully pleased. Perhaps one would be if one were a Persian, there seems nothing for it but to be European and so the sooner they do it the better from their own point of view, but it doesn't make it attractive for travelling.

14 *May*, 1930.

Dearest Venetia.

I wandered all over the bazaars this morning. At first I thought that people must be wrong and the modern Persian must really have a future before him for the bazaars were lovely—many white-washed arcades, many with beautiful domes in delicate brickwork and patterns of glazed bricks in colours. And all clean, without dust or great noise (the Persian isn't noisy like the Arab anyway). Khans, where the bales and sacks are stacked, down dim arcaded vaults with coloured gates, blue, peacock green and vermilion, the colours picked out with great brass or iron nails. The good things are old however, I am told, and the new régime has only polished and cleaned them up a bit. But it was very fascinating to wander in that labyrinth of faded splendours, which the business of Qazvin to-day can hardly fill, and watch the little pale-faced boys knotting their carpets with incredible speed; one could pick up heaps of treasures if one had money and time. All Persia is crazy for modernity and selling its old stuff, and there it all is, treasures here and there among the rubbish: but one ought to know a great deal. I hardened my heart, as I am so broke that I have to borrow off a kind Armenian here, and shall be on the verge of bankruptcy till I get back, and trust to Providence that some money may have turned up then.

In the morning I went and looked at the mosque of Hussein from outside, and found a lovely old khan with decorative gateway, and walked with a little shi'a girl to see the back of the great mosque, but, of course, could not penetrate. Then I had my Armenians to lunch, and so finished the business of the day. What a pleasant feeling it is to be all ready, with the road before and civilization already in your thoughts behind you. How sorry I feel for people tied by their silly motor cars to the long white roads that leave the huge plains of Persia and all its ranges undiscovered on either side.

My poor Armenian friend is trying to stop a man who has stolen £100 off him from getting across the border: he has been for three days trying to persuade the local justice to send a telegram to Teheran with this object, and has only now succeeded, so that probably the thief will be safe by now. For anything except serious business the people are charming; but I have come to the conclusion that to put off doing troublesome things is really a much more serious fault than it looks; I think it means a lack of will-power, for you will notice that *no* nation which has this defect will ever get on: it means that it hasn't got the backbone to make itself do something it doesn't like, and of course there is no hope for it.

CHALA, 16 May, 1930.

Darling B,

This note-paper gives me quite a shock as I pull it out on a steep hillside of wheat and grass and enormous walnut trees, looking out across the Shahrud valley below Chala village. I am so lucky: I have a guide who really wants to do what I like: I mentioned a wish not to eat in the stuffy but friendly village room, and he immediately took my quilt and the mule-cloth of grey felt with a black pattern stamped on it—and brought the lot out here—and though he will sit close beside to guard my sleep and his little boy is drinking tea with awful noises, I really have nothing to complain of.

It was pleasant to go to sleep with the stars through my net and the crunching of the mules in the yard. Then the three muleteers came and settled beside me on the ground with the saddle-bags in a heap in the middle: one hasn't got that feeling of absolute safety as far as one's property goes that one has as a guest of the beduin (and in fact my hostess's first question was where I kept my money). They are very poor, and one pays for one's lodging: but they were healthy and cheerful people and extraordinarily European in type, with straight nose or slightly curved, quite different from the real oriental sort of curve: and when they roll the sleeves up off their hands which are nearly black in the sun, their arms are as white as ours.

I didn't sleep well, partly because Ismail (who annoys me by always inventing the name of anything I ask for) had spilt the paraffin of the lantern over my sleeping-sack and I couldn't get away from the smell. The moon was large and bright and seemed to be in the same place right above me whenever I woke up. She was still up there when 'Aziz came and asked if I would like to go, and I went into the room and dressed with the gradually awakening interest of four pairs of eyes from the bundles which represented the children of the family on the floor. I don't think any peasant's house in Italy as poor as this and possessing so few things would be cleaner, and they had nice things: the copper basin, turned over, had a scalloped edge and carved pattern: the earthenware water-jars have a lovely shape which belongs to Qazvin—and the rough carpets had pleasant colours.

As I have the onus of making a precedent for any British lady who may ever come this way, I am trying to make her as comfortable as I can. I get my bed and net (so as to get some sort of privacy) put up in the open—roof or yard or so: then get hot water provided: then turn everyone out of the harem and have a good wash, and appear in my dressing-gown and go and sleep outside. In the morning I can't turn out the harem again, but I only wash with my own lotion and they are too sleepy to bother me. This is quite a comfortable way of doing it. It is hard to realize that here I am the first English, possibly the first European, woman who has ever come this way.

They make a little community: a good type, busy with their fields and knowing very little outside their own valley. There used to be a post, but "the two postmen died and so it stopped".

They usually sow rice one year and grain the next. This year it is grain, and therefore there are no mosquitoes—and anyway it is early. The place is infested later on. They make a little silk with their mulberry trees. But the villages and their green plots are tiny spots in the great bare valley. We have travelled up it from eight to eleven-forty-five, and only passed three tiny villages—and there are none in the side valleys: they roll down in treeless folds now covered with a thin grassy loveliness in the distance, which close by is thorns and flowers: the 'place of wolves' one of these desolate valleys was called, and so they say it is: they come in troops in winter and the dogs keep them out of the villages. Bears, too, and foxes, and a few which I take to be sables, but was not sure of the word. I lose most of this village Persian and find it hard to give medical advice—but I manage somehow.

SHAHRAK, 17 *May*, 1930.

When we came down into the Alamut valley we met huge bushes of wild roses everywhere against the grey boulders: white ones with very large petals, or pink like the English rose: the scent came in whiffs as we went by.

I have had a disappointment. Elias, the muleteer, was a real image of the Assassin descendant, with his wild locks coming out under his cap and brilliant eyes and thick eyebrows: I was waiting to get a good mountain background for him—and last night the wretched man came to supper, all spick and span with his three-weeks' beard shaved off and all his locks cut away, and shaved in front to the top of his head which gives such an intellectual look to the Persian peasant.

I have been slipping about in the native *giva* shoe: if you put your weight on the heel downhill, you come on the piece of slippery camel-skin and skid: but if you walk on your toes, it's all right.

ZAVARAK, 19 *May*, 1930.

We slept the night at Shutur Khan, and presently—before supper— had a visit from the one police officer whom here we simply call "The Government".

"Are you going to take tea with The Government?" they ask you. The Government was rather a nice little Persian with an enormous district all to himself—15,000 souls who all quarrel, he says, and says his hair is going grey. He was exercised over me, only I am now an expert with hostile police. It was amusing, so like a skit on Baghdad. What they could not understand was that I should go on taking photos and refuse to show them: why not show them? They didn't believe it could be impossible and they asked me whether what came out of the camera was a map like the one I had with me and which was so suspiciously well informed about Persian names.

I had really a great stroke of luck. A rather unprepossessing, unshaven man came in to call, with the pahlevi hat which looks very wrong here, and after salaams and all half rising, and all sitting down, and then all rising again to the newcomer and making little murmured polite enquiries, and settling down again to collect ourselves after the disturbance, we began to talk about the castle. The new arrival had seen us yesterday at Badasht. Badasht, he says, is corrupted from Bagdasht, which means a desert garden: and where there is a great stone in the river bed just below this place he says that there is an old building high up on the cliffs above: that there are seven reservoirs one below the other, and the remains of ancient chains which once carried a water conduit across the Shahrud valley. "There should be a garden somewhere," said I, "for it is written that Hasan as-Sabah kept a garden hidden in the fastnesses here." "Oh, that must be up in such and such a place," says this wonderful man. And he explained that in coming over a pass right at the back—exactly in the position one would expect—and about 11,000 feet up, he had been surprised to see fruit trees growing on a space of ground of about three to six acres as far as I could make out and far above the level of any cultivation now. The place is yet deep under snow and will not be clear for another two months—but it is a thrilling thought, isn't it? I got so excited I felt my fingers *trembling*. Ever since I went up to the castle and indeed came into the valley I have felt there must be a good deal in the old legend (as there usually is). People told me that there is no sign of the garden by the castle now, but the very meaning of the legend points to the fact that the garden was somewhere else, far out of the ordinary way: and this barren valley which looks like a desert until you come on some patch of incredible greenness and fertility is exactly the place where such a little paradise could be made.

ALAMUT

GARMRUD, 20 *May*, 1930.

From the Castle of Nevisar Shah in Alamut, you can see that the
valley is absolutely closed. I sat for an hour, finding the points of
the compass, getting the names of the hills sorted, and trying in vain to
disentangle the absolute wrongness of my map, which has actually
got the Elburz *range* in the wrong valley. It isn't easy to get correct information, and needs infinite patience. My doings too are
of course the sort that really upset all the authorities. However,
I have got about half a dozen new mountains and two really important
villages in the pass that figures as uninhabited in the maps.

It is so pleasant to be welcomed by the whole village: all the
relatives and friends coming in—and three women sitting round me
while I wash, which I could have done without, but it gave them so
much more pleasure than my own discomfort that it didn't seem
kind to interfere with it. The muleteer Ismail has become really
clever at setting up my bed and mosquito net. He is very rough,
but always willing and good tempered and I believe it is he who sees
that each mule has a blue bead tied into its tail by one hair: the harness
also consists of a little garland of bells round the posterior, which
tinkles nicely but must be very inconvenient.

There was a bit of old worship when we left the castle: 'Aziz told
me one must salaam to Elburz, whenever one leaves the sight of him.

The type here is purely Aryan, though not blue-eyed—but straight
noses, rather long, and good brows, and most of them might be
Italian peasants. Many of the children and young women very pretty,
though not the aristocratic arab beauty. They are quite well off: a
great contrast to the miserable poverty of the plains round Hamadan.
This house has good carpets and felt rugs with a pattern in black felt
laid on them and half beaten in so that it is like a fringe, only not
sewn but actually welded in, with a pattern also beaten into it in red
and black: these come from Mazanderan, but the others are all woven
by the lady of the house.

I have just been seeing how the women do their head kerchiefs:
they make themselves look like the heads of queens on playing cards.
They, and many of the men, have a round mark on their foreheads
where they are 'cupped' in their infancy against headaches. I am
getting to like the quaint dress of the women—their trousers and shirts
just like a man's and a manlike waistcoat (only usually one colour in
front and another at the back) and then the very feminine frilled

[169]

ballet-skirt coming out from under all this. Then they tie themselves round with a big cotton plaid with the point down behind them to the knees or lower, and tied tight round the waist, and into that the babies are tucked when they want to carry them, so that they look like snails walking round with their houses. The men look just like the medieval pictures, except that they have trousers instead of tights. But the rather tight coats with a white sash wound round the waist over them, and no collar as a rule, and sometimes a white or brown felt jacket over this, rather loose, and sometimes the sleeves open to the elbow over another sleeve of the same, and the round caps—are all as 'trecento' as can be.

SALAMBAR, 21 *May*, 1930.

I have crossed the watershed and am now on the Caspian side, still very high up (the pass just above is 11,290 feet) and surrounded by mountains and snow. *Such* a pass. Six hours from Garmrud and nearly all the time the magnificent massif of Elburz in full view across the valley. There are two villages above Garmrud, then nothing but rock and snow and water, and a really wonderful wilderness of hills. Mr. Watelin, who appears to be the only one across here, told me it was the finest thing he remembered after a life spent in Asia. We started at six o'clock. Such an affectionate farewell from the family. I wasn't able to pay for anything, but left a shawl and the half sack of sugar I was so uselessly burdened with.

Last night our guide and a few village people dropped in—the guide bringing the precious antiquity which his father had handed down and which he evidently thought might be worth great wealth, and what do you think it was? A glass marble, one of those with a curly pattern inside. How it came to the centre of the Elburz mountains is a mystery for ever, as much as my yellow silk powder sachet will be to the next people who climb and find it in Nevisar's castle. I gave my guide four krans (8*d*.) and he was very pleased; and I left, feeling very friendly to the little village piled up at the foot of its crags. We went through the eastern *serra*—one cliff sheer precipice, the other nearly so, and just room for river and path to tumble through together. Then up and up and up, and a chaos of river beds and narrow glacier courses to look down on—the barren red of the Assassins' rocks looking small now compared to the more awful fastnesses of the mountains. Half-way up we stopped: the two men to consume an enormous armful of wild rhubarb which may be gathered, while I tried to draw the lovely peaks of Elburz across the valley. They say that all the other mountains bowed to Elburz, acknowledging his superiority—except Syalan, who looks this way across the Caspian and said he was just as tall. But when the flood came he was submerged and only Elburz kept his head outside. At his feet, where two of these little lonely streams meet, is a shrine to another of the sons of Musa of Kadhimain. I find, by the way, that my having been there is a great asset and I am taken as a believer right away. Another thing I find very useful is when taking photographs to begin with Bismillah and end with Inshallah—and I hear the women murmur that it *must* be all right if I use these holy words.

I never seem to manage more than five days' tramping without some trouble and went to bed last night with shivers and a sore throat, making sure it must be the malaria before its time, just when I was as far away as I possibly could be from *either* end: however, it seems better to-day, although it has got worse again rather since a stone turned over and I went into a snow stream to well over the knees. It was cold enough on the pass, and when we finally got there and had tea in a little hovel of a *chaikhana* with three young boys in white felt jackets over their blue cotton clothes, we were glad to hurry down out of the wind. The whole pass felt like the very high hills. There were three sorts of little yellow flowers, one a tiny campanula, the other like a primrose, the third like buttercups with as many petals as a mar- guerite—and coming down on this side, big pale yellow iris were out in bloom and yellow tulips. They are so bad at plant names and it is only since I told them that one can make them into medicines, that they take my desire for information seriously. (Aziz is just stirring my tea with the big packing needle used to goad the donkey. It is so pleasant to sit beside a samovar in the grass.) Last night I tried to explain to the village people why I liked to know the names of hills and places: I showed them the mistakes in the map, and the omissions, and explained that when I next went to the shop where I bought it I would tell the people there what was wrong, and the next time they printed it, they would correct it: and I said that nearly all English people do this, and that so the maps are made better and better, and that is why it is so bad to give wrong information to travellers: and I believe it had some effect, for they have been trying to tell me about the country, and I feel I have been doing quite good work.

The Bolshies only got to the top of Salambar and were chased back to Khurramabad, being taken in the flank from either side of the pass. If they had succeeded in getting further down, I don't believe one would have escaped alive.

THE CASPIAN 'JUNGLE'; BELOW YUJ, 22 May, 1930.

It seems very strange to be here, in a narrow valley wooded with tall and beautiful trees, and no one near for miles and miles except the muleteers who have their packs stacked round and their sleeping figures laid beside them, while the mules with their saddles on are grazing about on the steep hillside. The air is filled with the noise of the stream rolling its boulders and the wind turning the shiny side of the leaves as it blows up the narrow gorge from the sea. We have been coming for hours down the long shaft of the valley— with hardly a side valley off it and no human dwellings except about four villages and here and there a little wooden *chaikhana* where the traffic of this road can have a rest. I have got a new pass for the map, and the name of two lonely villages, and a little village that no one has ever I believe heard of before, where the people of Khurramabad send their flocks in summer. It is all green here, kept so by the mists and dews.

At 8.10 this morning as we rode along, the bushes of hawthorn and sweetbriar threw heavy showers on to me as I passed. The track is quite good, like the way to Lago di Sais from Acceglio, with remains of old causeway here and there and a lot of traffic, for, before the new road along the sea was made, all that went from this part of the coast to Teheran or Qazvin had to come through this valley and then go either left or right when it got to the top of Salambar: and the road hasn't yet been built long enough to make any difference. The old man whose house we slept in last night in Maran said that in the old days the road was kept up by the Emir Sipahsalar (the one who committed suicide) and he would collect a special tax off the muleteers and see to the road. But now it is the government's job, and there is no special tax, but also no upkeep of the road: and in fact one of the bridges this morning was no use as a bridge and we had to ford lower down. We also had a narrow escape—about a dozen huge boulders fell bounding across our path five yards ahead of us in a narrow gully—a matter of less than a minute and they would have had us. Ismail with admirable promptness said "Ya Hussein" and headed off the donkey which wanders at leisure with our caravan apparently just for the sake of company. 'Aziz didn't come out very heroically for as soon as the stones had stopped he headed for the gully at a trot and got safe through, explaining afterwards by opening and shutting his fingers that his heart had been 'going like this'. I said "Al hamdu l'illah," and we went on again and have had no further adventures. Our host of last night joined us, a nice boy going down to Tunakabun as they still call Khurramabad, and they all advised me where to take photos on the way. I feel like one of this gipsy fellowship now: a moving sort of confraternity which lives on the roads, with its friends and gossips at the resting-places: the same sort of bronze faces, with black thick hair coming out from the felt caps, the sash tied round the waist over the coat and long thong wound round over with a leather satchel behind for knives, and two blue beads on the tassels to make it lucky: the same laden mules and jingling bells come up to meet us or wait for us to pass in the narrow places, or pass us as we are resting or greet us passing as they sit with the samovar by the wayside: and 'Aziz will say "They come from Garmrud, or Rudbar, or away over the hills of Talaghan", and greet them with every variation form cordiality to mere politeness.

We had a ghastly number of biting things last night—the first time I have really felt unhappy over them, and I have mislaid the Keatings. I have got an influenza cold from 'Aziz (one never knows whose cup one is drinking out of and must be grateful for catching only colds), and felt rather tired altogether, but now I have been sleeping in the sun with my head under my umbrella and am all right again—and was not too ill anyway to enjoy coming down steeply into the valley, with Solomon's throne shining up a side valley and all sorts of new flowers—wild sweet peas, rose coloured; red poppies with yellow centres; and every sort of tree as we came down. First stunted little things growing on the slopes, but now lovely timber—beeches and things like chestnuts only they have no fruit, and wild plum and pear and a blossom like honeysuckle. There is bracken, but here there are no longer so many flowers. I suppose it is too shady. There are white misty clouds drifting up too.

Last night we sat round the fire waiting for the pilau and discussed religion, 'Aziz having with a little self-consciousness got through his sunset prayer which took up all the available room in the centre of our small village group. I am quite an expert in shi'a theology, however, and was able to explain how Muhammad and Jesus and Moses are to meet and co-operate on the Day of Judgement. 'Aziz told me that Noah is buried in the right eye of 'Ali at Nejf—which I didn't know. 'Aziz walked from here to the holy places, taking a month over it. He was pleased with me for saying that we do not venerate Omar and Yezid. I felt feverish and in that state of contrariness when I should have liked to stick up for Omar whom I always admire; however I didn't.

I then sustained an argument that opium is forbidden: and quite impressed my gathering who divided into two camps and were evidently rather troubled about it. Then the pilau came and the women watched us eat it: they were a poor village, and dressed in tatters, but good-looking people. I give three krans as a present when I leave (6d.) and that leaves them very happy, so that feeding and sleeping, the two men and mules altogether come to about 8s. per day.

LATER AT GAVAR

—where there is a decent wooden house built by the Emir Sipahsalar and where he used to stay. I took one of the upper rooms, on a nice wooden balcony where my bed is being put up, but the glory is rather dimmed by having the two men and all their fleay possessions up too. The owner of the *chaikhana* came too to give tea which was not from a samovar but warming on an earthenware brazier. Then our host of yesterday turned up, and a strange old man who saw a tea-party and joined, as anyone may do, and so here we are in a circle again, and the caravans arriving one by one, depositing their packs in the various 'grangie' and rubbing down their animals. A pleasant feeling of leisure and the end of the day's work about it all.

This valley might be Switzerland now, or rather Pyrenees: the lonely woods and streams, and the few houses built of wooden trunks, with stones to hold the slates on the roofs, which slant. Very familiar it all looks and European: and the men are not foreign, but just medieval. Four Englishmen came here some years ago as guests of the Emir, and went to climb Takht-i-Suleiman and came back this way, missing the beauty of Salambar. The grangie here are very flimsy affairs built like skeleton rooms with a lattice-work of poles: so that all the winds blow through.

[174]

NR. KHURRAMABAD, 23 May, 1930.

It is a most extraordinary sight to come out on to the Caspian after all the forest—all yesterday afternoon and six hours to-day riding through it, lovely in the lower parts like some lonely bit of Pyrenees with its rushing streams, enormously tall trees—not the same as ours, but they look like enough—and the path goes wandering in and out of shadows among boulders and small streams. At the end it is not so good, for the trees turn to a thing called Qarad which is a sort of acacia: the steamy clouds hide the higher hills; and the landscape looks hot in spite of its green. But one leaves the big river, the two Hizars they are, which have joined their waters and rush down foaming together: one crosses a small col which the Emir Sipahsalar paved with boulders before he was asked by the government to commit suicide: then one crosses the Valmirud—a broad slow stream in a big bed: up another steep, short col—and there is the Caspian, and between you and it a landscape that has walked out of a lacquered tray: a flat landscape shining like a dull mirror with endless little sub-divisions of rice plots divided by tiny mud barriers: islands of green trees, oranges and pomegranates in flower, rise all among these water plots, and every island has a few houses under enormous beehive roofs of rice thatching. Little observatories on four pillars, also under a dome of thatching, stand about in the water, and beyond it all is a pale streak of sea without shadows that also might come out of a Japanese print. Blue dragonflies with the outer half of their wings velvety black, dart about doing their little best with the mosquitoes: but, of course, this is a perfect trap for malaria and even the poorest house has a veranda which you climb to by a ladder and are supposed to be out of their way. I am sitting on one now, after lunch, and the centre of an interested row of onlookers who look very much more Russian than Persian. The darker eyes, and pretty oval of the faces, and generally softer expression. Their language is quite incomprehensible— and especially to-day because my cold is so bad that I could scarcely understand English if there were any to be heard within fifty miles.

My coming has evidently been heralded by the muleteers who went ahead, for I was greeted with looks of expectant surprise by all we met. It is quite a shock when you are jogging along amiably absent-minded to see the people meeting you suddenly petrified with surprise.

I had quite a good night having rediscovered the Keatings; and a nice airy balcony: and in the early light could see the caravans getting under way, the mules being groomed down and the packs fixed on, all in the cold wet light with mist overhead and everything drenched in dew. The men wore woollen stockings and a bit of leather or fur gathered round their feet by way of shoes. The shepherds in the jungle are wild-looking people—with one of those square felt capes over their shoulder and a cap of sheepskin with the long fur worn like a busby. I got a photo of one boy, after some difficulty—but the light was rather poor. I believe these people used to be very wild and a man who is now political officer in Fars was kept a year or so as a prisoner tied to a tree: at least that is what Captain Holt told me, and said I should get to know him as he is as mad as me. Anyway they seemed friendly enough now, and let me look at their camp where a dozen or so wee calves were penned in a reed hut browsing off a great bunch of branches tied from the middle of the roof: they just strip the trees for fodder when they need it, and use the dry leaves like grass.

24 May, 1930.

I am waiting in patience to know whether or no a motor is going to take me to Resht or not this evening. I had been hearing so long of Tunakabun as the centre of all things here, and was thinking of it as a kind of metropolis where civilization, films, and chairs were flourishing. What it is, is a peaceful little village with a market twice a week where people from Resht spread awnings and all sorts of bright cheap cottons, buttons, beads, elastic, and such European oddments for the rice growers round to buy. It would be a charming spot with its green gardens and the row of wooded slopes rising to snow behind, if it were not a perfect death-trap of malaria—luckily the bad season only begins in a fortnight, but I do find it trying to sit with my hosts round a lamp on the open veranda, with silent insects flitting about. We catch them and I have been told how to distinguish the good and the bad, and I dose myself with quinine which may explain why I feel so peculiar—but I shall be glad to get away to a drier country.

RESHT, 26 May, 1930.

I had just got so far when a motor car finally turned up. Two in fact; one which had been ordered from Shahzavar came along, but

with the intention of taking me only half-way and then stopping:
so we took the other one, which had a charming chauffeur like a
Mujik with an enormous beard. The first car wanted to be paid
for coming so far, but even the easy benevolence of the Doctor
came to the conclusion that a car which comes to take you to a place
where you haven't asked to go to, needn't be paid. To make all
sure we appealed to a village Elder with a red henna'd beard: and
the verdict being in favour, started off without more ado. Most
affectionate farewells. I felt I was leaving quite a familiar place:
having sat under the orange trees, drinking tea in the Emir's garden:
and spent the morning with a little procession of Bahai notables
behind me, visiting the bazaar (and buying a silk bedcover which I
regret, for the sum would have just prevented me from being impe-
cunious now): and having visited the school, which is a lovely old
dilapidation in a garden with a tank and big trees where the little
boys read out short moral stories in high sing-song voices. It was
good to make for the coast and see the Caspian, grey in the grey
evening, stretching away shallow and flat, and a dumpy little village
which is the port of Shahzavar and which you reach by splashing
through the Seh Hizar river just below the piers of the new bridge
which is to be finished some time. We stuck: but the removal of
a boulder in the river bed set us going again. Evidently the Mujik
had been told about my thirst for information, for he told me the
names of all the villages we came to—and stopped the car to show
me the face of Adam in a wall of rock which is called Mere-Kuli:
the rest of the time he was busy in telling his sub-chauffeur to go
slow in avoiding the donkeys and hump-backed bullocks, all strolling
home in the evening. The mountains were hidden, and it was
drizzling now and then, but it is a magnificent coast. We got to a
place called Ab Garm, where some pools of steaming water spring
up by the roadside and you can see the skinny Persians bathing while
a little circle of *chaikhanas* and cars and crowd make it into a sort of
fair: there was even a conjurer with his wares spread on the floor
making the same jokes in Persian which his colleagues make in their
European languages. I lost my people, who disappeared to drink
tea, and when at last they reappeared it was with a fat blond chauffeur
and a really nice car. They extracted me from the conversation of
an Armenian lady and a horrid tourist man who asked for my visiting
card, and whom I could only shake off by asking if he belonged to the

police and if not why so many questions. I got rather annoyed, and at last hit on the device of asking questions back, so quick that they couldn't get theirs in: I found this quite a good way of getting rid of them.

It was now about seven o'clock, and I had discovered that it would be another four hours at least to Resht, and was not too pleased when it turned out that the old Mujik was leaving me and the fat chauffeur alone to take me through the Caspian jungle. It did seem very lonely: the forest here reaches almost to the water's edge; the sea lay very quiet and dull with a last light in it; and this road drifted along through sand or gravel, with not a soul on it. I asked what was going to happen to all the cars we left at Ab Garm: "They stay there," said the chauffeur, "as they have no permit for Resht at night." Neither had the old Mujik, so he knew all the time that he could not have taken me. Luckily the chauffeur was a really good man (and not a Persian by his looks) and not fond of talking: his only remark was as we came to a particularly shadowy bit under the trees, that there used to be a lot of robbers here. We met a woodcutter or two trudging home: a horseman now and then: and about one car an hour coming the opposite way. Here and there were clearings for rice-fields, their little tiny waterfalls where the water goes from one terrace to the next, shining in the last light. We punctured conveniently in one of these clearings—and the chauffeur turned out really capable and put it right quickly. After that I saw no more of the country; we went through like a dream, and it was extraordinarily like England—the green hedges, and trees, and thatched roofs. Only the little towns with their bazaars still busy—shoemakers and tailors stitching away at ten o'clock at night round a big lantern, and the tea-shops handing round their little glasses, looked foreign enough. About ten-thirty we waded up to the footboards in the first branch of the Safid Rud which I had crossed a week before near Chala: when we got across, a man in a little hut sounded a gong, and by the time we reached the second branch the ferry was waiting and a posse of men ready to get us across. It was so like a dream. I could not help wondering all the time how I came to be there on the edge of the Caspian in the middle of the night. A little after eleven, I got to Resht and asked for the Grand Hotel—having been told this name by the A's: it was a mistake, however, of theirs, for the Savoy is the one to go to, and the Grand is an awful little place with nothing clean except its notice board. I was too exhausted to care much however.

The rest of the next day was spent in meeting Bahais: a lady came who kept a school and carried me off to her house after lunch and let me rest in a room with four beds. Then we sat round in a circle while the Bahai leader and member of the Esperanto Society came and called—rather a nice little man: and a sad elderly female pillar of the faith. I imagine it must be very like the early Christian Societies, still tied closely together and with their common faith as the great bond and occupation, and it is interesting to see it. But when they informed me that the real time for my car to start would be six —I felt I could bear it no longer, and decided to go and call on the Consul—whether I knew him or not. I went and was passed at the door by a lovely vision in grey crêpe de Chine and pearls—me feeling the acme of shabbiness: into a lovely garden of roses, with tea laid with strawberries. The Consul came along—an intelligent-looking fair young man called Finch, who had heard about me in a note from Mr. Summerhayes. We had a French tea, the lady being Parisian with a Greek husband: Mr. Finch's French excellent—the tea a dream —I began to revive.

When the visitors left, the Consul kept me on to explain my route: we went and looked at maps: he had done some exploring himself— farther east—and, by the time I was going, he asked me to stay to dinner—and rang up Mr. Ward the bank manager: we filled in the time by talking about Dante, he being a good Italian scholar. So pleasant: dinner with candles and silver: and the two men so friendly. They discussed Valerian and the Persian wars, very agreeably remote— and by the time Mr. Ward took me back to my disgusting hotel and asked me next time to stay at his house, I was feeling much refreshed. The only redeeming point about the Grand Hotel is that a Caucasian with a long Mephistopheles face plays rather fascinating wild music on a *kamenja* with a piano accompaniment: quite a different thing from the Persian music, with a strong rhythm to it. Did I tell you what a pleasure it was riding down from Alamut suddenly to notice that Ismail was chanting Omar Khayyàm stanzas ul, -ul, -ul, ul, with the three rhymed and one penultimate unrhymed line?

KANGAVAR, 1 *June*, 1930.

The Williams', back again in Hamadan, were so kind—and so was everyone except the bank, which told me that quite distinguished-looking people, generals and such, come and pay uncashable cheques: I was not particularly pleased at being put in this category, and very glad when my money finally came.

Then the great excitement was the stealing of my Kodak. The coachman took a fancy to it while I went into the house and sent the man out for my things. So I went all on my own to the police station, and explained the matter (in Persian) to the head officer and spent a happy hour there watching the lavish way in which the Persian police scatter salutes. I was asked to choose my coachman from two walls full of appalling photographs: luckily he was deformed with a permanent stoop, so they were able to spot him; I tactfully promised a reward—and sure enough about eight-thirty a fluttering was manifest in the kitchen regions and a policeman rode up and presented the camera: such a triumph has never been known before in Hamadan. Out of my gratitude and riches I gave him two tomans, and Mr. Williams, and Mr. May, when they came home, explained in horror that now everything would be stolen so as to get a reward: and sure enough a sheep and a lamb and a bag of wool were taken this very night out of their stable.

It is very hot driving over these greeny-yellow plateaux. Baghdad will be awful. Hamadan now is a city of poppies; everywhere a field of great white flowers, with a few mauve ones among them, stands out in the foreground, with the mountains and their last patches of snow behind. Grain, with hollyhocks, pink, red and white, growing among it, and big tufty feathery yellow flowers and multitudes of poppies. The Persians gather their wild flowers in tight little bunches round a stick, so that they carry coloured staffs, very pretty: they will stick a rose anywhere—on their *leban* bowls, or in their mouths—but they could not understand that I just loved to look at them and not to pick them.

ON BOARD S.S. CARNARO, 18 *June*, 1930.

Dearest Pips,

Just before leaving I got your letter and the most surprising and altogether overpowering news of your present. I don't even know how one says thank you for such large sums. I am just £66 overdrawn, so my banker says, and suggested in a tactful way that one might sell securities: so you see it will be such a nice moral satisfaction to tell him 'nothing of the kind'. Thanks most awfully, dear Pips. Only *can* you really afford it? It is a most lovely present, and lets me get home without that awful feeling of having to economize so strenuously for ever so long to make up for Persian dissipations.

I had a very good trip across the desert, in a respectable manner in the huge six-wheeler Nairn car with all the British. There were no other women travelling so I had all the attention to myself. Left at 7 a.m.; got very hot by the time we were out in the open desert through the afternoon though it was all greener than when I came over in October. We had sandwich lunch at Ramadi, then tea out of kettles, very neatly done: the whole kettle is smothered in wood, and a little paraffin poured over, and it boils in no time, and tastes good. We reached Rutba about 9 p.m.—barbed wire, and the fortress walls, and great gate and sentry of the Arab desert police, looking very grim under stars. I got a bath of sorts, and had my arm dressed (septic mosquito, now all right). Then dinner, and back into the car the whole night: rather weary. I found my head resting on somebody's knee who didn't seem as pleased with it as he should. People with longer legs were worse off than I however. We had breakfast inside the Syrian border, in the desert among thousands of camels. Sausages cooked in their tins while a man of the Persian Oil told me how he came through this place some years ago when it was strewn with ten thousand dead Druses.

Then ages at the Damascus quarantine where a doddering old man looked slowly through our certificates and murmured "*pas de précipitation*". So that I had very little time in Damascus, and had to *rush* out to the bazaar and buy an 'abba' which I had promised to Mrs. Granville, and then just time for bath and lunch and off in another car with a young Air Force man who was also starting from Haifa.

ASOLO, 7 August, 1930.

I got home a week ago and have been having rather a bad time with enteritis—lying in bed and drinking milk. I am beginning to have something more substantial now and get up for an hour or so, and hope to be right by the end of the month when I start for England. It is probably from a chill through the absurd weather we are having: the cyclone must have thoroughly unsettled it.

We heard the other day of a poor priest in a village by the Montello: he left his church just before the cyclone began, and went into his house across the little piazza: then heard a great noise, came rushing out, saw the piazza and no church in it, and thought he had gone out of his mind. The whole thing had been lifted bodily by the wind.

Did I tell you of the Dronero priest's sermon against football? He says it is anti-Christian because it concentrates everybody's attention on people's legs. The poor little girls' lives are made a burden what with long sleeves and long frocks (and even necks are indecent now).

5

The Persian Summer, 1931

AT the beginning of 1931 a riding accident provided me with a few weeks of what must be one of the most delightful attributes of eternity—a sense of leisure.

I was spending a day or two in Wales with Venetia Buddicom on my way from Canada, and took a pony on the moors. Where the high hill meets the wind we pushed through a gate, and neither of us noticed a rusty pipe sticking out there. At least, the pony may have noticed, but did not care, for horses have gone through their millenniums of history without ever making an allowance for their added size when ridden, which shows them to be stupid, though charming. The pony pushed through, with the gate slapping to behind it in the wind; a deep triangle was cut out of my shoe and foot, and I myself torn off and dragged round a gorse bush, remembering early training and sticking to the bridle. The pony stopped with that bored air of asking what the fuss is all about; and I mounted, made for the gate again, had to dismount to shut it (which a countryman or woman will do at the point of death) and remounted, all without looking at my foot, for I guessed that the sight of it might make me sick: I rode home for over half an hour with no pain or sensation, with the sun pleasant upon me, and thinking, I remember, of all the wounded who must have been able to reach dressing-stations before the pain began. It only started about an hour after the accident, and I was stitched up with nine stitches and continued on my way to London and Cambridge in a few days' time; but here the trades' union of the body, which acts so much more like the United Nations than they do themselves, protested, and I was laid up for nearly a month.

I was in the house of Olivia and Ernest Barker, and they not only kept me with kindness, but were able to provide all the books I most wished to read. It was then, as far as I can remember, that I first came on that store of Mediterranean gossip—Heyd's *Commerce du Levant*. In the intervals of reading, the George Trevelyans came to see me, remembering the old war in Italy; and Guy le Strange talked about Persia in the days when he travelled post as a young man, changing horses and covering as much as seventy or eighty miles a day. He had called on the last husband of Lady Ellenborough, the handsome old sheikh of Palmyra; and he carried about with him, in the rather close atmosphere of Cambridge, a gay, eighteenth-century feeling of connoisseurship in life, of enjoyment, and spaciousness, and a friendly intimacy and disregard for time.

Nancy Lambton too I met here, and gave my small support to her desire for Eastern travel and freedom: when her first journey to Persia was planned, she asked me down to Newmarket for a week-end to do what I could to persuade her family. Sir Denison Ross had been there the week before; his wife had a cold, and he had a new book, and they both refused to visit the famous stables: orientalists were at a discount. Nancy and I, arriving by a late morning train, watched Mrs. Lambton, hard and handsome, leap up at intervals through luncheon to hang over the telephone for the betting on a race in progress, without a remark to her guest during the whole meal.

In the stables, my hostess continued to annoy me by giving advice, as if an orientalist could not be expected to know the head of a horse from its tail; I came away feeling how wonderfully well-bred the horses were; and though Nancy's father was charming, and her mother softened by Monday morning, I sympathized with her efforts at emancipation, and have continued to admire her, for she studied with a thoroughness which I never attained. Eventually, in 1940 I think, she became attaché to the British Legation in Teheran—the first woman to have this rank even temporarily in the British service. I believe I was the second, and was given temporary diplomatic status in

Baghdad in 1941; but I never dug into Arabic as deeply as she did into Persian.

Most of the early spring in London was crowded with the struggle to study geography in the short time. The year before, at Lionel Smith's suggestion, I had shown the Alamut records to Arthur Hinks, the secretary of the Royal Geographical Society, who received my timid approach in a benevolent but remote way—rather as if I were asking Dr. Johnson to take an interest in a new hat. Mr. Hinks carried a stout, eighteenth-century Johnsonianly definite atmosphere about him. He told me to leave my papers, and he would look them over with Prof. Kenneth Mason. When I returned to the secretary's room, I found both very encouraging, and had my first experience of the generosity of geographers and orientalists to each other: of all human toilers, they seem to me to be the freest from meanness and envy, perhaps because their work is so washed through by space or time. They thought that, before I travelled again, I should learn the rudiments of a survey from Mr. Reeves, a soft-spoken old enthusiast who lived in a quiet corner of the building, where almost every British traveller for the last fifty years must have been through his hands. I spent happy mornings here learning about triangles, and the distribution of error, difficult even in real life: and we met at Redhill Station to survey the Common, whose contours turned out to be surprisingly different from what the Ordnance Survey evidently thought. Mr. Reeves told me that he had put Rosita Forbes through this course in her time, and had found her outside Redhill Station, sitting cross-legged on the pavement eating a bun, in the middle of a crowd; which just shows that one can be oriental anywhere, if one wishes.

There was a Persian air about London that spring. The first and perhaps the most beautiful of a series of foreign exhibitions at Burlington House had started with Persia, and it gave one a singular feeling for the unity and harmony of that land—the same delicacy, specialized and remote, ran through it all, from carpets to maiolicas, and miniatures to brocades. Mr. Cooke was in London and took me through, pointing out the fakes, and I left with a harvest of new and exciting thoughts inside me. I had a Leica camera, and knew how to use a compass; and had met a host of people, of whom Sydney Cockerell and Sir Henry Lawrence became intimate and lifelong friends. In Paris I stopped both to call on Professor Minorsky, the most charming of all experts on Persia, and to buy a white evening gown of a satin they called angel-skin, which gave me a feeling of happiness, small but compact, whenever I put it on. The magic of art is that it inspires inanimate objects with some of the qualities of *life*, so that they can create pleasure, and satisfy obscure needs for colour, or rhythm, or form: the art of dress perhaps brings these qualities into the closest relationship with ourselves; and a woman who has no use for it must have some secret obliquity, arrogance or malady of soul. I suspect anyone self-satisfied enough to refuse lawful pleasures: we are not sufficiently rich in our separate resources to reject the graces of the universe when offered; it is bad manners, like refusing to eat when invited to dinner; and indeed I should call humility in religion the equivalent of good manners in ordinary life.

For my own part, I have not suffered from any reluctance to welcome enjoyment when it comes, and this spring was pleasantly full of it. Lionel Smith, reaching Venice, invited me to stay some days at the Danieli; we took all the gondolas we wanted, and liked looking at the same things at the same pace, as important in sightseeing as it is in mountaineering for climbers on one rope. Lionel then spent a fortnight in Asolo, walking about our little hills with sugar sweets in his pockets for the children, and showing me nightingales in the steep glades of the acacias.

When May was nearly over, I made for Brindisi through Rome; lunched under vines along the Appian way with Lolette and Gustino Biancheri and saw the 'imperial' city which Mussolini was hewing out of what we had known untidy and merely 'eternal'. Sitting with my old friends in the long afternoon light of the Campagna, I felt as one does in a ship that moves: though there is a gap between it and the shore, the hand stretches across—but the gangway is lifted, and the new horizon is there already, over the rim of the sky. My heart was now in the East for many years.

I felt this more than ever when I landed among new sights in Haifa, with a home-coming gaiety scarce damped by the British smugness of the Windsor Hotel. I felt it when I visited the Bahais, and saw their guest-house open to all who came; and spent a sunny day at Athlit, thinking, among the ruins, of the Crusaders as they departed, defeated, from the rocky headland through the striped blue sea: their palmers' shells lay all along the sands, and the wind hummed in the sea-lavender and salty scrub of the shore.

I made my way north by the castles of Belfort and Banias, to Damascus; and reached Baghdad in the summer heat of June. The Sturgeses, friends from the first, rescued me out of a kindly little hotel romantically placed but so smelly from summer lowness of the Tigris and the things on its shores that no oriental enthusiasm could make one forget them.

In less than a fortnight I was in Hamadan, in the beautiful Consulate now given up, where the Summerhayes were staying. I was there longer than I had intended, for Peggy fell ill with typhoid and we all shared in the nursing; and it was not till August that I managed to reach Qazvin, and not until the 9th that I finally set out for a pass on the northern skyline.

My journey is described in *The Valleys of the Assassins*. It brought the same enchantment as before, with an added knowledge, as the second rung of a ladder is added to the first and the height gained is a combination of the two. No one can ever quite recapture the feel of the earliest step upon the lowest rung, and the goal unknown: it is first love, or the morning gloss of a journey wet with dew. But I do not believe that with this the best of life is over, and all that comes later is retrospect or work. Things and people again and again are made anew and startle by their freshness; and memory pushes out into age with undefeated youth at its heart.

[187]

On this journey I first stood consciously on the edge of death. This I think is rarely done if you are attended by others in a sick-room, where it is their business and not yours to estimate your chances. But, alone and in the open, the trench where the world ends is very near, as if it were a part of the unexplored landscape around you, with love and fear and the days of your life in its dark. Later, I have been afraid, but this time all seemed a part of the far valley and its austerity, and I was subdued to a sort of timeless peace. I have thought of this since when travelling in the Western Desert and watching the twisted metal that marks the places of so many dead, and have been comforted by the hope that those, in their lonely ends, were visited by the same final gentleness, remote from men and their fatiguing ways. The thread that held my will to life in those days was the thought of my father: I must not die before him, I thought again and again, hoping to spare him a useless grief. And when I reached Teheran I found a letter, telling me of his death during those hours when I lay ill in the hills.

The Legation was in summer quarters at Gulahek, and they welcomed me and asked me to stay. From then on I never again had to suffer among my own people from a want of sympathy, encouragement or kindness in my ventures; and in fact I soon realized that a woman gets far more than her legitimate share of praise, merely because of her comparative rarity in the explorer's world.

Few things could be more pleasant than to descend from the uncomfortable bare mountains to civilization in the diplomatic enclosure. A sentry stood at a gate on the dusty road, and after that all was high avenues of trees, 'shades and whispering winds and gushing brooks', cool empty glades where the Chancery houses were scattered with no dividing boundaries between them, and a blue-tiled swimming-pool in common, with minia-ture blue pools in private bathrooms in the separate houses as well. Here Charles Dodd gave me dinner in a white tent lined with scarlet, with white and gold *cawasses* handling porcelain and silver; and I found my angel-skin, rather crumpled, in a

suit-case sent by road from Hamadan. The Lingemans took
me charmingly into their house, and showed me Luristan bronzes
in the Teheran bazaar; and I spent cool restful mornings plotting
out my map, which—thanks to Mr. Reeves and all his teaching
—came out of the mountains with only two miles of 'error'
to be distributed, after a month's wandering: Colonel Dodd, the
military attaché, told me that my map was the best of that region
so far produced, and I tasted the joy of the geographer, one of the
pure and unpretentious joys. If I could choose a reincarnation,
I should be a surveyor; even with my elementary knowledge, a new feeling for *form* in country, the climax of the watershed, the intricacies of contours that determine the meanderings
of streams, the tilt and exposure of slopes that mean woodlands
or erosions, gave and still give me an unspeakable delight. And
perhaps the things accomplished by myself that I think of with
most pleasure are the few trees I have planted and the few names
I have added to the map.

Teheran is a city I liked particularly, neither western nor
eastern, but with a character of its own, colourless but clear, like
water—and I do not mean the Teheran drinking water, which at
that time ran in open gutters through the streets and was not clear
at all; it is almost certainly now rectified and enclosed, and in
fact the whole city must have changed greatly in the last twenty
years. I left it casually, by lorry, packed with travellers and
bundles and water-jars slung from the cage, a dilapidated contrast to the *cawass* in uniform who came to put me in; and I
made my way by Qum and Sultanabad and Malayir, flattish
cultivated lands interspersed with dasht and desert, dusty yellow
mud-built villages, and croaking frog-filled ditches where a
weeping willow droops beside the stagnant pond.

I made this detour so as to visit the ruined medieval caravan
city of Saveh, now lost in a mountain bay where no road takes
the traffic, with only a fine mosque-ruin and two brick-carved
minarets, circular towers with inscriptions, to show the grandeur
of the huge enclosure of the dead town in its crumbled walls.
It was pitted with amateurish shafts where the people of modern

Saveh dug up bowls and vases for the antiquarians of Europe. My first Persian teacher came from Saveh, and his brother made me welcome, and I picnicked with the notables on *kilims* spread in gardens under pomegranate trees. Saveh is the only place I know where the pomegranate becomes luscious and fleshy and can be eaten with pleasure, and it is as famous in its own district as the melon of Isfahan is farther south.

There is a charm in this hill-encircled plain with the little town forgotten by the world where nothing happens; it lies still as a stream, and only the faintest ripple through the centre shows that it moves at all: this ripple was the mail car which took me back to Qum, a juggler's toy of odds and ends held by mechanical attraction, with a driver who was a friend-of-all-the-world. He took us past the nomad flocks whose winter quarters are villages in the plain. They perpetuate, in a mean way, the Sassanian palaces of the past, handed down through impoverished generations, with domes and barrel vaults of mud that still have a grand air at a distance.

After Qum the lorries deteriorated and the trip lengthened out to days instead of hours. They were mostly spent by the roadside in dejection, with the lorry strewn in the dust. Such wayside groups defeat the mechanical age, through the length and breadth of Asia.

A feeling of eternity depressed me by the middle of the second day; there seemed to be no reason for journey and breakdowns ever to end at all; and even the order of time was shattered, for we travelled at odd hours of the night so as to cool and pacify the radiator, and took snatches of sleep on hard chaikhaneh benches beside the road. I thought with longing of the comfort of the hills where no wheel is known. At every small town all our papers were shown at entry and exit, and, a little before arrival, illegal passengers would descend, make a circuit on foot, and be picked up in open country on the far side. My British passport was always handed out and returned to me by the driver, and I naturally assumed it to be unique in a region so conspicuously unprepared for tourists: opening it idly during one of the long pauses, I was startled to see the portrait of an old man with a beard inside, and the name of Hajji Abdalla, passed by the Criminal Investigation Department of Lahore on his way to Mecca. He was probably even less pleased with my picture than I with his. I handed him to an amused group of drivers who, with a feeling of unlimited time before them, were breakfasting on hard-boiled eggs at the ditch side; they selected someone travelling in the opposite direction from ours, and in less than a week, out of the halting network of the lorry world, my rightful passport emerged, to everyone's surprise. I was by that time rested and restored by the kind Williams' in Hamadan, and on my way across Elvand and the plains to Nihavend and Luristan.

That delightful journey, also described in *The Valleys of the Assassins*, lasted till the end of October when I reached Baghdad and settled in my room on the Tigris with the four months in Persia and all their memories to arrange in my mind: the unmapped hills and rivers, the saucer plains enclosing little worlds whose voice is never heard beyond their borders, the open hunted freedom of the southern ranges are always with me, and flit refreshingly through any dusty day.

In Baghdad Jamila's cooking seemed increasingly dingy, and I began regretfully to consider a new lodging. Things too were happening to my, and most other people's, income; there was a slump at the end of the year, and I saw nothing but a financial blank ahead. Vyvyan suggested work on the *Baghdad Times*, which printed a daily sheet of Arabic and three of English news interspersed with local advertisements. Mr. Cameron, the editor, was looking for someone to take on the English pages. I went to see him, and found that he faced the thought of a woman with reluctance. Hospital nurses and Miss Lucie-Smith, safely tucked away in the palace teaching the princesses, were the only independent women with jobs in the whole of Iraq at that time. Mr. Cameron was afraid, he said, of taking on someone to whom he could not be rude. I suggested that we might separate, if he felt rude too often. He also said that no woman in Iraq could be relied on to stick to a job for more than a few weeks: and I promised solemnly to stay for a year if I were given two autumn months—for I had already decided to try a southern route to Luristan. On this basis we agreed to begin at the end of March in 1932.

Meanwhile I transferred myself to a bedroom and sitting-room in the Y.M.C.A., on the eastern side of the river, among palm gardens which have long since disappeared. Mr. and Mrs. Lampard ran this place in an open-minded way. A stream of daily visitors, of R.A.F. from Hinaidi, of travelling missionaries or others passing through, took their meals at long tables, together with the staff and the lodgers, and brought an amusing variety of views to every discussion. Every subject could be tackled safely except drink, and on this point I think I was the only person brave enough to contradict Mr. Lampard; it took me a long time to recover from the sight of my little store (so very expensive to me) being taken kindly from me and poured down a sink. I cannot and never could see why teetotalism and religion should be linked together, and would quote the marriage of Cana, to which Mr. Lampard put up a feeble defence by saying that the liquor must have been 'unfermented grape juice'. "You can't tell me that unfermented grape juice also made those old bottles of the parable *burst*," said I—and Mr. Lampard would give in, unconvinced but amused. They were very kind to me, and I was fond of them both, and entertained by the unerring tactlessness with which Mr. Lampard steered under full sail into every topic liable to give trouble, and clung to it with bulldog tenacity: I believe it made him a menace at committee meetings, but added zest to conversation, and I suspected him of doing it on purpose with an obstinate twinkle. He was small, plump, and friendly, and his wife—quietly gifted and most capable—was small and sturdy too; and so was their terrier, Punch: the three would stand together on their doorstep like three slight variations of the same theme, compact, unpretentious, and kind.

*   *   *

Dearest B,

I had a fall from ponyback just before leaving Penbedw, and am tied to a sofa for a week—nothing serious. It wasn't even a real fall, but my foot got caught by an iron bar sticking out of a gate, and the shoe was ripped and a bit of the top of my foot torn. I came off, clung to the reins however, and the pony—being really not in a wicked frame of mind—listened to my ingratiating remarks and stopped after a yard or two and I was able to gather my stirrup off the ground and ride home wondering what was left me in the way of toes. They were all intact luckily and no tendons touched, and the doctor came and put in nine stitches, and next day Venetia's cousin Sir Henry Lawrence and his wife arrived, and he carried me about very kindly. He is a charming little ugly man with a great sense of fun: his wife is very delicate: she went to bed and left us to talk over Gandhi and India generally. It was such a luxury to be ill in Venetia's house; the little nurse took all the worries; I just lay and was comfortable, and suddenly wondered why it was so heavenly to lie with my toe stitched up, till I realized for the first time for I don't know how many years I had not a single decision of any kind to make, it was all being done for me. Bless that nurse.

They sent me off with bath-chairs to meet me (for I couldn't put London off). Viva looking well, though first so busy telling me I had been stupid to ride, and then that my trunk was impossible to put anywhere, and then that Bessie was not to be kept waiting: so that I fled and only got a harassed note next morning and found that she had recovered her equanimity next day.

I went and saw Mr. Hinks at the R.G.S., who was charming and told me that he liked my paper. He was very helpful, promising to get me otherwise unprocurable maps. I feel absurdly shy; as if I were about eighteen. But it was very nice. They really are good to women, making so much of all the things that a man wouldn't be looked at twice for doing.

Yesterday Mr. le Strange came to lunch, a gay old boy of eighty or nearly who once had tea with Herbert in Asolo.

To-day I had more or less to myself and have been writing a footnote to my article in the light of that of Mr. Ivanow, who comes out on the same subject and has been enraging poor Mr. Hinks, by insisting on spelling all the names wrong *including his own.*

20 *January*, 1931.

I don't know when I wrote last. All has been so vague and changeable because of my foot which is still keeping me here with poor Olivia. The bruise was too bad after all for it to heal: but with my usual undemonstrativeness in the way of temperatures, nothing showed till three days ago, when I had great pain and had to telegraph to cancel everything in London, and the wound had to be opened up again and now it seems at last to be in a good way, though it will leave a horrid scar. However. It is most trying for the poor Barkers, who are angelic about it. I just enjoy myself reading all the books I can't easily get at otherwise, and correcting proofs. I don't know what I told you of all my literary excitements: first of all, Dr. Huxley, to whom I sent two articles to choose from, has kept both, as well as the Persian Legends. The *Spectator* wrote telling me they liked my work, wished me a happy new year, and would I send more. And Ernest [Barker] has got my serious effort into the *Contemporary Review*. So that now all I have written is 'placed' except one little orphan: and I rather wish I had more. But I will make just enough to pay the fare to Baghdad and back, which is what I was trying for this year. I will not be able to go till later, with this delay and all, so I may get a week or two's quiet to write in Asolo. Here it is of course out of the question: I need all my spare time to *read*.

In London I was to have met Sir Percy Sykes and quite a lot of interesting orientalists: it is most tantalizing, and when I do go I will be so plain that I will merely be taken as a warning *not* to go to the East.

The Trevelyans are here. Wonderful people. I like her almost more than him, if that is possible, and two such fine, keen strong faces, the spirit shining through with a calm and steady light.

Then there is Mr. le Strange, a delightful old man, as keen as a schoolboy after a happy life misspent in doing all the things he liked, dabbling in embassies and oriental studies, wandering on the Afghan borders and reading Petrarch's Sonnets now for the first time. He has sent me a packet of books to Asolo (to await me) and is most anxious I should go again to Alamut and investigate more fully. He endorses my view of Marco Polo's castle and two mountains: says there can be no doubt about it, and likes my article best—though as a matter of fact I think this is mere illusion, Ivanow being *really* scientific and only spoilt by his crotchety spelling.

[194]

That was my last day out—in a bath-chair wheeled by Ernest, and we visited his college of Peterhouse and lovely panelled room looking out on one side to the quiet of the court and on the other out to the trees, the sunset and the river. What a luxury of civilization it is—their hall, all panelled and pictured with high vaulted carved ceiling, and common room with stone hearth and lovely fire and low chairs, and the library with old carved bookcases and Dutch tiles in the fireplaces, and the chapel in the court below. No wonder women, and all the agitations of ordinary life, are here excluded: it would not do to interrupt that perfect repose.

LONDON, 9 February, 1931.

Foot is covered over at last and I hope to begin R.G.S. work to-morrow. Am waiting for the doctor now. He is going to take a blood test and give me injections accordingly. I am really all right: it was only a bit of exhaustion, and this month of rest and good feeding and nothing to think about except the Mongol invasions has already nearly set me up again. How nice about Lionel Smith. I had a letter too. I think he will like Asolo.

I have got some good out of my reading. Some day I shall have to sit down in a library for a year and study the original sources. I think I am on the track of quite good work, only all far in the future.

18 February, 1931.

I am just home, tired, but having much enjoyed my visit. They were so kind to me. Sir Henry Lawrence likes me, I believe, and is going to have a whole twelve hours of my society when he comes up on Friday week. Lunch at his club and then we are going to the India Office to look into a trial about the Agha Khan's ancestry and his descent from the Assassins, on which his revenues depended: the documents are there, and only the Initiate can get at them, so I shall go as Sir Henry's secretary. Then dinner and theatre: I think I shall find it very hard to remain conversationable all that time and fear we shall both be exhausted. He is a charming man to talk to, full of a dry humour which flashes out suddenly in a quiet way. Lady Lawrence is very delicate and an invalid, but nice and artistic: her sketches have a lot of feeling, and she talks very pleasantly but in a vague way, and begins stories which hover about aimlessly till she resigns them into the capable hands of Henry who sits chafing inwardly but outwardly calm under this mismanagement and immediately takes them in hand. It is wonderful how a strong character makes itself felt, without speech or any apparent *action*: just by *being*.

There was also a retired naval man, Lady Lawrence's brother called George Napier: they are cousins of the Venice Napiers. He was pleasant with simple, charming manners of a sailor and a man who spends his life away from women a good deal. The house is right on the hill, with copses around, and Oxford country rolling about on the skyline. We went for a long drive this morning, to fetch a bull terrier which Lady L breeds, lovely strong white dogs. We came back by sandy roads and villages with thatch, and Abingdon with a spire, and the Thames flowing by.

Yesterday they took me to a League of Nations Union lunch to hear Mr. Noel-Baker speak: he is secretary to Henderson, a clever quiet young man, and very able speaker: says something for the Labour people that they can get this type of man. What he actually said was not so startling: the need for 'international' instead of 'national' fiscal policies, which, of course, is obvious, but no nearer for that.

ASOLO, 31 *March*, 1931.

Dearest Pips,

I am trying to write a few more articles before I forget it all. So you know what *that* means, and how difficult it is to get anything else in. I do manage however to go out and do a little map work, and the rumour no doubt has gone through Asolo that I am going to buy the Villa of Briseghella, for I have been measuring up and down the Foresto Vecchio these three days. It takes me about two hours a mile, so that if I do that in Kurdistan, not only will I be murdered as a spy, but I shall never emerge on the other side of it. I have now more or less concluded that I walk at 3 m.p.h. on a road and that my pace is 2 ft. 2 ins.: but even supposing this to be fairly accurate, I don't see how, in a hilly country, one can make up one's mind as to how far one has travelled *on the map*, and how much one must allow for hills, etc. It is very difficult. And then if one is on a wiggly road, one must take a new bearing at every change of direction, for if you once lose the record of your line of march, you are *done* for, you have no fixed point at all to go by. Apart from these obstacles, I am beginning to find my way over a plotting paper quite nicely and can remember that a mile is 63,360 inches without a second's hesitation.

16 *May*, 1931.

I have just seen Lionel Smith off at Vicenza and am now rushing through my packing to get off in time. I have to stop a few days in Rome, to try and get taken on as a correspondent by the *Oriente Moderno*. So I shall take it on my way and sail from Brindisi on the 28th. Next address will be c/o Ottoman Bank, Baghdad, and I will let you hear the next move when I know it myself. I do hope I shall find a letter from you there, for I am worried about that blood pressure of yours and do hope to hear of its being down again.

Lionel Smith had a nice visit. He said that if he stayed another week he would never have been able to go at all. We took him up by Asiago, picnicked by miles of little gentians, cowslips, and scented pink daphne, and back by Thiene and a lovely old villa of the Colleoni. I went to Padova one day, and saw your friend Gattamelata covered with pigeons and looking very fine. It is the Anno Santo there, and no one is to dance for the whole duration of it, and they are smartening it all up and painting new frescoes in S. Antonio: they are rather bright just now but will tone down I expect and look well in a few hundred years.

Here the garden looks nice, but it is full of beetles: I picked twelve out of one rose.

I am trying to write my Baghdad sketches—hope to do them on the voyage out.

Darling Pips, I do hope for good news of you. It is always such an anxious feeling if you are not well.

WINDSOR HOTEL, HAIFA, 9 June, 1931.

Dearest B,

As you see, my address is all that can be most respectable—only not of the sort I can keep up for long. I stay here to-morrow to go to Acre and then to call on the grandson of the Prophet of the Bahais.

I hate this sort of hotel. All expecting you to do the dull expensive things. The British are going through on leave, nice and clean and

[197]

talking in pleasant low voices and looking very much as if they lived in a private club in this foreign land.

It is so good to hear arabic again. Mine has all gone, and when I say anything it is usually Baghdad instead of Syrian, but it does to get along with. I drove up to Mount Carmel and saw the monastery of St. Elias, and he is not buried there as he never died, but is supposed to be hovering about Mount Carmel, and has a feast on July 20th when they bring sheep to sacrifice to him.

10 June, 1931.

I have had such a morning at Acre—first of all a delightful cool drive along the sea sand right round the bay (half an hour): it only cost 1s. in a little public car; we nearly turned over but not quite when the sand was soft. People were pulling at long ropes of the fishing nets and laid them down for us to run over: very exciting to see them do it *just* in time. Acre looks well with the mosques and houses showing over its old walls: but though there is more to see in a way it is not really so interesting as Athlit, because it has been so often retouched, and the walls are now comparatively modern and stood Napoleon's sieges. I am so lucky. The Qaimakan of the place was travelling on the car, an Arab, very cordial, who gave me a letter to Mr. Frew, the governor of the prison: I took it rather dubiously, but he had me into his office and was charming and sent a man to show me the old castle and church which are not open to the ordinary public at all: the church is only half excavated, enough to show immense columns of mortared stonework, and the castle has an English lawn and garden inside its walls, a delightful place, made by Mr. Frew and his prisoners and which he speaks of with pride. He is now busy with a pathetic little row of green benches surrounded by heaps of stones with geraniums stuck among them, which he hopes will become a tidy promenade along the old crusaders' reef. He has presented two benches to the municipality and induced them to buy the rest: they look so out of place, but after going all round the old walls I was rather glad to sit on one and thought with pride of our countrymen's disinterested efforts which no one ever troubles to thank them for. In the afternoon I went to call on the Bahais. The prophet had toothache, but there were lots of ladies. I sat in the place of honour beside a beautiful old lady dressed in white, with blue eyes rimmed with kohl and very humorous and kind, who kissed me before I left: she was a dear. The younger members of the family were nice, but more of this world: the daughter, a cousin of the Afnans in London, has a daughter at Westfield College. The house was filled with coming and going: a big airy room and then the divan with seats all round. Glasses of tea with little Persian spoons. A lovely garden, well trimmed, with box hedges, a pergola, a fountain and geraniums: and a seluki lying at the door. They gave me white flowers to hold in my hand, and the children had necklaces of orange blossom as I have seen at Resht: it was a little bit of Persia. I hope to call again on my way back and talk a little better.

WINDSOR HOTEL, HAIFA, 16 June, 1931.

Dear Mr. Smith,

I am sure you will approve of this very respectable address. I had better make use of it while it lasts, and tell you all about Athlit in case you are forgetting it. I went yesterday. It seemed a waste you should not be there. The viper's bugloss was still in flower over all the promontory, but the path to it from the station was nearly buried in flowering thyme, scenting everything in the sun and the sea wind. I took the early train and spent a happy morning there. You had not told me about the underground vaults and passages, nor that they were full of bats. Two Arabs turned up and took me down into pitch darkness and we admired the crusaders' work with matches. I believe the vaults must go right round below the inner battlements; I found more of them, used as stables in one corner of the village where I scrambled about trying to get a photograph of the bit of wall you drew. I recognized the places and felt as if you were there, and wished so much it were so. Then I got rid of my escort, and lay in the sun looking at the waves and the curious bay and wondering why one spends so little time in being happy and looking at beautiful things. It was a lovely sunny solitude. A chameleon came on to a rock—the first I have ever seen. I went back to the station and had nearly an hour to wait, and showed little Arabs how to make paper boats, but had no caramels.

RUTBA, 16 June, 1931.

Darling B,

I had a lovely day yesterday with Amatallatif and Ne'ma at Zebdani, a place where Moslems go to for the summer in the hills.

The Abana rises here and it is full of fruit gardens, and poplars which turn up the silver side of their leaves in a wind which blows constantly down the valley. Anything so delicious as the apricot—the kind they call of Hama—you have never even imagined: the flavour of the most delicious greengage and peach combined. It is worth the voyage only to taste it.

I find my arabic has gone so much to pieces. We went up in the train in the ladies' carriage, all veiled except me and a peasant woman, and all the ladies talked and smoked and did not really bother about their veils when the conductors came along: as they look at passengers' tickets by crawling along the outside of the carriages and looking in at the windows, one can't know when to expect them and be veiled.

Zebdani is about two hours away from Damascus: the valley is all one mass of green trees, with the green water running among them, and the red naked hills on either hand: looking down, was like a shimmering green velvet—figs, apples, apricots, pomegranates, walnuts, every sort and kind, and cascades of wild white roses. At Zebdani lives a bachelor uncle who is secretary to the Qaimakam and evidently a keen politician, and I was made to feel one of the wicked, though privileged as a guest: my arabic, however, was not good enough for politics, and they became a little less anti-British as the day wore on: he even told me the Arab proverb that: "What the English write on the earth Allah writes in heaven," which is taking rather a lot for granted.

It would be a lovely place to wander about in the shady lanes and the gardens, if they were not all locked. We, however, drove to the two villages higher on the hill—Zebdani is in a great shallow basin with Hermon far away over the southern rim—and sat in bare rooms being polite and quite shut off from the view, and saw the new hotel being built—a large place with columns very light and airy and a big *vasca* of water with fountain splashing in the flagged terrace in front of it: if it were in Europe, with that lovely view, it would be perfect, but the Arabs always manage to leave little slip-shod oddments here and there which spoil the general effect.

We got home at eight and the two girls refused a cab from the station because it would take them along a dark road where French soldiers might come and ravish them. In a way it is a comfort that nobody ever wants to ravish me. So we walked to the lights and parted. Amatallatif has got together £1,000 for her school and the house is being prepared and she is now trying to get teachers. The British missionaries are, as usual, the limit: the mistress of one school wrote to say that her girls preferred to teach in Christian places (so useful for these missionaries to want only to deal with Christians), and the other asked Amatallatif if there was to be any religion taught and when she said no (as it is difficult if you have a Syrian school to know which of the eighteen religions to choose), the woman said: "Then your school is without God." So now Amatallatif is going to try the German sisters who will no doubt be helpful and polite and of some use to their country.

BAGHDAD, 17 June, 1931.

Got here safely. Found quite a nice, clean-looking hotel on the river, just newly started, for 10s. 6d. a day. Rather tired now, motoring since ten last night, though I got a little sleep; but it was cold with the window open and made one sick with it shut.

26 June, 1931.

Captain Holt looked in yesterday to tell me that the Persian quarantine is quite impossible and that I *must* fly, and that anyone might have known that one would be ill coming here in the heat, "but that, of course, is what you say you like." I am so sorry to be enabling him to say "I told you so" in this way. However, I am much better to-day and will be perfectly all right in Mrs. Sturges' nice house, and will fly to Hamadan and so avoid quarantine.

I went to call on my Bahais and found them all well and most affectionate in their little courtyard cool but completely airless. I do realize why people's tempers go in this heat: it is extraordinarily trying.

HAMADAN, 6 July, 1931.

It is wonderfully green and bright up here, and good to see the ridges of Elvand. Everyone so pleasant and hospitable, and a nice house where one can do just as one pleases and I hope to get some work done. My old Mirza beaming all over with a set of new teeth which keeps him smiling as often as he can.

It was a marvellous experience flying up, with the Persian ranges opening out below one, first a little series of folds and wrinkles on the edge of the desert, bare as the skin of a hippopotamus, then high upland waterless villages with little ridges between, and then south-ward the wild country of Luristan and the broad valleys of the rivers east of Kermanshah flowing down into their unknown depths.

A fearful mess of my complexion creams—all *melted* away. Luckily I packed nothing important near them.

I have got two more Baghdad sketches done and sent to *Spectator* and hope to do more here.

18 July, 1931.

Dear Mr. Smith,

I have just got your letter. I thought one was due, and so waited to write. It is so lovely to get letters out here, and you can't think how remote Persia feels this year with the new anti-foreign policy which stops everything from coming into the country. I came by plane: I believe I told you I was going to. It was marvellous to see the mountain ranges below—not beautiful but interesting as W P once remarked about an anthill: one can see the skeleton of the land just like looking with X-rays at a body. The strip between this and Iraq is a desolate bit of landscape, very like the moon. I only came so expensively to avoid quarantine for plague, and to make Captain Holt happy as he felt that otherwise he would have to make arrange-ments for my funeral.

I feel I shall never be able to do what I really like again, as everyone has taken to a policy of Persuasion by kindness, which is so impossible to deal with. However no one makes objections to Alamut where I hope to return in a fortnight's time and thence find a Jungali to take me across a bit of country where the Survey have put nothing but trees and a few question marks, and so keep east, and down to Teheran eventually.

1 August, 1931.

My dear Rector,[1]

How very grand that sounds, but what is it really? I have just heard from Mama and am so glad. Is it just what you like? I hope so and hope to hear all about it, and that you will send me a proper detailed description, and tell me where it is in Edinburgh, and what sort of people you will have to look after. How nice it will be to be

[1] Lionel Smith, who had just become Rector, Edinburgh Academy.

a Dictator, and see everyone flatten out before you, after being a Mustashar [Adviser] with refractory Ministers. I am so glad. I wish I could see you to say so.

I have been helping nurse the little Summerhayes girl through typhoid and it has all been rather anxious and worrying, but better now. I leave for Qazvin in a few days, and hope the sight and breath of the hills will make me feel a little more fit than I do just now.

Persia and Iraq are talking about a war. I think I would back the Iraqis on the whole. The Persians started building a fortress about 300 yards inside Iraq territory and did not wish to pull it down: now, however, they seem finally to be doing so, while officially denying its existence. At least this is the account of the matter we get here.

The disgusting people open one's films at the frontier. They let the light into one roll of every three (I not being there to stop them) and I can't replace them as the importation is forbidden.

1 *August*, 1931.

Darling B,

I think I am really going to-morrow. I shall never get fit till I am right away, and I feel I can leave as they are getting a trained nurse to take over. I have done ten nights [nursing] on end, and feel rather worn out.

Just had such a nice note from Mr. Hinks wishing me luck and saying I must *lecture* to the R.G.S. when I get back: a nice suggestion but more terrifying than any Assassins. I feel everyone is so kind this year, something is bound to go wrong.

I have been seeing Luristan bronzes—a lovely little silver bodkin I should like but £2 is too much for me. They are very expensive— naturally perhaps as the last two people who went after them with a bag of money (very stupidly) got knocked on the head and killed.

I have a packet of medicines for distribution among the poor. An old Jewish doctor who deals in antiques did them up for me with a list of suitable complaints for each. It was a depressing sight to see his operating theatre: a sort of antique executioner's table with huge crank to turn it up or down and two grooves down the length for the victim's limbs, an ancient soiled cushion embroidered in gold and full of stains at the head, and bottles round about covered with the

[203]

dust of ages. His son an intelligent young fellow just back from America. They promised to let me attend the Sabbath prayers at the tomb of Esther.

QAZVIN, 3 *August*, 1931.

I suppose the adventure has started, though it does not feel like it yet, and Aziz is not here but only *expected* which in Persia is a dubious word. I left Hamadan at 9 p.m. and it was rather lovely going through moonlight with the barren open ridges very soft and dim on the horizon. The Public Prosecutor who sat with two friends at the back of the car offered me a rug, which I refused in my ignorance. We stopped at Rezan, where I had lunch last year : the gentlemen dined but I sat outside with a tumbler of tea and watched the process of opium smoking inside over a brazier : a talkative Bakhtiari with a little pointed nose and bristling moustache was doing the work, holding a coal to the hole in the bowl where the opium is and prodding it with a pointed bodkin at intervals, while his friend did the smoking and rolled his eyes about. It was a Rembrandtesque sort of scene with their shadows on the white-washed wall and I wished I could photograph.

We kept on breaking down and it was very cold, and my cold and fatigue returned so that I was glad enough when daylight came and showed us to be on the great plateau of Qazvin. I gave the three travellers bread and they gave me tea : and the Public Prosecutor invited me to call in Teheran, he being a philologist and possessor of rare books and M.R.A.S. printed on his card, which is Member Royal Asiatic Society. He had a nice face in spite of lots of gold teeth and little shaving, and the long, narrow fingers you think only exist in Elizabethan pictures but which one sees quite often in Persia.

I went to bed here and stayed there and feel a bit better to-day, and received a visit from Mr. Sookias and the doctor very charming —only my Persian is really inadequate. He tells me of the castle of Lamiasar in Rudbar which, if really *it*, is very important being one of the Assassin castles mentioned in the chronicles and not yet identified. So I shall go and look, if only Aziz will turn up. I am going to be short of money again I believe, but Mr. Summerhayes says he will come to the rescue anywhere where there is a telegraph office to send to.

I had lunch with the doctor and landlord, who took my volume of

[204]

Sa'di and started reading verses with great enthusiasm, not shared by the rest: he is an irascible impulsive little man with an eye to business, so the poetry was rather pleasant to discover.

Very hot here and mosquitoes and sandflies and noise. Nothing but a quilt on one's bed so that one is either suffocated or bitten. And the water supposed to be unsafe.

6 August, 1931.

Still here. One does learn to be patient in Persia—everyone so amiable and full of kindness, but nothing gets *done*. Aziz hasn't turned up, but I hope another *charvardar* will appear by to-morrow.

I had a nice morning in the bazaar with the doctor's son who is going to be a chemist: first we went and bought a rope and a little blue and white cotton saddle-bag to keep tea and sugar in; then we got six handkerchiefs of green and blue striped silks, and six towels woven in Yezd at 7½d. each (not very good cotton). Then a knife, a lantern and a mirror; then a lihaf, which is a dark blue cotton quilt for 4s. 7½d.: then almonds, raisins, tea from Lahijan that 'smells like attar'; candles, matches, and seven cones of sugar; then a little purse for cash and a porous water-jug and earthenware mug. All this took two hours and was very amusing. The ropes come from Isfahan: each place has its own industry.

I do wish I could be off now. The bank manager and his wife invited me to tea and they are very kind, though disapproving: it is funny, but my wanderings seem to be a test of most people's social status and some always disapprove. Mrs. — told me that for *her* part she liked looking after husband and children (quite nicely): "I have neither one nor the other," I explain humbly.

7 August, 1931.

I hope I really am off this time. Ismail—sent by Aziz—turned up, looking more dilapidated even than I remembered him: I have bought him a safety razor for when we part. He has tied up all my things in saddle-bags so I hope we shall really start to-morrow dawn.

I am just looking at some Persian pigs in the yard: they are fiercer than any domestic pig I have ever seen except the kind near Perugia. They are running amok among the cars.

I had a shock last night. Feeling very hot and rather out of

[205]

sorts I took my pulse: found it 88 instead of normal 72. Much perturbed on the eve of a journey, I pulled out thermometer: found temperature perfectly normal—evidently the height here affects one: shows what a difference it must make to people living here.

I have bought two knives, two purses, two dolls and 400 doses of quinine (as presents), five tins of biscuits and six of ovomaltine—so ought to be all right. One does get surprises. "You will like Takht-i-Suleiman," says the Hakim: "There is a watering-place with hot springs where people go from the coast," and it isn't even marked on the map.

I have just been interrupted by the dear old doctor coming to say good-bye with a tin of sweets and two handkerchiefs: he is such a nice man, and so like the Colonello.

Captain Peek has not been able to get me a bearing on the far mountain—fearfully annoying; it is too hazy. He was in Baghdad and told me about Lionel Smith who was offered a game of hockey: they thought him rather good, and were very kind and offered to put him in their eleven and asked where he had played before. "I have played for England," said he quietly.

IMAMZADEH, ZEINABAR, 11 *August*, 1931.

I will not be sending this till long after the trouble is over so may as well tell you that I *know* I have dysentery and may have malaria: it is inconvenient as it is out of reach of anyone, a little Imamzadeh looking out across the valley from a lovely little nest of fields and fruit trees to the absolute barrenness of the Rudbar hills. It is above the mosquitoes, and the village is some way off, and altogether a peaceful place to be ill in. I am only disquieted by the fact that my dysentery vaccine seems to be only half the first dose prescribed and the emetine has got lost: however, I have *mast* (Yoghourt) and hope for the best, though it is rather depressing. I fear I am getting too old for this sort of thing, alas—or too much of a crock anyway.

The castle was a marvellous find. I hope I may not die before writing about it, for it *was* the missing castle, and it is a grand place, covering the slanting top of a hill (about 1,200 by 400 feet) surrounded by cliffs, with battlements still left here and there and a passage built down to the river about 800 feet below. It is really a fine place. I hope the photos come out.

27 August, 1931.

Just breaking camp—my second night out above the villages, and very wonderful—a high corrie enclosed on three sides; a great drop to the river below whose noise comes up with the wind intermittently: absolutely no other sound except a little shriek of bats: and the moonlight spreading slowly like a fan first in the sky behind Takht-i-Suleiman, then down the walls of our amphitheatre and across the valley on to Narghiz and Syalan and Salambar. It was very cold. This place is over 10,000 feet and the col we are climbing is about 14,000 feet. I have renounced the climbing of Solomon's throne: the mules can get no nearer than eight hours away, and I cannot do it—but am sorry. I may get a more accessible mountain farther east.

It is a wonderful feeling to be here where the map puts only little trees (which don't exist), and to be plotting out my camp every night and marking the passes as I cross.

EVENING ABOVE BARIR.

Have got over the pass. Our camp was beautiful, but cold by morning—nothing to what this is going to be. A little circle of stones about 2 feet high set against a rock, where three shepherds live with 600 sheep or so. There is a wooden bowl for kneading bread, a cooking pot, a pewter jug for water and a bowl to scoop it with, an iron scraper for the pot, shearing scissors and sacks of wool, half a carcase to eat off, some sheepskins and a felt rug to sit on. The little shepherd boy in square felt tabard and black sheepskin cap is drowsing, and the Refuge of Allah is boiling up water for tea. But it is going to be cold: the valley steep and rocky, nothing but stone and water and lavender; we came down from the pass alongside a long couloir of snow. This is over 10,000, the pass about 14,000 feet. Marvellous view: all new ridges eastward, with pleasant dark patches of jungle and smooth white mist from the sea.

I was exhausted. It was four hours from our high camp, like a wall, so that the mules had great difficulty. I just couldn't go uphill because my heart is still so feeble, did it slowly and resting, and riding whenever possible regardless of cruelty to animals. It was worse because Aziz would get on to the other mule whenever I did—and is much heavier.

The wind blew on the pass and made all my bearings doubtful, and anyway it is very difficult to know what points to choose: I fear I shall make a fearful muddle, especially as I believe my map has put in one extra river and one extra range that do not exist.

28 August, 1931.

I was rather shocked to find yesterday, that instead of being on a little river so far, I thought, unexplored, I was on a pink dotted track which ought to have been farther east. To-day, however, I hope that the mistake is the map maker's and arises from the fact that there are two passes with nearly the same name which he has got mixed. And so I still hope that this is my own river, rushing along white and green through the first trees of the jungle.

I really hope this new pass is a discovery, as it is quite a good one. The valley most lovely, the trees seem to know they grow for their own pleasure, they stand so gracefully, well spaced on the hillsides and near the stream—and not too many, for the naked mountain-sides come in among them. They are all sorts, chestnut (without fruit), sycamore, wild medlar, old thorn trees, ash and beech. A warm wind comes up the valley: we are off the heights.

I feel thoroughly ill after yesterday's effort but hope it is just fatigue and nothing more: I am five days off Teheran now, the farthest I am going, so it is a bad place to get ill in.

Did I tell you that yesterday I saw the vision of Demavend, far away across many ranges, a great cone cut off by clouds and striped with snow?

LAHU, 29 August, 1931.

The pot is cooking over an earthen fireplace filled with logs in a place called Lahu, a big village in Kalar Dasht which is quite a well-known place. I feel sad, because I didn't come down the little road marked in red: the map maker put an extra range of hills in out of his head—very disgusting—but I have done a traverse that was not mapped and added about half a dozen villages.

They have had Captain Fortescue here some years ago: I suppose he made the red lines all over the place, but did not discover Kalar, which is an important place whose locality is I believe uncertain, but which I find is buried under a mound in this place. I have also got the contents of a grave for 5s.: two jugs and a spear head—very

[208]

fascinating and breakable. They added a blue jug from Teheran, which I bought though I did suspect it: then heard privately from Aziz all about it, so I returned it with a grand air saying I found it was not antique.

BRITISH CONSULATE, HAMADAN, 2 September, 1931.

Dear Mrs. Stark,

You know that after your daughter had so kindly helped us here with the nursing of our small girl, she left for Alamut.

From there I got a note on Saturday last to say she had been rather unwell but had got up higher to a village where a doctor was stopping and that she was much better already.

On that same day a wire came for her from Creston to tell of the death of Robert Stark. I wired then to Qazvin for further news of Miss Stark and on hearing good reports of her I sent on the bad news which may reach her in the mountains. I am also writing to her at Teheran.

As communication from her may be slow, I write to tell you of her whereabouts and to offer my sympathy.

Yours sincerely,

C. H. SUMMERHAYES.

PS. Our little girl is now much better.

DELIR, 3 September, 1931.

Darling B,

We have got over the high pass and are down to 9,500 feet again. I feel rather exhausted with height this year: I don't know what it was, but it was five hours up from 8,000 feet level and a marvellous view: Takht-i-Suleiman most beautiful in the N.W. with a semi-glacier curling down round him: a ridge of peaks joining us to him, and another ridge cutting us off from the rivers that flow into the Sardabrud, which we were going along the other day. I see where the map man's mistake was: he thought a ridge was a watershed and it is only a sort of spur: at least I think so.

Our guide had one of the first guns ever made, inlaid with horn. He shot it off and no disaster occurred. I was taking bearings. I was unable to walk much in that air: "The scent of the hills affects one's heart," said Aziz: anyway I had to ride, though it was hard on the mule: as steep as a wall, zigzag, the pass is only open a month or two, and used chiefly for salt from this side. We met donkeys with little green apples near the top and bought some. Spent three and a half hours up there looking at all the world, from the throne of Solomon to the Teheran passes and the far open valley of Talaghan shut in by a southern saw ridge like a wall rising in little waves. And the sky was clear with brilliant clouds throwing shadows : the Chalus valley under a sea of mist shredded itself against the hills there, and the great hollow of the pass was sand coloured with our track zig-zagging up to us, for it is one of those long passes, wearisome to go over, with a little barren world of its own of small bumps and hollows at the top.

A whole system of ridges comes down this side, spreading like a hand from our hill, and we came down very steep for three hours, with only a pause at some shepherd tents on the way. The man there was very friendly; sat with his long pipe by the tent-opening with women, children, puppy and baby kid nearby. The tents are poor things; only a bit of wool over a pole above one of the low compounds of loose stones: the hut circles of Dartmoor must have been such.

Ever so much love to you both. Am longing for letters next week. My watch stopped: I know neither the day of the week nor the time, and am not very certain of the day of the month.

DÒHTAR QAL'A, 8 *September*, 1931.

We are up by the pass to the plain—really near the end, about time, as I have to pick lice out of my clothes and my hands are all skinned by the sun. But the view from here is so beautiful, one forgets all the rest. Takht-i-Suleiman is high up in the sky about fifteen miles away, with a deep valley and six ranges between, all rising grandly up to him as if it were a crowd carrying him on their shoulders. He is the only one with snow running down his side. To-morrow from the pass I shall take my last bearings, and hope that they may turn out *probable*, when I come to work them out. I don't think I have got any result of any moment from my journey; but it has been wonderful practice and I have done useful though un-obtrusive work if my bearings come right, for I will have got the geography of the top of this valley complete and the names and position of Takht-i-Suleiman and his group—all of which were com-pletely wrong and their names not mentioned. It is a tiny piece of work, but I hope it will be good all the same. It will not be a lecture at the R.G.S.: a terrible fate pursues my photos—my three *best* films all spoilt: yesterday I discovered the last of these tragedies, all up the little unmapped valley of Shahrud: I nearly wept. We had a wearisome day, after leaving the pleasant leafiness of Joistan, which is a big village and has a lovely carved doorway (glass not being used at all and the woodwork pasted over with paper for warmth from autumn to spring). I had supper there with ladies who winter in Teheran: the girls sang to the lute, or 'Tar', and the old grandmother, with hennaed hair and blue eyes (a speciality of this Talaghan valley) sat on the floor smoking a hubble-bubble which reached high above her head.

It was a nice place to stay in: a charming gay old lady who had broken her shoulder smoked opium to cure the pain, and washed my clothes for me and gave me heaps of hot water in the cow-stable, my only really satisfactory wash except the rather doubtful bath at Bijeno. The only drawback was that the three children were all ill with a mysterious epidemic, and as one eats out of their plates and sleeps or sits on their rugs, it makes one rather anxious.

We had a two-hour walk this morning up to the famous castle [Dohtar Qal'a], which is only a little five-sided fort with a tower to guard the pass, but has at least the merit of not being entirely underground. Instead of going on as we should, to get to Teheran tomorrow, I let myself be deluded into a two-hour expedition to see a water reservoir: it turned out to be much farther, down a precipitous exhausting hillside, and was only a disgusting cave with bad stalactites. We crawled in through a hole and got wet, and I hate caves anyway. By the time we got back, Teheran to-morrow was done for, so I stayed here and trotted off with the old man who keeps the tea-shop to see a graveyard in a lovely neck of the hills—how it got there and whose it is, is a mystery, and I think it is not very old (nor is the castle): but there are some green stones, squared, with inscriptions which I photographed: they do not belong to this hillside, and *may* throw some light.

What really interested me was the legend of a man whose two sons died before him, and he buried them here and left the place: and as it happens, the first Assassin's two sons died before him (he had them killed) so I thought it worth looking at. It was a pleasant ride —along high, shallow grassy dips, a sort of shelf, with the big valley and its opposite ranges below and visible at every opening. And from the pink limestone rocks, five ibex, two mothers with three young, crossed our path not two hundred yards ahead, and stopped to look at us and ran up the opposite side into the rocks again. Little white crocuses are everywhere, even on the path; and buttercups in the green patches where there is water; and partridges clucking in the rocks and running along in dozens; and whenever a load of hay goes by it smells of sage or mint, or lavender or thyme, or other delicious things I don't know. But the grass is mostly thorns, and the colour of it yellow with the red earth showing through.

This lovely little castle has nothing round it for miles except the little tea-shop—just tall enough to get into with a stoop, with roof of thorns covered with mud: the mules stop on their way over the pass, and the old man is a keen old boy with blue eyes and a jolly smile, and a sportsman: can see ibex miles away and looks with longing at my field glasses. There are little patchy fields in the hollow where once the village was to which the near graveyard belongs, but the people only stay to gather their harvest and go and in less than a month the pass will be shut for the winter. At Parachan, they told me, they are imprisoned for three months: if they get sick they die, if they run out of anything they do without. They shut themselves in with their cattle and wait till the snow melts.

It is now cold again: and getting dark. I must go in with the little family of muleteers in the dark little house.

10 September, 1931.

Got down to the main road. The valley got dull and hot, and we ended by plodding along the semi-made road: I have learnt the art of sleeping on the saddle just not deeply enough to fall off. The Refuge of Allah went on with the mules, but Aziz and I stayed by the main road, bought a slab of bread with spitted meat and tomatoes, and waited for the bus. It is only 9½d. for twenty-four miles to Teheran, but not worth more: we broke down twice, and altogether felt that civilization is too much trouble.

DIARY. TEHERAN TO SAVEH

25.9.31.

Start 6.45 p.m. Long wait at Teheran gate; police at little tables with oil lamps either side lighting up a bit of mosaic. Lorries lumber-

ing by; white and green lights; mules; dust. Like the Via Appia outside; two men with a samovar sitting in a tomb. Dog-tooth Sassanian
brick-work: little round tombs, square, domes, all pale in the moonlight: hills sharp above the mist or dust.

A col crosses the barren little mountain range with telegraph poles.
Motor has to cool on the top. Cold wind comes in. 9.30 Hasanabad.
Good-looking caravansarai. Eating-place with raised platforms for
sitting under the trees outside, with rugs over them. People have
supper here. Steps up to rooms over gate. The caravansarais built
on the plans of the Sassanian palaces. All domes in this country with
little flat roof.

Mist over the lake of Qum.

Quarrel with the chauffeur whom they raced on the road; he
was driven off into the desert: police took them both—delay.

Reach Qum 3 a.m.

26.9.31.

Fellow traveller went to Teheran to pay fine for her son whose
car ran over small Russian boy of 12 by the gate and killed him. The
son in prison as well as fined. Lady says 'wa, wa, wa' with a shake of
the head but otherwise cheerful: nice capable managing woman with
black hair parted in middle and very sturdy: three sons and three
daughters married to various officers scattered over Persia. Takes
me through the chief street and back by bazaars to the door of Fatima's
mosque, where she leaves me. Friendly group nearly lets me over
the threshold; takes me round to side door; just letting me in to inner
court when young fanatic mulla comes out to upbraid them. No
Christians in Qum or Saveh, nor Bahai either. Qum so intractable
that it was given exemption from conscription for ten years by the
new Shah.

SAVEH, 27 September, 1931.

Darling B,

There is a most beautiful and famous old mosque here with a
minaret going straight up like a sausage on end, but all beautifully
covered with a delicate lacework of brick of which I hope to show
you photos. I had my first struggle with the police here, as I found

that one could not enter the mosque. I came here to get photos of
it, however, and get them I did, though I spent two hours in the
police barracks and two more sitting on the edge of a water reservoir
near the outside of the mosque. The police was one of those bullet-
headed officials with whom nothing is to be done: I saw that, if
I wanted to get anywhere, I must only make him more afraid of
me than of the populace. "Telephone to the Ambassador, if there
is any difficulty," I remarked in a lordly and unscrupulous way.
Finally he said I must get a permit from the governor. We went
this morning and found that my visiting card, sent last night, had
prepared a most amiable reception. I had refused to go without
knowing that he was ready to receive me, saying that: "I was not
accustomed to wait," and altogether made them put all the police
force at my disposal. The town by this time was quite friendly and
there was no sign of any trouble, and I spent over an hour in the old
disused mosque, photographing inscriptions. The mosques *can* be
entered now by very special people with government permits, but
it is still difficult otherwise.

This is Behruz'[1] native town. I did not find him, but two nephews,
and they are all very cordial and took me to lunch in their garden
of pomegranates. Saveh is famous for them and you never saw
anything more lovely than these wildernesses with the crimson fruit
and little streams running through. The carpet was spread; we sat
and ate water melons and figs and pomegranates so delicious you
would not know them for the horrid little things full of seed one has
in Europe. They got out their opium pipes, and a brazier was brought
and we were all as happy as can be.

They are all shocked and horrified at the price paid by the British
Legation for my place in the automobile—ten tomans instead of
three. I knew it was something of the kind, but could not say
anything about it—but it is cheaper to travel in one's own obscure
manner.

I meant to have left Teheran a day earlier, but the car was out of
order, at the last moment the garage put it off for the day. Nobody
worries about this in Persia and I have learnt the ways by now. The
five hours drive was eight, and we left at seven instead of five-thirty
so that I got to Qum at 3 a.m. and nowhere to sleep. A lady from
the back of the lorry took me with her to a sort of hostel for female

[1] My teacher.

[214]

pilgrims, surprisingly clean, so that I did not unpack my bed but slept on their mattress and pillow on the floor in a nice room with five doors which did for windows. As a matter of fact one comes up against insects and such far less often than one might expect.

28 *September*, 1931.

You would be surprised to see me now, sitting in a garage waiting-room for ladies, with a member of the Shah's family, her baby, little boy, servant, and six fowls in a cage. The Royal Lady has not combed her hair for the last week. I have provided a melon which we have shared; it was rather a mistake as all the skins are strewed about just off the edge of the rugs which the garage provided us with: perhaps it explains the proverb 'Do not put your feet out beyond your carpet'. The people have a fine reckless generosity in the way they put their rugs down for everyone on any occasion.

I had a hectic time leaving this morning, as the town of Saveh had just discovered that I bought pottery: the three best pots were got for 30s. while the Royal Mail and its passengers were waiting. Four are nearly complete, about a dozen more with large pieces missing: but all genuine and between A.D. 1200 and 1600: some really lovely bits, as good as the Persian exhibition—one interesting old tile of blue green glaze, a deer in relief, unfortunately its hind legs missing. They are all packed in two petroleum tins and I hope they get through. Anyway I know they are *genuine*.

The old mosque and minaret at Saveh are well worth a visit, but it *is* a business: a night on the road each way in places where Europeans don't often stop.

My host turned out an awful thief but otherwise nice. It is as my Royal travelling companion suggests when she says with enthusiasm: "The Moslems are *good*. They lie and they steal," she adds as an afterthought. Behruz was very nice, however, and not looking out for loot.

A good touch while we were having our picnic: the servant, a tall countryman with a red velvet skull cap braided with gold, came up when we had done and asked for a whiff of his master's pipe, which was given as a matter of course. It is extraordinary how much more democratic one could be if one did not worry about infections.

[215]

MALAYIR, 30 *September*, 1931.

I am *still* on the way to Hamadan—hoping to get there to-day for lunch, though by this time I have developed the sort of despairing fatalism which is the only way out of it in the East if you travel in the eastern way.

We finally left Qum at 7 p.m. after all sorts of affairs. I had arranged to go for four tomans and paid half: then the partner came and said it must be one toman more: I foolishly refused: we had a great deal of conversation and finally got a paper with the one toman added and a solemn promise to go soon: then I was misguided enough to follow somebody's advice and get a policeman to come and confirm the conditions: the policeman listened with a judicial air, went off with the garage people, and came back smiling: he had arranged everything, the fare was to be another toman above the last condition: so much for the assistance of authority. The motor however had now materialized: I was taken to its office, which is a sort of reception room where the passengers drink tea and the partners fight furiously over their accounts before every departure. I was furious too, but knew it was no good to do anything: I did get a small revenge however, for, when answering some question, I said in a loud voice that the bills at my garage were like babies—small to begin with and growing while you look at them: this joke pleased them all hugely and they kept on going up to the garage owner, clapping him on the back and repeating it to him, to his obvious annoyance. When the partner came and asked for a tip I was able to tell him with great politeness that I would have given it if I had been pleased with them but I wasn't: and so left, feeling better.

The next lorry has been my home for a day and two nights and is now laboriously getting under way for the next bit, as it goes south while I hope for another and better to Hamadan. You wouldn't believe so many different things would be wrong with one car. The first breakdown always occurs just outside the town and is a sort of indispensable beginning to a Persian journey. Then we had a more alarming trouble: the screw which kept the back wheel on, whether lost or only unsafe I don't know, but we went on, looking back at intervals to see if the wheel was still there. Then the clutch had to be changed—and so on. About midnight we stopped and I was given a bed made of two benches with quilts and was tucked in among all the sleeping passengers in the long room of the *chaikhana* by the *chaikhana* keeper, and very glad of the warmth. He pulled down one of his curtains to cover me.

In the morning early they all woke up and said their prayers: mostly pilgrims returning from Meshed, a patient and pleasant lot of people with a number of querulous veiled females whom one only heard vaguely asking for water to drink at intervals inside their cage, and hushing a little indiscriminate heap of babies. The passenger here is not a privileged being to be looked after: he has taken a share for the time being in the lorry or car and it is all one concern where everyone takes the good or bad as it comes: walks up the hills when the lorry is tired, and takes it as a matter of Fate when it breaks down. The driver was also the owner, a young Assyrian with a pleasant face but so much taken up with a young lady who said she was his wife that he was useless for anything else. We took a day more than even the local average over this bit of journey. It was an interesting land-scape for an hour or two—the waste salt lands with their domed villages at long intervals, built like the old Sassanian palaces, with little decorations in the mud that showed the trace of old beautiful brick models some time in the past. But I soon got tired of landscape of any description. We spent the morning mending the clutch: then five hours at the town of 'Iraq in a house where women walked about with very little on and where our driver's lady seemed much at home. They were kind and gave me a bed to sleep on and food to eat, but it was impossible to get the driver away until the afternoon: and two more breakdowns and a puncture, besides walking up the steep hill to save the lorry, made it night before we reached Malayir, where I still am in hopes of a car. It was annoying as there is an American doctor here, and if I had got in in time I would have gone and got at least a good bath and supper.

During the last puncture the lady and the Assyrian had a quarrel: the lady was pretty in a fierce and gipsy fashion: she had friends in Teheran she said: the driver tried to put his arm round her, and then being repulsed, sang Assyrian songs in a loud voice while the lady sat beside me in tears. They made it up however and decided to stay here the night instead of taking their passengers on to their destination. I found another bed like the night before and was un-fortunately given a lamp, which is always a mistake because of bugs. However, I was much too tired to set up my own things and further demoralized by discovering that my soap had been stolen. The landlord was distressed because I slept alone in the building. This was not really a worry to me and I slept like a log in spite of the dreary surroundings. But I *do* want a wash.

I came down into the yard and sucked a pomegranate on a carpet by the gate while my fellow travellers were getting into the car and the chauffeur was patching up a new puncture. "May you arrive to-night if it please God," said I, which pleased them, as it is supposed to be only an hour's journey away. The lorry is a Chevrolet and only a year old, so they told me: so that one wonders how it can pay them at a maximum of 1*d*. a mile per passenger.

HAMADAN, 2 October, 1931.

Dear Lionel,[1]

I have got your *lovely* bronzes. I went with a connoisseur in these matters to a little Jew in Teheran who collects them, and spent a glorious morning bargaining and have now had them packed up with my prehistoric pots and had them sent, as it means a long delay for permits. The bronzes came to £17 and a shilling or two, but I expect there will be about £1 more for the sending and squaring the customs, etc. (as it is more and more difficult to manage Persian regulations). But don't bother about this: I shall need the money far more when I come through England later on, and you had better see them first—and choose, for when I saw them I *couldn't* resist the temptation myself and got two knives and two axe heads. I enclose the pictures of both knives, practically exactly what I found, and one of an axe, though I was not able to get them with the animal mask on: you shall choose which you like best of both. Then there are two bodkins, and a bowl, and a little ibex something like the pegasus in the photo only not quite so good: and a bronze of two lions biting a mask which is better than this picture and very interesting because the face is so exactly like the Sumerian things. It was great fun, and it is nice to think that they will sit in your new house. I have also found you a present of blue silk for sofa cushions—so mind you leave room for them till I can bring them along!

I have just got here from a weary way round by Saveh and Qum; and travelling in lorries till I thought the landscape of Persia would never come to an end. But Saveh has a wonderful minaret of delicate

[1] Lionel Smith

[218]

brickwork well worth a visit, and I managed to induce the authorities to take me into the old mosque though it is closed to all Christians except those who are looking after Persian monuments. The population took it very nicely—even when the policeman carried out the 'minbar' for me to stand on and photograph inscriptions.

I am now going to Baghdad to await news from Canada and try to make plans. I thought I would go by way of Nihavend and try to get to Alishtar and see the Lurish graves, if I can dodge the Persian police: I think I can do it by going by mule instead of car: one will have to have a mule anyway from Alishtar to Kermanshah, as it is a desolate bit of country, and Mr. Summerhayes—who is a most encouraging Consul and *never* asks me why I have come to Persia— is looking out for a Lurish *charvardar* if possible who knows the tribes.

Arivederci.

TUSIRKHAN, 6 October, 1931.

Darling B,

This will be a surprise—it is to me, I meant to go quietly in a motor car, but a chance of a letter to a chief Lur was *too* much temptation and I am off to try and see where the bronzes are dug and to get photos and a skull. I think it can be managed if I dodge the police, and really the chief obstacle is my own feebleness. Mr. Summerhayes found me a *charvardar* called Hajji and two very lean horses who must be real optimists, for I can see no other reason for their continued enthusiasm in trotting with a pack over stones. We chose Hajji out of two others because of a charming smile minus one tooth; hope he lives up to it.

We went up by Ganj Namah and saw the cuneiform inscriptions, fresh as if cut yesterday. Mr. S sent his man in gold braid behind me, a funny mixture with my equipage: he will take back my news to-morrow.

We went up a 10,000-feet pass—very mild after my other ones: but then a long afternoon dipping into one shallow basin after another —a lovely fertile busy peaceful country, with no hard white roads: just blue figures digging or ploughing: the stubble strewn in the fields, the green autumn wheat sprouting, villages in vines and groves, and the long shallow bare ridges going away on every side to the horizon, all tawny. It has been twenty-two miles at least and I can hardly move, besides having a cold. But a chicken is cooking.

I am sitting near a mound which is being dug by two French archaeologists who have invited me to lunch and spend the night. I heard of them at Nihavend and walked up and presented myself, as it is on my road. I don't know what they are like, except that their appearance is almost as unkempt as mine.

I got to Nihavend after a very long exhausting day, tinkling along at a jiggly trot over one plain after the other, all shallow basins with rings of barren hills and long slow passes from one to the other. There was a wind raising high dust pillars and worrying one incessantly: my pack saddle rubbed my legs to pieces so that I have had to spend 7½*d.* on a new pair of stockings: and I had a cold in the head which made life a misery. A man we fell in with told us that we couldn't possibly get to Alishtar as the Lurs are shooting people on the pass. This didn't worry me so much, but my *charvardar* Hajji was very dubious because of his two horses I think. In spite of his assurances, I am convinced he has never been to Alishtar before.

However we got to Nihavend, a lovely green patch stretching across the head of a fertile plain, and an old ruined Moslem citadel on a spur of the low range. The hills of Luristan south in long barren ridges.

My first business was to manage the police. I went to Dr. Ibrahim, a Jew (there are near 600 in Nihavend and said to date from the Captivity), and found his son. Most helpful. There is usually something to be done with the young. He said he would find a Lur guide or one who knew the Lurs. The shooting is stopped either three weeks, one month or two months ago according to various versions. It wasn't the robbers' fault: they used to charge two tomans (4*s.*) for everyone going over the pass: two men with mules from Parisvan arrived with 5*d.* short, so naturally the Lurs shot them. This induced the government to put ten men with guns in the vicinity, so that—though unintentionally—the two men who tried to save their 5*d.* have made things much safer for me. This story cheered my *charvardar* and in the evening a man called Vali Khan, a nice-looking tall man with shiny eyes and eyebrows going upwards and nearly meeting over his nose, came along and offered himself and will take me as far as I wish to go.

The doctor's son meanwhile wanted to carry me off to the police

station. I had to use all my tact and most of my imagination. Told
him the police hated knowing beforehand if one is going to be killed:
if one did not go to them it is one's own and not their responsibility:
and it would mean telephoning to the Embassy at Teheran who,
though they would give all the orders necessary, might delay, and
meanwhile the Luristan governor was expecting me; and there would
be all sorts of questions if I was late—and I pulled out Dr. Cook's
letter to the governor and let them see the envelope, which finishing
touch settled the matter.

It was a very patriarchal Jewish household—grandparents, the
doctor, his daughters and their husbands and children; the patients
in a little outer room on one side of the court and the court itself
filled with maids who made pathetic efforts to sweep it at intervals.
I can't tell a Persian Jew from a Persian and they dress the same,
and say the Moslems are getting more and more tolerant of them.
They have two synagogues in Nihavend. They were so kind:
gave me sweets, manna, and nuts in sugar, and took me round the
bazaars which wind rather attractively up and down the hill, roofed
over with timber and full of people weaving or dyeing, or making
quilts, etc. Then up to the citadel where all the Lurs come with their
black cows carrying charcoal—but the suggestion of one for Alishtar
met with no response. If once one can overstep the boundary
between the townsfolk and the tribesman, all is well: but it is extraordinarily hard to do so. They see each other all their lives, do their
traffic and their shopping together, and yet have nothing to do with
each other.

My doctor gave me a glorious supper—chicken and rice and soup
and melons, with sour milk to drink. He had a room with chairs,
and stucco work over the doors, and painted glass cases for candles
over the mantelpiece, and pottery (rather a poor lot) in the upper
niches of the room: the lower were filled with all the oddments of
life, mirrors, books, dishes, lamps, clothes, and *never* dusted. Lots
of small tables and chairs and rugs. They put two sofas together,
and their best silk quilts and pillows, and I slept marvellously being
quite tired out. Left this morning after sunrise at seven-twenty, and
got here in less than three hours, over a low pass and along the fertile
land which is being ploughed for corn. Women were harvesting
cotton, and men preparing the ground for opium sowing, among
villages in trees here and there. Outside the villages are great mounds

of chaff where the winnowing is just over, giving an extraordinary feeling of opulence and contented life.

The mound here is all prehistoric. They are finding the simple patterns on the pots, and a rough clay, but hope to come lower down upon the birds and the fine pottery which is known as Nihavend. There are 100 men digging and it looks most fascinating; one of the Frenchmen lying on his tummy over a hole which is just being scooped out, to see what emerges. Dr. Contenau of the Louvre is doing this dig, but is away just now.

I told them of a beautiful tell I saw a day's ride from here, and they seem interested: it is a wonderful country where you can still ride about making archaeological discoveries.

It is very fascinating to sit here and look past the village poplars and willows to the ridge and the col beyond and think that is to-morrow's ride and all the unvisited country there—so near and so little known—though as a matter of fact the route is marked on the map and must have been done by two or three Europeans. But they are a wild people, the women with long shaggy ringlets and enormous head-dresses; the men in their white felt coats and caps with locks sticking out under them and fierce eyes and meeting eyebrows—driving down their little black cows.

ALISHTAR, 12 October, 1931.

I have discovered something. The plains of Alishtar and Khava, where I have spent four days, are *not* the site of the Luristan bronzes as Mr. Pope and Professor Godard think. All the things I have found are at very *earliest* Sassanian: the bronzes come from the hills—I shall have great difficulty in getting at them but hope to succeed. Another thing I believe is that the horse, whose origin is so mysterious, was *not* originally found here: none of the bronzes have horses, though cows, goats, and sheep figure largely and, of course, the horses were used as one can see by all their bronze bits: but I believe they were an importation which did not find its way into the very 'stylized' art of Luristan.

One can see the little goats browsing here now, exactly like their bronze effigies, and there are no horses here now. The goats are still drawn roughly on the walls of cottages. All the things are so pretty: two tassels where the tent is joined and makes an opening:

white circles and stars woven into its brown sides: the reed tent enclosure woven in patterns with canes and wool: the bright Khurramabad rugs: the tarnished gold round the ladies' jackets with their long sleeves hanging open from the elbow: and the enormous coloured head-dresses from Baghdad. It is interesting to see the Baghdad things, to show how Sumerian art once came up here.

This morning I called on the governor in the big square fortress dilapidated among its trees that once belonged (three or four years ago) to my host's brother. The governor was polite but suffering from malaria and spent the time asking questions about me in a sad voice. I was shown a coin, which I identified as Parthian with Greek writing. The chief of police was there, asking for my passport, but very amiable: the fact of my not being married was dismissed as usual—I am getting tired of it myself. The idea here is that I would make a nice second wife for Kerim Khan.

16 *October*, 1931.

We got at last to the tents of Abdul Khan. All the people friendly except the dogs. A pretty woman to whom I said good morning did not answer. "Your father a dog, did you not hear the Khanum's salaam?" said my guide, and the poor woman who had not understood couldn't get over it: she and another were walking along with little goatskins full of corn on their heads: they were both wives of one man, and very friendly about it. They look very pretty with their long locks and turbans and loose gowns, and the gold and beads worked on their sleeves, and strings of beads round wrists and neck.

There were a few trees near Abdul Khan's tents. He received me charmingly—though he is half a skeleton through malaria and opium and sits on a mattress in his tent with a bright rug over his shoulders and the little opium brazier before him. He knew a lot of Persian history in a vague way and reads translations of French novels. He was a great man in Dilfan: then had to flee from his enemy, the Emir Ophar farther south, who came and ruined the houses which his father had built—and he spent fifteen years in Nihavend and only came back with the soldiers three years ago—but laments the good days before government came to Luristan. It was rather pathetic.

"It will be well for those," he said, pointing to his two little nephews. "They will be civilized."

Yesterday I got a good photograph—a drove of mares over the plain—like the ancient days of Media: I hope it comes out.

I wish I could describe to you the beauty of colour here: the sky pink now, the land with a pink light beneath its faded yellow of grass or stubble—the glorious openness, these plains like great shallow bowls with ragged rims lifted to the sky. There are no particular places to put on the map, but the lands of this and that tribe; one does not know (though they do) where one ends and the other begins. And next year they will be wearing Pahlevi hats. Already Abd' Ali did not dare to come to Harsin because they would tear up his overcoat. The white felt coats are forbidden. And soon the first car will appear on the new motor road which now travels along with such pleasant loneliness.

I am now sitting cross-legged with two lanterns beside the Sardar (head of police), while the *mirza*, his account book on his knees, joins in the argument, and Sardar is trying to convince a stubborn-looking Lur, who is being told to do something he doesn't want. I like the wild Lurs, but also feel that it is a hard and rather fine job to try and rule with law and order. There are six posts of six men from the far col of Khava to here, about twenty or thirty miles. (The obstinate man is now looking very puzzled while the *mirza* tries to find a comparatively clean finger to put ink on so that he may sign his mark on paper.)

TUDARU, 17 October, 1931.

I have got here. To ride up a long empty valley knowing that there is a possibility of a bullet from behind a stone was very exhilarating though Hajji gets gloomier and gloomier.

Unluckily Amanullah is away at Alishtar and we sat in rather a dubious-looking crowd. One has to sit on one's belongings like a hen on her eggs. The sheikh's cousin is here, a merry old ruffian who has shown a distressing liking for Mr. Summerhayes' *abba*. And as soon as my guide got here he smoked three opium pipes, which makes him very unreliable.

They all smoke opium here. Keram says he took to it when government took his gun away and prevented his going hunting in the hills. "We are all made as women now," says he—and adds that I cannot believe the glory of Luristan three years ago: "one was murdered for half a toman."

[224]

There was an amusing instance of the civilization of Luristan the other day in the tent of Abdul Khan. An old bandit-looking Lur said affectionately to his neighbour: "You are *bendisi*."

"What is *bendisi*?" they all asked.

"*Bendisi* is a French word to express affection," said he.

Fantaisie was what he meant, it dawned upon me.

I took an affectionate farewell of the *sardar*—a really nice man, although he does have a picture of three naked ladies bathing pasted inside his silver cigarette-case. He very nearly proposed to me. All I could give him was my water-bottle, ginger biscuits, and condensed milk, besides a little cold cream.

I have just called on Amanullah's wife—a lovely creature under her enormous turban, with little plaits hanging down and fine black eyebrows like bows, so beautifully drawn. She apologized for having no furnishing to the tent: "as they have put it all in the part of the country where there are police." The way people examine one's belongings here is rather disquieting.

HARSIN, 18 *October*, 1931.

It is very disappointing—a grave is not forthcoming: the only way would be to stay here about a month and pay for a lot of digging. I hope I have found out something worth while, but not nearly what I hoped, and even if the skull is good I fear it is not the right sort of skull.

We did not have a very good night. Hajji in abject terror: came up as I was lying down to sleep to beg me to sleep lightly—that we were surrounded with thieves. He woke up Keram Khan at intervals to say he saw bandits on the mountain slope in the starlight, and swears that a woman was stealing round for the horses when he made a noise and frightened her away. I thought that as there was no way of escape, if one had to have one's throat cut it would be nice to have it done in one's sleep, but I was visited by insects, fell asleep late, and only woke with a gentle light of dawn on the mountains and all my belongings still safe around me.

The people were quite friendly by the time our supper came and we had all been sitting in a circle round the fire and talking about suttee, and astronomy, religion, the British constitution, and antiques —a most elevated conversation I thought to take place outside the pale of civilization. As a matter of fact the Lurs seem much more

[225]

men of the world than the people of Elburz. A rather pretty touch: one of the little Lur girls saw my map case, which looks very like a Qurân in its cover, and took it up and kissed it, asking me if it was "my book?"

We came down rather late in the morning to this famous graveyard—while Keram walked along and told us about the war here three years ago: how he was on the Government side and nearly died of hunger and thirst, as the other Lurs surrounded him and held the water; how he made signals, and food was dropped in bags from aeroplanes, but the *other* Lurs picked it all up while Keram's people could only look on. "It was a good time then," he ended up unexpectedly.

The little black Lurish cattle were all over the hills among looted graveyards. I asked the price: a horse is 50 tomans (£5), a cow 15 (30s.), sheep and goats 5 (10s.) a pair.

I can hardly understand anything the Lurish women say. They came to look at me yesterday, and refused to believe that I was a woman, to dare to come among them. "She is more than a man," said Hajji with really pathetic conviction. He does not dare to say that he is afraid, having been teased.

All this bit of country used to be jungle and has been burnt for charcoal. It is quite warm, with tamarisks in the valley bottom. The zone of the horses ends with the warm country, so that I feel inclined to think they came from the south after all. There seems no trace in the flat cold plains which would have been so suitable for them if they came from north or east.

HARSIN, 19 October, 1931.

Got to Harsin down the pass from the plateau—rather sad to come away from it all, but glad of the prospect of a little civilization. Even Harsin, however, seems never to have seen an Englishwoman and we had a procession of small boys trying to pull my pony's tail as we went round searching for the motor road and garage. The garage was so full of donkeys with packs that there was no room at all for a car. One car seems to go to and fro in the day, but not till tomorrow, so it looks like sleeping here on a little ledge above the donkeys, as the one room is filled with travelling Harsinis.

I got rescued from my garage by the director of the Harsin telephone who came to call and took me to his house where a nice young wife and two infants live. From there I telephoned to Mr. Hoyland the consul and asked him to send a car—regardless of expense. The car couldn't come the same day as it was late: there is a mountainous stretch along the road, and a cavern overlooking it, whence five days ago some robbers came and looted a car, so that they only go by daylight now. In fact Harsin is a lawless neighbourhood: it was near here that the two Jew merchants were murdered five months ago: the murderers were caught, but denied, but one of their wives gave them away.

Anyway it was a lovely drive from there early in the morning. We forded the Gamasiab, a big river full of water now that there is no irrigation being drawn off for the fields: we had to wrap up the machinery in thick felt so that the water should not get through, as it washed well over the footboards.

During my last night in Luristan the horses got hungry and the Lurs went off to get straw for them at about 1 a.m. The horses here eat straw, maize and corn when oats are scarce. But the Lurs love them, and treat them like people and when a horse dies they say to its owner: "But you are in health," and condole with him just as they do for the death of a relation.

We rode away on very friendly terms and the Kadkhuda's son rode with us to the next camp to sell a plate he had there. He looked very fine on a good black pony with green shagreeny leather bridle and pistol cases and silver pommel. We still went over great downs, with the shoulder of 'Forty Thieves' on our right and groups of oak (?) trees here and there, up over rolling passes towards Harsin, with my valley and the country where the bandits are not domiciled all spread out behind us across the Ghizarud valley.

Keram went along telling me stories. First of all about our night among the Ittivend which really was more dangerous than I had realized as one of the guests there was an Ittivend whose brother Keram had killed. Keram did not feel happy about it and asked him to be removed to some other place for the night: the man apparently put his hand on Keram's back to feel for his money; Keram quickly asked, "Why do you put your hand there": "I didn't,"

[227]

said the man. His brother had been banditing at the time of the incident; he came up to Keram on a pass and asked for his horse and gun. Keram was in a bad position for shooting, so turned and fled, and his horse got shot under him from the back: he turned as the horse fell and killed the bandit; but it was unfortunate meeting his brother in this way. He got up and left, however, and the disturbance at night was not his doing, but was a woman creeping up to steal from my luggage. Keram told me that the Lurs pride themselves on their stealing: when they were conquered two years ago and the Persian general was camping with 1,800 men at Tudaru where I had slept, the Lurs crept in at night and stole his gun and all his clothes. In spite of the guards, they got in again the night after, and took his blanket off him and got away just as he woke up.

When we got near the col which overlooks Harsin, Keram asked me if I would mind his not going right down as he had not been into the town since two years ago when he and the inhabitants had a fight.

"If I had a gun I would not mind: but I am a woman now," said he.

"How was the fight?" said I. "Who began it?"

"I did," said Keram; "but it was their fault; they said things they shouldn't: it was a caravanserai, we had words, I shot one of them, and went home to a house I had in Harsin. All the Harsinis came round in a crowd and asked me to leave the lands of Harsin. I said I wouldn't and we began to shoot, tik tak, all night: the house had high walls, they could not get in. We went on shooting all day long. They knew I smoke opium and hoped to get me then, but when the time came and I wanted my pipe, I put my wife at the little hole through which I was shooting and told her to go on: and so she did, and killed one man while I smoked my pipe of opium: then I went on again. When it was dusk I sent a friend to slip through and tell the tribe to come down to help. We kept it up all night: early in the morning we heard shooting from the hill: tik tak—all the Kakavands were coming down to help me. The Harsinis scattered away and my wife saddled my horse and I went up to the tribe. But since then I have not been again among those Harsinis, may their fathers burn."

"I hope you have kept your wife," said I, "she seems one of the right sort."

"I have her now," said Keram, "I am very fond of her. She fights like a man. Those days were good," he added sadly.

I was sorry to part with Keram. He had a charming twinkling smile, and was quite fearless, and a real connoisseur in raiding.

Did I tell you the story of the Armenian governor's seven pigs? I'll repeat it anyway: it is so like Benvenuto Cellini! The governor was Sarhangi Gaukhan, the man who betrayed Mir Ali Khan at Alishtar, and then lived in his fortress there. And he kept seven tame pigs and sent them out to root about among the rocks. Keram saw them there, and never thinking that even an Armenian would keep such abominations, thought they were jungle pigs: he shot six, but the seventh got the bullet in its leg and went limping home to the castle. "What is this?" said the governor as he came riding out. "One of seven jungle pigs I have just shot," said Keram innocently. And that is why his gun was taken away from him for the second time.

I gave Keram my old fur coat and my watch to take to the police sardar, who apparently expressed a liking for it (shows how convenient it is to travel with only 3s. 6d. watches), and we parted on the col with Harsin and its gardens below and the downs and peaks of Luristan behind me.

BAGHDAD, 24 October, 1931.

It felt very like coming home to reach Baghdad yesterday morning: the river sparkling in the sun, and New Street looking quite neat and smart when you come to it from Persia. I had a good night in the train, but am not yet beginning to feel really rested: it always takes about a week. It is nice to come to a comfy house, and Léonie (Chapman) is a nice child—just twenty and very serious over her housekeeping. I found her at breakfast, having been up since four o'clock getting her husband off for his shooting. They came back with large quantities of black partridge, Mr. Chapman, Captain Woodhouse (a brother-in-law), and Mr. Oxford—Major Young's A.D.C. —who had a message inviting me to dine on Monday to meet King Ali who is supposed to be the future King of Syria. Kind of them to ask me so soon!

Léonie took me to lunch with Jamil Bey Baban, a Kurd of the family of the lords of Suleimania, and a delightful man who luckily talks Persian, for my Arabic has gone for the time being. He said that when I come out again, he himself will take me to Kurdistan.

We sat for hours, for it turned out that the invitation to lunch was invented by the Chapmans' servant, who had belonged to the Babans and was anxious to show his old master's hospitality but had omitted to tell them so. All went well however: they made great efforts, and by two-thirty we had rice and a hastily murdered chicken, and little greasy rissoles, while the daughter and son, a boy of twelve, fair as an English boy and just as keen on football, sat and talked. We came away feeling rather fatigued, and this evening have to go to dance at the Carlton with Wing Commander Grahame whom I don't know (beginning ten-thirty, when I should like to go to bed). My Alamut came out in *The Cornhill*, October.

28 October, 1931.

The dinner at the Youngs was great fun. Besides them and their brothers-in-law the Woodhouses, and a nice relation Miss Olivier, there were the Drowers, the Lloyds, and the King, Ali. We all curtseyed. It is extraordinary how a chair or something always gets just behind one when one wants to curtsey. The King is a rather sad, most gentle and dignified little figure in his long black *abba* and white *keffieh*: he has charming manners, and a beautiful sad old face not meant for fighting. I sat opposite him, on Major Young's left, who talked about mountaineering and antiques all through dinner. Sir Kinahan Cornwallis, Mr. Edmonds and the A.D.C. completed the party, and after dinner we had an Indian conjuror who ate fire and did a horrid trick, fastening a big stone by little metal cups to his *eyelids* and lifting it up. What I liked best was his pet mongoose tied to a string by which he pulled it out of a bag: the mongoose as soon as it got out turned round and ran back into the bag, looking so like a mechanical toy that it was absurd. He was a very good conjurer, and King Ali looked really nervous by the time we reached the fire eating.

My room is being whitewashed. I hope to be in next week. Meanwhile am here in luxury at the Drowers'. What contrasts I do live in. But I do enjoy a private bathroom of my own when I get it.

Dearest Herbert,

A terrible tragedy has just occurred—the day before yesterday. There is a very nice Iraqi girl, a daughter of the Sa'dun who was Minister and committed suicide two years ago. He had arranged a marriage for her with a good man of Baghdad. The rest of the family and tribe however were against it, as they said the man was of a family originally slaves and not fit for a Sa'dun: they made a formal protest to government, asking that the girl be married to one of her cousins as is the custom. However the protest did not succeed, and the girl's mother and some others carried out Sa'dun's wish and married her in Stamboul to this Abdulla, and they came back a month ago most radiantly happy.

On Saturday a cousin, an old man about sixty, walks into the office where Abdulla was one of the heads of the Ministry of Interior—sits down, waits till the people there go out as is customary: a clerk enters with a letter to sign: Abdulla turns away to read it: and the old man puts five bullets into him at close range, nearly blowing his head off, and killing him on the spot: then, while the clerks all bolted from the building, sits down and smokes a cigarette and waits. The question now is whether he is to be hung by Civil Law, or whether he will get off under tribal law. The feeling in the town is rather in his favour then otherwise— he is only criticized for having done the deed in a government office. "He might at least have waited till Abdulla was leaving the building and getting into his car." Apparently the family had planned to kill also the girl, her mother, and another relative who had encouraged the marriage, but so far have not succeeded.

14 *November*, 1931.

I am still in hectic work over my map, which has to have all the heights and form-lines fixed by Tuesday. A nice man, the map expert here who is off to do the Southern desert, came and looked at it; he took it quite seriously, and said I had done all I could to fix the positions, though I ought to have relied less on the actual maps and found more certain fixed points.

Captain De Gaury told me he was a talker, but I did not expect his call to last from 5 p.m. to 9 p.m. I got faint with hunger and did not know what I should do when it came to bedtime.

The High Commissioner elected to arrive just in the middle of the polo match: the A.V.M. was supposed to meet him and, as the landing-place is quite near the polo ground, they were to dash off as soon as they saw the aeroplanes. Two aeroplanes came sailing down one hour before the expected time: Mrs. Ludlow Hewitt sure it was the H.C., but the A.V.M. was just umpiring the game and refused to be torn away till the A.D.C. rode up to remonstrate, and they dashed off long after the H.C. must have landed.

3 December, 1931.

The river was so lovely to-night in the sunset—very still and full, and yellow with mud from rain up north, and three little boards filled with candles floating down in mid-stream, a votive offering to St. Elias.

4 December, 1931.

My dearest Venetia,

I am just off now to see my map: it is being done by the R.A.F. here, and to be sent to the Survey of India: I feel it is like the Day of Judgement: one's mistakes being recorded into a permanent form.

We had great excitements here over the visit of the French colonial minister: all the heads of departments waiting three hours on the aerodrome for his arrival before M. Lepissier the French representative produced a telegram which gave the hour as G.M.T. (Greenwich Mean Time): he had paid no attention to these alphabetical details and got the whole programme started three hours too soon. Altogether there was one fiasco after another, including the borrowing of the High Commissioner's launch without asking him and flying the French flag on it: the first he knew of it was looking out of window and seeing the phenomenon on the Tigris outside. And that was not even the end, only the rest is kept as a private joke for the secretariat.

I have a fear this may be my last year in the East. All my money except £80 a year or so, seems to be in Brazilian loans. I don't know what will happen. But it is no good to worry—and meanwhile I feel that these last three years have been thoroughly well spent: that is always a satisfaction.

[232]

Darling B,

They have had great Economy meetings these days. First one for the men, where the only brilliant suggestion seems to have been that of reducing the *servants'* wages: and now the women, who wish to reduce the consumption of whisky but seem doubtful as to its feasibility. Meanwhile they had a very expensive tea at the Residency. I was not asked, being I imagine considered economical enough as it is.

They are having a little war in Kurdistan: it has been a secret for some time so I did not write, though Mrs. Chapman told me about it. The Sheikh of Barzan, near Suleimania, got the Iraqi rear-guard, killed some, captured twenty-nine, and prevented the bombing of villages by tying the prisoners on the roof. It is a good time for him as winter is coming on.

20 *December*, 1931.

Rather depressed at the prospect of an almost total absence of income. I must say Captain Holt is a brick: he was so distressed when I informed him of the sad circumstances, and instantly began to think of means of making money and sent me off with a letter to the Editor of the *Baghdad Times* who had asked him to suggest someone to write the resumé of the year in Iraq, which always has to be sent to *The Times* for their supplement. So do look out for it, though I expect it will be cut to bits before printing. I have to do 1,500 words (for £1). I say *I* but as C.H. came with all the facts in a dossier and dictated the paragraphs I feel I have not really done much to deserve my £4.

So we buried the hatchet of the golf and are in harmony just now, and sympathizing over each other's troubles, as he hasn't yet been able to please H.E. by finding a lodging this side of the river and is getting very furious about it all. We went out riding yesterday and had an exciting but undignified time trying to make my pony do figures of 8—rather deplorable exhibition I felt, and got so nervous that I completely forgot whether you put your right hand down and press your left heel or vice versa, and made the poor pony cross and bewildered and C.H. quite hoarse saying things but with self-restraint considering—and I believe rather enjoying me making a fool of myself.

I get amusing news now from various people, but all too confidential to write about.

New Year's Eve, 1931.

Dear Lionel,

We had a cold Christmas here, with ice in all the ditches, and a dust storm on Christmas Eve. Bad for the war in Kurdistan which they insist on waging in the winter in spite of advice: I don't know if it is supposed to be talked about, but three wives have been telling me about it, so it cannot be *very* secret. It is Sheikh Ahmed of Barzan: is he a friend of yours?

I spent Christmas at the Drowers and Christmas Eve at the Youngs, and have twice been in bed with cold—and rather troubled, for all my plans have to be altered as I cannot afford to get back to Europe yet: my income is going to be only £60 instead of £160, and the least expensive thing will be to stay here and perhaps go into Luristan where one can live for nothing at all among the tribes. I am sorry to have to give up the thought of seeing you and your new house in the spring. It is *'forza maggiore'*. (By the way please do not mention these troubles, especially to the Kers as they would want to *do* things.) I hope that all will smooth itself out later in the year, and meanwhile Mr. Cameron is going to make a book of my Baghdad Sketches and Colonel Prescott's artist son to illustrate it. This is great fun.

NOTES FROM MY LESSONS WITH MIRZA HASAN IN HAMADAN

'Ali, born in the Ka'aba. When Fatima went to pray for an easy delivery she heard the voice of the Lord telling her to go into the 'house': as soon as she was inside, the walls shut upon her for three days. At the end of this time the people who were standing outside saw the wall open again, and Fatima came out with 'Ali held close to her breast. The place of his birth is shown on a stone of red and white marble.

'Ali's burial. Before he died, 'Ali said to his sons: "When you accompany my body, whoever speaks to you, give no greeting, nor answer his questions." When Hussein and Hasan went with their father's corpse to burial, a horseman met them by the way and greeted them: they gave no answer. He asked them whom they were burying. They gave no answer. When he asked the servants, they replied and told him of 'Ali's command. Then he lifted the 'liwa' from his face and lo—it was 'Ali himself.

Shah Shahbender heard of the splendour of 'Ali's tomb in Nejf and came to plunder it. When he approached the tomb, two fingers appeared from it and touched him at the waist: instantly he fell asunder in two pieces. The place where the fingers appeared out of the tomb is now decorated with gold.

The wall of the mosque of Kufa is now slanting because it bowed at the passing of 'Ali's funeral.

Salman Muhammadi of Ctesiphon: one of the Ansar. When the two tribes of Aws and Khazraj were digging the trench round Medina, Salman would go first with one tribe on one side of the town, then with the other. One day the two began to quarrel, each saying "Salman is ours". Muhammad came and asked the reason of the dispute, and settled it by saying: "Salman is mine."

'Ali sent him as governor to al Medain (Ctesiphon). He went riding a small donkey he owned. When the notables of Medain came out to meet the new governor they saw only an old man on a donkey: they asked him: "Have you seen the governor?" "He is hastening towards you," said Salman. They went past him to search along the road and found no one, and finally realized who the old man must be.

When he reached Medain he refused to go to the Government's house but settled in the mosque: "The house of God is for the servants of God." He refused to have any of the usual employees and dignitaries—but one day he called a dog, "four-eyed because it had a white spot over each eye." The dog came, and they spoke together, and the dog called and all the other dogs came and spoke. Then Salman gave the order that every door and shop was to be left open that night, and if anything were stolen, he would pay. The thieves thought this a great chance, but as they came at night to the open houses, the dogs leaped up and slit their bodies open—and next morning seven hundred dead thieves were found in the streets.

One day a woman came to complain that her butcher had given short weight. "Send him to me," said Salman. The butcher refused to go. "Tell him to come," said Salman, "and if he does not, tell this stone to *make* him do so." The woman went, but the butcher refused to come. Then she told the stone to *make* him. The stone, when it heard Salman's order, leaped up and hit the butcher on the back of the neck: when he wanted to turn to the right it hit him on the right cheek; when he wanted to turn left, it hit him on the left—till the butcher found himself in Salman's presence. Then Salman admonished him, and told him that if ever he gave short weight again, the stone would punish him.

When the time drew near his death, his servant asked Salman who would wash and shroud him. "He who washed the Prophet will wash me," said Salman—and the servant wondered for 'Ali was in Kufa. Then one day Salman went to the graveyard, and talked with a man there, and when he came back he knew death was upon him, and he told the servant to have a cloth ready to cover him, and he lay down and died. And the servant covered him with the cloth. But he had scarce done so, when the door opened, and Hazret the Amir ('Ali) came in, and asked, saying: "Is this my friend Salman?" And the slave said, "Yes." Then 'Ali took away the cloth, and the body of Salman sat up to honour him. And he called him back to life and told him to live. But Salman said: "I would rather be with my friend, the Prophet of God"; and his spirit went from him and he died. And 'Ali washed him, and as there was no saffron he provided the saffron, and a shroud—and then he disappeared: and when the people of Medain came with shrouds and all necessary, they found it had all been done, and wondered. And his body is still in Salman Pak (Ctesiphon).

The wall of Ctesiphon arch fell when Muhammad was born.

Nushirvan the first. He is in Hell as a misbeliever, but because he was so just, his justice turned into a fan in his hand and he fans the flame away so that it does not touch him. 'Ali said: "Better one act of justice than seven years' prayer."

Nushirvan had a chain from his bedroom to the four cross-roads:

anyone could pull, and a bell rang in his room and he heard the complaints.

The story of the serpent and the scorpion: in its gratitude it brought seed of sweet basil to cure the Shah's headaches.

Eve was created out of the three ribs of Adam. And when he saw her, he called to her to come to him. But God said: "If you make her come to you, it will be the woman who will choose her men for ever after: but if you go to her, man will ever choose his woman." So Adam went to Eve.

Adam was shaped out of mud by the angels and then lay for 200 years before God called to the spirit and it entered in at his head: and when it reached his eyes, they saw; and when it reached his nose, it smelt; and when it reached his mouth, it tasted; and his ears, they heard. But when it reached his heart, he did not realize that the rest of him was not yet alive, and he tried to sit up and fell back. And when it reached his waist, again he tried to sit up, and fell back. And God said: "Man is a creature of haste."

And when they were chased from Paradise, Adam wept for twenty years. Then he was hungry. And Gabriel brought him wheat from heaven. And Adam began to eat it. Then God said: "It is not eaten so." And Gabriel brought a mill, and they ground the wheat to flour, and Adam ate it. And God said: "It is not eaten so." The writing has reached us, that Gabriel taught Adam to mix the leaven and make dough: and Adam ate it. And God said: "It is not eaten so." And Gabriel brought an oven and they baked the bread. Then Adam ate and burnt his mouth and God said: "Be patient: Man is a creature of hurry."

Jesus, when a child, was left by his mother as an apprentice to a dyer. One day the dyer was invited to a wedding. He had four different colours to dye and left his silks in four heaps telling Jesus to put each heap into a separate vat—green, red, yellow, and blue. When he had gone, Jesus put all the silk into one 'hub'. When the dyer came back and saw this, he put his hands to his head in despair. Jesus pulled out the silks, and each came out dyed in its separate colour, green, red, yellow, or blue. Then the dyer kissed Jesus' hands and feet and when his mother came, asked, saying: "Who is this?"

[237]

"It is 'Isa," said Mary.

"It is I and not he who should be the servant," said the dyer.

Water, because it gives life; the Qurân; the mirror, because it is as the eye; and a bit of greenery—are the first things to be brought into a new house.

Gabriel came to Noah with date stones, and told him to plant them and wait till the trees bear fruit, while he exhorts the people to leave their idol worship. When the trees bore fruit the people still had not turned from their evil ways. Then God told him to take the stones of the date trees and sow them, and wait till they grow, and to exhort the people—and still they did not listen. When these trees bore fruit, God told him to take their stones and sow them, and still to be patient. But when the third trees had grown, then Noah begged God to destroy the people.

Story of the two dervishes from Khorasan taken for spies and put into prison. After a week it was found that they were not spies, and the prison was visited to see if they were still alive. The thin one was living and the fat one dead. A doctor was sent for to explain the phenomenon, and told the authorities that a thin man has a contented nature—has not grown fat by eating all he wants—and therefore can do without things when necessary.

The Mirza says that our hands and eyes and ears are ordered to speak on *The Day* to bear witness about us.

Story of the man who murdered 199 people, and asked a Hermit if there was any hope for him. The Hermit said no. The man murdered the Hermit also, making 200. Then he asked a wise man. The wise man said: "Yes. But go and see so and so, wiser than I am." The man set out, died half-way along the road, and angels of mercy and punishment came from opposite directions to claim him. As they argued, the voice of God said: "Do not quarrel; but measure the road, and see if it is more or less than half-way to his place of repentance." Found that it was one span beyond half-way (and some say that God contracted the road behind him to make it less) : so he was admitted to Paradise.

Mirza tells me a cold is an excellent thing as it prevents madness.

The Caliph Ma'mun came riding along, and the other boys fled, but one of them stayed; the Caliph lifted him to his saddle and asked why he did not run away. "I have done no evil to fear you, and the road was wide enough for both," said Muhammad. The Caliph asked who he was. "I am the son of that Riza (of Meshed) whom you killed," said he.

The Mirza says it is well to rise early, for the hour between dawn and sunrise is taken from Paradise.

When Gabriel came to Muhammad one day, he saw two poor men quarrelling over a piece of ground. As he saw it, he smiled. Muhammad asked him why he smiled. Gabriel said: "I have seen forty thousand kings quarrel over this same piece of ground : and they are all dead. Now it is the turn of these men—and they too will die. But the ground remains."
"For the earth" (says the mulla) "belongs to God and not to men."

The owl used to be a tame bird and live among the dwellings of men: it used to come into Sayyid Hussein's tent and sit there. But after his death it fled and ever since has lived only in desolate places.

When Noah was in the ark, they were dreadfully bothered by mice, who multiplied and spread. There were no cats then. And Noah asked the Lord what to do. The Lord said: "Pass thy hand over the lion's face, and a small lion will spring out of his mouth and kill the mice." And Noah did so, and the cat was created.

Two angels came while David was praying: they were refused admittance but entered through the wall: David feared, but they sat down and said they had only come for a talk. Then they told him the story of the ewe lamb: and when David exclaimed that the man who took it was a tyrant, they smiled and disappeared—and David saw the reproach and wept, so that the grass sprang up from the ground where his tears fell.

6

Journalism in Baghdad, 1932

IT is wise to discover what our happiness is made of. Of the
ingredients of which mine is made I think the presence of
goodness comes first, and the affection of a few people I can
understand and care about is second. The third is sunshine.
After these, and close upon them, comes some sort of daily
beauty, preferably a spacious view; and after that and side by
side—expressions perhaps of the same desire—domestic servants of an old-fashioned friendly sort, and an atmosphere of
sequence in time, a regular procession and not a disorderly
scramble towards eternity. I like to have as much as possible
of the background of this procession in sight, and could never
live happily for long in a country where no winding footpaths
have been made by the steps of my predecessors. That is why
I care little for deserts, unless a caravan route, crossing them,
makes the long human endeavour, the slow repeated victory,
more plainly visible by the nearness and constant obvious
possibility of defeat. United to this feeling for time as it passes,
so that I will not even separate it, is a delight in learning as much
of the world as I can before I leave it. I think that these pleasures
—all receptive—are more essential to me than my own work.
They mean more than any applause or esteem, for the voice
of other people only touches if it carries affection; and I can
imagine nothing more barren than to be admired and not
loved.

Though human loves come second on the list, coupled
with the sun, I have also had, ever since childhood and no
doubt in my very bones, a curiosity due to detachment. It is

not really detachment but rather a *wideness* that makes me feel intimately about a number of things that to many people are remote and strange. Every view, to appeal to me, must have a distance; every friendship, a depth below the surface; every work of art, some quality brought out from the unknown. The absence of this quality makes me generally dislike newspapers, debates, or the knick-knacks made for tourists: it makes me like things like telegraph wires (especially when they hum in the wind) or corners that turn *outward*, all skylines, all mirrors of water great or small, an orchestra tuning in, or the funny snatches of random voices that the wireless picks up as you turn it about—so different from its set orations; the sudden remarks of unexpected people, and the little involuntary gestures that move, as a leaf moves, and reveal what is so much greater than themselves.

In this intimacy I long ago discovered a refuge from loneliness, and I suppose it gives me a certain independence, for I know that, if my own sort of life fails me, I can still take a genuine delight in the mere passing of the world along its way. This is a lucky capacity, if one does not use it to escape, but faces closer relationships with their ecstasies and sorrows and welcomes them when they come, knowing only (through what heartfelt experience) that there is a sanctuary in case of need. And I have often wondered whether this sort of detachment is not a humble workaday relative of the undeserved and unexpected grace by which the contemplative are visited, which brings with it a security of union not only with human, but with intangible things as well.

The year 1932 in Baghdad lacked some of my six essentials and therefore did not remain in my mind enchanted, like the first winter, with Lionel Smith on Sundays, or the spring in Hamadan. But there was much busy pleasantness, novelty of work, a constant interest of news told me by all the men who were carrying the burden of Iraq upon their shoulders, and a host of friends, varied, affectionate, and amusing.

In the summer I moved into a little house near the Embassy

lent to me by the Sturgeses. This took away a great deal of the physical strain of living and gave coolness and space to the beginnings and ends of my days; and I had a Turkish servant of my own who prepared a small dinner for four people on Fridays, included in the pound a week which he received for marketing. He was faithful and devoted, and said he would never have done it so cheaply for anyone else. He knew my income, which was £20 a month from the *Baghdad Times*, and he arranged his budget to suit it, in the decent eastern way, where the servant feels his master's opulence or poverty as a part of his own life, and shares accordingly. The habit of fixing a weekly dinner-party, and merely filling in the names, I have followed ever after in the East, and found it a great simplification; and indeed I think it is a good thing to turn as much of the machinery of living as possible into a routine, to preserve energy for other things. Perhaps this is due to my long years of illness. My mother, with a vitality never tarnished in eighty-one years, looked upon meals, house, and parties as if she were ever meeting them for the first time; nothing was taken for granted; she would suddenly and absent-mindedly sit at a new place at the dinner-table, alter the hours, or move the furniture about, with never a need to think of any physical frontier to her strength. I have had to save and choose between one thing and another, unable to suffice for all—and it has made me careful about the accessories of life. The Baghdad summer put a strain upon me; it was only with the help of the little house, and half a bottle of stout at luncheon, that I came through. The discovery of the stout was due to Mr. Hogg, the financial adviser, who lived with his wife just opposite: they were pleasant neighbours; and he told me how husbands in Egypt keep up their strength through the hot weathers when their wives have gone home—and we shared a bottle between us every day.

My fatigue came from the office work, added to all the other things I was doing. I began in April, and as I had no car and could not afford a conveyance every day, I would walk across the bridge of boats to New Street, now called Rashid, which at that hour of the morning was being sluiced recklessly, with danger to one's ankles, in water as dingy as itself.

I would turn into a door where our messenger was lounging, waiting for the energies of the day to collect themselves, and would climb past printing presses where the Indian compositors worked, to a hot little office crowded with promiscuous stores. The skeleton of the news, B.B.C., Reuter, and *Daily Mail*, was lying on my table; and I would spend the morning piecing it together, turning its language into English, and arranging it under headings in a symmetry pleasing to Mr. Cameron, who had been trained in the classic tradition of *The Times*. I learned the art of spacing, and the types that go suitably together; and soon grew so quick at my work that my six hours were reduced to three. The badness of the telegraphese was shown by the fact that as often as not I could improve it by shortening, a shocking reflection when one considers the price of every word. It never knew the meaning of its own adjectives, and threw about verbs like *allege*, or *state*, or *declare* as if there were never a difference between them. I think I should have felt less tired by the end of the morning if this nauseating language had not stared me in the face.

In a room even smaller, but with more air and noise because it had a window on the street, sat the office boy and the clerk, and Mr. Tewfik the Arab editor, a round and cheerful little man who really shared my office, but stayed away out of delicacy when I was there. On my first day, no one rose to greet my arrival, and I made a little speech in the clerk's room explaining that office women are to be thought of as queens, and men stand when they come in: and stand up they did, for the whole of the year that followed.

Mr. Cameron lived in his own flat, beyond a door close by, a sort of private Olympus, visited by a stream of business people through the morning. He was a most thoughtful and friendly employer, and always generous, suggesting extra payments for things I had expected to do for nothing, and quick to appreciate any literary art: he had indeed a delicacy both of taste and feeling unexpected in a stout, huge man, rather like a friendly full moon in appearance who spent most of his free time on the race-course, and was often ready to think the 'commercial community' right and the 'Embassy' wrong. He soon saw that I took an interest in the work and gave me more or less a free hand. He once asked me to shorten an article, and I told him it could not be done.

"Nonsense," said he. "There never yet was an article that could not be made shorter."

"Read it," said I, "and take out what you like."

He did so, and admitted handsomely that there was nothing to cut; and indeed I find even now that I am far more inclined to tighten up my sentences too much rather than to spread them out prolixly.

When Mr. Cameron went to England for the summer, Ernest Main took his place in Baghdad. He had been brought up with the *Daily Mail* under Northcliffe. He was a small, tough Scot full of cheerful truculence, ready to fight anyone and the Embassy for choice, and with an endearing love for the *Odyssey*. I was happy with both my editors, and much touched years afterwards when Mr. Cameron told me that my job was always there if I should want it. For the first time since the days when I nursed in Italy, I worked not alone but with my fellows, and realized the pleasure of it—the pleasure a drop might feel, sparkling down on its way with all the other drops beside it to give an air of familiarity even to the waters of Lethe in which we unconsciously travel. When the morning's work was over I walked back over the bridge with eyes as nearly closed as possible under the fierceness of the sun, and heels sinking into the melting asphalt.

At this time I made friends with the coolies of Baghdad— small boys who, for a coin or two, carry parcels in their baskets, and are such a nuisance, so clamorous and persistent, that I once slapped one of them on his fat and tempting cheek, thrust out towards me, when he refused to go away (it is the only time I have ever used violence in the East). Now, every morning, I saw these children asleep about the pavements in some scrap of shade and was sorry for them—doomed to every vice and temptation from their infancy—and once ordered a dinner for those of our neighbourhood. It was carried on round copper trays to the doorstep of the printing press, and procured me smiles and greetings all over Baghdad for the rest of my stay.

Even the squalor of my daily walk to office had some charm of incident about it. I once saw a horse being led along the pavement, crowding us all out into the traffic, and protested to a passer-by who looked at me in surprise. "Of course it can walk on the pavement," said he. "It is a *race* horse."

Until late in the year I hardly left Baghdad except for a visit to Kuwait with the Hubert Youngs and Juliette Huxley, before my work began; a day in Mandali with Evan Guest; and a week in summer after sand-fly fever, driving to Persian Kurdistan. My companion on this trip suddenly wished me to run away with him to Samarkand. I should have liked to do this, but alone. He was a clever, interesting man, but his voice spoilt the moonlight of Persia, talking of careers, and other masculine prescriptions. The secret of travelling is to leave one's past behind, and to keep a mind a little blank and empty for the new to be received. There is a difference even in a mere stroll, if the outer world seeps in with silences and leisure, and words are not thrown like stones into a pool, to break all the reflections with private affairs. Companionship lives far below words: it is more primitive and more profound; and nothing can be mended with words, if the other level is not reached and touched. On this particular expedition, the deeper level was completely unaffected. I was sad at heart all that summer with my own troubles, and the masculine picture of my sex, sitting disengaged and eager for *anyone* to take an interest, seemed preposterous. My companion had another masculine delusion and thought he could organize mountain travel in a strange country better than any mere woman—and this landed us, extremely separate, on a cold hillside without food, blankets, or guide, where I slept among the rocks in a small uncharitable cave as chilly as my feelings.

The best of the expedition was the Chaldean Bishop of Senna, a prince bishop of the old school who—in March 1917—saved the Moslems of his town from extermination at the hand of the Cossacks, of whom 40,000 came down from the north. They sent messengers ahead, to tell the Christians to put white flags on their houses and save their lives. The Bishop rose early, prayed —fasting—and dressed himself in his crimson gown; with a crucifix in his hand and the Sheikh al-Islam beside him he rode to meet the Cossacks in the snow. He saved the Moslems. The Persian military governor in his turn had recently rescued the Christians from a tax on wine, imposed by the municipality, against which the Bishop had complained. The municipality was deposed, and the Bishop presented with the proceeds of the tax, which he reduced to six shahis and used to pave the Christian streets in Senna. These happy results of mutual toleration between Church and State made a friendly atmosphere in the mountain community, though the views of the Kurds—who had just failed in a rebellion—were not so easy to ascertain.

I came back in the summer to the end of the Iraq mandate, and to her treaty with Britain; and I left again in autumn, for two months according to my agreement, to climb, alone this time, into southern Luristan. This journey was filled with rumours of bandits and murderers and was interrupted by policemen who returned me under escort to the border, regretful but relieved to reach Baghdad, where I now felt happily at home. My little house again had its rightful owners, and I settled in the Y.M.C.A.

Of the friends I made in this year many have remained. Tich Bamfield in the Assyrian levies brought his bride, a tall and lovely Juno with something of the goddess in her walk, and they settled in one of the little mud houses near the Diyala river, whose source I had visited at Senna. Evan Guest and they made a pleasant easy-going colony, free of official stiffness; and indeed some of the people who lived in the other mud houses nearby, and took an interest in Central European dancing girls, gave to the local atmosphere a strong Bohemian flavour. One of the dancing girls appeared—in a jockey cap and rather pathetic continental finery—on a picnic trip up the river; quite a large party was invited, and confined for hours on one of the flat-topped barges called *shahturs*: they split instantly into two portions, respectable and non-respectable, separated by a space of deck, with a few like myself acting as liaison between them. We wondered whether the angels on Jacob's ladder had to traverse a greater distance than that which separated Mrs. X from the Hungarian dancer; one could only hope that their efforts at reconciling were more successful than ours.

The Tigris was beautiful to look at on summer nights, and the tents of city dwellers escaping from airless alleys nearly touched each other along its banks. But it was better to look on at a distance. The smells and heat of the day seemed to distil into a bouquet that hovered on the surface of the stream; and it was sheer imagination that made one enjoy the Baghdad pastime, of bonfires sunk to embers, and stuffed fish—*masquf*—filled with spices, eaten on some mud-bank far enough downstream to be clean, with boatmen rowing long and hard against the current to get one sleepily home. It was pleasanter to watch the river sinking into the swiftly closing arms of night from some high terrace on the east bank—the R.A.F. mess, or the A.V.M.s, where I stayed now and then and felt happy. Sir Edgar Ludlow Hewitt was head of the Air Force, and General Sir Rowan Robinson was adviser to the Iraq army; they were both friends, with wives as delightful as themselves, and they were both busy through this summer with one of the usual sporadic Kurdish wars. The great days of the duel with Sheikh Mahmud were over, and this time the trouble started to the north of his territories, with Sheikh Ahmed of Barzan. The underlying fact was the dislike of Kurdish hillmen, with their separate languages and origins, for the Arabs of the plain, who were supposed to rule them and yet scarcely crossed the border without fear. It was the old story of highland and lowland; and I think a good deal more could have been done at that time to satisfy the Kurds by encouraging their separate costume, customs and traditions, and so incorporating them, with a difference which need not touch their pride, into the general picture of Iraq. The problem was very like that of Scotland after the '45; and it kept the Iraq army and the British Air Force busy every summer for many years, as soon as the season for mountain warfare began with the gathering in of the harvest. Incidentally, it provided me with the only chance I have ever had of being a war correspondent for *The Times*.

Except for Cairo in war-time, I have never been in a city smaller than Rome where there were as many varied, amusing, interesting and adventurous people as there were in Baghdad in 1932;—road-makers in difficult places, like Archie Hamilton in Kurdistan; or gatherers of news, like Pat Domvile and Jope-Slade; or passers-by to their digs and explorations, like the Leonard Woolleys or Sir Aurel Stein. Him I now met for the first time—a little gnome of a man with apple cheeks and the eyes of youth, and with the gentle deceptive manner of those who always get their own way.

The person I still must mention is Gerald De Gaury, whom I first met in the summer of this year. He has changed very little in the eighteen years that have followed. He might still come dropping in as he used to do, to my office in the morning, vague, with some bit of gossip, most amusing when merely invented, with a teasing way not devoid of malice, and that pleasant easiness of space around him which the mere worker can scarcely understand. He asked me to teach him Italian, and made a habit of calling twice a week, attending to anything but the book in his hand. He would look round my little tunnel of a room at the Y.M.C.A. wondering 'how can you stand it?' I liked him because he lived in a world of imagination, much as I did. He had been caught young by the war and the army in 1914, and they had turned him from his natural path of writing or painting, either of which might have made him happy, and had given him the uneasiness of two worlds to live in uncertain of his home.

My own adventure this year, apart from the treasure hunt in Luristan, was the writing of 'Baghdad Sketches' for the

Baghdad Times. I still keep them, in their newspaper dress, in a bundle, drafted week by week among the local advertisements and bits of Arab news. They were accepted kindly by both British and Arab, and I think it was Mr. Main who suggested printing them in book form, with drawings by 'Copper' Prescott, son of the head of police, a young man full of talent, now dead, who surprised his parents by preferring art to the army.

The little volume came out, printed by the Indian compositor who always helped me with football results in Reuter, which I could not understand. I have been told that the bright red binding is vulgar; and the pages are apt to fall out if roughly handled: but to me the little book looks as charming as a walk in some eastern town through the market of spices, where every whiff calls up—not a picture—but some piece of the life I have lived.

* * *

BAGHDAD, 19 January, 1932.

Dearest Herbert,

I wonder when I shall get to you? My finances seem very groggy and now I have had an offer of £20 a month and possibly £30 later to work here for the newspaper: and am wondering whether to accept or no. It seems wicked to refuse and to fly in the face of Providence these hard times. But I do dislike the thought of being tied to a job. I am going to think it over for a little and perhaps see if they will have me just for a few months' experiment.

I have been working hard at Baghdad Sketches and there are now fourteen excluding the one that they refuse to publish about the mosque; but I find it's hard work to write to order and am not at all good at rapid modern journalism.

The High Commissioner is going to Geneva to-morrow—everyone busy getting him off.

25 *January*, 1932.

Darling B,

I am still in the throes of indecision and have been unable to think of anything these days, with an upset tummy too. I went yesterday to Dr. Sinderson who says it is something in the food. I rather think Jamila will have to be left *anyway*, though it goes to my heart.

This unbecoming state of mine, of course, coincides with four dinner-parties : it is unfortunate. I enjoyed three of them all the same. I sat next to Sir Kinahan Cornwallis at the Chapmans and thanked him for sending me partridges : I like him with his kind eyes and big nose and gruff voice, though I hardly know him.

A very gay and nice old lady, Mrs Rowan Robinson, asked me if I didn't mind being criticized and I told her that as one *has* to be criticized anyway, one may as well be so for doing things one enjoys.

To-day also had the visit of two Chaldean priests bringing me a history of theirs to read. They were rather nice with their long beards and voluminous garments—especially the one who *hadn't* been to Europe : the other had been to the College of the Propaganda in Rome.

I am beginning to understand very elementary sentences in Russian; I don't work much but am letting it sink in unconsciously. After my lesson this morning I came back across the Tigris, which is getting very muddy and slowly rising, and went to call on the Sturgeses; found them sitting on their roof in the sun.

2 *February*, 1932.

My dear Lionel,

Your letter has been here a long time, but I have been feeling depressed lately. No doubt if you were here I should go and weep in your office and add one more to the number of ladies who did so. But, as it is, all I can do is to get cross with Jamila who *will* look awful with her head wrapped in a shawl, so that I sometimes long for a Neat British Parlour Maid, or even for Emma from Asolo.

However, I am really rather lucky. I have been offered a job on the *Baghdad Times* which will solve all my financial troubles and enable me to get back to Europe after a few months. So I shall hope to see your house after all this year, though probably I will not be able to get there before the vacation; you had better come to Italy first.

It has been so cold here and all the poor people's sheep dying from hunger in the north. The poverty they say makes the roads unsafe and a young man in Mespers called Brinton was shot the other day between Mosul and Shergat, and killed. It is the second tragedy, as Dr. Litten had just died a few days before of heart failure.

I was asked to the Residency the other night to talk arabic to the Amin-el-'Asimat and the Director of Health (a fat man from Mosul who arrived forty minutes late for dinner, but when Lady H apologized for beginning without him, said "it doesn't matter"). He told me that the Yezidis are the remnants of the Ommayads in Iraq and that they took to Devil worship because their patron saint and teacher was in favour of general toleration and once told them to curse no one, not even the Devil. So that will teach people to preach toleration out here.

12 February, 1932.

I *did* go off to Mandali with Evan Guest after all, and *no* chaperone. At the very last Mrs. Young gave out and we decided to go off only for the day: then it was a glorious morning, Evan arrived and said he had packed his bed and it was mere foolishness to give up the trip: I packed in haste, we rushed round buying chocolate and petrol; we stuffed little Yusuf as chaperone in at the back, and set off looking like an expedition to the North Pole, and met Mrs. R. Robinson on the bridge, who threw up her arms and shrieked with laughter. We had a glorious day: lunch in a river wadi in the shelter of the sheep backs; evening with the Naqib of Mandali, a nice man with a green turban and a cashmere gown: we sat round a brazier and talked, and found out a lot about how to get into Luristan. Next day we drove up to the border: you can't imagine anything more lovely than the snow ranges and the palm gardens in front, all sliding down into the desert so that it looked like a little coast town on the desert instead of on the sea. Next day we returned, lunched with a Dutchman who manages a huge estate which has been established here since 1887; and got home for late tea with the Drowers.

c/o Y.M.C.A., BAGHDAD, 20 *February*, 1932.

My dearest Venetia,

It seems ages since I heard from you. I don't know if it is your fault or mine, but it is not any slowness in my *thoughts* at any rate,

[252]

for they are so often with you. I have been and am going on with a harassed time, with more to do than I can cope with. For one thing I am ill with some internal thing which means X-rays and next week in hospital, I hope no more. Then I have taken on a job on the local paper, which means eight hours a day at least for a time. Then I take some Russian lessons in the evenings, and all my writing to get in somehow. And besides this everyone is being nice to me just now and asking me to delightful trips in the Persian Gulf or Kurdistan, so that I am torn every way at once.

By the end of the summer I hope my book will come out. The illustrations look very attractive. I hope it will be readable. You shall have a copy, but I hope you will make an enquiry all the same at your bookseller's and stimulate their interest in the unknown author. It will be called *Baghdad Sketches*, and printed here by the *Baghdad Times*: I have no share in it till 500 copies are sold, so that I don't expect to get very rich on it.

I am spending a week-end with the Ludlow Hewitts. He is A.V.M. out here and is Irish, and interested in plants and birds and nice quiet things. I feel rather like the Prodigal now that I am to leave my native lodgings: the High Commissioner's wife pressed my hand and said: "I am so glad we are rescuing you from going native," and everyone beams upon me as if I were a brand from the burning —as if I had ever been 'going native', but such is the human slavery to labels.

The other day I drove to the border and looked at the snowy ranges of the Persian hills. On the other side is Luristan. No impossibility in getting across I do believe—only this miserable want of money. But by the autumn I hope to do it, and also to be perhaps fitter in health than I am now. And meanwhile I have got lots of information and made the acquaintance of the Chief Lur in Baghdad, a nice old man with a beard who says he will come as guide.

The spring seems here at last. Orchards full of apricot and apple blossom. It makes me sad, I don't know why—perhaps because the spring makes one feel the fragility of life so much more. I feel I have wasted so many years just in learning how to live, and now the machinery is all a bit worn and creaky and all the beautiful new gloss gone off it.

Such amusing things happen in this country. If you go to one of the most fashionable receptions you meet the lady who monopolizes all the brothels of Baghdad: apparently she keeps the master of the house in motor cars and his wife in diamonds. A League of Nations commission on the White Slave Traffic is here just now, but I don't imagine this will figure in their report.

26 February, 1932.

Darling B,

I have begun work, and to-day is my first day on my own. Mr. Cameron says he notices 'a great difference' and will 'begin' me at £20 a month, and extra for any little things of my own I find time for. Now if only my health will stick it, I can make a decent living and get fun out of it too later on. Just now I am still a bit thin and weak, and so plain.

Vyvyan is furious with me: I think he would like to shake me, all because I won't go home. He can't bear the thought of my going to an office every day, says that it is quite ridiculous.

4 March, 1932.

I have done nineteen sketches now, and they are supposed to come out on Tuesday. I am now writing about the Jordan and Banias— I think it will come well. But cannot get the time.

Lunch to-day with the Ludlow Hewitts and yesterday with the Breeses (they kindly prepare milk puddings for me). There were two rather pleasant elderly men to-day, one coming to regulate Civil Aviation, who told us that the ancient British coracle—*exactly* like the *gufa* only smaller—is still used at Shrewsbury. He also said that he measured the tracks worn by the ancient Roman chariot wheels at a garrison gate of the Great Wall in Northumberland, and found that they are exactly as far apart as the present distance between the two wheels of a hansom cab.

Mr. Cameron apologizes for giving me so *little* pay, so I suppose he is pleased with me?

9 March, 1932.

So tired, and no energy left to write after five hours of it in the way of business. It is a poor sort of an occupation dealing with bad English all the time.

To-day I lunched with the Youngs and Mrs. Julian Huxley. Major Young tells me that my editor has published something he shouldn't (anti-British probably)—and that everyone instantly said "He never dared to do it till Miss Stark went to his office"—and I am as innocent as a babe, and don't even know what it is.

On Monday I lunched with Mrs. Drower, Lady Humphrys and six Arab ladies—quite gay though language rather difficult. Lady H. said she had settled my career: I was to show off Baghdad to tourists (what a *horrid* thought). I took the A.D.C.'s mother round into two mosques and all sorts of corners, and it was great fun; but we had to keep it dark as H.E. disapproves of going where one has to take one's shoes off.

The Cornhill has taken 'River of Adonis'. Only one thing of mine now without a publisher and I could write more if I had more time. But I find it is necessary to lie flat and rest when I get in and then get exercise out of doors, and there is *no* time left for other writing.

SOUTH OF KUWAIT, 20 *March,* 1932.

It is so lovely out here and I am feeling fitter and better in the good light desert air.

The Dicksons (he is British Agent at Kuwait) brought us out to their camp: two white double tents and one beduin one, very gay with white and black and yellow woven patterns and tasselled saddle-bags; looking out on to the low desert ridges where the sand shows through bushes of 'arfa' which will be full of little yellow daisy flowers in a day or two, but are still just brown prickliness at present.

We flew down to Basra: I couldn't talk much as the air made me feel very queer: I looked out at intervals over the brown emptiness of South Mesopotamia, the river winding in the curliest curls imaginable and no vegetation. Then over the green marshes, cut through by little straight waterways: and then finally down at Shaiba—the world standing nearly upside down to meet us as we came down. We had a luxurious dinner and night at the Consul's there in Basra, and came on to Kuwait next day.

This is miles out in the desert—the Nejd border quite near. There are only a few beduin tents and sheep and lambs. We have all been camel riding this morning, a very pleasant hypnotizing swaying motion, not unlike my mule on a pack saddle.

The air is buoyant, one does not mind the heat. The Dicksons love the Arabs and it is not a bit 'touristy'—we had our dish of rice and sheep and ate it with our fingers. The women come to talk—they have black veils with two holes for the eyes.

I do wish I could jump off from here into the middle of Arabia. It is good to be on the very edge. The desert has its extraordinary fascination, quite inexplicable—the emptiness and thin buoyant air.

They are Wahabis here and very particular about drink and morals—though smoking seems to be allowed now. They pray more than in Iraq. The two women who accompanied us to the wells of water stayed behind to pray while we strolled home and met an adder coiled up on the sand.

The Youngs are charming to be out with: so pleasant and pleased with little things like beetles or sunsets or food.

Lunch here—must stop. A green kettle just brought to wash our hands for the meal.

BAGHDAD, 26 March, 1932.

Ever so many happy returns of the day. My holiday to-day, and your two letters to cheer it up. I do so like to receive all the gossip, and so glad to hear you are better. Do take as much care as possible—you know it would be just the last straw in the way of troubles if you let yourself get ill: so *do* if only from this altruistic view, *prevent* it, and if necessary take a holiday right away. I can always pay at a pinch so that need not worry. My experience is that prevention is the only useful cure for illnesses; they are the devil if they get hold.

I am now convinced that it is using my brain in a sedentary manner which makes me ill; I was perfectly well in the beduin tent. It is annoying as there is no way out this summer and I do enjoy earning a little money and could make lots if only I could physically write more. But I will take it all as easy as I can and hope to settle into the business before it gets very hot. At present it is very trying: one day a dust storm, everything under an *inch* of dust: then hot enough for muslins: then an icy wind from the north with hot sun. One doesn't know what to wear.

I am looking very ugly—and thin: it depresses me, but what can one do? I shall ride with V.H. to-morrow—the poor man is being terribly hard worked, with a little Kurdish war on and all. I shall take him the Italian articles on Baghdad: do send any more in the *Corriere*: I believe it is the Italian minister here who writes them.

2 April, 1932.

Mr. Cameron has just asked me up to-day. He discovered one of my adjectives in a Reuter telegram. It said that the money from death duties was less than had been expected owing to the abnormally low mortality in millionaires. I thought 'abnormally' a poor sort of adjective and substituted 'regrettably low mortality of millionaires'. I was so sorry to be found out before it was published.

10 April, 1932.

Your letter just come with two questions. Y.M.C.A. *is* my address. They take in p.g.s and it is really quite comfortable, though difficult for entertaining as one can't drink. I had the Staffords and Evan, and got in a bottle of whisky for them, but omitted to buy a corkscrew: so we sat in my room after and just looked at it sadly as they said it would smell too much if they knocked the heads off, and also look bad to have the tops of whisky bottles just below my bedroom.

Your second question as to my work—'tis very dull: just putting the Reuter telegrams into decent English—nothing creative about it, and when there is it is discouraged. All I can do is to invent the headings and that does not allow a free rein. A Professor in Liverpool at a Science lecture drank a tumbler of acid instead of water by mistake and died on the platform: I called it "An Absent-Minded End," but this was suppressed by the editor I am sorry to say.

I am writing my article on Kuwait and hope it will come. But it is 105 in the shade already, and my only writing time before tea, when one is not energetic. I think I shall not mind the heat however. I like it so far.

The Kurds have managed to snipe poor old General R. Robinson in his foot. He is here in hospital. I will take some flowers this evening. I asked the minister last night why they are so secret about it all, so that we have to wait for all our news from German sources, and he said with engaging frankness: "When it is bad, we do not like to talk about it."

10 *April*, 1932.

Mr. Hamilton came to lunch and told me all about the Kurdish affair. It appears they had an awful smash up—two battalions involved in the mountains, cut off from their fodder, food, ammunition, over 1,000 horses, all their baggage, all of which Sheikh Ahmed's people carried off. General R. R., who is supposed to advise, but does not get his advice taken till all is in the soup, rushed up with a small force to try and extricate, and then got his wound in the foot —and very nearly got cut off with the force to be rescued, for they were all surrounded and only disentangled by some very strenuous bombing by the R.A.F. So now they are where they were before except that the Kurds have lashings of stores and ammunition. This is rather sad for the first effort of Iraq to manage the Kurds on her own : I suppose it will be kept from the League of Nations, or 'arranged' at any rate—and I don't think you had better mention it around, though it was as a matter of fact given me as quite public here.

Mr. Hamilton is very pro-Kurd—a nice young man, who says he hasn't talked to anyone as interesting as me for years (because I hardly spoke at all), and wants me to go up and stay with him and explore Kurdistan. He came to lunch and stayed to tea, and then I didn't know what to do as I *had* to come to the office, so I weakly consented to go to dine to-morrow—rather fun at the Levy Mess.

25 *April*, 1932.

I am in bed with a cold—such a nuisance, and brought on by these vile dust-storms. But Mr. Cameron is awfully considerate, and is doing my work this afternoon. He found me working late on Saturday (not from any misguided devotion to work but merely to save myself on Sunday) and was deeply impressed and sent me back in his car. When I get these undeserved bits of Credit I always accept them thankfully as a Compensation offered by Providence for all the occasions on which one's real merits are misinterpreted.

I spent last evening dining at the Reeds', nice people in a funny little house right in Baghdad—a party of ten, and no bridge after, so that in spite of my hostess, who is very gay and able to keep things going, I found myself drifting off asleep and only hope it didn't show; but I *know* I lost consciousness twice. The dust was so thick that we all wrote our names on the table in it before leaving, and could hardly see the lamp-posts on the way home.

[258]

Somebody took a fancy to the Italian flag while it fluttered on the Chargé's car and carried it off (the chauffeur having sneaked in to see a play). It was only six inches square, but Rulli made an awful fuss, and came rushing up to the A.V.M. for an apology. The A.V.M. was not a bit inclined to bother, and Rulli rushed off to the High Commissioner. Finally an unimportant Flying Officer was found, put into parade uniform and sent with an apology. Now Rulli has presented his chauffeur with a huge revolver, to *shoot* anyone who comes to steal the flag, to the great amusement of everyone here.

26 April, 1932.

Dearest Venetia,

I lost my little niece years ago, nursing her mostly myself, and cannot think of it even now without a tight feeling at the heart. It seems a terrible waste: and yet now I do believe it does not matter, any more than it matters whether the drops of water in the river are out in the sunshine or swallowed down in the current below: all are moving to whatever is our mysterious goal. Of that I feel more and more sure. I think I would like to have been born a little later: we are to discover so much in the next few hundred years. Your talk about marriage—I used to feel that I had missed the real reason of life by not marrying, and was out of the stream in a backwater as it were. But now I feel this is not so. I think the human being is just coming to that point where sex is no longer the only means of progress, as it has been so far: we are just stepping into a wider world and need not feel lonely, except in the way that pioneers are lonely. Life is easier for married people: but I think it ought to be if anything richer for us, so long as we take it with full hands and not with the inferiority sense which has often ruined the lives of spinsters. Don't you think this is so? Anyway it is a comfort to know that all the greatest thinkers are with us; I think there is not one who considers marriage as a necessity to the fullness of life, though personally I would like to be married, having a fatal devotion to *habits* in my affections, so that I hate to be torn away from the people around me.

I *hope* to get home this year. But do read the financial papers and remember that nearly all my income is either in South or North America. I am now living on my own efforts, and dare not give it up till I know I have something else to live on. When we 'are old and grey' shall we settle together, half at Penbedw and half in Asolo?

I think it would be fun.   And we will have time to talk all the talks we are missing now.

This climate is most trying.   The dust-storms fiendish, and lay me low instantly with a bad throat.   And—you will be horrified—I am to lecture to about fifty men on Saturday.   I go sick with fear at the thought.   It will be a dismal failure.

28 April, 1932.

Darling B,

Mr. Cameron is very kind and said I could take to-day off.   He made me take so strong a whisky and lemon yesterday that I was *completely drunk*.   Rather a pleasant feeling: I felt as if I was quite irresponsible and had nothing to do with what I myself was doing and saying: I hope it was not too visible.   Anyway I slept it off and was given tea, and felt much the better, but have not mentioned the scandal to this respectable establishment.

30 April, 1932.

Two letters from you to-day; that is so nice of them—to come just when I am feeling so nervous—quite incapable of doing anything at all.   We have the slides, and the map drawn on the blackboard.

10.30 p.m.   The blinking thing is *over*.   I *am* so tired.   They had a larger audience than I have ever seen before, and had to get in heaps more chairs—over 100 people.   I thought I should die when I went in and looked at all those rows of faces.   V.H. came to dine and bucked me up, and Evan, and Professor Jordan—otherwise all airmen and a few Iraqis.

They say it went well: that I stood with great composure and every word audible, and just the right length.   As for me I know nothing: only that I had one ghastly moment when I thought my heart would suffocate my voice, and then somehow or other got started, and had practised so much that the thing went off by rote and I referred only once to my notes.   But what a terrible ordeal.   And no one provided anywhere for me to melt away into when it was all over, and the stick was too short for me to reach the places I wanted on the map.   But never mind—it is over.   And I *have* lectured to 100 people all at once and not collapsed.   Oh dear.

It seems I disgraced myself at the races—by leaving and going to play golf just as 'the horses were coming down the straight'.

Gerald de Gaury tells me that the news was going about that I could not be a real racing enthusiast. Anything more dreary as a matter of fact I can't imagine.

8 *May*, 1932.

Such good news of Vyvyan Holt. He went up to the Kurdish rebels in Barzan (being sent off from our bridge party on Sunday) and got off the two British officers and brought them away with him. He had nothing to offer the sheikh in exchange—but went up and talked of this and that, and said he would explain the Kurdish grievances to the government here, and then eventually added that he would take away the two prisoners. Of course they thought it a joke. But he said he could not go away without them. If they would not give them, he would stay too. They sent him out of the room and finally had him back and agreed, and he and the two (one wounded) and the doctor went back a long trek. Had a bad moment when a message came after one whole day's journey to tell them to turn back. There was nothing for it—they were marched back and spent a night in great suspense, but it was only because something else had happened meanwhile which made the sheikh (Ahmed of Barzan) anxious to see V.H. again: so they set off once more and have got here safe with great kudos. I am *so* glad.

Evan took me to an arabic play the other night, *beautifully* acted, though a dreadful crude composition with a lady on a bed dying of syphilis and dreadful to look at all through the last act. The best thing was the old Baghdad poet, Jamil-az-Zahawi, about seventy, with one tooth or so and a little wild fringe of hair round his baldness, reading a long 'Qasida' from the platform, half-way through. At the end of every line he beckoned to his audience, who all applauded and went quite wild, and said 'Allah', while he thoroughly enjoyed himself and a young man stood behind his chair to see that when he flopped back after any particularly emotional bit, he met his chair again. The play went on from 9 to 1.45 a.m., and then there was to be singing; but we left.

18 *May*, 1932.

Dearest Venetia,

I have had an interesting time watching the Muharram procession. You must have read all about it, but nothing can give you the intense emotion of those wailing crowds, beating their breasts, their heads daubed with mud. From the roofs around, the women shriek in high voices as one after another the incidents of the day of Husein's death are presented before them: the dome of Mecca; the bridal chamber where his cousin (I think), who was killed with him, had slept; the two children tied to the wrist of a great bully in red with a drawn sword who stops at intervals to kill them, while the crowd sways and shrieks around, and the water that is brought to them is dashed from their lips. Then come the women in their howdahs; and the enemy, in red, in beautiful old armour handed down for this occasion. And the horse of Husein, trapped with silver, shaking its bells, all draped in rich brocades. And then the men in black who beat their backs with bunches of chains so that they bleed: they do it to a cadence, with a very slow sort of dancing step, turning half-round backwards every time. And after them comes the body of Husein, when passion rises to an incredible pitch—and a horrid sight it is, with its feet sticking out and a bloody sheet over it, and a truncated neck showing (the man really has his head tucked away under a box under the sheet, and I suppose a sheep's neck is pushed on top of him): two doves sit on his breast, and a knife is stuck at each shoulder.

I had my little camera under an *abba*, and was able to photograph it all, though it is a risky business: and Mr. Chapman, who went with me, added to my difficulties by being terribly fussy. However I think I have a complete series of pictures to show you when I get back.

After the body come the men who beat their breasts, also in rhythm, stripped to the waist, while their mulla chants the terrible story. It was an awesome sight to look down on to that crowd of brutal faces —all the lowest dregs of Baghdad join these crowds, and the pain and the excitement turn them into animals: at Kadhimain they are still allowed to cut themselves with knives. The police hover about anxiously and are glad no doubt when the day is done.

                    .   .   .   .   .

Just this minute comes nurse's note. *So* sorry, my dear, you are unwell again. Oh, dear, I am so sorry when I hear of these set-backs. I think as you about this life. It is up to us to make it a success— and there are so many ways of doing it; it does not matter very much *what* our circumstances are. If we fail in one part, it is a bad plan to waste time in regret: just to give it enough thought to realize, honestly, that we *have* failed and how; and then turn to the future again and make *that* a success. I see people all the time brooding over their *past* mistakes, and then doing them all over again in the present, just because their thoughts are not turned forward.

I regret so much in my youth—so much time wasted, and health unnecessarily wasted. But there is always time to conquer one's universe; it is only the matter of seconds, a matter of seeing, after all.

c/o MRS. STURGES, RESIDENCY ROAD, BAGHDAD,

27 May, 1932.

Darling B,

Well now I have just been doing some real journalism. We have this war going on and nothing but the meagrest news, and *The Times* in London clamouring to hear about it. My editor unable to get them to allow him to write anything (or hear anything for the matter of that). I had a happy thought and suggested going up into the enemy country and getting news there, but Mr. Cameron was not bold enough for this and said if I went it must be officially: so I asked the A.V.M., and of course could get nothing satisfactory, and went to Vyvyan who said it was a 'monstrous' idea. But then he suggested I might get leave to look at all the despatches and get an article that way, and that is what I have now got leave to do. The A.V.M. most kind; will let me copy the maps and get the news, and may even get some photos taken of the actual fighting area, and says he will give me the bits of 'local colour' himself. To get first-hand help from the British Commander of Operations is no bad start for a journalist, is it?

Mr. Cameron says he would like me to stay on permanently. He says the paper is much improved. I do feel rather pleased, to feel that my first effort gives me a chance of £240 a year or more in these hard times.

I gave a little bachelor dinner to Mr. Chapman and two young men—Mr. Bailey and Mr. Oxford, with bridge after. It was great fun. We talked all about the war, and how a Turkish frontier patrol had been bombed in mistake for Kurds and so on—and they did not leave till midnight.

Then I dined at the A.V.M.'s, and sat next the Prime Minister and opposite the German Chargé d'Affaires, and enjoyed that evening very much. But I get awfully tired if I go out twice running and must refuse invitations.

29 May, 1932.

My article is started. I do hope it will be a success. It is a big thing to do—to give a resumé of even a small war for *The Times*, and to be read by all who were concerned in it and able to point out any inaccuracy. I spent yesterday morning at A.H.Q. and Wing-Commander Garrod explained all the despatches to me (not quite all I suspect) and showed me the photos—*very* interesting. I have all the plan of operations in my head now, and see the sort of country. Vyvyan is coming this evening to tell me about the negotiations and about his part of the show. I am being charmingly helped—and I hope to get some photos out of them for *The Times* with the actual village and the defile where the chief battle took place.

9 June, 1932.

Dearest Venetia,

I have a sad story to relate apropos of Germans. The Director of Antiquities here is by way of being a friend, and a really most charming German. An old dealer, quite illicit I find, comes round to me with antiques now and then and brought me a Greek statuette the other day—a very lovely thing, I thought. I took it to the museum to show my friend and left it a day for him to look at; went back and was told it was not worth more than thirty rupees at the outside: now the dealer comes and tells me that they sent the police to him, took the statue, and are offering him sixty-five for it. I went to see the Director this morning, who admits all except the offering of a price—and seems not to see in the least that he ought to have told me if he was going to pinch my statue. He is obviously quite at ease with his conscience—so what can one do? It is one of those National Abysses, and I have taken it for such and not broken off my friendly relations—only made a mental reserve to show him no more antiques.

Did I tell you I had been doing War Correspondent for *The Times*: I'm told anyone can tell it's a woman because there's so little blood-shed (a bad psychology I think), but as a matter of fact all the best

[264]

bits were struck out by the authorities. It is a sad job to be correspondent: what the military leave you the politicians take out.

What fun it would be if we were housekeeping together. I am
craving for female companionship. Now I have not a single woman
left whom I can talk to at all properly, and anyway I have no one at
all intimate. There is a nice woman interested in history and things,
but so much so that she meanders off on Islamic books when I am
longing for something human. I do think one should cultivate a
responsiveness to other people's moods—it is such a lovely and
precious gift.

15 June, 1932.

No letters from you this week. The posts are dotty, but I am
always afraid of your poor old head and that you may have been
giving it too much work. How lovely it must be at Penbedw now.
Sometimes I am just overwhelmed with homesickness so that I know
why such an unattractive name for the feeling was chosen. I long
for spring in England and to wander somewhere just on the edge of
a little copse with last year's leaves still on the ground and the new
green all about me. And here it is 113 in the shade and fans going
steadily.

There is a great to do with the Assyrians just now. They are
terrified of getting into the hands of the Iraqis now that British rule
is to cease, and the Assyrian Levies, very fine troops under British
command, have threatened to strike: the officers have threatened to
resign, and the rank and file show signs of following suit, and all the
nation, men, women and children, mean to move up to the north.
What they are to do when they get there remains a mystery which
is causing no little discomfort all round. Every levy, when he leaves
the service, is given a rifle and 200 rounds, so that they are all armed.
On the other hand, their income in the service is enough to keep
the whole nation going, and when it stops they have *nothing* else
except robbery to fall back on.

If they were to join with the Kurds, the Arab is simply helpless:
and the British taxpayer is not going to pay for a war against a people
who are homeless and destitute merely because they stuck to us through
thick and thin before. So that they really have a very strong position,
and they are being led by a remarkable woman, the Lady Surma,
aunt of the young head of the nation who is a religious chieftain.

[265]

She and her nephew are sitting up at a place called Amadia (old Roman fortress) in the north, and refusing all blandishments to come down. I think they have every chance of forcing people's hands so long as they make reasonable demands: on the other hand they seem to want quite unattainable things, such as a mountain kingdom of their own, when there *are* no uninhabited mountains to give them. Meanwhile days and nights are filled with conferences and rumours —and this by the way is not information to be scattered about as they are trying to keep it out of the Press (a foolish attempt, I think).

23 June, 1932.

Darling B,

I do want to beg you again not to suggest borrowing from the bank. Already twice I have tried to tell you that it is really *insane* just now. If one *had* to borrow, of course, I can do so myself at about half what it would cost you. But in the very same letter you quote Lord Iveagh: you say yourself that all we have is as likely as not to vanish at any moment—and then talk in this irresponsible way of borrowing. I suppose we have it in the family and I shall be doing it when I get older, but I do feel depressed when I have already written two long letters to explain what I think of it, and they have no effect at all. What one must do now is to save, if possible, and in something *not speculative*: one is trying not for interest, but for the safety of the capital in case all the rest goes smash as it seems most likely to do. If these conferences end in failure, even the Tessoria will not go on for very long: there will be a very hard time coming. Do please believe me, B, and not forget it all a week after you have put away my letter: or ask *anyone* who knows about these things and hear what they say.

It is a terribly harassed summer out here, what with Assyrians and Kurds. British troops just been flown out to take the place of the Levies, who have all resigned.

5 July, 1932.

Dearest Venetia,

I have just sent you the last batch of my Sketches. They have come to an end—rather sad: they were bringing me in quite a nice income. I am trying to write about Mazanderan in a feeble way and remembering it all—that strange week lying as I thought dying in the hills: a thing quite unforgettable and which seems to set a seal of quite different values on all one's life. It is strange how these land-marks of deep feeling stand out, and one does not know them at the time: they go so much deeper than one realizes. And afterwards even those that have meant such sorrow are worth while: it seems to me that I only regret the sordid and nagging things over which one has wasted time—none of the real joys and sorrows.

7 *July*, 1932.

Darling B,

I am now busy with prostitutes. It appears that the Colonial Office classes Prostitutes and Artistes under one category—and the municipality here has made a law for having all the cabaret artists medically examined at intervals. This leads to great abuses as it gives too much power to these doctors and is unpleasant to think of with European women (though I don't think most of them are very far off the Colonial Office definition).

Still, one of my friends is interested in one of these ladies and says he will kick the medical officers downstairs and would I get something about it in the paper? So we had an interview this morning and I hope something may be done. I prefer messing about with military matters.

Group Captain Garrod, who is the R.A.F. information bureau, has been very good in getting my articles off. I must say I should love to do a little soldiering, but it is nothing to the passion these military people seem to develop for writing.

14 *July*, 1932.

Yesterday Franks the A.D.C. came along to see my Editor because he had got something all wrong and we told him it was their job to give us the right news if they didn't want the wrong stuff in the paper. I am beginning to feel quite as if it were 'My' paper and stick up for it, much to V.H.'s amusement, who says I think I am everything now I am on this 'dirty little rag'. He got terribly annoyed with me because I wrote him an invitation to dinner in the style of an official memorandum (it took two typewritten pages and was awfully like the language they use).

15 *July*, 1932.

Dearest Venetia,

I have too much to do. You can't think how much I feel like one of those squirrels in a cage. If I leave for Luristan in six weeks I *must* get up a little Persian, so have added three lessons a week with a very fat dignified gentleman in a khaki-coloured turban, with rosy manicured hands and the face straight off one of the miniatures—placid but not good-tempered. He has assisted four High Commissioners and their Secretaries in turn, and no doubt knows a lot. He and I are to read the poems of Sa'di.

Let us make plans for a holiday sometime next year. Except that I shall be penniless and you will have to pay. But let us find some quiet *green* place and sit about there. I am not going to allow you in the East till you are very strong again—it is a horrid place when things go wrong. Do you remember lying in a coma at that village on the edge of Leja, and eating larks? Isn't it good to think we really did all that? Where shall we go? I have a very open mind, but it will depend on the season. It would be rather nice to sit in a boat and travel up or down a river, wouldn't it?

I have had a charming letter from the R.G.S. Secretary, saying lovely things about my literary style and telling me that one of my efforts is to be out in their Journal in July and the next in September.

I am trying hard to finish Mazanderan before I go off again, but it is too much to expect of the female brain. And I seem to have a different young man to tea every day: as I can't illude myself as to youth and beauty, I fear it must be that I am getting too middle-aged to matter. Anyway they are all very pleasant, and I am learning to switch off my affections about four times a week.

We have dust-storms nearly every day. It is terribly harassing to the nerves. However, I feel better to-day having bought a Luristan bronze I feel sure is worth £80 for £3—a lovely idol with two ibex heads, and two lion and two bulls' heads. They are not known here as they are in Persia. If I can sell it, we will go and rejoice on the proceeds.

24 *July*, 1932.

Darling B,

I think R is going to take me to Persia for a week. I need a holiday—everyone does just now. We are having the third dust-storm this week. You must be tired of this bit of news but not near so tired as I am of the dust-storms. R has bought a lovely car which I am to learn to drive. It will be great fun. Such nice things do happen to me.

Vyvyan came to tea. He is very indignant because a cat has chosen to have kittens in the cupboard where the secret documents are kept.

2 August, 1932.

We leave on Thursday, all being well. It will be nice, and R very pleasant to go with. He is teaching me to drive. I forgot which was the brake and a beduin seemed unable to realize this fact, so got gently pushed along. He didn't mind, but turned to smile apologetically and seemed rather pleased than otherwise to see R and me overcome with laughter. It is great fun, only I do find it hard to think of three things at once.

I think I have found a good site in Mazanderan. Am looking into it for the first time and it all seems to fit with the references and may be quite an important historical discovery. One never knows. Anyway I have done a tiny bit of real work: I mean finding something new, not just other people's sayings and ideas rechauffés.

KERMANSHAH, 6 August, 1932.

Dearest Venetia,

Here is a new address for you. I am in Persia for a week, invited by an old friend of ours, who is in Baghdad and decided to bring his car up (which he is now regretting owing to Persian roads). I could not resist and we are here on the way to Senna in Kurdistan, to stay with the Chaldean Bishop. I hate cars I decide more and more: all one's time is spent tinkering at the million things that go wrong with them, and everyone who has to do with cars in the way of commerce becomes a criminal, and my camera, the most precious possession I had in this world, is lost and done for. I was dreadfully disagreeable all yesterday afternoon, and realized how trying a honeymoon must be when there is no one to be annoyed with but an uncomprehending man whom one feels one ought to be nice to. I think it is a dispensation of Providence that has spared me (and him) this experience.

We had quite an exciting drive from Baghdad to the frontier at Khaniqin, getting caught at night out in the low desolate Jebel Hamrin where one is not supposed to be after sunset. I didn't mind the chance of being shot at, but did not want to be held up by police and kept all night in one of their solitary little towers for safety, so we put the accelerator on whenever we came into their neighbourhood, and finally, after a last breakdown, reached Khaniqin and only discovered a puncture in the morning.

I am practising driving. It is fun, but not travel I consider—and barbarous to have to rush along with one's eye on the road all the time. We had lunch in a pleasant thicket by a stream, under willows, and sitting on scented mint, and then began climbing up, a wall of a pass, but not as bad as the Alps, and not so beautiful. A road does spoil a pass, unless you can see it winding away in ribbons far into the distance below.

BAGHDAD, 13 *August*, 1932.

Darling B,

It was lovely to get up into the fresh air, and an amusing ride, and lovely to get to Senna and see the edge of Kurdistan. But I really *do* prefer to go alone. R is going to be so tiresome; and he refused to believe what I told him about the difficulties of getting into the frontier hills from Senna and went and blurted it all out— so that we were very politely and suavely turned away from any westward expeditions. We had no difficulties in getting through the customs, but came along very slowly as something was always going wrong with the car. You can't imagine what a troublesome thing a car is when there is no Beppe to look after it. I drove it for one and a half hours. I must have been bad for it, as it seems I went too fast.

We drove up to Senna and got there late at night over a good road but with very narrow bits—beautiful wide valleys with streams but very little trees. The Bishop received us most cordially—a man about sixty—very much used to command, and pleasant. We went to mass in his church and then were taken to call on the Governor, a very civilized Effendi. But Senna was disappointing, as the men's dress is Europeanized by law and we did not see a single Kurd whom one could recognize at first sight as such. They are building barracks, and the soldiers are out in all that district settling it after the rebellion of Ja'far Sultan and Mahmud Dizli last year and the district where they are is just the one where we wanted to go to. So we stayed and played about with the Bishop instead, and took him to the north where the Diyala river rises: but just before reaching the last villages, the outer cover burst and we had to come back very careful and make the bishop and his two friends walk up the hills.

We came away after three nights there and, having to go so slow because of punctures, had to sleep out in the open and only got to Kermanshah next day. Then I was so tired of R, always saying we could do this or that and that I was wrong to imagine difficulties—that I let him try. We started off to climb the mountain of Bisitun —or rather Parau behind it. All seemed well: then the taxi-man missed the road. We got out and found two donkey men—but one had to go to the village and get food. So we arranged to meet him and went on with the other—rested a little by a spring, saw no one coming and went on in the moonlight up to the meeting-place, the last spring of water under the snow. It was a lovely ride, but we only got up about 10 p.m.—and no sign of the donkey with our beddings, wraps and food. R wanted to go up to the snow: this I refused to do however—as it was quite cold enough where we were. He says I was very disagreeable, which is possibly true. Anyway we got very cold. I found a small cave where I could lie with only my head out in the wind, and I wore the donkey man's coat. Then from one to four we made a fire—and then at last daylight came. R and the donkey man went up to the snow and I remained and fell asleep and woke up to find a circle of Kurdish villagers looking down into my face and Mirza the donkey man arriving with lots of provisions and a charming smile, and no explanation except that he had thought it late the night before.

We left that same day and got to Karind at night where the A.P.O.C. have a summer camp and tents in a lovely gorge of walnut and fruit trees—and so home next day—after a glorious bathe in a river—all green strong water lined with oleanders.

20 *August*, 1932.

Darling B,

I am going to be left alone with the paper next week-end as Mr. Main takes four days' holiday. It means a lot of work and no time to do it properly, and there is just now a heat wave on—but, of course, it feels very responsible to run a newspaper all by oneself for four days.

Do you know V.H. really is the most disarming person. I left some money in an envelope in his office when I went to Persia—and

[271]

went the other day to retrieve it and said: "I have come for some money." He had forgotten about the envelope, and was going without a word of enquiry to produce some of his own money for me out of his desk, as if this were the most natural thing in the world.

I am getting quite clever with R's car. It is rather fun; one always wants to go faster and faster. R is beginning to become sensible again. I think I will have to try and see if I can help patch things up with his wife: he must have *some* woman—I really don't think it much matters who it is. I find myself with mid-Victorian ideas of morality, and no one to share them with except V.H., who persists in thinking me fast and modern. It is hard. And R has been suggesting travelling together to Bokhara and Samarcand. He says he has never met anyone so virtuous as me. Such a pity one gets no credit for it.

28 *August*, 1932.

Darling B,

Evan spent the day yesterday. He came to do some German in the morning and stayed till seven-thirty, with an interval during which he slept in the room downstairs and left his tie and studs in the drawing-room, so that I nearly had a fit when the bell rang and I expected a caller: my poor reputation gone for ever. (V.H. says I needn't worry—I haven't got any.) I asked him what I *could* do for a respectable holiday and he suggests going by train to Basra with female friends—of all drearinesses: I said I hadn't got any: and he said: "I don't wonder." Life is hard.

The boy who sweeps the floor has just been sacked for washing his head with my soap.

8 *September*, 1932.

Darling B,

Most exciting thing has happened. I am on the track of a hidden treasure. Don't please mention to *anyone* for a few months.

One of the people here came up to me, said he heard I was leaving for Persia, and would I like to go with a young man who wanted a reliable English person to help him get this treasure which is hidden in twenty chests in a cleft in the mountains. They had a map in the family which he came upon as a boy and showed to a school friend of his: the friend's father seized on it and now refuses to give

[272]

it up, but the boy has a copy. His family was a big tribal one and the tribes are still loyal to him, and one of them came to him one day and told how he had come upon this treasure while taking refuge in a cavern from a storm. He brought several specimens—and I am to see one to-morrow. It seems and sounds quite genuine, though fantastic. It is worth going to look anyway, and sounds too alluring altogether for this prosaic century.

Captain de Gaury back from Jerusalem looking very fit. Came to see me first day he arrived and told all about the rebel Ibn Rifadha. They were horribly massacred, and his head impaled on a spear, and the few survivors, nearly starved, crossed into Palestine where Captain de Gaury saw them arrive. Among them was the rebel's secretary —a man with a romantic story: he was a Hejaz merchant, travelling with all his goods in a little ship in the Red Sea when he was wrecked and cast away, with nothing, on the Arabian coast. He was picked up by Ibn Rifadha's tribe and the chief took him in and made him his secretary and promised to make him wazir at Mecca if they succeeded. So he played and lost and now is completely broke and a marked man too. All still very like the Arabian Nights out here in many ways.

I have got £8 for my Tunis article, all going in carpets.

R told me it would be better not to quarrel and to go on seeing each other, or people would talk. He wrote saying he longs for some firm courageous mind on which to lean. He little knows what a mistake that was: if there is one thing I am tired of it is being treated like a pillar for leaning against. It is *I* who would give I don't know what for someone who would consent to prop me up for the rest of my days.

9 *September*, 1932.

Darling B,

This letter is not to be posted till I return, so as to spare you unnecessary qualms—but I must put it all down now before I forget.

I have just had a visit from the owner of the treasure, an engaging youth who is, however, getting more and more into a funk. He was implicated in the last Lurish rebellion at Deh Bala, and is doomed if the police once catch him. He finds that everyone knows he is going, and is afraid: but tells me that he will go separately by himself and *meet* me there—and meanwhile dodge the pursuit by pretending to

[273]

be leaving for Syria. He is only twenty, but with a nervous face that makes him look older: a very determined little man, not too open. He knew an old man who would have been able to get us safely through the intervening tribes (between the frontier and his own people) but the old man refuses to take *me* because he says he has just done his pilgrimage and he might accidentally touch my cloak or something and be polluted and all his trouble for nothing. But the young man will give me letters and guides. I decide to-morrow.

11 *September*, 1932.

Darling B,

The treasure hunt is planning out nicely. Even Vyvyan seems grudgingly to acquiesce and admits its charms. I have the map of the place—a valley—a big rock; three oak trees in front—and the cavern behind it. Only skull and cross bones missing. It is fun isn't it to come upon this in 1932?

Lovely to think I shall be coming back to new clothes.

11 *September*, 1932.

Captain Hare, Abdul Kerim the owner of the treasure, and I, have just finished a long two-hour conference. He brought the man who is to take me to the hills, a dear old man with ears like an elephant's sticking out under his turban and eyes pulled up a little at the corners so that he might be a benevolent mandarin. He seems just the right sort and I feel very happy with him. His name is Shah Riza.

BEDRAH, 14 *September*, 1932.

I have started on the venture, but whether I ever get across the border and on my way is still a problem. I am here in an empty house belonging to one of the sons of the Vali of Pusht-i-Kuh with a courtyard and closed gate that keeps out children but not flies. I had a sleep on the floor of a nice room with windows surrounded in red, green, blue and yellow glass and a wardrobe with a mirror. The house is empty—the man's wife having died and he moved to Kut —but his steward, a handsome but untrustworthy young man in a turban and wavy locks under, with a rosary in his hand and a jaunty manner suitable to a retainer in Great Houses, has been installing me— and sits outside smoking cigarettes, squatting on his heels against the courtyard wall while I rest. The yard has a high wall finished off

[274]

in points over which tops of palm trees are swishing in the wind and sun, with date bunches all dry because of Bedrah's want of water. Like Mandali the Persians are cutting it all off upstream.

I like my guide—Shah Riza: he sat in front with the chauffeur and little serving lad, who was sleepy, and the old man put his arm round him to make him comfortable. I would go on a thing like that rather than on lots of recommendations. He has been saying his afternoon prayer in the yard while a pigeon drinks at the brick-work tank: all very peaceful.

15 *September*, 1932.

I am trying to learn patience again. This is good practice. Yesterday we sat in lantern light under the six palm trees by the little tank in the yard and discussed our policy: it was quite in the right style. I watched the four organizers of the expedition, all squatting in a row, each very eager with a policy of his own, and all interesting faces. Two typical Lurs, with the pointed face and thick eyebrows; my old guide, a nice old face with the neat straight features that seem only to belong to the Moslems here, and his uncle, an old Moslem peasant type, very wrinkled and positive with a manner of evident authority. Finally it was settled that Hasan, the Lur, should go for a friend who has mules early this morning and come back so that we could get off by night. Now it is 11 a.m. and I have discovered he has not yet gone: so it is very doubtful if we start till to-morrow—and it is a wearisome business waiting with nothing to do and also a tempting of Providence. However we hope for the best.

This house has the inestimable advantage of privacy. Only my immediate retainers so to say, the family and friends of my guide, have the entrée, and I have a good big room to myself and a complete wash in big copper basin. In fact I felt so secure that I was combing by the open door—which won't shut anyway—when two sayyids appeared to be shown over the place, on their way from Kadhimain to Pusht-i-Kuh to fetch a wife for the son of the Vali.

We had a quiet night—with a lot of loading of rifles before settling down, in case of beduin after the dates: but no noises agitated us except the falling of ripe dates from the trees with a loud whack, and then in the middle of the night an eclipse of the moon with banging of tins and barking of dogs from the village next door.

I had an amusing chat this morning with an old scamp of a barber, with a long nose falling over his face and twinkling eyes rather near together, and a curly mouth under a grey moustache: he comes from a place where there are said even now to be idolaters in secret, and where they all used to worship idols, and the bronze statues they worshipped have been taken away and sold to dealers: but there is still a temple in the mountains with inscriptions. He was a gay old man and sat smoking Persian tobacco and telling stories from the *Arabian Nights*.

Old Shah Riza the guide told me the story of a judgement. Two babies, a girl and a boy, got mixed up at birth: the boy's mother, though she did not know it to be her son, always felt a pang when she heard it cry: so at last her husband asked the tribal sheikh: and he ordered milk to be drawn from every available sort of animal—two ewes, one with a male and one with a female lamb, two mares, one with a male, one with female foal and so on: and the mother of the male was always found to have heavier milk: and so the same experiment was tried with the two women, and the babies restored to the right mothers.

16 September, 1932.

If there is one thing more exhausting than the other, it is the waiting which always precedes these expeditions. This is my *third* day here: I hope we start to-morrow. There is nothing to do but to wait, learn a few Lurish words, and read *The Pilgrim's Progress* which luckily I brought.

I paid a call on the authorities this afternoon—a long walk down to the other end of the gardens of Bedrah, where there are a few little 'city' houses and buildings round the police station, and the doctor and judge were sitting in what is to be a garden later on. All very cordial and pleasant except the judge, who never looked in my direction and was heard to say "Allah" when I left. I have told the people here to murmur to him that I knew the Drowers, so as to make him feel unhappy. The others were all pleasant and say there should be no trouble in getting over the border: but I shall try to get through incognito all the same in my Kurdish dress, so as to avoid being shepherded all over the country later.

We came back, my old guide and I, about two miles along the desert edge, with a tiresome wind, which has been knocking the dates

down these three days, worrying us—while he beguiled the way with
stories. He told me that Alexander the Great said: "If there were
five men like me the world would know no trouble": but his friend
said: "If there were *two* people whose hearts are as one, they would
do with the world as they like."

His other story was a long one about the king and his vizier
who went hunting alone in the desert and the king's horse threw and
killed him. The vizier said: "What shall I do? No one will believe
it was an accident." And he saw a shepherd boy almost exactly like
the king and put the king's clothes on to him and took him to court;
and told the queen, and they managed the matter so that in a year or
two the new king had learnt his trade and no one noticed. Then
one day the shepherd king said to his vizier: "Buy me a horse made
of stone," and then the vizier knew he was to be killed because he
knew the king's secret. So he got a horse cut out of stone and brought
it to the king—and the king said: "Now ride it." And the vizier
said: "How can I? It is only stone." And the king said: "You
must." And the vizier got on, and pricked it with his spurs, and the
horse stamped its feet, "because the vizier was lucky." "And,"
said my guide, "without luck one can do nothing, but Inshallah your
luck is *good* and everything is possible to you." And with this moral
we reached our manzil.

17 September, 1932.

I really thought we would get off early this morning, but while
I was sitting over my tea and Shah Riza squatting and meditating
with bowed head as if time were non-existent, it suddenly appeared
that he had neither a hat nor trousers to go in. He must be dressed as
a Persian if he wants to go about unquestioned. He wasn't doing
anything about it and I got rather cross. "Here have we been three
days," said I: "time enough to get twenty trousers. I am tired of
sitting in this courtyard." He opens his hands with a pathetic expression. "And I?" said he. He is off now with two rupees to get
trousers, and I hope will not be too late—but it will be grilling
travelling as it is eight o'clock already.

Besides Shah Riza I will have Keram Khan, the real smuggler
lad who owns the donkeys, and looks a regular young scamp. Alidad,
a middle-aged man with bushy moustache, rather like an Italian
peasant, I think will be all right, though he says, sitting here in a

[277]

meditative way, that "with you, money runs like water," and tells me that when he went to see his brother and ask him for help he found him working in the house of an English lady at Khanikin. The brother would give him nothing, but the English lady enquired into the matter, wrote his name down, told him to serve in the house for four days, and when he left gave him some notes of which he did not know the value, but which turned out to be fifty rupees, a fatal generosity which it will give me a lot of trouble to counterbalance. I said: "That lady was better than your brother." "My brother," said he and spat on the ground: "That's what I feel about my brother."

I am suffering from the fact that my papers are too much in order and they all want to go in a lawful way for once. That will mean an escort and lots of questions, which I don't want. But anyway I hope in my luck, as the old man says.

There are lots of thieves about here at night—night before last they carried off a ewe, and last night shots going on all round.

17 September, 1932.

I am almost worn out with delays and very annoyed with my doddering old guide who is quite useless and can't even manage to buy his own trousers. He came along this morning with a quite inadequate piece of black alpaca saying that someone would be found here at this first Persian village to sew it up. This turns out to be about fifteen mud huts without a shop, and the women unable even to weave carpets which they do nearly everywhere. Shah Riza sat looking sadly at the useless piece of stuff: but when a second-hand pair of trousers was offered in exchange, he was for refusing them as not sufficiently beautiful: and only a positive intervention on my part, supported by the village which was naturally on the side of the owner of the trousers, carried the day. A long piece of red string was found, wrapped round a stick, and run through the waist of the voluminous garment which has now, together with a Pahlevi hat, turned Shah Riza into a legalized Persian.

I paid extra to be taken secretly into the country, but the three men came to another conclusion and have gone off with my passport to the police—so I expect every sort of trouble and delay.

20 *September*, 1932.

I can't write because we have to do long days, leaving early with scarce a midday rest and reaching shelter at night. It is such an uninhabited country—we have ridden nine hours to-day, and no habitation on the way. A high range with a col of 8,300 feet: that has been surveyed by an Englishman; but now we are in new country —a lovely pastoral valley with lower hills dotted with oak trees and high cliffs behind, and a river, and we are sitting for the night round a fire under an oak: the old man of the mill rode off on his horse to buy us flour. There is the mill, and a few tents higher up—otherwise no dwelling in the valley: but there is life in it, for shepherds have also fires under oak trees here and there, with their flocks around them. I said I would rather dodge police and trust to the tribes alone, and it is a true remark besides having been popular: I find everything much easier and more friendly. It is so pleasant camping here. The mules with intelligent faces join the circle, the big tree is all lit up above us; there are crickets; it is nice to see a few crops again after the savage highness of the hills: and the old miller, and a young man who has worked for the Anglo-Persian Oil Company in Baghdad, are pleasant people.

As we came down a very precipitous valley we saw quantities of ibex, grown and baby, scurrying up the tossed-up strata of a point of rock opposite which ran straight into the sky in the sunlight; the ibex ran as it were upstairs, a pretty sight. We have been 3,000 feet and more up to-day and as many down.

There is something very pleasant in these clear forests with nothing but rock or gravel under the trees, and each separate, like a primitive drawing, sitting on its own shadow on the hillside. Some are fine trees, but mostly have had to struggle too hard in their youth not to show traces of wear and tear.

I hear great tales of castles and graves and hope for luck. According to my map I am in a white piece of country called "unsurveyed' and hope to put in a few names. But there are no villages—only tents.

My old guide used to live here, and had not been for years and years. He sits and talks for hours about old friends and enemies.

I have presents of thimbles and needles for the women—seem popular. Everyone friendly—the only trouble is that my men seem to think all I need to eat is flour and water baked in ashes, and I have only five sardine tins. Light gives out.

[279]

27 *September*, 1932.

I was discovered by the Commander of Police in a little group of tents out in the blue yesterday about lunch-time, and it now remains to be seen whether I can get rid of him or not. There seems to be no particular obstacle to going by way of Tarhan; I hope for the best; I was able to show him, with pride, the whole of my collection, it being nothing but old stones and a skull. I have, I think, discovered an interesting place: the city of the Larti, who may be the originals of Lur, and have a ruined site on a precipitous spur in a defile, very fine and romantic, with a delicious spring of water. The Larti still live in their defile in small numbers, but most of them have fled during small feuds, and gone to Kermanshah, and their lands been taken over. They were settled up in the defile in little tents arranged each round the trunk of an oak tree with a woven screen of reeds around. They are wonderfully hospitable, and never expected anything for the night's hospitality, and gave their tea and sugar, which are now the scarcest things in the country. I spent three nights out, finding an old city and a lot of mounds, and a wonderful defile where a Sassanian fort must have barred the way. I was in despair as to dating it, till at last, after making my mind up to go once more on the way home, a boy came up with a cornelian bead stuck in a bit of plaster column—and three spear heads and a broken dagger were brought from the foot of the pass. I hope this business may be of some use to archaeologists—for I don't know what use it is to anyone else, and I am finding it a little solitary, though it is pleasant in many ways, and nice to ride through the oak forests and see their dull green against the blue sky. They have bigger leaves and acorns than ours, with pretty cups frilly at the edge, and the people are making bread of them this year, as the rain has not come to grow the corn.

DEH BALA, 2 *October*, 1932.

I am here in the capital of Pusht-i-Kuh kept waiting for a telegram from Teheran to hear if I can continue my journey. If only Prof. Godard is there I hope he will send me all sorts of permits. If not, I shall be interrupted just in the most interesting part, and have to go sadly back. Meanwhile this is my second day wasted, and only consoled by the chief of police, whose guest I am and who is very pleasant, and by the wife of the Governor's Wazir, a pleasant jolly lady who yesterday brought five other Kurdish ladies (two being other wives of her husband), all dressed in their best—a gorgeous sight, with the enormous head-dresses of black and red Assyrian silk all hung about with beads and tassels and pendants, and an abba laid over the top, and bright flowery dresses under. They are very handsome, two with marvellously sparkling eyes in long colourless faces with black eyebrows painted very thick.

We arrived here in a sad little procession, the police officer reclining on the baggage mare and I riding his white horse, as he was laid low with dysentery. Then I was taken to the house of the chief of police, washed myself, and spent the evening being asked about antiquities in the most intelligent way, so that if I had not been genuinely up in it, I would certainly have come to grief. The only safe thing is to stick to the truth in this world. Next morning I was taken to the Governor, in a fine new villa, all whitewashed Corinthian columns and water and petunias in the garden—and drank tea out of silver cups with spoons instead of with a bit of wood to stir it. The Governor was a big, pleasant, slow man, rather florid with black eyebrows and greenish eyes that were consumed with amusement at the appearance of my retainer, Shah Riza, whose coat is all in tatters and his locks sticking out with the air of those of a distressed philosopher, and who when asked what his business was announced himself as a maker of quilts. They have sent telegrams to Teheran. Apparently to wander about in those mountains with nothing but a skull in one's luggage is too much for local resources. But I hope to get off by to-morrow or next day.

This is an interesting place just now—a town in the making. Houses and boulevards springing up with the black tents still scattered among them.

BAGHDAD, 9 October, 1932.

I have just got back and had a bath, and send this off at once.

The reply from Teheran came at last (after four days) to say that 'with the perfection of courtesy and honour' I was to be escorted the nearest way to the border. I feared as much. I begged for a little less 'honour' and only one policeman escort, but they insisted on four: a sergeant and three men. Whenever I got off to walk a little, they all four got off and walked too, the sergeant ten steps behind me with his gun; and it took us four days to ride back across the hills. They were very nice policemen and it was a lovely country and

[281]

most enjoyable if it hadn't been just the opposite direction to what I wanted to go in. However, being so well guarded no one asked about my skull at the frontier, and I hope to have got some interesting information though nothing to what might so easily have been— and me on the very edge of it all.

It was the fault of the treasure. I hung about waiting for my accomplice (and knowing he wouldn't keep his promise). I can't remember if I told you about how I went to the place, recognized the valley, but the actual spot was indistinguishable among a hundred others exactly alike: I could not go alone, as it is not a safe place, so had two tribesmen and a policeman, and had to slip away from them after their lunch: all managed successfully, and I had a bag round me under my skirt, and torch and candle all ready. If the wretched man had come we could have brought lots of it away—but no one can possibly find it without. Will let you know developments later. Dearest darling, love dear B. So many things to think about. Hope lots of letters waiting for me.

Y.M.C.A. BAGHDAD, 10 *October*, 1932.

Dearest Venetia,

Five letters waiting. What is nicer than to get back to civilization and find one's friends' news all waiting. I wonder if you got my letter written from the capital of Pusht-i-Kuh? And did I tell you that I went treasure hunting? And found the locality, but not the exact site? And then was providentially interrupted by the police, and after four days waiting in Teheran, escorted in a polite manner by four policemen across the border the nearest way? And meanwhile the enemy, who knew of the treasure and that I had gone, sent men 'to see I did not come back'. The people here have been in a great state, unable to do anything or get at me, and expecting never to see me again. It was rather nice to hear their voices all so relieved at the ends of the telephone. What happens next I will let you know in due course. It is all very Rider Haggardish. I think I have brought back enough material to map two unsurveyed valleys—not as much as I hoped. What pleases me, is that ten men should be thought necessary for my elimination: such is one's vanity.

I come back longing for things like clothes and books, etc., and to lie in nice white sheets.

I liked your distinction between the 'end' of the multitude and

[282]

the 'ideal' of the individual. I think it is true—and it must be of use to live rightly, and not to compromise with what one holds to be the best truly. Sometimes it is difficult to know—and one gives up what seems a great deal for what is only a dim possibility, never probably to be realized: and yet I think it is better to do so.

15 *October,* 1932.

Darling B,

I lunched yesterday with Sir Hubert Young and heard all about the solemnities of Iraq's entry to the League, and how the F. O. delayed so long in deciding *what* Sir H was to be (as he is only temporary here, and if they made him merely Chargé d'Affaires he would have had to be the last at all the receptions), that when the great day came his credentials hadn't arrived and he was nothing at all, and Britain was the only country not officially represented at the termination of her own mandate.

17 *October,* 1932.

There seem to be very few letters of yours: I hope you are not neglecting me. Am now waiting every day anxiously for the arrival of *clothes*: do long for them with genuine *hunger*. All Baghdad is to be filled this winter with young and lovely débutantes—about half a dozen. So I shall not have a look in: but still it will be nice to have clothes all the same.

Yesterday, at tea, I met Sir Aurel Stein the great explorer, a charming little old man of seventy, as keen as a needle, and as obstinate —and with a misleadingly benevolent smile. Very interesting to talk to. I don't think he approved of my expedition, and he told Gerald de Gaury, whom he met to-day, that it was a great pity to waste time over Luristan bronzes—which are quite late—and only hoped I had not spoilt his chances in Eastern Persia. I, of course, feel terribly pleased at being considered *able* to spoil anyone's chances, and de G came along much amused at these archaeological pre-occupations.

He comes two times a week for Italian and it is very pleasant— he is a charming interesting man and tells me all the gossip. I shall sit in my little study this winter and just lead a quiet life, seeing the friends who take the trouble to come to me.

[283]

25 October, 1932.

The garden party was in honour of four female delegates from the 'Women's International League'. I saw them before at Mrs. Drower's: one talkative old Englishwoman, a tall Frenchwoman like a Grenadier just spoilt in the making: a little Syrian, very small and shrinking like a drowned rat, only obstinate: and the President, a fat plain lady Druse from Lebanon with little corkscrew curls under a black veil, always worrying about being first. They are having meetings and making a great flutter about women's rights and progress, and the Arab men, I hear, all dislike it very much. The garden party was a great success, however, and was on the lawns of the king's palace, all pleasantly set out with little tables, and, when the two queens arrived, the band (which the king had lent as a great concession) struck up the national anthem, for the first time for a woman, and the queens with a select circle sat at the chief table where they had a chocolate cake with a crown on it.

1 November, 1932.

Darling B,

The treasure story is getting too wildly improbable. It seems now that the man sent to rescue me and the six sent to murder me, met out there and had a wild scrimmage near the site: the six were caught by the tribe, and had their heels put into a wood fire till they confessed, and are now home again in Baghdad. Whether to believe it all, or how much of it, I don't know. Anyway I hope I am clear of them for good. I don't like being involved with these very peculiar people. Anyway I am sure anyone who tries to get the treasure now will be in for a lot of trouble from one set of people or the other, as it is being carefully watched.

The Y.M.C.A. is full up with a mixture of Service people and missionaries. I really am there very little, as I have three evenings a week talking Russian. I feel such a brute always with poor Mme Halutin who is one of those affectionate females made to be unjustly trampled on. She is so well trained by V.H. that nothing in the way of a pupil's impatience surprises her any longer. Yesterday she was nearly in tears because she had made V.H. read an 'interesting' story which he threw aside after a few minutes saying "It is interesting for you, but not for me", whereupon she, unwisely, said: "But it *is* interesting." Whereupon he repeated his former statement more emphatically: and she told me that he was of a "nervous disposition". I am sure there is something wrong in being as meek as all that. Anyway I'm not.

I must stop now—I am busy with my book, which comes out to-morrow. Am sending you and Herbert copies. If you can tell me how many you want for yourself and anyone who wants them in Asolo, one can make all one parcel. I think it looks quite nice, but V.H. says the print and binding are appalling. I don't think them so bad. Anyway it appeared to me a most impressive sight.

19 November, 1932.

I had to go over the museum and write an article: it was very interesting and Dr. Jordan himself took me: I had Mrs. E with me. She is a peer's daughter and a bride—the former spoils her a little as she would be very nice if she was not so very sure of herself: but no doubt Life and a Husband will eventually teach her that she is not so very important and the niceness will remain. Well, we went over the museum: they have done wonders with it and arranged it all chronologically which makes it far more interesting, and they have an Islamic room (owing to Mr. Guest's and my remarks). I would have had a better innings by myself with Dr. J because he had to explain such silly things—but it was a good morning. Then, walking back we saw an accident: man knocked over by an *arabana*, he fell between the front and back wheels, and first the driver drove on and went over him with the back wheels: then pulled up and drove back and so went over him again with the front; then was going on again to go over him a fourth time when I managed to make him stay still and the man was got away. I hope not dead: the human body seems unpleasantly soft when it gets under unyielding substances.

30 November, 1932.

Such an agitated week. First of all I was feeling rather coldified and cross anyway, and inclined to be snappy—and on Sunday, instead of finding V.H. to ride, he turned up with the new Councillor and the Second Secretary, all in comitiva. I thought that, if he liked my society at all, he would not go spoiling it with a crowd of people on the one day we had, so went along talking to the Embassy and feeling crosser and crosser. Poor V.H. noticed something was wrong and came along in a conciliatory mood remarking on a bull-dog by the roadside. "I don't like bull-dogs," I said, "nor Alsatians, nor poodles, nor lots of other animals." Before I left he asked me what was the matter, but I didn't tell him and left him distressed and completely puzzled—and I do think it served him right for being so stupid. However, the very next day my editor went and published something about the new spelling of Baghdad as arranged by the Foreign Office. This would not have mattered, only he put in something that sounded as if it came from a confidential source. V.H. had spoken to me about it and he rang up and asked in the voice of an inquisitor *where* Mr. Main had got his information. I had not seen the thing in question, but the tone of voice alone made me feel guilty: I was really *dreadfully* upset, and only in thinking it over after realized that I was quite innocent: I telephoned to Mr. Main, and found out the real source, and yesterday when I went to the office, told my editor what I felt about it all so that he appeared quite cowed under the unexpected onslaught. V.H., evidently still worried over Sunday, asked me to go and help him choose his furnishings: which he did by going to one shop, seizing every object on his list, pushing it into a heap, and buying it all— and then saying that it was an expensive business. And so we left on a restored basis of tranquillity, though he still feels a little insecure I believe.

*　　*　　*

ARTICLE BY F.S. IN "BAGHDAD TIMES" OF NOVEMBER 1932.

Foreign Office Drops Its "H's"

When I came to my office the other day, with that anticipation of instruction and delight, which the prolonged study of Reuter telegrams may be presumed to foster, I saw among the papers on my desk a type-written sheet signed with a rubber stamp, "British Embassy, Bagdad"— —just Bagdad, without an H, as it might be Ollywood or Little-ampton.

I was shocked.

Can it be possible, I thought, that this august document has lain so long among the Reuter telegrams that it has acquired their peculiar notions of the English language?

Or is it a Diplomatic Incident? Without its H, Bagdad means nothing at all; but with it, it is derived by Arab historians from the Persian as signifying a "Garden of Justice". It is nice for a place to be called a Garden of Justice, whether it is one or whether it isn't. The Foreign

Office might of course not think of us as a Garden of Justice: and it might, of course, always want to say exactly what it thinks: and so it might be saying it in a diplomatic way through a philological insinuation.

Or perhaps it is just that the Foreign Office does not know how to spell?

Spelling, we admit, is one of those accomplishments that Diplomacy need not trouble about: and Geography is often proved to be beneath the notice of Public Men. With any other letter of the alphabet it would not matter. But H has a peculiar position all its own. It has acquired the dignity and mystery of a symbol. Years of expensive ancestors or training are necessary to its proper management.

"The little H, and how much it is." Put it were it is not whanted and nobody whill believe that you have been educated at Arrow or Heton.

It is really very important. And to see our Foreign Office forgetting itself in a body as it were, dropping its h's and giving us a cockney Bagdad on its own rubber stamp, is a humiliating experience for British patriots in Iraq.

Gh has long been recognized by all the Best People as the only possible transliteration for that Arabic sound which otherwise can only be expressed by the clearing of one's throat before a cough.

The Foreign Office cannot be expected to discover such minor details all by itself, especially now that it is chronically busy with these Conferences that are always beginning so well. But there must be some little office boys in Downing Street who could rush into the Library between one thing and another and turn over the leaves of an Etymological Dictionary: and at the worst, could run round and ask the Royal Geographical Society, who have a committee thinking out Transliterations all their lives, and apparently enjoying it. They are only too delighted to help one to spell the most difficult names, and since they are capable of reading even a German transliterator without fainting, they would be sure to listen with patience and urbanity to whatever enormity the Foreign Office might put before them.

7

The Last of Baghdad, 1933

THE year 1933 began with sorrow. The eldest of my
little Italian nieces died. She developed appendicitis
and, following the family way of wrestling with illness
in private, told no one, dosed herself fatally with castor oil, and
almost at once turned it to peritonitis which killed her. She
was only fifteen, and the third in our family whose death might
have been avoided by theories of health a little less spartan than
ours. My mother wrote the news to Vyvyan Holt, who told
it me in my dark little room at the Y.M.C.A., and I remember
feeling as if a wide black lake were there on the floor before
me, with opaque waters hiding one after the other the heads of
those I loved. In the end, it is well to be familiar with the
contemplation of death. We follow him, as he carries our
friends away, until the strength of the world bids us turn back and
live; the shadows then sink into the dark more gently than
seemed possible at first. Yet I carried the sadness of that
waste of youth and unnecessary pain about with me for a
long time.

The early months of the year, till March, were spent with
the *Baghdad Times*; and when I left it, having trained someone
to follow in its mystery, I spent some weeks visiting parts of
Iraq as yet unknown to me, and staying with the Sindersons.
These were the kindest people, who looked after the welfare,
bodily spiritual and political, of the royal family and of anyone else who was in need of comfort or advice. One of the
most shocking things that happened in the rebellion of 1941 was
the looting of their house, where so many sick Iraqis had been

[288]

cured for nothing, and so many young students looked after, entertained, and counselled.

At this time there was no sign of such a cloud; Iraq and Britain basked in a post-treaty honeymoon, and the summer massacre of the Assyrians was unsuspected. Such little shadows as there were, gathered themselves round German and Italian embassy intrigues. Herr Grobba was the German, a man unscrupulous but pleasant, who bore no malice for his own sins nor for those of other people, and kept a first-rate cellar. I suspected him of liking his British enemies much better than most of his friends. He used to give two parties a year—one for the Germans and one for the Jewish-Germans in Iraq—and the latter, even in 1937 when next I visited Baghdad, was being attended as completely as the former, in spite of all that happened in the Fatherland during those years. In 1941 Herr Grobba came to direct the anti-British forces, and was disappointed to find how little enthusiasm all those good wines and planned hospitalities brought him in: the unexpectedness of the Arab is that he does not allow himself to be much influenced by the bribes he takes. Worse damage was done by Professor Jordan, a charming man and beautiful musician, with an ascetic face, whom Lionel Smith had suggested as Director of Antiquities. We all liked and admired him; but he kept a private Nazi printing press.

This was all in the future on March the 26th, 1933, when I left Baghdad at ten o'clock at night, with no menace visible except that of the rain; it lashed almost horizontally against the little glass cage of the lorry in which I sat. Vyvyan Holt sat with me, seeing me off, as gloomy as the weather, distressed at the sight of discomfort which he thought I enjoyed. Finance, as usual, was the simple explanation. My lorry seat cost £2 10s. from Baghdad to Amman, and I wanted to be economical so as to go on to Petra and back by Jerusalem. My friends have always seemed to find it difficult to understand this easy motive, or to realize that, as pleasures must be paid for, one cannot humanly speaking embrace them all. Most people let them come indiscriminately, and often miss the best: but I was glad to buy Petra with a night of shaking and cold, in the company of a black-bearded, spectacled Swiss professor, who had means as slender and a curiosity greater even than my own.

One of the pleasantest of all days was spent in the desert train. It travelled once a week from Amman to Ma'an. Turkish slit trenches still showed round stations where T. E. Lawrence had hovered with his sticks of gelignite. But there was now no feeling either of drama or hurry: the wide white sky, the pale earth like an embroidered tent below it, no trees, but here and there a ruin, or fort, or well; outlines of camels, and riders with their striped cloaks in the sun; and, when the train, puffing its smoke like a leisurely pipe, came to a standstill, the song of larks above it clear and high: all these things built their harmony in the desert elixir of air; and the train, washed through and through with light, surrounded by emptiness, seemed to lose that feeling of congestion which we associate with the mechanic age. I think one may become fond of machines, as one becomes fond of people, if there is space enough around each one to see it clearly, so that its individual dignity remains. A plough is beautiful on a hillside of furrows, or a car alone on the loops of its road; and there is all the difference between crowds and processions, merely because in the latter every creature has a place and space to move in. The same may be said of most vehicles, and of a fleet at sea. The feeling for space, which is respect for the individuality of objects, is an invention of humanity unknown to nature, who crowds all things regardless of individual perfection: and that is why I like open landscapes best, or else an arranged view—a park or tidy cultivated slopes—where the struggle is either invisible to us, or has actually been done away with by the selectiveness of men.

Dust-devils whirled through the streets in a Dantesque perpetual wind in the afternoon emptiness of Ma'an, with the feeling of the greater emptiness of the Hejaz beyond it just across the border. Here Pat Domvile appeared with Savile Row elegance, silk handkerchief and smooth sleek hair, extremely individual in the beduin solitude around him. He had mislaid Lady Irwin and her party in Sinai, and was perturbed but still charming, unselfish and affectionate; he has those fairy gifts that, however tattered by living, one carries to the grave. It was our first meeting, and, next day, the professor and I reached the ravines of Petra, blossoming with scented broom.

All this, Amman, and Jerusalem, are described in letters that follow: the ruins of M'shitta, which still hold the charm and wonder of the Ommayad caliphate, its combination of Byzantium and the desert; the Nebi Musa pilgrimage winding by the Bethlehem road and the Jaffa gate and the pool of Siloam to the whitewashed enclosure so small in the wilderness of Judæa; the day in Hebron, said to be dangerous, and then so friendly, with coffee and the sheikh of Abraham's tomb; and the Passover, where fifty or sixty guests were gathered, women in evening dress and men with their hats on for the journey from bondage, and the youngest child asked the ritual question, the history of the ancient delivery from Egypt. Looking at all the faces, Jews from the United States or Spain, converted Tatars from the steppes, the bitter ideologists of South-East Europe, or more moderate products of the West, it would have been difficult, even for an anthropologist, to unravel the racial strands. The only thing that seemed to unite them was an absence of perspective, purely oriental, which gave a contemporary pungency to the sayings and doings of the Pharaohs, and to all the details of so long ago: I have often noticed this quality among various eastern races, though I suppose among Europeans it only exists in Ireland.

By this time I was poor, and travelled to Trieste third class, in a cabin for seven people, with Jewish women from Germany and the Crimea: we would have been happy and comfortable if they had not been sick in such unexpected places. I was anxious to see the last of them, and the squalid details of the voyage are forgotten. On my arrival in Venice, a suit-case rolled off the platform under the train which should have started some minutes before. I hesitated, but the thought of the treasures I had collected decided me, and I climbed down among the wheels and retrieved them, thankful that the famous fascist punctuality was now only a cliché of the British Press. In the evening I reached our railhead at Castelfranco, and found my mother and Herbert Young waiting with a car. As we drove up by the familiar road, damp with the smell of ditches and with the plane trees like sentinels beside it, they told me that the Back Grant had been awarded me by the Royal Geographical Society for my travels in Luristan.

The most complicated sensations were caused by this announcement; it came as unexpected as a Visitation to someone who has no reason to think himself a saint; I felt as if another world, whose existence I had never thought of, had suddenly inserted itself into my small, self-contained and solitary orbit, destined now never to be again the same. My mother had to repeat the news to me; I thought there must be some mistake; and I then contemplated it with awe, not far removed from fear, but with pleasure too—a gentle pleasure, for it had little to do with myself, but welled up warm and thankful for the delight of the two old people beside me; what chiefly remained was wonder, and gratitude equally distributed between destiny and the Royal Geographical Society—that I could procure such happiness merely by walking by myself in the Persian hills.

As for the awe, and perhaps the fear, they were justified, for this news marked a threshold over which I passed that summer. I was made much of in London; there was a presentation at the Royal Geographical Society; I was made to speak on the B.B.C.; was interviewed by the Press; was asked for sittings by misguided photographers; lectured to the Royal Central Asian Society, and in 1934 to the Royal Asiatic Society, which presented me with the Burton medal. I was the fourth person and the first woman to receive it, and am still astonished when I think of those who received it before me—Philby, Bertram Thomas, Harold Mac-Michael—and that I came to know them all as friends.

People were delightful that year. London was gay, and I was well, and I had no idea that there were so many attractive human beings to know all at once. I lunched at the Allenbys, sitting with the Field-Marshal on one side and Sir Ronald Storrs on the other, talking alternately of Palestine and Cyprus. Sir Ronald and I had a link, for Queen Cornaro, the last queen of of the Island, ended her days in Asolo, and her castle still stands in view of my windows, on the hill. Lord Allenby, with his great domed head and tall stoop and hot blue eyes and deafness inspired awe, until I found that he liked to talk about finches, of which he kept a many-coloured aviary in a little court outside.

General Sir John Shea at this time described to me the battle for Jerusalem and how, at the last push, as our troops fought their way up the steep hill exhausted, a gleam of sun pressed out through clouds and lit the city in its grey walls, and with the radiance of that sudden lighting made perhaps the difference of the day.

It is one of the regrets of life that we forget so many things that people tell us (though, of course, it would be far worse if one had to remember *all*). What remains is not what people say but what they are. Many of those I met became friends in the years that followed—almost dearest among them Admiral Sir William Goodenough, who was president of the Royal Geographical Society and handed me my grant, and soon invited me to Coulsdon. Here everyone who travelled or explored, young or old, would gather. Lady Goodenough, with blue eyes and white curls, sat at one end of a long cheerful table, and he at the other, talking of remote places from poles to equator, with a zest and innocence of enjoyment. He had sailor virtues— integrity and conscientiousness and selfless humility and kindness. When the last war came, while his wife did most of the house- work, the old Admiral set himself to keep the garden and clean the silver, and fill his days with a simple hospital job to free a younger man; and when I went for the last time to see him, showed me, in his study, his flag of the battle of Jutland, care- fully put away. Whether he had ever had to think the matter out, or whether it came by a happiness of nature I do not know —but I feel sure that he never hesitated in his life between the right-hand and the left-hand path, and served—as he is surely serving now—in perfect freedom.

In and out among the new, were old friends from Baghdad for the summer, busy with King Faisal's visit and, later, with the massacre of the Assyrians in Iraq. In our paper civilization in which we tried so hard to feel secure, this was an opening on chaos and old night of a sort we liked to think confined to Asia; and, even there, we were surprised to see it following so close upon a British administration. This was a general feeling. But for those who knew the country and its neighbours, it was no great surprise; and perhaps one of the most useful things learned east of Suez even in those days, was an awareness of what lies under the hollow crust of words.

On the 13th of July I signed an agreement with Mr. Murray for *The Valleys of the Assassins*, which, in the document before me, is called *A Treasure Hunt in Luristan*. I signed with feelings almost of religion, at the great desk in the room in Albemarle Street where Scott and Byron, Moore and Lockhart, and all the most accomplished of their day, had gathered.

My friend in that house, Leonard Huxley, editor of *The Cornhill*, had died some time before, and I received a letter from Jock Murray, telling me that my MS. had been found in his safe, and would I call when next I came to London?

I went, expecting the return of the MS., and walked upstairs with an 'official interview' feeling, immediately dissipated by J. M., a slender young man in tweeds, who leapt up from his desk, brushed back a *mèche* of straight, untidy hair, and said, without any preparation: "I am glad you have come. We like your book. It *is* peculiarly typed, isn't it?" (This was my mother, who had done it in love and devotion, but with obvious tension between her and her machine.)

The friendship with the house of Murray began with that interview, and has continued ever since. It would leave an emptiness in my life if it failed. It has added to itself unnumbered days of companionship, affection for the older generation, intimacy with the younger, to which Diana Murray added

[294]

herself in the course of time; and interest now in the youngest, four small Murrays, all different and all the same, as is the way with happy families.

My book was to pay me 10 per cent rising to 15 per cent after 1,000 copies. These figures had no meaning to me. I had cleared £55 on *Baghdad Sketches* and, beyond this, during five years since I first published my article on the Druses in *The Cornhill*, I had made £226 by writing in the *Illustrated London News*, the *Spectator*, *The Cornhill* and *The Times*. Even in my poorest days, finance has had nothing to do either with the planning or the writing of my books: what they have brought was welcome, but they were written for their own sakes, nor have I ever debated whether this thing or the other might be what the public wants; when anyone makes suggestions of this sort, which they sometimes do, it grates upon me. I think of the Public as a friend, who may like me for myself alone, and not as a Cerberus to whom cakes must be given to soothe it from biting. If I had to work for my living altogether I would not be a writer but a cook—and would write for my own pleasure after the dinner was served.

Two episodes stand out in the summer of 1933 with a vivid light against the years which followed. One was a June afternoon with Charles Ker, who drove me to St. Albans; we strolled about the empty cathedral and its green enclosure and stopped by the wayside for strawberries and tea; and came back with the quietness of England in our hearts. Sometimes all our centuries, from the Neolithic days, the first chippings of flint, the monolithic temples, the rumours of Phoenicians, Greece and Rome, the first rude mason's chisel on Gothic saint, the wool merchants and men in small boats on coasting ventures, the excitement of learning, policy and politeness and the new subtleties of faith and the hiss of steam—all gather together to press within us to our Present, like the strength of a rower gathering to his stroke: and to us who live so much away from England, perhaps these moments come with a particular intimacy, reminding us of that to which we belong.

[295]

The other memory is a visit with Minnie Granville to Geneva, our only sight of the League of Nations at work.

Looking back upon it, from a world in which discrepancy between paper and reality is ever more apparent, the remarkable thing about the atmosphere of Geneva was an element of hope. It was not obvious at the time. Long speeches—in English and French—first in one language, then in the other, had the same irrelevancy which every generation finds peculiar. Milton was probably justified in dating it before the creation of this world, in the first Parliament of Hell. Real business, mixed with most excellent feeding and an expert knowledge of restaurants shared by every delegation, was carried on in quiet little corners after meals. The same jokes were made as now, debunking what the next day's papers would dress in *clichés de cérémonie* and offer to a world that, when it asked for bread and was given stones, liked to hear them called by some less pessimistic name. In and out of the delegations, owners of all the hotels and of all that was eaten, drunk, driven in, and paid for, the Swiss bourgeoisie, anchored on a defensible frontier, domestic conformities and safe investments, walked up and down on small and inexpensive walks along their quays, well aware that the great art of self-preservation must outlive all the experiments around them.

The delegates themselves had not yet reached the sharing of this view. Their cynicism was more apparent than real. They smiled over the Turks who objected to sitting in the great hall opposite the Austrian tapestry, which pictured their defeat under the walls of Vienna. But it was a kindly smile, meant only for the passing of time. The Germans had left the Disarmament Conference, and few recognized the tempest in that little cloud. In looking back upon it, it was perhaps the same world but with a difference—the difference between the throwers of dice who have a comfortable income still left them, and those of our day who know that with every cast they are throwing all they have.

With the end of the summer and the parting from friends at Geneva, my stay in Iraq and Persian exploration come to an end. I had long thought of more general travels in Arabia. One day, in the Alwiyah Club in Baghdad, I chanced to see the first photographs of the Hadhramaut published by Rickards in the *Illustrated London News*. Those high and strange medieval buildings filled me with curiosity, and my thoughts were now turned to South Arabia.

*　　*　　*

BAGHDAD, 3 January, 1933.

Dearest Venetia,

It is bitterly cold here. Ice in the ditches and a wind straight down the Tigris from the Taurus or something equally chilly. Nothing but a horrid little paraffin lamp to get warm by. But I have had a black velvet dress made and bought a hat with an orange bow, so that the morale is all right. I went to a dance, too, in fancy dress on New Year's Eve, but I feel rather sad always at large shows and like the man who wrote Ecclesiastes.

The worst about working is that one gets into the habit of it, and remains at a loss with one's holidays: not that I have reached that petrified stage as yet.

10 January, 1933.

Darling B,

The Lampards took me to call on Mar Shimun, the high priest of the Assyrians, a young man of twenty-four or thirty who has no easy task before him. He is just back from Geneva, where he hoped to get some concession of land for his people, and of course got nothing but polite words, as anyone might have told him before he went. He had very pleasant manners, though he had a cold and kept on rolling his handkerchief into a ball with both hands and passing it about under his nose; and laughing whenever he mentioned anything which he felt strongly about, such as the treachery (he considers) of Sir Francis Humphrys who made him promises which he did not fulfil. He has a curious Assyrian face—the nose with high bridge almost like the Greek, but then going on into a slight curve, and soft gentle brown eyes with pleasant wrinkles, a rosy complexion, and a little curly stubble beard. His under-lip a little protruding and a curious pulling back of sides of the upper lip when he laughs.

[297]

He had a black gown and crimson silk sash and a gold chain and cross, and his manner was like a Country Parson in Piedmont.

He is now going up to break the news of his failure to his people, who had saved up all their pennies to send him to Geneva. It is very sad and hopeless. The Assyrians want to remain a separate independent nation, and, of course, that is the one thing they cannot hope to obtain—especially as they are not united among themselves. They made an effort at resistance last year, very stupid, as they were not strong or decided enough to follow it up, and now the other people have had time to disunite them even more. They are a heavy peasant people, not with the sharpness of Arab or Kurd.

I am going out hardly at all, and do not mind it. Yesterday I dined at the Hoggs', a pleasant evening with the Minister of Finance, a man who learnt English as a prisoner of war in Egypt, Nusrat al Farisi. And I met the First Secretary at the Embassy, Mr. Bateman— also pleasant, blunt, not at all like a diplomat and with a curious mouth. He twinkled a little when, as someone was complaining that now in church we are made to pray for the American President, I remarked that it wasn't the President but his better guidance which required praying for.

16 January, 1933.

Dearest Herbert,

I must tell you that the *Baghdad Times* is suppressed. We published an extract from a London paper to say that the Persian premier, Taimurtash, now in disgrace, taught the Shah how to eat with a fork and how to use a toothpick. Probably true but not polite. The Persian Minister here made a fuss: the editor apologized handsomely, but did not mollify him: the Council of Ministers, the Ambassador, and poor Captain Holt, all sat and cogitated and diplomatized. The Persians insisted on suppression: then it was found that by Iraq law one could not suppress Mr. Cameron, but only fine or imprison him for a year: so they asked him to be a sport and suppress himself—which he has done for a fortnight, during which time we are no longer the *Baghdad Times*, but the *Times of Meso- potamia*. It has had to be kept rather quiet as it would cause a great to-do if the British papers get hold of the incident. I wrote a nice obituary notice for the *Baghdad Times* but Mr. Cameron is too pusillanimous to publish it.

16 *January*, 1933.

Dearest Venetia,

This is a very sad week. Mama wrote from Dronero to say that my little niece Angela died suddenly from some poison. It seems hard to believe, and is such a great grief. She was just coming to her best age, and sweet and happy, and very like my sister to look at. What can one say or do? Perhaps in time one may reach a serenity which these sorrows cannot shake.

It is pouring with rain. The first proper rain for a year. I am crippled with lumbago. I should like to spend a week in bed in a warm and pleasant room—a thing quite out of the question here.

19 *January*, 1933.

Darling B,

A letter begun to you is lying about somewhere, but my lumbago is too bad to allow me to get it. I have been like a semi-cripple all the week, and a kind woman next door rubs ointment into me. V.H. is so sweet when anything is wrong with me, and wrapped me round with his scarves and never forgets to come along with cushions, and really seems to mind my being laid up—but never comes in to see me unless he happens to know that he has been really aggravating the day before. He said that trotting was the best thing for lumbago so we trotted—with the result that it was quite agonizing all the afternoon.

I had a very interesting morning to-day going to get an interview in arabic from a Druse friend of King Faisal's, the Emir Arslan. We conducted the whole thing in arabic and he told me his ideas on the French in Syria with remarkable indiscretion (no joke to get it all correct). He is a delightful man: good manner, most charming presence, very good European clothes ("Looks like Sir Francis Humphrys," said my Arab colleague); a man of the world with a sense of humour. He talked for over an hour, discussing the Syrian question from head to foot. I went away and put about half of what he said into English—leaving out all the most indiscreet, and Mr. Cameron was delighted. Just now Captain de Gaury rings up and says the Emir has been to him in an absolute panic, very perturbed at the idea of the interview; I was anyway going to send him a copy of what I meant to say, but he may not want to publish anything at

[299]

all after all. He appears to have said nice things about me to Captain Gaury. You can't think how difficult it is to go up to a perfectly strange man in an hotel and interview him.

29 January, 1933.

To-day I called on the Queen, as it is the 'Id, the Moslem feast. There were dozens of people to curtsey to—first the Queen, sitting on a throne in a gentian blue tailor-made with silver buttons. The wife of the Emir Abdullah of Transjordan beside her in a sky-blue tailor-made with a native head-dress of white muslin with blue flowers. She has a heavy, sallow face, enlivened by a gold tooth, and beautiful eyes when they had less cheek around them. Then a visiting cousin princess very well dressed in brown with pearls, who looked European. And then the two princesses, sitting about, and lots of Iraqi ladies and only three English.

4 February, 1933.

Evan told me a story of one of the Muntafik sheikhs who are so strict that their wives are *never* allowed out of the tent, not even for the most necessary purpose, except at night and with a black slave beside them so that no one can tell which is which. Well, one of these sheikhs was sitting with his wife drinking coffee in his tent when a beduin from another tribe, crossing the desert and light-headed through the sun, smelt the smell of coffee, and, without realizing, blundered into the tent. As soon as he saw the wife, he knew he was in for it. The sheikh however said very quietly "Salaam 'aleikum." The beduin was so overcome he didn't reply. He flung himself at the feet of the sheikh and begged for forgiveness. The sheikh called his people and had him bound and kept in a separate tent. In a day or two he sent for him. The man still thought he was to be killed, but the sheikh let him go. "At first," he said, "of course I meant to kill you. But then I gave you the greeting and you did not reply, so I knew you could not be in your right mind, and I let you go." It is a good story, showing the great value of the greeting among the Arabs.

9 February, 1933.

Dearest Venetia,

We are more or less marooned, and all letters and passengers stuck in the desert. It is amusing to see American globetrotters arrive here, accustomed to having the elements under command and amenable to time-tables, and furious at being kept for days beyond their time by the mere potency of Mud. I have no news of you for the same reason—and after this you had better only write once more here, to get me before the 15th March, and then write poste restante Jerusalem. I shall spend a day or two there, going either by Aleppo or Amman. I can't afford much lingering on the way, but either of these routes can be managed without extra expense.

The book that has moved me very much is Edmund Candler's *Long Road to Baghdad*, but very sad reading. We spend our time creating a magnificent *average* type of Englishman, the finest instrument in this world: which we then fritter away because we have no *super average* to use him: none of our education sets out to produce great men.

18 *February*, 1933.

My dear Lionel,

I believe you owe me a letter, but it is just possibly the other way round, so you shall be given the benefit of the doubt. This is my last on official paper, as I chuck this job on Friday week and once more become (I hope) a lady. It is rather a soul-killing business, and I think that earning one's living is sordid though I suppose necessary. When I stop this work, I shall have a little holiday—will go down to Warka and Ur with the Staffords, and possibly to Kirkuk, and do a little russian and arabic here before going back to Asolo.

24 *February*, 1933.

Dearest Venetia,

I am living in luxury. Such an unfamiliar experience. Bath salts every morning, masses of violets on my dressing-table, a mirror in which the hem of my skirt appears, and a car wherever I want to go (very bad for me as I get no exercise). I do wallow in all these fleshpots, and feel all at once how Spartan I have been all this time. I am staying for ten days with some charming Scotch people, a doctor called Sinderson: and then with the Financial Adviser and wife called Hogg—and altogether am *slacking off*. One's capacity for civilization gets atrophied like anything else, and I feel it was high time I came to live like a lady again for a bit.

Next week my work in office stops. I shall be sorry to leave. How often, I wonder, will I look back with wistfulness to these two years, full of so many strange new things. I feel I may never come out again, and every moment becomes significant. But then on the other hand I may—and you and Penbedw are there to look forward to at the other end. I do long to sit and talk to you.

I have been having tea at the Embassy. I don't know why it should make me shy, but it does. I think it is because one is rather expected to feel shy; and so one does so because one is naturally responsive. Anyway I find I get more and more shy instead of less as time goes on. Do you know we are thinking of cotton frocks already? And your snowdrops only just out, I expect.

KIRKUK, 8 *March,* 1933.

Darling B,

This is a pleasant little town, spreading and overflowing off an ancient mound by a stone bridge of many arches on to the flat ground, surrounded by ramshackle bazaars full of colour and Kurdish costumes and Turkish baggy trousers, and with a far rim of low hills on three sides and a foreground now faint green with young crops.

I have been this morning to see mosques, churches, and the Carpet of the Prophet. I first went to call on the Mulla 'Abd al Qadir, whom Mr. Cooke wrote to me about. He is the head of the Waqf here, and was very friendly and sent along an old Turkish servant in a turban to take me to the great mosque which is on the top of the mount, in a quiet quarter of little lanes and houses round courtyards of orange trees in pots. The mosque had a pleasant little quiet churchyard round it, with one smart grave in a sort of ironwork cage, and a portico at the mosque entrance with coloured stucco carving round the door. There is a lot of soft Mosul marble about here and they carve it with incised patterns, and the portico of the Hedgecocks' house is all lined with these to a height of seven feet or so, like the old Assyrian palaces.

Inside our mosque were the tombs of Husain, 'Assar and Daniel. The Jews come there to Daniel's feast, but not the Christians. The old mosque, they say, was once a Christian church. The tomb of Daniel is covered in green brocade with beige flowers, and Husain is tucked away under the pulpit beside a minbar with more coloured stucco, white on a blue ground. The Assyrian church is quite near—

a long building with low pillars painted light green. The front half is for the men and the back for the women, and there is a sort of loft at the top for the girls. There are 200 Christian families here and about as many Jews, a few Ali Ilahis in the villages about and a little group of about forty belonging to a sect like the Yezidis.

The place of Muhammad's carpet is on the other side of the mount. We drove in an *arabana* all through the bazaars, which lie round the mound and below. The houses, built to the edge above, look like a citadel: an eagle or big kite was sitting on the corner of one against the blue sky. The bazaars were *great* fun. In one of the little shops, stacked with pots white, blue and green, to the ceiling, a young man was reading his Qurân. I got up quietly and photographed him without his noticing, to the great joy of all the neighbours. The bazaar ended in a series of caravanserai yards and the street went on between two raised mud pavements with a dirty stream down the middle till we came out into more open spaces, with a graveyard on what looks like another old mound, and small houses; and there behind an open enclosure, with orange trees and leafless rubber trees, and a stork's nest and a tank of water with tidy cement pillars round it, behind it, up steps, was the old sheikh's house and the room of the holy carpet.

The old sheikh was a nice old Moslem, with small features and trim beard, and white turban—he was sitting with spectacles on his terrace writing a letter and very cross at being asked to show the carpet as he had done so a week or two ago to the Hedgecocks and it is only supposed to be shown at the feast. He softened however and took me to the room, which was very simple and bare under a blue cupola, with rugs on the ground and a table by the side of the wall-cupboard where the relic is. The doors of the cupboard are all wood and mirror work, and locked over by a green iron grill, and when these two things are opened one sees a red box bound with brass and also locked and covered with one cover and a quilt. Inside the box, wrapped first in white calico then in white satin, then in silk and silver, was the relic: it was an old camel-hair rug with two lines of darker wool running round it, and so old that all the folds had been eaten away and fell to pieces. Muhammad gave it to the Caliph Abu Bekr and his family took it to Damascus till the Abbassids came to power: then they spread in Sistan and Shiraz, and the carpet-branch went to Shiraz and then finally to Kirkuk, still with the precious carpet.

There is nothing else said to belong to the Prophet extant except a banner and a clock in Stamboul.

The old sheikh is a descendant of Abu Bekr. The Caliph's belt is under the carpet and also a little cap belonging to another ancestor. The old sheikh and my guide said prayers as they opened the wrappings and then put everything away again still praying—I was not allowed to give any money. But I mentioned Mr. Cooke, and the old man became still more mollified and we parted on excellent terms. Hardly any tourist who comes here knows or asks for this carpet. Near the place is a Christian church built on the site of an old one where lots of Christians were once massacred: it is a place called Tamasiar, but they say there is nothing but the new church to see and I did not go.

Yesterday I saw an amazing sight. The testing of a drill hole for oil. It meant burning a lot of waste oil as it poured from two pipes at the rate of 50,000 barrels per day. The flame rushed out in two jets roaring like tumbling stones in a mountain torrent. One felt the great heat about 300 yards off, and the actual fire must have risen to about 150 to 200 feet, pouring out in yellow masses with dark rolls of smoke on one side, which then stretched away right over the sky. The yellow fire was soft and frothy as new milk, or the snow of an avalanche, and covered with these rolls of smoke like transparent leafless woods on a hillside: now and then a black shadow thrown on the brightness made a strong contrast; the two jets showed against the fiery mass by darker shadow and blue light playing round them. Dark light shone on the lake of oil on the ground over which the fire swept. It looked wonderful in the middle of the peaceful empty landscape, throwing its long shadow over the shallow hills. People were ploughing, taking their teams of horses to the nearest possible point so that the fire rose like a curtain behind them: they said the heat in the ground would ruin their melons. All this waste of fuel was to test the pressure from the oil well. They have thirty-six wells ready now, all sealed down till the pipe-line is laid to take the oil to Haifa. Two lines go to Haditha on the Euphrates, and there divide into four, two for Alexandretta and two for Haifa—and they hope to have finished in eighteen months more. About a thousand people are at work now, one way and another.

Yesterday morning I spent in the bazaar, watching the silversmiths heating their metals from little beaked metal lamps like the old ones in shape. There was a head-ornament for sale called *tappeh*, a round thing like a plate with a turquoise knob and little dangly things all round. It is Kurdish, but I haven't seen anyone wearing it. The women here have big trousers gathered in to the ankle. The men, too, wear the full Turkish trousers and all sorts of jaunty turbans. Kurds come wrapped in sheepskins on top of all the rest of their costume, so that they take up most of the road. There is not much to be got in the bazaars, and the best comes from outside—but they are nice to look at: the rugs come from Suleimania and Erbil and the shoes from Mandali; and Kirkuk seems to make nothing but blue and green bowls and pitchers. On the flat side of the bridge it has a school, a *crèche*, the Government Serai and public garden (a very nice new one), and an enormous barrack, one-storied with buttresses, where there are now 2,000 troops. One of the pleasantest things about the place is that its flat roofs are interspersed with proper trees, not palms, but trees that change their leaves. There are rickety towers about, made to protect the mills: the man on guard used to sit up there while the flour was ground. In the mosques are perforated windows, mud or stone. There are lots of bits of carving about on doors, but no wooden carved windows jutting out as in Baghdad. One climbs up on to the mound by a road with lines of steps on either side of it—and the whole feeling is that of a little mountain town, head of a country district.

9 March, 1933.

Darling B,

We went yesterday to see them drilling a new well for oil out in the plain beyond a little village of mud which must be a pattern thousands of years old. The wells as they are drilled are surmounted by a sort of Eiffel tower of steel scaffolding at the top of which are the pulleys by which the enormous shafts that hold the drill are pulled up in sections of 80 feet. It is a most thrilling affair to see. This drill has only got 700 feet down, and the maximum here is 3,000, but oil wells somewhere in the world go down to 13,000 feet and it seems incredible that any single machine can be strong enough to pull up a shaft of that weight. At the bottom of the shaft is the drill, which has two steel blades that rotate and eat their way down, bathed all the time in muddy water which helps to grind the rock and is pumped up and thrown away together with the small

[305]

stuff ground by drill. After a few hours, the sharp edge of the drill is blunted and has to be changed, and we were lucky to come just as this operation started: four Kurdish coolies stood by the shaft; two more climbed up to the top of the scaffolding 80 feet above, and the American driller moved the levers of his machine so that the shaft started to come up. He was a strong, intelligent-looking man, and told me that he could tell from the sound and feel of his machine what sort of stuff it was eating its way through down below. The smooth shaft came up, while one of the Kurds turned water on to it to wash off the mud: it ran down it in little pointed ripples like a pattern. The Kurds looked extraordinarily handsome and agile and strong: when 80 feet of shaft were up, they clamped it in two enormous iron clamps at the join: the machine gave a twist, the screw came undone; a Kurd seized the bottom of the shaft length in an iron hook and swung it to one side. The machine that held it above was released and let down to clamp up the next length of shaft, while the first—80 feet of steel bending about like a reed, fell carelessly against the top scaffolding. It was all done with wonderful speed and precision. The Kurds had been at it three years and liked their job, smiling as they handled those great masses of metal. The machine was made to go by steam, produced by six huge boilers where oil was lighted under pressure and spread in beautiful fans of white flame impossible to look at long. Water is mixed with the oil in the ground: in the great fire the day before, a lot of steam lay along the ground below the black smoke.

As we went along to the drill we passed the beginning of the pipe-line—a steel pipe on the ground and the telegraph beside it, going out straight without a swerve into the desert. It is the conquest of mind over space and desolation—made visible by that thin line of poles and wires, losing itself among the mirage and the sand. If this had been done in older days, poets and sculptors would have celebrated it: it would have been looked at in proper perspective as a symbol of Power.

After all these excitements we went to tea with a geologist's wife and saw the view from her roof. It is a pleasant town: the mound like a citadel catching the sun, and gardens of olive trees here and there among the suburb houses; and a blue rim of faint hills far away on every side.

To-night I leave for Nasiriyah.

14 *March*, 1933.

Darling B,

Mr. Woolley took us all over Abraham's village in Ur and it was very interesting, and extremely like the back streets of Baghdad. The houses were two-storied, but very small, and there was the same absence of piazzas: the streets so narrow that the corners were rounded to make it easier for loaded mules. Mr. Woolley said that now, from clay tablets of bills, letters, etc., left about in the houses, he knows the names and occupations of nearly every one of them. One was a school, with all the exercises left about, arithmetic, and calligraphy, etc.

Then we went to the Ziggurat. It is impressive from its size, and the three great stairs that run up in a triangle meet at the top. It is rather curious that this is the only public building found (except for a temple or two): there must have been offices one would think, in a place of 500,000 inhabitants, as Mr. Woolley estimates. He thinks the climate was different then, owing to the amount of cultivation. It is certainly different here by the river, which is much more gentle than the Tigris and bordered with palm groves for hours and hours, and with slow waterwheels, often still provided only with waterskins, that pour the stream into irrigation channels. A misty humidity hangs over it and here in the Rest House garden one might be in England on a steamy summer morning. The summer they say is awful, but now it is relaxing but not unpleasant. We went up in the launch to Suq-ash-Shuyukh, a little brick town with long dark bazaar in a district of reed villages and palms.

AMMAN, 28 *March*, 1933.

Darling B,

I am moving about again after so long, feeling quite strange at it, and not as if I wanted to be very energetic, but very glad this morning to see the big grassy hills of Transjordan as lovely and solitary and gay in the sun as I remembered them. I shared the mail lorry from Baghdad with a Swiss Professor of Persian dialects— couldn't have been more of a Professor—with black beard, glasses, soft hat and peculiar buccaneering clothes finished off with a white shirt and what looked like an evening collar (but may not have been) —and a note-book always ready. Rather nice man, only he kept on falling asleep on my shoulder. The lorry started at 9 p.m. and poor

V.H. had to interrupt his dinner to see me off and came and sat with me in the Drowers' car in an empty custom house with an icy wind, while we waited for the departure to materialize, and he told me I enjoyed being uncomfortable for fun. The lorry came along—a huge affair full of fish I believe at the back, but I did not go into the matter closely. It seems peculiar to take fish from the Tigris, which is horrid anyway, 900 kilometres over desert to the Mediterranean coasts, but this is what they do. Anyway we had a good place in front shut off by glass, and a capable and placid Russian driver with a round face and smile like the full moon and his machine in good order; so that we had no hitch, and lost the consort lorry and her Arab chauffeur very soon, and have not seen them since.

The night was cold; rain-streaks horizontal across the lights; and icy wind in through many cracks. But after three hours of it we got at midnight to Ramadi and spent the rest of the time in a semi-native hotel, quite comfortable.

Next day, yesterday, we got up at 8 a.m. and left at 9 a.m., a fine day, and pleasant, for the desert was blossoming in its transitory spring, all faint green in the distance with the brown earth showing through like copper in old Sheffield plate. It was covered with a pretty yellow flower, little candlesticks of six petalled blossoms standing up stiff out of fatty pale leaves, about half a foot all over the ground, and very charming in the smallness of all else. We had it all to ourselves, especially when our convoy left us and got lost. There were only a few birds, a flock of fifteen wild pigeons, resting all together on the sands, and innumerable hairy caterpillars when we got out and examined Nature closely. They have marked the track now with elegant black-and-white signboards and an arrow at the back of them to mark the direction—a comforting sight it must be often.

We kept along the usual road to Rutba, and got there about 5 p.m. That square fort with its little group of beduin huts around, built up out of petrol tins filled with sand, is a most cheering sight so far from anywhere. We were still the only travellers out except for a lorry or two in the opposite direction, and we had tea quietly before the Damascus convoys came along. The Professor was a pleasant companion, used to adapting himself to discomfort and with a disinterested passion for facts for their own sake. I like him, but would not mind his taking journeys to Persia now and then if I were his wife.

After Rutba there is an unobtrusive fork in the tracks that now at this season show brown in the grass. One is the Damascus road, the other is ours to Amman, only open again these last eight months having been closed after brigandage six years ago. As we turned on to it we met an armoured car with three very cheerful desert policemen inside it, and stopped for a little chaff and a photo. The armoured car looks useful with the machine-gun on a swivel ready to turn in any direction at a moment's notice.

We seemed to get into greener desert here—lovely soft lines like open bits of Dartmoor; little bulbs shot out thin spikes of leaves, sparse close at hand, but bright and beautiful seen sideways in the sun. We climbed the low, imperceptible cliff steps of the desert and were now at about 2,000 feet without noticing the rise from the Euphrates. And as the night came we began to reach the lava country, the Harra, which has poured in a black sheet over this flat, and then has crumbled into black surface stones. We only saw the bits of this desolation that came under the lights of the car, but felt the bumps. It was a weary night—the only comfort my lovely watch that showed the passing of time in the darkness. At 3.30 a.m. I suddenly saw what looked like small temple columns of black stone arranged like a gallows by the wayside—not a hallucination I believe, for there are many old ruined sites lost here on the desert fringe. The bumps got worse and worse: I nearly concussed myself by hitting the wooden ceiling with my head. Luckily the wind has lessened: we were not so terribly cold, though cold enough, and then we met a lorry that came the opposite way, derelict in the middle of the tracks, just where a series of sandy hummocks made it difficult to circumvent. The Russian driver was sleeping: his Arab assistant, with usual native optimism, tried to get by on a miracle basis and stuck, and we nearly came to grief then: a depressing thought, as the derelict lorry had been there four days already. Two sleepy inhabitants crept out and assisted with advice: the Russian woke up, and set them more usefully to work with a spade, and we got by with not much worse bumps than the usual.

Then the dawn came: we were out on the stony desert with the far familiar outline of Jebel Druse on our right, and in daylight we came to the first Transjordan post, in a new grey stone fort with two square towers, at Azraq.

We had long delays as the Transjordans were conscientious, and everything was wrong with all our passports, and we spent the time drinking tea and coffee with the beduin in a small tent. The Arab police look fine: we passed a camp of them along the way at night and were stopped, and they look wilder than anything else in the desert, with their long curly locks falling over their face under the red *kaffiyas*, and their blackened eyes and usually a gold tooth or two. They wear khaki gowns, a red sash, bandoliers of cartridges, a carved bone-handled dagger and a white long-sleeved shirt.

I knew that there was an old ruin at Azraq, having read about it in Gertrude Bell, and also knew it was the place where the Druses took refuge. So I asked (although everyone told me there was no such place)—and sure enough the beduin police showed us the old Azraq away on the edge of black country that here pushes out into a swamp. The Professor, too, longed to examine it. It was only ten minutes by car; we used all our blandishments on the amiable Russian, and took the mail vain and all its contents sightseeing out of their course: and no sooner were we down in the hollow near the swamp, with Azraq showing ruined black walls quite near, than the ground opened beneath us, spurted out a mass of disgusting liquid grey clay, and swallowed one wheel completely. I must give credit to the Russian: he said not a word, but continued to smile in rather a thoughtful way, while the Arab assistant launched into a speech on the non-necessity of sightseeing. I said I would get men from the village and strode off, and opened conversation with the first Druse we met. They live in little black houses, recently built, round the old fort, a large ruin Roman and possibly older but touched up by an Izz-ad-Din in Saracen times who gave it a portcullis and arched door. The two old doors of single stone slabs are still there in their sockets, and a bit of the old stone raftering. And there were two pretty Druse girls in their white veils, all just as we knew them five years ago. I wished Venetia were there. I sent a note to Mut'ib Bek al Atrash by hand to Suweida, and saluted an old kinsman of his, and wished I could stay longer to make friends again. But we had only time for a few photos. Fifteen men had lifted out the wheel and filled the hole with boulders and we dashed back at great speed and out over the desert, strewn with flints and sandy in patches, until we came to this big land of grassy stony shoulders with scarce a tree. We stopped to photo a domed building about half-way from Azraq: Moslem probably, but early, made with square un-mortared stones.

A square ruined fort was above on a hill on the right. All the country is full of castles and ruins. It is nice to come to a land built with stone. Along our track here and there were signs for aeroplanes, and the road through the lava was marked by the simple expedient of aligning the stones on the side of it.

We saw what looked like a small grey crested ostrich but of course it can't have been.

29 March, 1933.

Amman is a most attractive little town, poked down into a steep hollow. One side was built into an amphitheatre which still forms the hillside. It goes up in tiers just opposite this hotel, which is very clean, new, European, and expensive, with tennis court and all modern sanitation complete. The little town goes along the valley in two narrow streets filled with modern shops and Arabs in white *kaffiyas* and *abbas*, and then clambers up the steep valley head, with new houses built in the squared stone that is such a pleasure to look at after the mud of Iraq. The Chapmans are on the brow of the hill, looking down at night on the lights of the town arranged like a theatre scene, and with the old citadel and remains of temples on the left-hand height. The whole place is like a funnel, steeper than a bowl, and very fascinating. On the next height beyond the temple is the Emir Abdullah's palace. It all looks much more solid than Iraq and less shoddy, and the land too. The rolling high shoulders all cultivated with thin corn. It is solitary as I remember it: one wonders where the cultivators come from, as there is hardly ever a village in sight—only ruins of Roman watch towers and forts on the heights.

TRAIN, 29 *March*, 1933.

Now we are on the way to Petra, jogging in the slowest train I have been in, and supposed to do it in eight hours to Ma'an: the ordinary train takes twenty-fours hours, but how it achieves such a miracle of slowness I can't imagine. We have been four hours on the way, climbing slowly up till we have left the valley and its thin sprays of fruit trees blossoming, and come over higher shoulders ploughed to young corn, with rounded hill horizons and clouds travelling; and are now on a still higher bare plain in the land of Moab, with great uninhabited spaces, a few tents, no cultivation; from the train it looks still and basking in a bright sun, because there is no vegetation tall enough to show the racing wind, which one can hardly stand up in as soon as one gets out. If one looks close, one can see all the tufts and grasses quivering and hear the whistle of the air. There are flowers, many and minute—tiny poppies, and all sorts of little delicate things clinging to the ground, and tufts of flowering asphodel in the limestone. It is fun to think this railway goes on into Arabia. A strong, nice-looking lot of Arabs, wrapped up to their eyes in *kaffiyas* against the wind, get in at every station.

There is only a house or two, if that, at most of the stations, and often not even the name painted on them—just a little square block of well-built stone, the same colour as the wilderness. Sometimes a square old fort, with battlemented top and a portcullis over the arched door on a blank wall space—probably Turkish. The pilgrim road to Mecca runs along somewhere.

The country is a light beige colour, not as red as Damascus, and looks limestone; the clouds have space enough to throw lovely patterns. It gives one a feeling of great height and solitude. So does Persia, but there the mountain-ringed plateaus give one a feeling of something dead and finished, outside and above the world: here it is rolling land which seems to share in the life of the winds and skies and seasons, though it has little to say to the actions of men. We are going towards Edom, which is the land of the Ishmaelites, and one can see that they were nomads from the beginning, dwellers in a country that never could be made for settled life.

We are doing the last hour in this desert train and have just been through a sandstorm—nothing much but the low sand flying along the face of the desert in this terrific wind. The pilgrim road to Mecca runs along our left, and the low hills are covered with ruins of watch towers. The desert stretches away, stony, with scarce a shrub, hard beaten earth on which the sand blows about. There are strange little hills, eaten away at the sides like the hillside at La Mortola, and looking nicer in the distance than close at hand. They stick out in a meaningless way. It is just earth as far as one can see, but with a strange fascination of freedom about it.

PETRA, 30 March, 1933.

I am actually writing this among all the Nabatean tombs in Petra, on a very comfortable chaise-longue in Cook's camp. Being given the choice of a tomb or a tent as a sleeping room, I chose the former.

It is a very roomy tomb, partitioned into three bedrooms, with all complete down to mosquito nets.

I must go on from where I left off, arriving at Ma'an, a dreary place in the desert with only a few small white-walled gardens half eaten by desert winds. The hotel and station are far from the town and have not even these advantages. I tried to get at Captain Domvile the S.S.O. on the phone in the police station, but he was out, so I sent my letter and waited in the hotel, kept by a very quiet friendly little mouse of a man from Jerusalem, who had high ideals about hotels but found it hard to live up to them in Ma'an. The table-cloths were Damascus *abbas* and the curtains held by Damascus *'agals*, and pictures of the Versailles Conference, Lloyd George and Clemenceau interspersed with a sentimental landscape, a copy of Sacred and Profane Love by a beginner in oils, and an advertisement of rapid travel by express train, which is rather an irony there where the weekly train comes to its slow end every Wednesday. In the Turkish days it used to take pilgrims from Damascus to Mecca and back for £4 in three days, but since Ibn Saud came to Hejaz it stops altogether at Ma'an.

Captain Domvile came as I sat rather sadly listening to philology by an oil lamp. My Professor is really like a caricature of what one expects of a professor. His note-book is always ready and he drinks in information like a child, taking such a long time to get at the obvious, but *very* intelligent. But I was longing for something lighter and welcomed Captain Domvile, sleek-haired in grey flannels, and most kind but unable to put us up as his cook and his house-party had gone to Akaba and he was following this morning. He has just sent Lady Irwin across Sinai by car and was waiting for news. He arranged for a car this morning for us—all terribly expensive here, as always under British and tourist auspices combined. We left at seven-thirty with a Turkish chauffeur who had fought with the Turks, been taken prisoner, fought for Faisal, married the Yemenite widow of a Turkish Qaimakam so as to prevent her two sons from being orphans (so he said)—and therefore did not mean to return to his relatives in Anatolia any more. He remembered Sir Hubert Young out here with Lawrence and showed me the hill where he, or one of the British officers, suggested shooting a few shells and wiping out Ma'an—but Faisal refused, as the town was the property of his friend the Abu Tai.

[323]

Captain de Gaury had told me that the view from the Akaba road is one of the finest in Arabia, so we went 30 kilometres out of our way, by Abu Lisān, where Faisal's camp was, to the Ras al-Naqb, where the high Arabian plateau (1,400 metres) falls away suddenly to the Red Sea. It took one's breath away; down below, the flat ground lay with isolated hills and farther ridges rising out of it suddenly like islands. There is no house in this land, but the road runs by a beduin place called Quweira to Akaba, and, on the left of it, white winding beds of dry torrents look like tracks. One could see, tossed about wildly, the rocky sides of the Wady Rum far off, which Lawrence describes and where Venetia and I had meant to go. Mist was trailing about the farther ridges. It was the sort of landscape you would imagine in a Burne-Jones tapestry, only without trees; a few thin patches of beduin ploughland here and there were almost indistinguishable in the brown patchiness of the desert. On the ridge, the names of Petra and Batn al Ghul, to east and west of this place, were written on the ground with white stones for our aeroplanes.

The road is now as good as most roads in Persia, but when our chauffeur was there with Faisal's army they had to manhandle the guns up that ridge which now has fourteen hairpins. A little below, at Abu Lisān, we saw the place of the camp, the hospital and the gun place on the left, Faisal's tent, and Lawrence below him on the right. A few stones of the guardhouse opposite Faisal's tent were still standing, and a well of green, most uninviting, water. All this valley was gentle and green, covered in parts with lily-like plants and spreading leaves of a sort of rhubarb, sweet to eat and very juicy, and with red flower bunches they call *camthūm*, and another little bulb with thin streaky leaves they call *shahūm* and also eat. I am just having one roasted now to try. There were lots of little flowers —cranesbill, and alyssum and several sorts I didn't know, little iris and poppies, very tiny, and everywhere tufts of an aromatic frilly-leaved plant like vermouth. The sun was bright, the air icy: I know nothing more deadly, invisible and merciless than the Arabian wind. Here and there on the ground we still found traces of war; shell-cases, and an English button—strange scatterings of Empire on the Arab desert. One can't help feeling pleased at being English when seeing this peaceful holding of the land, the police and roads, and air routes where before were only desert raiders. All the country belongs to the Howeitat, a big tribe now weak after Ibn Rifada's

revolt against Ibn Saud and death last year. One sees them, very
poor and black and wizened, burnt to nothing in the sun, taking one
camel or two donkeys, and some black little woman hung round with
trinkets of no value—always a gun over the shoulder of someone
in the party. Men from Ma'an were mending the road, carrying
earth in small baskets and patting it down in a half-hearted way.
Their overseer had on a white sheepskin coat, a red *kaffiya* and black
'*agal*, and a Caucasian worked knife, all over a woollen cardigan
with zip fastener. These workmen were from Ma'an and wore the
baggy Turkish trouser and not the Arab gown. They sang differently
from the Iraq beduin, the rather pleasant wild sort of beat we heard
in the Jebel Druse. They came and brought the edible plants and
were very friendly.

Then we came tearing up here, back on to the Arabian plateau
until it again breaks away in the Wadi Musa to the wild crags of Petra.
It is terribly tourist-managed, and the fussiness of the British for one's
safety is manifest in the most painful way, as one has to pay £1 for
being guarded and is not allowed more than thirty paces from the
camp without a guide *and* a soldier (guide 10s. a day). It is indeed
so ruinous that I should not have come if I had known and will never
come again, but now that I am here I am very thrilled to see it, for
nothing can spoil the wonder of the place.

Imagine an amphitheatre of red sandstone cliffs, cut through by
seven or eight converging defiles. Up the defiles, and where they open
out in the amphitheatre, on the rock faces, are cut the façades of the
tombs, columns and ornaments in rather bad taste of the early Christian
era, when the Nabateans held their impregnable capital here and
the land as far as Damascus, and all the trade from Red Sea to Syria
came here in caravans. An empty stream-bed runs through the
place, which in winter is full of water; one can see on its edge foundation stones of palaces which must have lined a way through the
middle of the city. The entrance is by the defile along the stream,
which used to be carried in small aqueducts cut in the rock on either
side, and in brick pipes of which the half are still in place. It is a
wonderful way in. We left our car at Wadi Musa—all green terraces
of corn and blossoming trees and pomegranates with sticky new red-
tipped leaves and Howeitat tribesmen ready to swarm like locusts on
the tourists, all this tucked down between two shaly slopes of stone,
with the wild Petra ridge to close the view. The police were very

polite, thanks to Captain Domvile's having telephoned, and we got one poor old horse to ride in turn and two small boys with the hand-bags, and a guide who was forced on us, and a policeman on horse-back, and so in file we entered under the first of the tombs into the red rock defile, not wider than eight feet in many places and higher than several cathedrals superimposed. It was all lovely shade and sunlight, red like stained glass on the rock; and white flowering broom and asphodel plants and little flowers, with fig trees with tiny shining leaves here and there in the crevices, and then at sudden corners the rock carved into a façade of tomb—until we came out of the defile into the open circle, with a theatre cut in tiers in the rock and the remains of a triple gate very ruined, and the white pointed tents of the camp grouped round a ruined square castle belonging to Pharaoh's daughter (or so they say). One goes between hillocks made by the crumbled houses of the town, with the tombs looking down from the cliff sides wherever a smooth space offered itself for carving—and feels extraordinarily intimate with these vanished householders who were so blatantly and vulgarly showy over their dead.

A sad contretemps happened when I arrived—for my coat which the guide was carrying had £3 10s. (all my remaining money) in its pocket and it was no longer there. The very courtly gentleman in a fez who runs this place and gives one a welcome something between a home-coming and an ambassadorial reception, says that it is sure to turn up again. I do hope so. But it is no use to worry. We had tea (with four sorts of jam, and the table decorated with ingenious bottles filled with sands of all the local colours—yellow, white, black, and red—in geometric patterns, the only local product for sale except antiques). Then we went for a stroll—a soldier instantly leaping to attention and coming with us; up one of the seven defiles to an ancient stone altar and floor of sacrifice, and climbed to the Crusaders' little castle, which defeated the Professor who quailed before a sand-stone corner, but I got round by taking off my shoes.

On a high hill at the back is the tomb of Aaron, where the beduin go for sacrificial picnics, and where the careful British have forbidden tourists to go. A light is always kept burning there, and incense, and that and all his provisions are brought to the old priest by these poor tribesmen—and they go on pilgrimage one day in spring. The policeman chatted away all the time. They love to have someone who can speak arabic, and this got us 10s. off the pension straight away, as the courtly gentleman said he saw we were 'of the country' and not tourists—and so we only pay £1 a day. (My money just been found, handed to the police in Wadi Musa by alarmed guide.)

When we climbed down, the policeman and I, from the Crusader fort from which all the converging defiles are visible as if one were a spider's body looking at all his own legs, a beduin woman came up to me to sell antiques and I got a hideous little debased Greek terracotta of a dog's head, quite amusing. She was such a pretty little beduin: their dusty black head-dress and draperies, and black curly hair and long black eyelashes and dark brown skin make them look like little furry dark animals. I took her photo against the rock wall; and then the photo of a handsome guide called Jesus; and had the pleasure of watching them walk, for their carriage is one of the loveliest things one can see in the human body and such a contrast to the two tourist ladies who have just arrived.

31 *March*, 1933.

Dearest B,

It is most fearfully exhausting to share an expedition with an enthusiastic professor. He has been sightseeing conscientiously since we had breakfast at 5 a.m. in the hope of seeing the sunrise, which was a tame affair after all, though pleasant. Last night we sat up to watch the poor Arabs of a little local tribe called Bduli (because they were once Christian and changed to Moslem they say) dance by a fire here. They are wizened and ragged, but they are the real beduin all the same, with fine little curved features, and they danced with great spirit, a line of nine of them swaying back and fro in front of a woman who led them on and swayed from side to side and tossed her long sleeves that reach the ground, holding a little twig in her hand: and the men beat their hands to the usual rhythm, eight beats, while one made up the verses, and the others ended in a chorus, and at times they all beat more wildly, growling out: "*Hai, hia, hai hulua.*" That is "she, she the sweet one," and advanced on her in a body while she retreated; till they all knelt and she knelt just opposite, and they continued the beating and swaying, a wild and primitive affair. I always like to see it, and it was done well, and she was a pretty little thing, though only a tip-tilted nose was visible from all the black swathings. There were only the three unattractive tourists and us, so that they only got 5s. for all the display, though I gave 1s. specially to the poet, for his inventiveness. These beduin live here in the old graves. To-day with their 5s. they bought barley, and we saw them grinding it between two flat stones. One little girl of the family had a very peculiar face arrangement: a black cloth covering her to the eyes, all sewn with small silver coins.

We had a lovely morning, climbing up for about an hour and a half to the high place of sacrifice, which must have a very old origin. It is a mountain top of flat stones, cut into an altar, and killing table, and eating table, and washing place, so that all the old ritual of sacrifice can be followed; and the way up is hewn into steps and water channels, and down on the other side by huge precipice faces smoothed by hand in the soft sandstone. And all this overgrown with flowering white broom and asphodel, and pine trees in the crevices and many little flowers. We were on a sort of plateau, which had been broken away by clefts and defiles and eroded so that it stood about in jagged pinnacles, but all more or less the same height. We spent over an hour up there in the still and sunny remoteness: one felt all the fascination of the High Place which used to worry the Hebrew prophets. Down below we had come by tombs and temples, ornate Greek and Christian efforts, up to this older and more direct religion; hardly anything was changed, since everything was made simply for use, cut out in the rock: the only ornaments were two obelisks of orange sandstone on a lower terrace, which were probably worshipped, as there seemed to be an altar beside one of them. If the people of that time could return, they could climb up again to their high place and sacrifice without being at a loss. We descended on the other side, where the way is better kept, cut out in sandstone with ribs of steps still across it. There, in one of the long waits which the Professor inflicted on me, I made the acquaintance of the largest black centipede I have ever seen, with so many legs that it moved them in little groups, five or six at intervals all down its body, while the others seemed to rest. It was shiny like boot polish and curled up like a catherine wheel when I talked to it, and the beduin said that its name was "Moses' Rod."

I have now got the geography of Petra quite familiarly, and feel I can see the old main street beside the stream, banked up with an embankment of great sandstone blocks and covered with bridges, and in the low middle ground all the houses, a temple and acropolis on a small southern height, and the cliffs all around worked into façades of tombs. They must have been a horrid rich commercial people, all out for display, and with a very coarse taste in their sculpture: the older tombs are the best, just decorated with a sort of parapet and a plain door; but the later Greek and Roman effendis went in for columns, urns, pediments and all the worst Mid-Victorian ornament. The biggest are near the entrance of the town, opening out at the defile which the Arabs call the Mother of Boxes—and there they are most impressive, with their high windowless walls lining the immense cliff sides. The Arab policeman and 'Ali the guide chatted about their versions of the antiquities, until the Professor exhausted them also, and I believe they began to prefer the Ordinary Tourist who does not insist on seeing everything.

We had one and a half hours rest after lunch, and then went up another of the defiles to look out over the Wadi Araba to Sinai. This was a wild place, towering precipices of rock, and the Nabatean road cut in it, reminding me in its ups and downs quite absurdly of paths in English resorts made to look picturesquely wild for the city population. This is quite unfair to Petra, which looks wild all on its own, but I think it was in self-defence against the Professor.

We get a car to-morrow afternoon, which will take us back to Ma'an and then back to Amman next day. We will have seen most of the sights, but I should have liked a few more days to sit about and think. Though it is only the situation and not the spirit of the place that makes it lovely—this enclosure of rock holding the ruins of so much pomp and now filled with flowers: the ruins themselves have no soul, except the sadness of dead vanities: none of the lovely tenderness of the Appian way. But of the high place this morning, and of our climb by the half-obliterated steps, I shall always think as a short excursion into the early life of the world.

1 *April*, 1933.

I don't know what sort of letters I am writing—I just jot everything down as it comes, as there is so little time after energetic sight-seeing to tell you all about it. This morning I renounced a rise before sunrise and view over the Wadi Araba and imagined it from my very nice bed in the cave while the Professor leaped up the rocks to the disgust of the exhausted policemen and was back here with his

photos taken and his soul satisfied for breakfast at eight. It is marvellous to be so methodical: he never eats when he is hungry, but
when he sees me pull my sandwiches out at any old time he looks at
his watch and eats according to whether it is 'drei stunden' since his
last meal. After breakfast we went to the narrow entrance defile to
photo the temple of Isis with the morning sun, a wonderful rose-
coloured sandstone Corinthian façade carved in the rock wall. There
was another sort of cave room nearby which I spotted and identified
without any trouble; but the Professor thought it did not 'bestimmen'
with Baedeker—though quite obvious to the mere uneducated mind.
So I said will you bet? Ten shillings, said he. And, of course, he
lost.

These poor Bduli beduin keep on coming up, women and little
shepherd girls and boys, to sell bad coins; but I got two nice ones,
a Crusader silver coin and one with Nabatean writing. We came
home by the valley where the caravans used to come from Shobek—
probably a very great highway for the Egyptian trade—and looked
at a big tomb there with a Nabatean inscription, rather untidy script
not so decorative as arabic. All the valley along the old road was
filled with white broom and leaves of asphodel, and oleanders and
a few tamarisk in the stream bed.

We refused a horse to ride back on, thinking to save ten precious
shillings. The horse came walking after and we were told later that
we were entitled to it anyway—but then pride forbade us to change
our minds. We walked with three small beduin porters, about
twenty-five years between the lot of them, crunching along the defile
with our baggage. Whenever I drew near, the littlest one began to
pant loudly with fatigue, but otherwise he forgot. A car which has
to go back to Amman is taking us for £4 10s. by the Crusaders' fort at
Shobek. I was pleased to find myself discriminating types: the
chauffeur seemed different from an Arab, not podgy like a Christian,
and not an Armenian: I asked at last and he turns out to be a Circassian
—with a lovely car all fitted with springs and windows, unusual for
the East. He made some fuss over the price and said he got £4 from
the Duchess of Bedford (who turned up in Petra last night) for only
going to Ma'an, but when I pointed out that she was rich enough
to come in a private aeroplane and I wasn't, he saw the point at
once. He has brought us back to this little station hotel at Ma'an
and we leave early to-morrow. We took photos in the town

as we came through. There are real beduin here, walking in to shop with their camel led by a string, wild and thin-faced and brown, with knife and gun, and with the intelligent finely cut features; the Professor, wandering about with his cinema camera and his black beard in the air while he looked through his glasses at them, annoyed one and got a furious harangue, till a policeman all in dark blue, as it might be Piccadilly, interfered. I was so annoyed, and talked to the Professor about asking before snapshotting and about not giving trouble to the authorities in a way which would have given Vyvyan unexpected pleasure if he could have heard.

Now we have been sitting in this little inn and I have cleaned my coin, and think it is Venetian.

AMMAN, 2 *April*, 1933.

Dearest B,

We have just got back to the Philadelphia hotel and found the manager precipitating himself on our car to say that we were not to worry about prices or anything, that Mr. Chapman had telephoned, and we would be pleased with our hotel in the end. So I live in faith and will stay here till the 5th or 6th, leaving a week for Jerusalem.

I saw a wonderful picture-postcard sun rising up in the desert of Ma'an. The little Palestine innkeeper was as nice as before and prepared a lovely lunch all in little packets. I hope for his sake more tourists will come to Ma'an. The Circassian chauffeur came at six-forty-five, and we settled in our luxurious shut car, which made me feel rather ill at once, and went along to Shobek, keeping to the high downs, where Arabia, which lies like a shelf tilted up to the west, begins to roll big waves before breaking away to the Dead Sea rift. All this makes Transjordan a lovely bold country for riding over, and apparently very nearly uninhabited—for we did not even see tents. Only one beduin family on three camels, the man with a baby son before him and a gun behind. The sky was wild with black and white clouds and squalls of rain, and the figures looked very fine on the black stretch of lava stones, with the hills before Petra showing in a streak of brilliant light. We kept on over these downs till Shobek appeared, a little walled place on an isolated hill like a volcano, the same bleached colour as its surrounding landscape, but with green barley and blossoming trees in little patchwork terraces in the valley below, and the cloud cumuli piled up on the hills beyond.

This was first a Crusader castle (Mons Regalis) and then an Arab fort; and now there are twenty to thirty families left in it, all wrapped up against the murderous wind which seems to have an edge as sharp as that of all the little flints scattered about the ground. You can't think how icy it was—a real work of heroism to get out and take snapshots. There were small yellow lilies about (called Abu Swei), very pretty, and a little beduin wrapped in an *abba* asleep in the shelter of a rock, whom I was just stepping on as part of the landscape.

Tourists do occasionally go to Shobek, and all the inhabitants were ready to take us down the well which descends about seventy metres by three hundred and thirty steps into the ground and has a clear pool at the bottom. The people said they do not use it, but did so lately, when enemies surrounded them. There are two good towers, one round and one square, with arabic inscriptions and a few bits of wall and arrow slits left, but it is only the position which makes it worth coming to see now, and the fact that once it must have lain on the great desert caravan route. This was almost impossible to find to-day. First we had tea and then coffee as guests of the six policemen, who were delighted to have visitors as they say they live like prisoners. They have no telephone, but a big-mouthed pistol which shoots red, green, or white signals to aeroplanes to tell them of danger, safety, or to ask them to land. I noticed for the first time that this flag is the same as the Iraq one, and they told me that the black stands for the Abassid, the white for the Ommayad, the green for the Fatimite—the three great divisions of Islam—while the red bit with a star is Faisal and his brother's family.

We photographed them all in a row, and came away, hunting about among the flints and little scented tufts for the road, which was almost imperceptible and not at all good for tyres. We finally got back to the main road, which goes drearily along the flat of Arabia or nearly, by the railway and Lawrence's old trenches, and is the pilgrim way to Mecca, now scarce used. Another bit of railway was built by the Turks to bring them wood for their advance through Sinai, and stopped at Shobek, and its embankment is still there, but all the rails were lifted off again either by Turk or English. We got along in a rather dreary way, I being quite exhausted by professorial thirst for exact knowledge. I do feel I am not meant for honeymoons. I can't *bear* people in such exclusive doses; anyway breakfast should be excluded.

Lovely little tiny iris were all about; I shall try and bring Herbert some roots. When we had spent hours in the dull country, only brightened by light rainstorms, we came back to the edge of the green bright barley in the sun, and there turned aside and saw M'shitta, an old palace which the Ommayad caliphs, desert bred and lovers of the desert, made for themselves in the wilderness: domed halls of brick with grey stone columns carved in delicate flower capitals, surrounded by a stone wall where towers once stood all along. Here was the carved façade that was presented by the Turks to the Kaiser and carried to Berlin. The grassy land rolled away into sunlit and cloud-shadowy distances, and if it had not been for the icy wind, one would have liked to lie on one's back and meditate a little on the Caliphs' holidays there, on the very edge of their desert lands.

I feel such a bad conscience for having been snappy with the poor old Professor—but don't you think it is hard to be made to contemplate everything from an instructive angle on a holiday? Whenever I say anything such as that there is lots of snow here in winter or some harmless remark of that kind, he pulls out his note-book and writes it down, and *never* notices himself what live people are thinking of all round him.

5 April, 1933.

It was fun calling on the Amira yesterday. Léonie [Chapman] invited a local lady whose husband is minister here to lunch and to take us afterwards: she was a pleasant Syrian woman, educated at Beirut, speaking very good English, and had spent three years or so in Mecca where her husband was Hussain's foreign minister. He got wind of the Wahabi attack under Ibn Saud and got himself and his family away just in time on an excuse of summer leave: the Wahabis massacred quantities of their friends who remained. We took a taxi after lunch and motored down into the well of the town and up again to where the new palace stands on a windy hill with very new little gardens and trees planted round it. The door was banged: a little tattered black maid opened and said welcome: we went up bare stone stairs very like a back entrance, into a gaudy drawing-room, all full of velvets and carpets, and there saw a little round princess with a most amiable expression, the eldest daughter, very plump, with black hair parted down the middle and round black eyebrows over round black eyes, and a little round nose and nice full little

[323]

mouth, all most attractive. Here, like Baghdad, there are too many daughters and no one for them to marry.

The Amira came in presently—very like Faisal's queen (who is her twin), and all bunched up in woollies. I presented my letter, and we talked arabic quite successfully and I told her about Petra, to which she has never been in all these nine years. She had a very kind face. While we were in the middle of it all, a knock on the door, and the appearance of a beard and *kaffiya* announced the Amir himself, who, however, did not come in (as our Syrian lady was unveiled), but retreated hastily. He has another wife in the other wing of the palace, but we did not call on her. We got up to go, were made to sit down again and finally spent about an hour there, and then walked home in a lovely afternoon, like a clean-swept and cold spring day in England.

JERUSALEM, 8 April, 1933.

It was so lovely to find a packet of letters waiting for me when I got here yesterday, after a motor ride where the beauties of the landscape were rather interfered with by the fact that two Arab passengers were sick. One was such a nice countryman, with a fair reddish moustache very crusader-like, all got up in grey flannel jodpurs, a mackintosh, woollen gloves and a white *kaffiya*, for the pilgrimage to Nebi Musa and his first visit to Jerusalem. We had to stop every ten minutes or so while he went very discreetly to be sick outside, and came back saying in an apologetic way: "There is nothing better than riding on horseback." The other was a fat and plain Christian lady who finally burst into tears, which made a most unpleasant combination. This all went on behind me however, as I had the front seat. A young American archaeologist had appeared, to travel with me from the hotel, and we spent the morning together, from eight to eleven, waiting for our automobile to find one more passenger, and finally laid in a stock of oranges and biscuits as our hopes of arriving for lunch vanished. It was the great four-day feast, and everything upside down, and all cars very expensive, so that we had to give 10s. instead of 6s. for our places: but all was pretty to look at as everyone was wearing something new, and the white spotless *kaffiyas* were flapping about everywhere. The young American is a talkative charming person full of kindness, and when I said I might be stuck for a lodging with all these Easter pilgrims about, he suggested introducing me into this school—which is just as well, as the German hospice I meant to go to was quite full, and everywhere else also. There is a sort of ascetic comradely feeling about the place, a little pleasant garden with cypress, lilac, and goldfish in a cement pool, looking out to the Mount of Olives. Nothing can take from Jerusalem her magnificent position and clear beautiful atmosphere: one sees her against the skyline as one climbs from Jericho through the dead hills; and as we came, the sky was full of sun and clouds, throwing big shadows.

As we came down towards Jordan, and below sea-level, the flowers burst open in masses, wild lupins, sheets of poppies, asphodel, yellow marigolds, and lowest of all, oleanders. At Jericho itself the bougain-villia was out. We climbed up again the other side into the same icy wind we had left at Amman.

Ever since arriving here, my American has been showing me round. The streets are full of colour and emotion and hatreds, with all these festivals; the little narrow bazaars are scarce changed since the Crusades; the same priests in the Holy Sepulchre. I got a picture of one close to the door of the church, with a notice "Beware of pickpockets" on the wall just above his head.

I spent the morning looking in an old Crusader house at a model of Solomon's temple, worked out through years of study by a German engineer. He was employed by the Turks, and asked for permission to measure out the present Holy Places as his only salary, and with this help he reconstructed the whole place, and whether accurate or not it is a most interesting effort. His daughter shows it, a dear old German lady whose one anxiety is not to receive too much money, which makes her more unique in Jerusalem than her own models. I think I now have an idea of the old city.

9 April, 1933.

Dearest Venetia,

I, too, feel that freedom you speak of, a sense of safety in oneself independent of others and also largely independent of circumstance. The knowledge I think that the secret of life does lie in our own hands and need not elude us unless we ourselves allow it to do so. And also the discovery that life is so infinitely rich, that whatever happens we can always find in it enough to keep our spirit busy. You have more time to think than I; that is one advantage of illness.

[325]

But I feel now that, although I am swamped in many things and cannot sit aside and observe myself and them, I *will* be able to get a quiet happiness out of contemplation some time when this rush subsides. That is a very peaceful feeling.

I am now going to the Citadel by the Jaffa Gate to see the Nebi Musa procession come in from Hebron. All the police taking precautions in case of scraps.

Here I am taking life easily. I spent a quiet morning yesterday in the Mosque enclosure, sitting about under the olive trees, and enjoying the peaceful atmosphere of the Moslem religion after all the competitive Christianity round about. The old mullas were charming to me when I spoke arabic, and one old man went so far as to pat me affectionately on the shoulder. But the little boys are horrid, clamouring bakshish, until I turned on one and prayed Allah to bestow intelligence upon him, which reduced him to a surprised silence. I have been studying the old geography and getting an idea of the Temple and City of Solomon and Herod, and have got Josephus' Wars of the Jews to read on my way home (3rd class, as I am reduced to my usual final state of penury). But I saved enough to buy myself a sheepskin coat in which I live, it is so cold.

ASOLO, 24 April, 1933.

I found all well here and it is a luxury to sit still at home, and have room to put all one's things, and generally to be civilized again. And I found a nice review of my book in the R.G.S., and a grant to be made to me for exploration: I know nothing about it yet, but hope it may enable me to go to Yemen next. It has had the surprising effect of inspiring a note from *Who's Who* with a questionnaire: I don't mind telling them my private life—all except my age, which I think is quite unsuitable for the general public to know. What do you suggest as Recreations? And where, if anywhere, was I Educated? And what is my Career?

I have got to try and finish two articles, and to get on with my neglected Russian. I can just get about with it and talked to a woman from the Crimea on board ship. I came 3rd class, and made up for discomfort by learning a lot about Zionism; and realizing how much Communism is gaining ground in Central Europe. Do you think we shall live to see the end of Capitalism? I sometimes wonder.

L'ARMA, 7 August, 1933.

It is so lovely and peaceful down here; a light and warm air, not a bit too hot, and the sea with silver streaks trailing about it, like Shelley's Ode to the West Wind.

We have just discovered a new iniquity of Mrs. Hanbury's. She is trying to plant trees in the Roman Road so as to block it up gradually. It was almost impassable, so Mama asked the gardener if he would not have it cleared: he said that Mrs. H had given orders to leave it. So I went myself to cut a way through, and after destroying various robust little plants, I suddenly noticed that they were all evenly spaced, and it dawned on me that this was a real plantation. We consulted all the neighbours, and the advice is to cut away and say nothing. It rouses everything Bolshevik in me to see old rights being trampled on in this way, and they have already appropriated one public path here with no protest from anyone.

I am reading a little Russian and just on the edge of beginning to understand it, a tantalizing time when a few months of hard work would make a real difference. But this writing is always in the way, and I feel so depressed about it and as if my book were going to be too dreary for words. I console myself by thinking that I shall be well out of the way in the Yemen by the time people begin to notice it.

15 August, 1933.

One loses all dates here. I too am so hard at my MS., just getting to the end of the revision now, that I find it difficult to do any other writing. I hope I have improved it: it is wearisome going over and over one's own words, and one ends by hating them; and they seem so inadequate. It seems far less a waste of time just to lie about and look at the sea through the branches of olive trees. One cannot see the horizon: the sky and water melt into each other and the olives seem to be some dreamlike plant that rises out of them.

I have just seen the proof of my review for the Archaeological book, and it reads very learned. You will see it in the September number of the R.G.S. Journal, together with my effort on the Pusht-i-Kuh. The Illustrated London News have taken four photos. Would you be able to send me a copy when they come out, for I shall never know?

The other day a friend here remarked that a big headline "Check to the League of Nations" was a complete contradiction of what was said in the article below. So he made enquiries and was told that the news belongs to the paper, but the headlines are sent by the Italian Government, and they could not help it if the two happened not to agree.

I am going to be all alone here till the 29th as Mama leaves earlier. Then I shall have a week in Dronero and then go to Asolo. I am fixing my lecture for the end of November, and will have my little time of London life then and retire secretly afterwards to hospital. I don't mean to tell *anyone* except you and Minnie.

ASOLO, 20 *September*, 1933

I have all sorts of anxieties of my own just now. First of all my eyesight is suddenly giving trouble—apparently strain due to fatigue: but no doubt it will be a rest to have an operation—at least I hope so. Anyway I have got glasses and a tonic. Then the question of Canada is rather troublesome. I am waiting to hear from the London solicitor but it is just *possible* I may have to go at once, though I *hope* not. Anyway it is keeping me in the discomfort of indecision. I will let you know as soon as I hear: but I still hope not to have to go till February as I intended.

I am doing a piece of medieval research trying to locate a vanished city. It may have been done already, but it is fun anyway, and necessary for the accuracy of my book—but difficult to do as I have so few of the references here at hand.

It is all very tragic in Iraq. I have not heard the full story of the Assyrians, but there is enough material for years of bloodshed ahead. When the war ended, the people at home were begged to take an interest in the Assyrians and they could have been settled in their old mountain home: but no one could be bothered at that time, and now it is an almost insoluble problem. Napoleon was quite right when he said that foresight is the whole art of government.

GENEVA, 21 *October*, 1933.

Dearest B,

We had an excellent journey, though we got to Milan one minute after the Lausanne train was supposed to leave. However, I had Minnie and all the eight packages waiting at the end of the corridor, so we nipped out into the arms of the first two porters who saw us into the train just before it steamed out. The registered luggage of course did not get through, but I talked to the inspector at Domodossola who took my word for it that we had no Works of Art and sent it on after.

Vyvyan got us lovely rooms, a little suite with bathroom, and a balcony looking out to the *place* and lake beyond. He and Major Edmonds came to dine last night.

24 *October*, 1933.

Minnie and I are enjoying this place. It is very luxurious and restful, and we are staying on till Monday next. Vyvyan came yesterday to take me for a walk, but I couldn't go because the Assyrian patriarch, the Mar Shimun, was coming to tea, and he and Mr. Edmonds were both slightly astonished at our getting hold of this controversial personage within three days of our arrival. It happened very simply, as we went to church on Sunday morning and there was he blessing us in Aramaic and giving a little address on his massacred people and the fact that now his only hope is in the League of Nations and the honour of the British Government. He was very nervous, sitting by the altar through the service in a black robe with magenta stole and sleeves, and fiddling at his collar, till the vicar introduced him in a deplorable little speech about Assyrians 'massacred almost to death'.

Major Edmonds is here for the Iraq Government, and Vyvyan with a Foreign Office man for the British, and the case is to come up on the 26th.

28 *October*, 1933.

We went to the meeting of the Disarmament Conference. We were up in a sort of dress circle above and looked down on all the delegates strolling about, smoking, and evidently having quite a good time except when they *had* to listen to the speeches. It was not very animated and Mr. Henderson in the chair said all there was to say and they all hoped to have done with it and go to tea when a delegate from Jugoslavia started a quite irrelevant discourse, and the Persian followed at enormous length.

[329]

Dearest Venetia,

Agostino made such a nice epigram on the English in general without knowing it. I asked him what he thought of Mr. Henderson. "*Mais*," said he, "*il est comme tant d'Anglais: il a l'air bête, mais il ne fait pas de bêtises: alors on doit penser qu'il n'est pas bête.*"

3 November, 1933.

Dearest B,

I have done great things to my appearance by waving my hair and discovered a woman here who gives excellent advice and has introduced me to a really good face cream—so that I looked quite right and I do notice what a difference it makes—even with the nicest men—though it takes a lot of time and trouble.

Index

Index

[333]

Stark, Freya (*contd.*)

327–8; ecstasy some sort of discovery, 4; *Letters from Syria*, 4; necessary ingredients of travel, 4–5; Damascus, 6, 11–16, 65, 76–7; "subversive," 7; value of affection in itself, 7; "a life of my own," 7–10; Rudolf Steiner's books, 8–9, 41; first article published, on Druses in Syria, 9, 30; Jebel Druse journey, 17–19; visits Pyramids, Sphinx and Cemetery, 20–1; reflections on leisure, 23; the Atlantic, 24, 29, 31; reads *Odyssey*, 25, 31, 48; Shakespeare and other classics, 25; Canada and Asia contrasted, 25; journey across Canada to Creston, 25–6; life in Creston, 26–9, 32–8; Niagara Falls, 29, 49; *Canada and the Odyssey*, 30; not really meant by destiny to be an author, 36; Wild West dance, 36–8; clothes and women, 38, 186; Canadian note-book, etc., 23, 38–60; reflections on chess, 39; personal object in life, 40; abstract thought, 40–1; veracity of *Arabian Nights*, 42; influence of casual words, 44; common figures of speech, 45; reflections on Yugo-Slav and other dictatorships, 47; *Wings over Europe*, 49; *Bridge of S. Luis Rey*, 49–50; Moorish cure for whooping cough, 54; in London, 54–5, 65, 185–6, 195–6, 292–5; British Museum reading room, 54; despotic governments and neatly planted trees, 55; music at Temple Church, 55; Thornworthy, 57–8; bliss of riding, 58; difference between wild and tame, 62–3; Zionists on S.S. *Carnaro*, 64, 70; *Valleys of the Assassins*, 66, 92, 187, 191, 294, 327; Brummana to Damascus by Sannin, Fakhra and Afka,

72–5; reflections on harem life, 77–80; Damascus to Baghdad, 80–2; British Civil Service in Iraq, 83–6, 89, 111–13, 121–2, 145, 147; in Baghdad, 83–132, 144–7, 187, 191–2, 201, 229–34, 242–74, 281–6, 288–9, 297–302; Iraq feeling towards British, 1929–30, 88, 101, 103, 105, 112, 119, 125, 127–32; objection to Philanthropy, 90; learns Persian, 91, 115, 120, 123, 149, 153, 155, 160, 268; description of Persian landscape, 91–2, 148–51, 157; regime in Persia, 156, 161; in Hamadan, 91–2, 147–63, 180, 187, 191, 201–4, 218; Hôtel de France, 92, 147; unrequited affection, 93–4; Baghdad note-book, 96–7, 99, 101–3, 105–6; Iraq Prime Minister's suicide, 100–1; Stark the orientalist, 104; disadvantage of calling oneself Christian, 105; Ctesiphon, 109; Csarevitch, 115; Kadhimain, 116; visits Queen of Iraq, 122–3, 300; Palace of Abbassids, 123–4; Akhar Kūf, 124; visits Queen 'Ali, 125–6; Kerbela, Nejf, Kufa and Qifl, 132–5; Babel, Babylon and Kish, 135–8; Mosul, 138–9, 142–4; Nineveh, 139–40; Shammar tents, 140–1; Baghdad to Hamadan by Paitak Pass and Kermanshah, 147–51; Bahais in Hamadan and elsewhere, 155–6, 179, 198–9; Hamadan to Caspian by Qazvin, Chala, Shahrak, Zavarak, Garmrud, Salambar and Gavar, and back by Resht to Hamadan, 163–80; riding accident Penbedw, 183, 193–5; in Cambridge, 183–4, 193–4; generosity of geographers and orientalists to each other, 185; "rudiments of survey" and map making, 185, 189, 196, 207–8,

Stark, Freya (*contd.*)
210, 231–2; Hamadan to Teheran by Qazvin, Zeinabar, Barir, Lahu, Delir and Dohtar Qal'a, 187–8, 204–12; on illness and death, 188, 206, 266–7; in Teheran, 188–9, 212, 214; *Baghdad Times,* journalistic work on, 191, 233, 243–5, 250, 253–4, 256–8, 267, 271, 286–8, 298–302; *Persian Legends,* 194; Acre, 198; Athlit, 199; Zebdani, 199–200; Diary Teheran–Saveh, 212–13; Teheran to Baghdad by Saveh, Malayir, Hamadan, Tusirkhan, Nihavend, Alishtar, Tudaru, Harsin, Kermanshah, 212–29; origin of horse, 222, 226; Notes from Persian lessons, 234–40; six ingredients for happiness, 241–2; secret of travelling, 246; *Baghdad Sketches,* 249–50, 253–4, 266, 285, 295; learns Russian, 251, 253, 284, 326; *River of Adonis,* 255; on spinsters, 259; lecture on Assassins, 1932, 260; Muharram procession, 261–2; War Correspondent to *Times,* Kurdish war, 263–4, 267; feelings about cars, 269; journey in search of hidden treasure, 272–82, 284; Women's International League, 284; *F.O. drops its "H's",* 286–7; Passover, 291; R.G.S. Back Grant and Royal Asian Burton Medal, 292; lectures to Royal Central Asian and Royal Asiatic Societies 1933 and 1934, 292; finance and planning and writing of her books, 295; visits Geneva and League of Nations, 296, 328–9; Kirkuk, testing and drilling oil wells, 302–6; Ur, 307; Baghdad to Jerusalem by Amman, Ma'an, Petra and Shobek, 320–4; visits Queen of Trans-Jordan, 323–4; *Pusht-i-Kuh,*

R.G.S. Journal, 327; letters to her father, 11–21, 55, 59–60, 65–9, 80–2, 97, 99–101, 104, 108, 110, 114, 120, 124–5, 141–5, 147–51, 163–4, 180–2, 196–7; to her mother, 19, 21–2, 31–2, 34–5, 48, 56–7, 70–80, 95–6, 102–3, 111–18, 120–3, 126–7, 138–9, 144–7, 151, 153–5, 157–61, 165–80, 193–230, 233, 251, 254–61, 263–4, 266–86, 297–300, 302–25, 328–30; to Herbert Young, 32–4, 36–8, 106, 118, 141, 231–2, 250, 298; to Venetia Buddicom, 68, 94, 98, 107–8, 116, 119, 155–6, 161–5, 232, 252–4, 259–70, 282–3, 297, 299–302, 325–8, 330; to Car Ker, 99, 140–1, 152–3; to Penelope Ker, 109, 125–6; to Lady Barker, 123; to Sir Henry Lawrence, 127–32; to Lady Drower, 156–7; to Lionel Smith, 199, 202–3, 218–19, 234, 251–2, 301.
Stark, Robert (father), 3, 5, 8, 11, 23–4, 26–8, 33, 35, 48, 53, 62, 68; his reading, 27; death, 93, 188, 209.
Stein, Sir Aurel, 249, 283.
Steiner, Rudolf, 8–9, 41.
Stevenson, R. L., 42.
Storrs, Sir Ronald, 293.
Strange, Guy Le, 184, 193–4.
Sturges, Mr. and Mrs., 111, 187, 243.
Suleiman, 99.
Sultanabad, 189.
Summerhayes, Mr., Consul, 151, 161, 179, 187, 204, 219; letter to Mrs. Stark, 209.
Summerhayes, Mrs., 151, 159, 187.
Summerhayes, Peggy, 187, 203.
Suq-ash-Shuyukh, 307.
Surma, Lady, 265–6.
Syalan, 171, 207.

Taimurtash, 298.
Takht-i-Suleiman, 206, 209–10.